The Master in Egypt

Studies in the Bábí and Bahá'í Religions
Anthony A. Lee, General Editor

Studies in Bábí and Bahá'í History, Volume One,
edited by Moojan Momen (1982).

From Iran East and West, Volume Two, edited by Juan R. Cole and
Moojan Momen (1984).

In Iran, Volume Three, edited by Peter Smith (1986).

Music, Devotions and Mashriqu'l-Adhkár, Volume Four,
by R. Jackson Armstrong-Ingram (1987).

Studies in Honor of the Late H. M. Balyuzi, Volume Five,
edited by Moojan Momen (1989).

Community Histories, Volume Six,
edited by Richard Hollinger (1992).

Symbol and Secret: Qur'an Commentary in Bahá'u'lláh's Kitáb-i Íqán,
Volume Seven, by Christopher Buck (1995).

Revisioning the Sacred: New Perspectives on Bahá'í Theology,
Volume Eight, edited by Jack McLean (1997).

*Modernity and the Millennium: The Genesis of the Baha'i Faith in the
Nineteenth-Century Middle East,* distributed as Volume Nine, by
Juan R. I. Cole, Columbia University Press (1999).

*Paradise and Paradigm: Key Symbols in Persian Christianity and the
Bahá'í Faith,* distributed as Volume Ten, by Christopher Buck,
State University of New York Press (1999).

Religion in Iran: From Zoroaster to Bahá'u'lláh, distributed as
Volume Eleven, by Alessandro Bausani,
Bibliotheca Persica Press (2000).

*Evolution and Bahá'í Belief: 'Abdu'l-Bahá's Response to Nineteenth-
Century Darwinism,* Volume Twelve, edited by Keven Brown (2001).

Reason and Revelation: New Directions in Bahá'í Thought, Volume
Thirteen, edited by Seena Fazel and John Danesh (2002).

Bahá'ís in the West, Volume Fourteen, edited by Peter Smith (2004).

Search for Values: Ethics in Bahá'í Thought, Volume Fifteen, edited by John Danesh and Seena Fazel (2004).

Táhirih in History: Perspectives on Qurratu'l-'Ayn from East and West, Volume Sixteen, edited by Sabir Afaqi (2004).

Táhirih: A Portrait in Poetry, Volume Seventeen, trans. and edited by Amin Banani, Joshua Kessler, and Anthony A. Lee (2004).

Alain Locke: Faith and Philosophy, Volume Eighteen, by Christopher Buck, (2005).

Church and State: A Postmodern Political Theology, Book One, distributed as Volume Nineteen, by Sen McGlinn, Leiden University (2005).

Resurrection and Renewal: The Making of the Babi Movement, 1844-1850, Paperback Edition, distributed as Volume Twenty, by Abbas Amanat, Cornell University Press (2005).

The Baha'i Faith in America, by William Garlington, distributed as Volume Twenty-One, Praeger Publishers (2005).

Baha'i and Globalization, distributed as Volume Twenty-Two, edited by Margit Warburg, et al., Aarhus University Press (2005).

The Baha'i Faith in Africa: Establishing a New Religious Movement, 1952-1962, by Anthony A. Lee, Brill (2011). Distributed as Volume Twenty-Three.

Religion and Relevance: The Bahá'ís in Britain, 1899-1930, Volume Twenty-Four, by Lil Osborn, (2014).

Being Human: Bahá'í Perspectives on Islam, Modernity, and Peace, Volume Twenty-Five, by Todd Lawson, (2019).

The Master in Egypt: A Compilation, volume Twenty-Six, compiled and edited by Ahang Rabbani, (2021).

'Abdu'l-Baha (1844–1921) in the Holy Land, photographed signing a Tablet.

Studies in the Babi and Baha'i Religions
Volume Twenty-Six
Anthony A. Lee, General Editor

The Master in Egypt

A Compilation

Compiled and Edited by
Ahang Rabbani

Kalimat Press
Los Angeles

Copyright © 2021 by Kalimát Press. All Rights Reserved

First Edition

Library of Congress Control Number: 2021930121

ISBN: 978-1-890688-01-1

This compilation includes excerpts from
Bahai News (later titled *Star of the West*) and from *Abdul Baha in Egypt*
by Mírzá Ahmad Sohrab (New York, 1929).

Abdul Baha in Egypt was approved for publication by the
Publishing Committee of the National Spiritual Assembly
of the Bahá'ís of the United States in 1929.

Republication of Mirza Ahmad Sohrab's book, *Abdul Baha in Egypt*, has been
undertaken with the permission of the National Spiritual Assembly of the
Bahá'ís of the United States, 2007.

Photos of Alexandria, Ramleh, and Port Said © iStockPhotos

Cover design by Erinn O'Dear
Cover photo courtesy of the New York Public Library collection
Sphynx et la grande pyramide. Circa 1860–1929

Manufactured in the United States of America

Kalimát Press
1600 Sawtelle Boulevard, Suite 310
Los Angeles, California 90025

www.kalimat.com
kalimatpress@gmail.com

CONTENTS

In Memorium: Ahang Rabbani (1956-2013) | xxix

Editor's Foreword by Ahang Rabbani | xxi

From *Bahai News* | 1
  October 16, 1910; November 4, 1910; November 23, 1910; December 12, 1910; January 19, 1911; February 7, 1911; March 2, 1911

From *Star of the West* | 23
  April 28, 1911; September 8, 1911; June, 1913

From *Abdul Baha in Egypt* | 27

PORT SAID, EGYPT, JULY 1, 1913 | 29
  1. To look back and survey the activities of the month. 2. The Bahá'í path and its pilgrims. 3. Tablet of 'Abdu'l-Bahá the magazine "Theosophy" in Scotland in regard to divine civilization. 4. Article in "Egyptian Gazette" about the Bahá'í Pilgrims. 5. Home of 'Abdu'l-Bahá in Baghdad and its keeper. 6. 'Abdu'l-Bahá's talk to the Pilgrims on the evidences of the Cause. 7. Experiences of a pilgrim and how he was robbed on the way.

PORT SAID, EGYPT, JULY 2, 1913 | 35
  1. A Talk of 'Abdul-Bahá on spiritual cultivation and teaching. 2. Departure of the pilgrims and remarks of 'Abdu'l-Bahá on music. 3. Quiet association with 'Abdul-Bahá. 4. Progress of the Bahá'í Cause in Germany and letters from that country. 5. Appearance of Truth.

PORT SAID, EGYPT, JULY 3, 1913 | 37
  1. The Bahá'í Cause is in need of earnest workers who will defy all opposition. 2. Life in Port Said, and fleas but no mosquitoes. 3. Husayn Rúhí and his Bahá'í school in Cairo. 4. Palace of Bahá'u'lláh in Nur, Persia. 5. Talk of 'Abdu'l-Bahá on Bahá'u'lláh's imprisonment in the Prison of 'Akká, and on real happiness. 6. Remarks on the war waged between Greece and Bulgaria. 7. Story about Bahá'u'lláh's shepherd. 8. A joke with Husayn Rúhí.

PORT SAID, EGYPT, JULY 4, 1913 | 42
  1. Story of the Hájí Abdu'lláh and his conversation with 'Abdu'l-Bahá. 2. 'Abdu'l-Bahá dictates Tablets for many Bahá'ís. 3. Tablet to the International Congress of Free Christians. 4. Poem by Mr. Chase read to 'Abdu'l-Bahá. 5. Story about Abraham's hospitality.

PORT SAID, EGYPT, JULY 5, 1913 | 49
  1. World's conflict and its remedy. 2. The departure of a Zoroastrian Bahá'í for Bombay and 'Abdu'l-Bahá's Tablet about his Western trip. 3. 'Abdu'l-Bahá's interview with the Indian Editor.

PORT SAID, EGYPT, JULY 6, 1913 | 51
   1. The Bahá'í heart is a cool fountain. 2. Another interview with the Indian editor and 'Abdu'l-Bahá's talk on education. 3. The Bahá'í Cause in Paris and Tablets for the friends.

PORT SAID, EGYPT, JULY 7, 1913 | 53
   1. Importance of correspondence between the friends. 2. 'Abdu'l-Bahá's talk on the enemies of the Cause. 3. Arrival of Hájí Niyáz, the old patriarch. 4. Tablet to the Editor of "The Christian Commonwealth" on Universal Peace.

PORT SAID, EGYPT, JULY 8, 1913 | 58
   1. What is the function of real religion? 2. 'Abdu'l-Bahá's perennial cordiality and courtesy. 3. The joy of serving 'Abdu'l-Bahá. 4. There is a power in this Cause. 5. Hájí Niyáz and the story of the king and Ayáz.

PORT SAID, EGYPT, JULY 9, 1913 | 61
   1. Our life in Port Said. 2. The death of a Bahá'í child and the ceremony of her burial. 3. The Christian and Mohammedan cemeteries. 4. Visiting Taqí Manshádí's tomb in the cemetery. 5. Outline of Taqí Manshádí's life and his services to the Bahá'í Cause. 6. Manshádí's epistolary style and his peculiarities. 7. How to conduct Bahá'í meetings and the importance of public speaking. 8. Tablet by 'Abdu'l-Bahá regarding delivery of eloquent speeches.

PORT SAID, EGYPT, JULY 10, 1913 | 67
   1. Sayyid Asadu'lláh departs for Russia to spread the message. 2. Sayyid Asadu'lláh's talk with 'Abdu'l-Bahá and his glowing resolution. 3. Farewell to Sayyid Asadu'lláh. 4. 'Abdu'l-Bahá's expectation to go to Ismailia. 5. Poems of Mr. Moxey read to 'Abdu'l-Bahá. 6. 'Abdu'l-Bahá speaks about the *Star of the West*. 7. Talk on his tour to America.

PORT SAID, EGYPT, JULY 11, 1913 | 70
   1. 'Abdu'l-Bahá's departure for Ismailia. 2. He praises American Bahá'ís. 3. He tells the Persians about Fred Mortenson who traveled from Minneapolis to Green Acre in order to see him. 4. The absence of 'Abdu'l-Bahá is noticed everywhere. 5. Tablet on 'Abdu'l-Bahá's trip to America. 6. The Power of the Bahá'í Cause.

PORT SAID, EGYPT, JULY 12, 1913 | 73
   1. Telephone message from Ismailia about 'Abdu'l-Bahá. 2. Mírzá Mahmúd prepares three volumes on the tour of 'Abdu'l-Bahá throughout Europe and America. 3. Translation of Tablet to the believers in Kerman, Persia. 4. How to deliver Bahá'í public addresses. 5. How great movements have advanced. 6. About 'Abdu'l-Bahá's American tour to a Persian Bahá'í.

PORT SAID, EGYPT, JULY 13, 1913 | 75
1. Tablet of 'Abdu'l-Bahá on progress. 2. A Tablet by 'Abdu'l-Bahá on personal illumination and guiding others to the truth. 3. The day of the glorious bounties of the invisible beauty of the Kingdom of Abhá. 4. Mrs. Stannard may go to India to teach the Bahá'í Cause.

PORT SAID, EGYPT, JULY 14, 1913 | 78
1. The French Day of Independence in Port Said. 2. 'Abdu'l-Bahá's life in Ismailia. 3. What constitutes everlasting fame?

PORT SAID, EGYPT, JULY 15, 1913 | 80
1. The message of 'Abdu'l-Bahá to the Unitarians. 2. 'Abdu'l-Bahá's conversation with Bishop Birch of New York City. 3. Some churches are free from prejudices. 4. 'Abdu'l-Bahá expresses the desire to visit the shrine of his father in 'Akká. 5. 'Abdu'l-Bahá praises the faith of German Bahá'ís.

PORT SAID, EGYPT, JULY 16, 1913 | 84
1. The scope of 'Abdu'l-Bahá's talks in California. 2. The program of a day's activity in Port Said. 3. Permission comes to visit 'Abdu'l-Bahá in Ismailia. 4. What is real friendship? 5. A prayer for the friends. 6. For me to be silent, for you to be singing.

PORT SAID, EGYPT, JULY 17, 1913 | 87
1. A prayer of illumination. 2. The dawn of the Sun of Reality. 3. People are heedless. 4. The duty of the followers of Truth. 5. Our journey to Ismailia. 6. Visit to 'Abdu'l-Bahá in the hotel room. 7. Formation of habits. 8. Bahá'u'lláh's life in the prison barrack of 'Akká. 9. 'Abdu'l-Bahá's room in prison. 10. The fleas of 'Akká. 11. 'Abdu'l-Bahá leaves for Alexandria. 12. Ismailia is a clean city.

PORT SAID, EGYPT, JULY 18, 1913 | 92
1. 'Abdu'l-Bahá's bust, made in Vienna, is sent to Port Said. 2. A Prayer for the success of the Bahá'ís. 3. Prayer for illumination. 4. The Covenant is a lamp.

PORT SAID, EGYPT, JULY 19, 1913 | 95
1. Arrival of 'Abdu'l-Bahá in Ramleh. 2. The presence of 'Abdu'l-Bahá holds the people together. 3. Brahma, Krishna, and Buddha taught the oneness of God. 4. The law of change is universal. 5. In the Bahá'í Cause no one holds religious office, titles and ceremonies. 6. Who are the sanctified souls?

PORT SAID, EGYPT, JULY 20, 1913 | 98
1. Who is 'Abdu'l-Bahá? 2. A Catholic procession in the streets of Port Said. 3. First journey of the Persians to America. 4. Material and spiritual food. 5. Steam a marvelous energy. 6. 'Abdu'l-Bahá's welcome in New York. 7. Interview with the newspapermen on the steamer deck.

PORT SAID, EGYPT, JULY 21, 1913 | 102
   1. There is no diary of Baha'u'llah's and 'Abdu'l-Bahá's words during the long years of incarceration. 2. Teaching the Cause is the most im- portant of all services. 3. It is the day of action and happiness.

PORT SAID, EGYPT, JULY 22, 1913 | 104
   1. The spiritual lesson drawn from the material progress of Port Said and the Suez Canal.

PORT SAID, EGYPT, JULY 23, 1913 | 106
   1. Possible departure for Ramleh makes us happy. 2. Arrival of Mrs. Getsinger in Port Said. 3. Translation of an interview between 'Abdu'l- Bahá and the reporter of the "San Francisco Examiner."

PORT SAID, EGYPT, JULY 24, 1913 | 111
   1. Our departure from Ramleh. 2. Thinking over meeting 'Abdu'l-Bahá. 3. Scenes along the railroad. 4. 'Abdu'l-Bahá calls on us. 5. Real love attracts divine confirmations. 6. Teach the Cause through deeds.

PORT SAID, EGYPT, JULY 25, 1913 | 114
   1. A call on Mírzá Abú'l-Fadl. 2. Alexandria is a progressive city. 3. 'Abdu'l-Bahá talks with the Persian followers. 4. Abú'l-Fadl, a great Bahá'í teacher.

RAMLEH, EGYPT, JULY 26, 1913 | 116
   1. The fragrances of God and their marvelous results. 2. Now is the time of the union of all the nations and religions. 3. In the Bahá'í revelation there is no limitation. 4. Become ye as kind fathers to the children of humanity. 5. 'Abdu'l-Bahá ready for the last call. 6. Letters and news from America. 7. Eloquent speeches must be delivered at public gatherings. 8. Persian American Educational Society. 9. Many Tablets dictated for believers. 10. Pray with an attracted heart.

RAMLEH, EGYPT, JULY 27, 1913 | 121
   1. The effect of association with 'Abdu'l-Bahá. 2. 'Abdu'l-Bahá dictates Tablets for the Persians. 3. Tickets for Charity. 4. Importance of cleanliness in all things. 5. Description of a charity bazaar in Alexandria.

RAMLEH, EGYPT, JULY 28, 1913 | 123
   1. First one must teach himself, then others. 2. Heralding the Kingdom of God in the cities of Europe and America. 3. While encircled by the whirlwind of calamities, blossom ye like a rose. 4. 'Abdu'l-Bahá sacrificing his life in the path of Bahá. 5. 'Abdu'l-Bahá tells of his early life. 6. 'Abdu'l-Bahá tells the Arabs about his Western trip.

RAMLEH, EGYPT, JULY 29, 1913 | 127
   1. Glad-tidings of the Kingdom of Abhá from Minneapolis. 2. Modern hos-

pital in Alexandria. 3. 'Abdu'l-Bahá takes the French Bahá'í doctor for a drive.

RAMLEH, EGYPT, JULY 30, 1913 | **129**
1. The Cause of Bahá'u'lláh is the mainspring of Love and Peace. 2. 'Abdu'l-Bahá tells about his health and work. 3. Oriental Bahá'ís anxious to receive the news. 4. Mírzá Abú'l-Fadl and his position in the Bahá'í Cause. 5. Mullás and their hair-splitting metaphysical discussions.

RAMLEH, EGYPT, JULY 31, 1913 | **132**
1. The progress of the Bahá'í Cause in the Orient 2. 'Abdu'l-Bahá tells about Rashíd Pasha and his system of extortion. 3. The episode of Rashíd Pasha and Madame Jackson about 'Abdu'l-Bahá's Freedom. 4. The infinite patience of 'Abdu'l-Bahá in answering the trivial questions put to him.

RAMLEH, EGYPT, AUGUST 1, 1913 | **137**
1. What can we do to spread the Bahá'í Cause? 2. The difficulties of Western journey have left their impressions upon 'Abdu'l-Bahá. 3. Now the importance of the station of the believers is unknown. 4. Service of the believers of God. 5. The Bahá'í meeting in Alexandria. 6. Bahá'í detachment and independence. 7. Arrival of members of 'Abdu'l-Bahá's family.

RAMLEH, EGYPT, AUGUST 2, 1913 | **140**
1. The "Greatest Holy Leaf," the daughter of Bahá'u'lláh. 2. 'Abdu'l-Bahá talks with two pilgrims. 3. This is the day of teaching. 4. Mr. Atwood, an Englishman. 5. Filial piety. 6. The future of Persia. 7. What 'Abdu'l-Bahá saw and did on his Western tour.

RAMLEH, EGYPT, AUGUST 3, 1913 | **144**
1. Spiritual sustenance distributed in the morning. 2. Spiritual receptivity 3. 'Abdu'l-Bahá sang a new song in every garden. 4. The Muslim month of fasting. 5. What is the real object of fast? 6. 'Abdu'l-Bahá writes to an Indian Prince.

RAMLEH, EGYPT, AUGUST 4, 1913 | **147**
1. The blessings of the universal mind. 2. 'Abdu'l-Bahá and the family morning prayer. 3. 'Abdu'l-Bahá and Shoghi Effendi. 4. The Persians delight with the pictures in the American magazines. 5. Universal homage paid to 'Abdu'l-Bahá. 6. Life during the month of Mohammedan fast. 7. How eager are the Bahá'ís of Persia for martyrdom. 7. 'Abdu'l-Bahá confounds the Mullás in the Mosque. 9. Story of Mullá Sadiq, the fanatical Shaykh. 10. 'Abdu'l-Bahá's love-pat.

RAMLEH, EGYPT, AUGUST 5, 1913 | **153**
1. 'Abdu'l-Bahá does not rest. 2. The significance of spiritual meetings. 3. The world is a farm and the people are farmers. 4. Spiritual guidance. 5. Be

seekers of Truth. 6. Divine confirmations. 7. Selfish people are tied with iron bands. 8. How 'Abdu'l-Bahá built a bath for Baha'u'llah. 9. Spiritual humility and the story of the king and the Arab. 10. 'Abdu'l-Bahá's generosity.

RAMLEH, EGYPT, AUGUST 6, 1913 | 157
1. God's favors measureless. 2. Spiritual relationship. 3. A walk through the streets and the radiance of the star of hope.

RAMLEH, EGYPT, AUGUST 7, 1913 | 159
1. The beauty and charm of the palaces of Ramleh. 2. The Egyptian Pashas are proud of 'Abdu'l-Bahá and his philosophy of religion. 3. A call from 'Abdu'l-Bahá and his encouragement.

RAMLEH, EGYPT, AUGUST 8, 1913 | 161
1. A practical lesson in cleanliness. 2. The story of the Dervish and his resignation. 3. 'Abdu'l-Bahá amid the roses. 4. 'Abdu'l-Bahá raises the Call of the Kingdom.

RAMLEH, EGYPT, AUGUST 9, 1913 | 164
1. The Bounties of God. 2. A Tablet for the believers of Isfahan, Persia. 3. Contrast between Oriental and Occidental houses. 4. 'Adu'l-Bahá gives money to the poor.

RAMLEH, EGYPT, AUGUST 10, 1913 | 167
1. How 'Abdu'l-Bahá dictates Tablets to his friends in all parts of the world. 2. 'Abdu'l-Bahá speaks on Theosophy.

RAMLEH, EGYPT, AUGUST 11, 1913 | 169
1. The spread of the Bahá'í Cause similar to the spreading of early Christianity. 2. 'Abdu'l-Bahá's Tablets are the never-fading roses of the Kingdom of Abhá. 3. The most great sin is backbiting.

RAMLEH, EGYPT, AUGUST 12, 1913 | 172
l. The Bahá'ís must start a forward movement of teaching. 2. Mrs. Getsinger and her forthcoming trip to India. 3. 'Abdu'l-Bahá praises German Bahá'ís in Tablet.

RAMLEH, EGYPT, AUGUST 13, 1913 | 173
1. The story of the man who made it appear that he was a Bahá'í in 1830, while the movement began in 1844. 2. The story of the fifteen robbers in Baghdad. 3. 'Abdu'l-Bahá talks about helping the poor and the needy. 4. The story of the Mohammedan Mullá and the questioner. 5. Arrival of a new pilgrim. 6 With 'Abdu'l-Bahá in the rose garden.

RAMLEH, EGYPT, AUGUST 14, 1913 | 177
1. Bahá'í schools in Kashan and Tehran and their examinations. 2. The Orient-Occident Unity. 3. Talk of 'Abdu'l-Bahá to the writer. 4.'Abdu'l-Bahá

praises Mrs. Goodall and Mrs. Getsinger. 5. Difference between 'Abdu'l-Bahá and others. 6. 'Abdu'l-Bahá and three roses.

RAMLEH, EGYPT, AUGUST 15, 1913 | **180**
1. How are you today? 2. Talk on religion and atheism by an illiterate Bahá'í. 3. 'Abdu'l-Bahá sends his secretaries to Nouzha Park. 4. Attending a Bahá'í meeting with new pilgrims. 5. 'Abdu'l-Bahá and the Khedive of Egypt. 6. A sweet Tablet to the little darling Mona.

RAMLEH, EGYPT, AUGUST 16, 1913 | **182**
1. 'Abdu'l-Bahá writes to a Hindu Bahá'í. 2. El Yahou arrives from Cairo. 3. 'Abdu'l-Bahá dictates Tablets in the garden. 4. Walks and Bahá'í reminiscences. 5. 'Abdu'l-Bahá gives Persian names to two German and Austrian Bahá'ís traveling in Persia. 6. The believers must summon the people to the Kingdom. 7. Acquire complete concentration.

RAMLEH, EGYPT, AUGUST 17, 1913 | **185**
1. 'Abdu'l-Bahá and the Khedive of Egypt. 2. A traveling companion for Mrs. Getsinger in her approaching visit to India. 3. Story of the French Ambassador and the Turkish Minister of Foreign Affairs about Christ's resurrection. 4. The principle upon which 'Abdu'l-Bahá's journey was based. 5. America cannot be compared to Europe.

RAMLEH, EGYPT, AUGUST 18, 1913 | **188**
1. 'Abdu'l-Bahá and his attitude toward humanity. 2. 'Abdu'l-Bahá and Abdu'l-Hudá, a favorite of the Sultan.

RAMLEH, EGYPT, AUGUST 19, 1913 | **190**
1. The coming of Isabel Fraser to Egypt. 2. 'Abdu'l-Bahá attends to his mail 3. "Thou must be firm and unshakable in thy purpose." 4. Abdu'l-Bahá and his talk with Miss Hiscock.

RAMLEH, EGYPT, AUGUST 20, 1913 | **192**
1. Strange customs in different countries are not tokens of the inferiority of the people. 2. On Divine Guidance from a Tablet of 'Abdu'l- Bahá. 3. Lack of trustworthiness. 4. Persecutions in the path of God. 5. Teaching the Cause. 6. Faithfulness at the Holy Threshold. 7. Arrival of a new pilgrim. 8. 'Abdu'l-Bahá's photograph in Constantinople. 9. 'Abdu'l-Bahá talks on his meeting and conversation with a Persian general in Paris.

RAMLEH, EGYPT, AUGUST 21, 1913 | **197**
1. The qualities of the members of the Spiritual Assembly.

RAMLEH, EGYPT, AUGUST 22, 1913 | **198**
1. Story of the woodcutter and his wife. 2. Story of the sinner and the Mullá. 3. Story of the Baktashi and his strange death amidst the laughter of his friends. 4. 'Abdu'l-Bahá goes to Mosque and gives money to the poor.

RAMLEH, EGYPT, AUGUST 23, 1913 | 202

1. The Bahá'ís must embody their teachings in their lives. 2. The story of the man who did not know the window in his own room. 3. No power on earth can withstand the Cause of God.

RAMLEH, EGYPT, AUGUST 24, 1913 | 205

1. How Tablets to the American friends are spread all over Persia. 2. An eloquent Tablet to Mr. William Hoar of New York. 3. The minute questions asked of 'Abdu'l-Bahá. 4. 'Abdu'l-Bahá jokes and beats his secretary. 5. 'Abdu'l-Bahá says that if people wish to sneeze they ask him about it. 6. A talk by 'Abdu'l-Bahá on creation. 7. Explanation on free will. 8. 'Abdu'l-Bahá talks to Shaykhs and young Egyptians on his trip to the West.

RAMLEH, EGYPT, AUGUST 25, 1913 | 211

1. International Bahá'í correspondence conducive to unity. 2. The weather in Ramleh. 3. Receipt of Bahá'í reports from America. 4. The story of Foad Pasha, the Grand Vizir of Turkey. 5. Qá'im-Maqám, the Persian statesman. 6. The story of the sick soldier and the watchman.

RAMLEH, EGYPT, AUGUST 26, 1913 | 216

1. The Bahá'ís must raise a new voice. 2. The article of Arthur Brisbane on "Science" translated and published in Arabic daily and discussed by students. 3. This world is dark, it must be changed into a universe of light. 4. Attraction is not realized save through teaching the Cause of God. 5. Confer upon everyone spiritual joy. 6. A poetic tablet like a bouquet of fragrant flowers.

RAMLEH, EGYPT, AUGUST 27, 1913 | 219

1. This is the seed-sowing time. 2. This is the day in which to lay the foundation of the house. 3. All efforts must be centralized around the spreading of the Cause. 4. Hope for the union of the East and the West.

RAMLEH, EGYPT, AUGUST 28, 1913 | 222

1. The life of the East and the West, and of how the Bahá'í movement unites them. 2. 'Abdu'l-Bahá writes on the future condition of women.

RAMLEH, EGYPT, AUGUST 29, 1913 | 225

1. The college life and its expected results. 2. A talk by an old Bahá'í on the sins of backbiting. 3. Permission given to Persian Bahá'í students to come to Ramleh. 4. 'Abdu'l-Bahá praises Mrs. Besant, President of the Theosophical Society.

RAMLEH, EGYPT, AUGUST 30, 1913 | 228

1. Spread of the Bahá'í Cause in the interior of Turkey. 2. Let the American friends wait. 3. Story of how a Bahá'í feast was given in Baghdad. 4.

'Abdu'l-Bahá writes on nineteen day feasts. 5. The Mohammedan month of fasting comes to an end.

RAMLEH, EGYPT, AUGUST 31, 1913 | **230**
1. The story of the blind man and the serpent.

RAMLEH, EGYPT, SEPTEMBER 1, 1913 | **233**
1. The watermelons of 'Akká. 2. 'Abdu'l-Bahá and the story of the policeman of Ramleh. 3. 'Abdu'l-Bahá talks on the power of imagination. 4. Oriental Bahá'ís portray natural spirituality.

RAMLEH, EGYPT, SEPTEMBER 2, 1913 | **236**
1. Moving picture theaters in Egypt. 2. The feast of Ramadan and its spirit of joy. 3. Talk on education and the story of the selfish mother. 4. Story of the theologian and the sea captain. 5. Story of a metaphysician and the correction of his book by a teacher. 6. Study of science and true religion must be combined.

RAMLEH, EGYPT, SEPTEMBER 3, 1913 | **240**
1. Persian Bahá'í students of the American college arrive. 2. Persian students in Paris and London. 3. 'Abdu'l-Bahá tells the students how to study. 4. The students read 'Abdu'l-Bahá's talks in America. 5. 'Abdu'l-Bahá calls on the Persian Consul.

RAMLEH, EGYPT, SEPTEMBER 4, 1913 | **242**
1. The story of the royal bird of Qidam. 2. Purity and chastity are foundations of spiritual life. 3. The brother of the Khedive calls on 'Abdu'l-Bahá. 4. American ice cream for the students; their visit to the national park. 5. Their love for the Bahá'í Cause.

RAMLEH, EGYPT, SEPTEMBER 5, 1913 | **246**
1. Who is 'Abdu'l-Bahá and what is he doing? 2. The Persian students and prayers. 3. The story of a man who was hired to build a wall around the garden. 4. In the Cause of Brotherhood there are no titles. 5. 'Abdu'l-Bahá inquires from the Persian students about their teachers. 6. People are not awake to the danger of war. 7. 'Abdu'l-Bahá dictates Tablets for the American Bahá'ís. 8. Program of a national or religious feast. 9. Driving around with 'Abdu'l-Bahá.

RAMLEH, EGYPT, SEPTEMBER 6, 1913 | **250**
1. The American Bahá'ís must make great efforts teaching the Cause of Peace. 2. Prof. Armenius Vambery's letter to 'Abdu'l-Bahá. 3. The Persian students meet Mrs. Getsinger. 4. 'Abdu'l-Bahá speaks to them on the Power of unity.

RAMLEH, EGYPT, SEPTEMBER 7, 1913 | **252**
1. The story of the mythical republic and a curious way of electing a president. 2. 'Abdu'l-Bahá spends a busy day.

RAMLEH, EGYPT, SEPTEMBER 8, 1913 | 256
1. The Arab Bahá'ís give a feast to the Persian students. 2. How an Arab became a Bahá'í. 3. Importance of agriculture. 4. A prayer for the illumination of mankind. 5. The object of the coming of Bahá'u'lláh.

RAMLEH, EGYPT, SEPTEMBER 9, 1913 | 259
1. A bird's-eye view of the general conditions of the world. 2. The spread of the Bahá'í Cause in Germany makes 'Abdu'l-Bahá happy. 3. Photographs received from America and Germany distributed among Persian Bahá'ís. 4. The silence of 'Abdu'l-Bahá is eloquent.

RAMLEH, EGYPT, SEPTEMBER 10, 1913 | 262
1. Good news received from America and Europe. 2. A few Arabian proverbs. 3. A prayer by 'Abdu'l-Bahá for detachment.

RAMLEH, EGYPT, SEPTEMBER 11, 1913 | 264
1. How the Persian students lived together. 2. An important Tablet revealed by 'Abdu'l-Bahá for China.

RAMLEH, EGYPT, SEPTEMBER 12, 1913 | 269
1. Departure of the Persian students. 2. Russian Count meets 'Abdu'l-Bahá and talks on the two aspects of reincarnation. 3. Strive that love may increase day by day. 4. Tablet of 'Abdu'l-Bahá to the author of "Modern Social Religion." 5. Pure intention is the magnet of heavenly assistance. 6. "Strive to quicken the dead souls."

RAMLEH, EGYPT, SEPTEMBER 13, 1913 | 272
1. From Ramleh the mysterious power of God is silently quickening the world. 2. Story of the German Consul in Haifa and how he became the victim of "Bravo." 3. 'Abdu'l-Bahá dictates many Tablets for Russia.

RAMLEH, EGYPT, SEPTEMBER 14, 1913 | 274
1. The law of Universal Love and the Bahá'ís. 2. Tablets for German Bahá'ís.

RAMLEH, EGYPT, SEPTEMBER 15, 1913 | 276
1. A busy day for 'Abdu'l-Bahá. 2. The story of the king and the thorn-picker.

RAMLEH, EGYPT, SEPTEMBER 16, 1913 | 279
1. Arrival of pilgrims and other incidents. 2. Translation of a Tablet giving the keynote of the Bahá'í movement. 3. Give hearing to the deaf, sight to the blind and speech to the dumb.

RAMLEH, EGYPT, SEPTEMBER 17, 1913 | 282
1. The spiritual palace of International Brotherhood is being built by the peacemakers. 2. "Christian Commonwealth" and Bahá'í articles. 3. Tablet to the Editor of the "Christian Commonwealth." 4. The sojourn in Ramleh has been fruitful.

RAMLEH, EGYPT, SEPTEMBER 18, 1913 | **284**

1. 'Abdu'l-Bahá writes to the believers in Russia. 2. In the Bahá'í Cause there are no salaried teachers. 3. Wit is the salt of conversation. 4. The second party of the Bahá'í students arrive. 5. Mrs. Fraser arrives from America. 6. Mrs. Fraser is welcomed at the station by Shoghi Effendi.

RAMLEH, EGYPT, SEPTEMBER 19, 1913 | **287**

1. The American Bahá'ís will be going to India. 2. The importance of the art of translation. 3. The past glory of Persia and her future opportunity. 4. The Bahá'í students meet Mrs. Getsinger and Mrs. Fraser in the home of 'Abdu'l-Bahá. 5. Bahá'í meeting for the Americans. 6. 'Abdu'l-Bahá amid a profusion of thousands of roses. 7. Description of the garden of Bahá'u'lláh in Tehran. 8. A single rose in the garden of Constantinople.

RAMLEH, EGYPT, SEPTEMBER 20, 1913 | **291**

1. Thoughts on the Mediterranean shore. 2. 'Abdu'l-Bahá talks to Mrs. Fraser and Mrs. Getsinger about their trip to India. 3. Mr. Hooper Harris and Harlan Ober's journey to India.

RAMLEH, EGYPT, SEPTEMBER 21, 1913 | **293**

1. The story of the king and his search for the fountain of life. 2. The simplicity of life and how the Arabs live in the desert. 3. 'Abdu'l-Bahá talks with Mrs. Fraser.

RAMLEH, EGYPT, SEPTEMBER 22, 1913 | **298**

1. 'Abdu'l-Bahá's spiritual moods. 2. Dr. Getsinger's arrival in Alexandria. 3. Tablet from 'Abdu'l-Bahá to Bahá'ís in Leipzig, Germany. 4. Another Tablet to a German Bahá'í asking him to teach.

RAMLEH, EGYPT, SEPTEMBER 23, 1913 | **300**

1. Speeches to be delivered at public meetings. 2. History of the life of Armenius Vambery.

RAMLEH, EGYPT, SEPTEMBER 24, 1913 | **304**

1. A Persian Bahá'í student delivers a lecture in English. 2. 'Abdu'l-Bahá wishes the Bahá'í students to take postgraduate courses. 3. The mission of the Bahá'í Cause is universal, not local.

RAMLEH, EGYPT, SEPTEMBER 25, 1913 | **307**

1. An Analysis of the Letters of Unity by a Persian student. 2. Story of the stork, fish and prawn. 3. Letters received from and Tablets written to different parts of the world.

RAMLEH, EGYPT, SEPTEMBER 26, 1913 | **308**

1. 'Ishqabad, Russia, an important center of the Bahá'í Movement. 2. Tablets for the Bahá'ís of 'Ishqabad.

RAMLEH, EGYPT, SEPTEMBER 27, 1913 | 311
　1. Tablet in handwriting of Bahá'u'lláh. 2. Prayer for spiritual strength by Bahá'u'lláh. 3. Someone must arise to write the life history of Bahá'u'lláh. 4. Pilgrims arrive from India, Persia and Russia. 5. 'Abdu'l-Bahá urges the students to practice public speaking on all subjects.

RAMLEH, EGYPT, SEPTEMBER 28, 1913 | 314
　1. Farewell words to the students. 2. I desire that thou mayst be filled with Bahá'u'lláh. 3. Mrs. Stannard, an earnest Bahá'í. 4. An address delivered to the students.

RAMLEH, EGYPT, SEPTEMBER 29, 1913 | 315
　1. The Persian Bahá'ís are anxious to know all about the Western Bahá'ís. 2. "Mahmal" or the Holy Carpet. 3. 'Abdu'l-Bahá speaks to the students before their departure for College. 4. Mírzá Jalal and wife arrive from London. 5. All the pilgrims are gone and the house seems deserted.

RAMLEH, EGYPT, SEPTEMBER 30, 1913 | 317
　1. The procession of Mahmal in Alexandria. 2. Mahmal, a great annual event. 3. Qur'an verses woven in Mahmal. 4. Mahmal or Carpet, is a sacred object. 5. People from all over Egypt come to visit and touch the Mahmal. 6. How Mahmal was originated. 7. Many Mahmals mentioned in history. 8. Hardships of Bahá'u'lláh to become the cause of the awakening of the people.

RAMLEH, EGYPT, SEPTEMBER 31, 1913 | 320
　1. What it means to be with 'Abdu'l-Bahá. 2. The students consist of a large delegation. 3. The students sing Mrs. Shahnaz Waite's anthems. 4. Happiness and tranquility of heart. 5. Lasting enjoyment is for the moral man. 6. The meaning of Faith. 7. The basic principle of the good-pleasure of God. 8. The successful student. 9. Light and Knowledge. 10. Letter to the students from the President of College. 11. The Bahá'í Cause as interpreted by 'Abdu'l-Bahá.

A Report from 1913 by Isabel Fraser | 329

PUBLISHERS' NOTE

In Memoriam
Ahang Rabbani, Ph.D. (1956-2013)

Ahang Rabbani became friends with everyone he met. His jovial nature, his loving smile, and his unforgettable laugh drew everyone close to him. He easily made conversation with strangers. In minutes they were laughing together. He was never at a loss for words or friendly gestures.

With a doctorate in statistics, he pursed his career on multiple continents. But his true passion was Bahá'í scholarship, which he worked at with diligence and endless energy—always after hours, and sometimes deep into the night and early morning. The products of his scholarly labors were many and important. He filled his personal website with his own articles and translations. His book, *The Genesis of the Bábí-Bahá'í Faiths in Shiráz and Fárs* (Leiden: Brill, 2008), the memoir of Mirza Habibu'llah Afnan, which he translated, edited, and annotated, is a major contribution to early Baha'i history, and one which is still underappreciated.

After noticing online his edited version of *'Abdu'l-Baha in Egypt*, by Mirza Ahmad Sohrab, Kalimat Press asked Ahang to prepare the book for a new edition. He liked the idea and threw himself into the task, working every night to annotate this edition. He was able to finish the manuscript in November of 2007. How bitterly disappointed he was when, due to unforeseen circumstances, the book could not be published in a timely manner. Kalimat Press certainly shared his chagrin. We regret that he was unable to see the book published before his premature passing in 2013.

However, after a delay of many years, we are happy and relieved to witness the manuscript in the light of day in this edition. We offer it in tribute to Ahang Rabbani's intellect, his diligence and dedication, and to his late-night hours of scholarly labor. May Baha'u'llah rain blessings on his radiant spirit.

The Publishers
Los Angeles, 2020

EDITOR'S FOREWORD

In the mid-1860s Baha'u'llah, living in Edirne, encouraged several Bahá'í merchants to settle in Alexandria and Cairo, thus opening Egypt to the Baha'i Faith. Among this group were Hájí Báqir and Sayyid Husayn, two natives of Kashan, who took up residence in Egypt.[1] Bahá'u'lláh also sent Hájí Mullá 'Alí Tabrízí, Hájí Muhammad Yazdí and Mírzá Haydar-'Alí Isfahání to that region and they lived in Mansuriyya, where they brought a number of people into the Faith, including Hájí Abú'l-Qásim Shírází.[2] In 1888, at the instigation of the Iranian Consulate, the Khedive, Ismá'íl Pasha, deported Haydar-'Alí to Sudan.[3] However, other Bahá'í merchants from Iran arrived, and by early 1890s a sizeable Bahá'í community was flourishing in several towns, including Port Said. The community was led by Áqá Mírzá Áqá Núri'd-Dín and Mírzá Hasan Khurásání.[4]

The arrival in 1894 of Mírzá Abú'l-Fadl Gulpáygání (1844-1914), a renowned Islamic scholar who had converted to the Bahá'í Faith, reinforced the Bahá'í community in Egypt. He started lecturing in association with Al-Azhar University and soon a large circle of students surrounded him. He taught philosophy, logic, history,

---

1. Shoghi Effendi, *God Passes By*, p. 176.
2. E. G. Browne, *Materials for the Study of the Bábí Religion*, p. 33.
3. Mírzá Haydar-'Alí, *Bihjatu's-Sudúr* (Bombay: Parsi Press, 1912); partial English trans. by A. Q. Faizi, *Stories from the Delight of Hearts*, (Los Angeles: Kalimat Press, 1980).
4. Mírzá Habíbu'lláh Afnán, *Memories of the Báb, Bahá'u'lláh and 'Abdu'l-Bahá*, chap 3.

dialectical theology (*kalám*), Qur'an commentary, and geography. He gained the trust of some of his Sunni students and soon was able to win many of them to the Faith.[5] This first influx of native Egyptian intellectuals into the religion gives evidence both of the appeal of the Bahá'í teachings for this group and the persuasiveness of Mírzá Abú'l-Fadl himself.

In 1896, an assassin, who was a disciple of Jamálu'd-Dín Afghání, killed Nasiri'd-Dín Shah. Both in Iran and among Iranian expatriates, many blamed the Bábís for this incident (few Iranians at that time, or even at the present, made any distinction between Bábís and Bahá'ís). Until official word came from Iran through the Consulate that the Bahá'ís were not involved, a number of Shi'i Iranian expatriates were calling for a retaliatory massacre of the Bahá'ís in Egypt. It was during this period that at a gathering in the Iranian Consulate, Mírzá Abú'l-Fadl openly declared himself to be a Bahá'í. He had by this time established contacts with the Egyptian press. When news reports containing charges that the Bábís were behind the Shah's assassination began to circulate, Ya'qub Sarruf and Farís Nimr asked Mírzá Abú'l-Fadl for an article on the Bábí and Bahá'í movements for their secular-minded journal, al-Muqtataf. Mírzá Abú'l-Fadl complied, and as such brought the history and teachings of the Faith to the attention of intellectuals throughout the Arab world.

During this period, a number of early treatises were published in Cairo, including: an Arabic polemical history of the Bábís by Mírzá Muhammad-Mihdí Khán, the Za'ímu'd-Dawlih, was printed in Cairo in 1903;[6] numerous titles in Persian, including collection of Tablets, prayers and poetry of Bahá'u'lláh, His *Epistle to the Son of the Wolf*, *The Seven Valleys*, *The Four Valleys*; three volumes of *Makátíb* [Letters] 'Abdu'l-Bahá; Mírzá Abú'l-Fadl's *Kitáb*

---

5. Ibid.
6. *Miftáhu Bábí'l-Abwab* [The Key to the Gate of Gates]. Supposedly this was a dispassionate account of the Bábís and Bahá'ís, but in fact a distortion of truth, and in effect, as attested by 'Abdu'l-Bahá, intended to arouse passions against the Bahá'ís.

Fará'id, *Dawra'l-Bahiyyih*, and *Hujaju'l-Bahiyyih*; and Hájí Mírzá Haydar-'Alí's *Dalá'ilu'l-'Irfán*. Publications in Arabic included Bahá'u'lláh's Ishráqát, Tajallíát, Tarázát, and Kalamát. Myron H. Phelps completed his work, *Life and Teachings of Abbas Effendi*, when in Cairo in March 1903.

In addition, starting 1899, Egypt had become a transit point for Western Bahá'ís coming to and from the Holy Land for their visit to the Shrine of Bahá'u'lláh, and attaining the presence of 'Abdu'l-Bahá.

Against this backdrop, we find 'Abdu'l-Bahá's visit to Egypt. The years following Bahá'u'lláh's Ascension, brought intense pressure on 'Abdu'l-Bahá instigated by his unfaithful half-brothers. For the first five years, He tried to conceal the actions of Mírzá 'Alí-Muhammad and other siblings in undermining His authority and bringing about divisions, but their own deeds finally brought their rebellion into open. They continued with their constant harassments and machinations against 'Abdu'l-Bahá, but the latter pressed ahead with developments both within the Holy Land and elsewhere.

In Haifa, 'Abdu'l-Bahá supervised the construction of the Shrine of the Báb and establishment of a larger Bahá'í community in Haifa, which also included His own residence and family. In 1904, He encouraged the immediate reconstruction of the House of the Báb in Shiraz, to the same design that it was during the time of the Báb. He continued to guide the ever-expanding Bahá'í community of 'Ishqabad and under His directions, the first Mashriqu'l-Adhkar was raised there. In the United States, land was purchased and dedicated for the first Temple in the West. Bahá'í communities were established in a number of towns in Europe and the North America. And all during this time, 'Abdu'l-Bahá endured the investigation of two Commissions of Inquiry sent from Istanbul to 'Akká as result of Mírzá Muhammad-'Alí's lies that he was spreading through local officials. The second Commission's visit, resulted in 'Abdu'l-Bahá's confinement in the city of 'Akká.

But, as 'Abdu'l-Bahá has described it, "God's cannon roared" and the Commission was withdrawn and His imprisonment ended. Soon after that, as result of Revolution of the Young Turks, all political prisoners are pardoned, including 'Abdu'l-Bahá.

On hearing that he was free, His first act was to visit the Shrine of His Father since during the years of His incarceration, He had been denied the opportunity to visit that Shrine and this weighed heavily upon Him. No sooner was He at liberty to visit Bahjí than He resumed the task which He had so diligently pursued in days past, namely, carrying water for the gardens to that Sacred Spot every Friday and Sunday.

But now He was sixty-five years old, and His health was failing due to years of hardships which He had endured. Resident Bahá'ís and pilgrims begged 'Abdu'l-Bahá to spare Himself physically difficult tasks, but He thought it was important for Him to continue with all His services.

Subsequent to the entombment of the remains of the Báb on Mount Carmel, 'Abdu'l-Bahá transferred His residence to Haifa, where a house was built for Him. Soon He ceased to set foot within the city gates of 'Akká.

'Abdu'l-Bahá's health continued to decline. Sorrows and tribulations pressed hard upon 'Abdu'l-Bahá, and weakened His frame and made Him a prey to various ailments, which at times were severe. Physicians advised Him that He ought to seek a change of air, and leave the region. "But subsequent events demonstrated the fact that 'Abdu'l-Bahá, when He did this, was not just embarking on a journey to improve His health in a different setting, or to prevent its further deterioration. He was indeed taking the first step to reach the world of the West and deliver, in person, the Message of His Father. There was another purpose evident in 'Abdu'l-Bahá's journey. Mírzá Muhammad-'Alí and his partisans were now thoroughly discredited. In the absence of 'Abdu'l-Bahá from the Holy Land the violators would have the field entirely to themselves, but their utter inability to make any move to impair the unity of the Bahá'ís would set the final seal on their downfall.

'Abdu'l-Bahá particularly stressed this fact in a Tablet addressed at the time to a Bahá'í of Iskandarun, Turkey (Alexandretta)."[7]

'Abdu'l-Baha stayed in Port Said for nearly a month. Once again, without previous announcement He took a ship, first intending to go to Europe, but it became obvious that the state of His health did not permit the strenuous journey. Instead He disembarked at Alexandria. Here a complete change occurred and all the work of last two decades began to pay off. Egyptian journalists, who had until then shown open hostility, began to ask for meetings with 'Abdu'l-Bahá and significantly changed their tone and often wrote in terms of high praise. Shaykh 'Alí-Yúsuf, the editor of the Arabic paper, Al-Mu'ayyad, had previously made harsh attacks on the Bahá'ís, urging that they be severely constrained. He visited 'Abdu'l-Bahá and in the October 16 issue of his paper he published an article under the heading, "Al-Mírzá 'Abbás Effendi." These are the opening lines of that remarkable article: "His Eminence Mírzá 'Abbás Effendi, the learned and erudite Head of the Bahá'ís in 'Akká and the Centre of authority for Bahá'ís throughout the world, has reached the shores of Alexandria." At first, related the writer, 'Abdu'l-Bahá stayed in the Victoria Hotel, but after a few days moved to a rented house. Then he went on to say:

> He is a venerable person, dignified, possessed of profound knowledge, deeply versed in theology, master of the history of Islam, and of its denominations and developments ... whosoever has consorted with Him has seen in Him a man exceedingly well-informed, Whose speech is captivating, Who attracts minds and souls, dedicated to belief in the oneness of mankind ... His teaching and guidance revolve round the axis of relinquishing prejudices: religious, racial, patriotic.[8]

---

7. Hasan Balyuzi, *'Abdu'l-Bahá: The Centre of the Covenant*, p. 133.
8. Ibid., pp. 136-137.

Other newspaper editors visited him and had the same remarkable transformation. This period of stay in Alexandria also coincided with the month of Muharram, which is observed with great fervor, recalling the tragedies befallen on Imam Husayn. 'Abdu'l-Baha participated in these observances and contributed to holding of commemorative meetings on His behalf and to feeding the poor.

Lady Blomfield writes: "A doctor, who had been in Alexandria, where he saw 'Abdu'l Baha and witnessed His Christ like life, told me that for the first time he was able to understand what the Lord Christ must have been like. 'Now I am able to believe,' he said."[9]

Early in May, 'Abdu'l-Bahá moved to Cairo and took residence nearby in Zaytun. As His stay in Egypt lengthened, newspapers showed increasing friendliness. In Cairo, 'Abdu'l-Bahá was able to meet with many liberal Islamic thinkers and win their support. During this stay, He also renewed His friendship with Muhammad 'Abduh, who had met Him in Beirut during the 1880s. The two had subsequently maintained a correspondence on the subject of Islamic reform. On his return to Egypt, 'Abduh was appointed Grand Mufti and became a leading professor at Al-Azhar University. He extended a particularly warm welcome to 'Abdu'l-Bahá. Many other notables, including many clerics, administrators, parliamentarians, intellectuals, journalists, politicians, foreign dignitaries, and Arabs, Turks and Persians, sought His presence as well and were deeply impressed by His vision. The poor and the deprived also had access to Him and left satisfied.

His visit to Egypt a complete success, 'Abdu'l-Bahá turned His attention to Europe. On August 11, 1911, He boarded *S.S. Corsica* bound for Marseilles, France.

Over the course of the next two years, 'Abdu'l-Bahá visited many major Bahá'í communities in Europe and North America—a story that is told in great depth in other available sources.[10]

---

9. *Star of the West*, Vol. 17, p. 354.
10. There are several volumes of 'Abdu'l-Bahá's talks in Europe, most important being *Paris Talks* and *'Abdu'l-Bahá in London*. Most of His talks in North

After completing His journeys, on June 13, 1913, 'Abdu'l-Bahá left Marseilles for Egypt on *SS Himalaya* arriving in Port Said four days later, June 16. On June 19, 'Abdu'l-Bahá cabled the Baha'is in the United States, "Arrived safely, Port Said, with joy and fragrance. Abbas."[11]

Port Said was hot and humid and the travels of the last three years were taking their toll on 'Abdu'l-Bahá. Shortly after arrival He wrote: "Praise be to God you are spending your days in a delectable, verdant and refreshing place. We too are, praise be to God, enjoying ourselves in the hot weather of Port Said with its excessive humidity, dust and dirt, while suffering with nerve fever. As the friends are comfortable, Abdul Baha is in the utmost joy."[12]

> 'Abdu'l-Bahá had decided not to travel to the Holy Land immediately. Pilgrims assembled in Haifa were called by cable to come to Egypt. As the hotel in which they were to be housed proved too small for their numbers and activities, a huge tent of the type which Egyptians used for public

---

America were collected as a single book titled *The Promulgation of Universal Peace*. Though much has been written on 'Abdu'l-Bahá's visits to America, little has been published about His travels in Europe, except such short accounts as "'Abdu'l-Bahá Meeting with Two Prominent Iranians", or pilgrim's notes such as *The Diary of Juliet Thompson*. The most complete study of 'Abdu'l-Bahá's visit to North America, Allan L. Ward's *Two Hundred Thirty-Nine Days: 'Abdu'l-Bahá's Journey in America*, and a detailed chronicle of 'Abdu'l-Bahá's trip is provided in Mírzá Mahmúd Zarqání's, *Mahmud's Diary*, vol. 1. Hasan Balyuzi's *'Abdu'l-Bahá: The Centre of the Covenant*, chapters 12-18, also provides a summary. Other sources include: Memoirs by Thornton Chase and Juanita Storch about 'Abdu'l-Bahá's visit to North America, describing the impact he had on Bahá'ís, (World Order, 25.1, Fall, 1993); *The Diary of Juliet Thompson* also includes a wealth of information about his visits to America, especially pages 223-395, and some of his time in Europe, especially pages 147-222; Agnes Parsons' *'Abdu'l-Bahá in America: Agnes Parsons' Diary*, and the biography of Lua Getsinger by Velda Piff Metelmann, *Lua Getsinger: Herald of the Covenant*, also cover much of the same ground.

11. *Star of the West*, Vol. 4, Chicago (June 24, 1913) Rahmat No. 6, "Cablegram from Abdul Baha."
12. Marzieh Gail, *Arches of the Years*, p. 124; received in America July 25.

functions was pitched on the roof of the hotel. There were constant gatherings under the shade of that tent. Meetings were held there at which 'Abdu'l-Bahá oftentimes spoke. Soon after His arrival at Port Said He remarked that, at a time when the heat of the summer drove people to Paris, He had come away from Paris to Egypt. He recalled that in the days of Bahá'u'lláh cholera broke out four times in the Holy Land. It touched the environs of 'Akká and reached Lebanon, but within 'Akká there was no cholera. Immediately after the ascension of Bahá'u'lláh there was another outbreak of the epidemic, this time inside the city walls. 'Abdu'l-Bahá, feeling that He could not stay at Bahjí and leave the Bahá'ís of 'Akká to themselves, returned to the city, only to find that other people had fled 'Akká and put their homes in the care of the Bahá'ís. He appointed watchmen to guard these houses. All the Bahá'ís escaped the ravages of the epidemic. Then cholera died down in the city, but appeared in the neighborhood, at which the people who had abandoned their homes rushed back to 'Akká.

Another day, under that tent, 'Abdu'l-Bahá, looking at the ranks assembled, said it was truly remarkable that such a gathering had been made possible. The issue of the Egyptian Gazette for Friday, June 27th, carried an article under the headlines: "Abdul Baha in Egypt. Wonderful Scenes in Port Said. Eastern Bahais Assembled in Force."

'Abdu'l-Bahá was now kept more occupied than ever. There were so many pilgrims, so many Bahá'ís of Egypt to meet and converse with, and a great many letters to answer. Letters, petitions and cables came pouring in from the East and the West. All the Tablets belonging to this period are in His own handwriting.

And there were not only Bahá'ís to meet. On June 24th, He had written and spoken much. At the end of the day, greatly fatigued, He was on the point of leaving the house for His daily walk, when a group of Christian missionaries, men and women, appeared at His door and asked to meet Him. 'Abdu'l-Bahá received them with His usual courtesy and kindness. Before long, they were harshly criticizing the Muslims and Islam. 'Abdu'l-Bahá told them that what they were talking about was not the true Islam, but imitations and trivialities; and He reminded them of a verse in the Qur'án about Christ: "Those who have believed, the Jews, the Christians, and the Sabeans, who believe in God and the Day of Judgment and do righteously, have their reward with their Lord. Neither is there fear for them, nor are they to grieve."[13] One of the missionaries said that in the Gospels Christ is extolled as the Son of God—the highest possible station—whereas in the Qur'án no such reference is made to Jesus. To this 'Abdu'l-Bahá replied that the term 'Son of God' was current in the days of Moses and Jesus, and was applied to the whole of Israel; He referred them to Exodus (iv. 22-3): "And thou shalt say unto Pharaoh, Thus saith the Lord, Israel is my son, even my firstborn: And I say unto thee, Let my son go, that he may serve me: and if thou refuse to let him go, behold, I will slay thy son, even thy firstborn."[14]

'Abdu'l-Bahá's family then joined him on August 1. In this party included His much loved sister, the Greatest Holy Leaf. Also included was Shoghi Effendi who had been studying in Beirut and after the school had ended in the first week of July, had traveled to Haifa and then with the rest of family to Egypt. For their stay, 'Abdu'l-Bahá rented a villa in Ramleh. Rúhíyyih Khanum, the wife of Shoghi Effendi, has written about these days:

> So many times Shoghi Effendi would say "the Master was like an ocean," meaning He could receive everything and give forth no sign of disturbance. This immense self-control

---

13. Qur'an 11:59.
14. H. M. Balyuzi, *'Abdu'l-Bahá: The Centre of the Covenant*, pp. 397-399.

is nowhere better shown than in the diarist's[15] report that 'Abdu'l-Bahá, after hearing of the arrival of the two people He loved best in the world, sat for an hour with Bahá'ís and friends before returning home to greet them! On 2 August the diary notes: "Today the Beloved did not come to see us in the morning because He was entertaining the Greatest Holy Leaf and the rest of the friends who had come with her." When one imagines the joy of the reunion and reads this trite indication of it one realizes something of the dignity and reserve which always surrounded the family of 'Abdu'l-Bahá. Nevertheless we have some indication of Shoghi Effendi's life there: the old custom of prayers in the presence of 'Abdu'l-Bahá was resumed and Shoghi Effendi would chant too, with his lovely young voice, and 'Abdu'l-Bahá would sometimes correct and instruct him. There was nothing unusual in this; I myself often heard older members of the family correct the tune or the pronunciation of someone who was reciting verses or poems out loud; no doubt the Master must have done this many times over the years to Shoghi Effendi. Intensely active and always capable, Shoghi Effendi, during the months he was with 'Abdu'l-Bahá, before he returned to his studies in Beirut, made himself constantly useful to the Master, taking down His letters to the Persian believers, which He would dictate to him as he sat in the garden of His villa, where He was wont to drink His tea and receive His guests, waiting on Him, doing errands for Him, being sent by Him with others to receive visitors or meet them at the railway station. We are told how 'Abdu'l-Bahá sent Shoghi Effendi to show some of the friends the famous park and zoo of Alexandria, how he visited Cairo—where one imagines he lost no time in visiting the pyramids, for Shoghi Effendi had an adventurous spirit and longed to visit distant places,

---

15. A reference to Ahmad Sohrab's account, which is provided in full later in this compilation.

as witnessed by the keen interest it is recorded he showed in some "Travel" magazines sent from America.

There was tremendous movement about 'Abdu'l-Bahá; pilgrims arriving from East and West, amongst them such famous old Bahá'ís as Lua Getsinger and Mírzá Abul Fazl [Abú'l-Fadl], who were to eventually rest, in Egypt, under the same tombstone, many, many years later; believers departing for India to spread the Message of Bahá'u'lláh; delegations of young Bahá'í students from Beirut and Persia; interviews accorded by the Master to press representatives and people of distinction and standing. One of His secretaries [Ahmad Sohrab] who had been with Him in America wrote at this time of what infinite joy and bounty these precious days in the Master's presence were. And if this registered itself so vividly on his mind and heart then what must have been the effect on Shoghi Effendi, so disappointed when he had been denied the bounty of accompanying 'Abdu'l-Bahá to the West, so starved for His presence and news of Him during almost fifteen months of separation? The heart at sixteen is capable of a kind of joy that seldom repeats itself later in life; in spite of the war years so soon to come, I believe that this period, up until the Master's passing in 1921, was the happiest of Shoghi Effendi's entire life.

I remember two stories associated with the days Shoghi Effendi spent in Egypt with the Master, which he himself recounted to me. He said that one day, after partaking of a particularly rich repast, the Master had recalled the days in Baghdad when His Father had returned from His self-imposed exile in the mountains of Sulaimaniya, when they had all been so poor—the days, however, when from Bahá'u'lláh's pen had streamed such a torrent of exalted writings which night after night until dawn the believers gathered to hear chanted, in ecstasy at this wonderful Revelation—and the Master said that the taste of the dry bread and dates of those days had been sweeter than all the other food in the world. The other story surprised me—and enlightened me—very much; I heard it more than once: Shoghi Effendi said that one day he was driving back from Alexandria to Ramleh with the Master in a rented carriage, accompanied by a Pasha who was going to the Master's house as His guest; when they arrived and got out the Master asked the strapping big coachman how much He owed him. The man asked an exorbitant price; 'Abdu'l-Bahá refused to pay it, the man insisted and became abusive to such an extent that he grasped the Master by the sash around His waist and pulled Him roughly back and forth, insisting on this price. Shoghi Effendi said this scene in front of the distinguished guest embarrassed him terribly. He was too small to do anything himself to help the Master and felt horrified and humiliated. No so 'Abdu'l-Bahá, Who remained perfectly calm and refused to give in. When the man finally released his hold the Master paid him exactly what He owed him, told him his conduct had forfeited the good tip He had planned to give him, and walked off followed by Shoghi Effendi and the Pasha. There is no doubt that such things left a lifelong imprint on the Guardian's character, who never allowed himself to be browbeaten or cheated, no matter whether or not this embarrassed or inconvenienced him, and those who were working for him.[16]

While in Egypt, after "short visits to Isma'iliyyih and Abuqir, and a prolonged stay in Ramleh, He returned to Haifa, concluding His historic journeys on December 5, 1913."[17] During these two stays, in 1910-11 and 1913, 'Abdu'l-Bahá became quite well known and influential—as evidenced by extensive press coverage in Egypt of His funeral in 1921. For Bahá'ís around the world, the extended visits of 'Abdu'l-Bahá gives Egypt a special significance.

---

16. Ruhiyyih Khanum, *The Priceless Pearl*, p. 21 ff.
17. Shoghi Effendi, *God Passes By*, p. 281.

Comments on the Present Volume

There is a large body of materials on 'Abdu'l-Bahá's stay in Egypt during 1910-11 and 1913, and much more to be gathered. The present volume is only a small step in making some of these materials more accessible to students of history.

The first section provides a series of extracts from *Bahai News*, which was renamed *Star of the West*. These are all from the 1910-11 period. Since these extracts used a system of transliteration no longer current (often making the names difficult to recognize), all the eastern names were edited to make them consistent with transliteration method presently used in Bahá'í publications. Several footnotes were added.

The second section provides a detailed description of 'Abdu'l-Bahá's activities during the summer of 1913. The source used here was *Abdul Baha in Egypt* by Mirza Ahmad Sohrab (New York: J. H. Sears & Company, Inc., 1929). This publication was written by Ahmad Sohrab before he was declared a Covenant-breaker and Shoghi Effendi had no objection to its publication. The book was approved by the Publishing Committee of the National Spiritual Assembly of the Baha'is of the United States and Canada, and the author's dedication read, "These records of the perfect life of 'Abdu'l-Bahá are dedicated to His ever-present spirit." The *Foreword* to 1929 printing stated:

> Around the great figures of the Prophets in all ages have been woven stories and records, often in the remote past clouded by myth and allegory, which nevertheless, constitute a witness to the light.
>
> In this age when the influence of Bahá'u'lláh and 'Abdu'l-Bahá is universally felt and their writings are being studied and translated into many languages, this intimate diary record should meet with wide response.
>
> Mírzá Ahmad Sohrab served for more than eight years as one of the private secretaries and interpreters of 'Abdu'l-Bahá; he accompanied Him on his journey throughout the West in 1912 and was with him during the World War. In this

diary he has vividly portrayed certain aspects and events in, the daily life and surroundings of the "Master" not found elsewhere, thus adding a document of human interest and appeal to the ever expanding literature written around the Bahá'í Cause.

Through his great love for 'Abdu'l-Bahá, Mírzá Ahmad Sohrab has given us a glimpse into that divine life of servitude and sacrifice, whose imperishable traces are written in the history of this age.

In preparing *Abdul Baha in Egypt* for inclusion in this volume, great care was exercised in ensuring authenticity. However, it was felt that a light editing would make the text more accessible:

Several misspellings or punctuation errors were corrected.

Transliteration of Persian names were brought in line with current method used in Bahá'í publications. Some now out of date terms (Mahommetan) have been updated (Muslim).

Subtitles at the beginning of each day's entry were removed as they contributed no extra information.

Several footnotes were added to facilitate identification of individuals or provide a fuller context.

Ahang Rabbani
Houston, Texas
November 2007

Bahai News and *Star of the West*

The *Bahai News* of the Bahá'ís of the United States begun its life on March 21, 1910. Later it was named *Star of the West*.

Editor's note: In the original publications from *Bahai News*, *Star of the West*, and *Abdu'l-Baha in Egypt*, original footnotes are indicated by this symbol †. Ahang Rabbani and the publisher have added footnotes to clarify points or identify individuals.

Bahai News, vol. 1, Chicago (October 16, 1910) Ilm, No. 12

First of a series of special news items pertaining to the tour of 'Abdu'l-Bahá. Portion of a letter from Mr. Sydney Sprague to Mrs. Isabella D. Brittingham.

Mount Carmel, August 29, 1910.

Dear Sister in the Holy Cause:

I have a very big piece of news to tell you. 'Abdu'l-Bahá has left this Holy Spot for the first time in forty-two years, and has gone to Egypt. Think of the vast significance and importance of this step! By it many prophecies of the sacred Scriptures are fulfilled. The Light and Life of 'Akká has departed and we feel as though we were now left in obscurity while Egypt is illumined, and that ancient country which has seen the prophets Joseph and Moses and even the infant Christ is now to see the Consummation of all the prophets. Will it appreciate and realize this Bounty? Everyone was astounded to hear of 'Abdu'l-Bahá's departure, for no one knew until the very last minute that he had any idea of leaving. The afternoon of the day he left, he came to Mírzá Asadu'lláh's[1] home to see us and sat with us awhile beside a new well that has just been finished and said that he had come to taste the water. We did not realize that it was a good-bye visit. Then he took a carriage and went up the hill to the Holy Tomb (of the Báb). That night, as usual, the believers gathered before the house of 'Abdu'l-Bahá to receive that blessing, which every day is ours, of being in his presence, but we waited in vain, for one of the sons-in-law came and told us that 'Abdu'l-Bahá had taken the Khedivial steamer for Port Said. We could hardly believe it was true, so great was this news. Think how happy we must be that after forty-two years in this cage, the Divine Bird has spread His wings and in perfect freedom flown away.[2]

---

1. A reference to Mírzá Asadu'lláh Isfahání, who was 'Abdu'l-Bahá's brother-in-law and had been entrusted with the conveyance of the remains of the Báb from Iran to the Holy Land. Later he followed his son, Dr. Amín Faríd, in rebellion against 'Abdu'l-Bahá.

The same issue includes the following:

SPECIAL.—Word has been received from Port Said that 'Abdu'l-Bahá has sailed from that port on a steamer for an unknown destination.

Bahai News, Vol. 1, Chicago (November 4, 1910) Qudrat, No. 13

Egypt, Port Said.—'Abdu'l-Bahá is in Alexandria and enjoying his sojourn in Egypt most heartily. Mírzá Ahmad Yazdí, just returning from Europe, has received permission to go to Alexandria and meet him.

Bahai News, Vol. 1, Chicago (November 23, 1910) Qawl, No. 14

Second in a series of special news items pertaining to the sojourn of 'Abdu'l-Bahá in Egypt.

"Out of Egypt have I called my son."

To those who are familiar with the sacred prophecies and the history of the Bahá'í (Glorious) Revelation, 'Abdu'l-Bahá's "going down into Egypt," after forty years' confinement in the Holy Land—in the prison town of 'Akká, near the foot of Mt. Carmel—is an event fraught with wonderful and tremendous significance; for it is, undoubtedly, that event whereby the Word of God, as uttered by the Prophet Hosea (11:1), finds its complete fulfillment—although foreshadowed in the sojourn of the infant Jesus in that land nearly two thousand years ago (St. Matt. 2:15).

It is an event that has stirred the Bahá'ís everywhere, for when it became known that 'Abdu'l-Bahá had departed for that ancient country of Joseph, there swept over the Bahá'í world a mighty

---

2. The author of this letter, Sydney Sprague, was married to the daughter of Mírzá Asadu'lláh and had been one of the early pioneer tachers. His book, *A Year With the Bahais of India and Burma* was published in London in 1908. Sprague rendered valuable help in the running of the Bahá'í Tarbiyat School in Tehran.

spirit of activity. It is an event that will, doubtless, soon command the serious attention of the Jewish and Christian world (especially those who await the coming of the Son "in the glory of his Father"), as it has already commanded the attention of the Mohammedan world; for, at present, the Egyptian newspapers—the most influential in the Mohammedan world today—are divided into two camps: some praising 'Abdu'l-Bahá's work; others trying to stop the floodgate of his irresistible influence.

Moamid, a paper respected by all the Islamic world, says: "Although he ('Abdu'l-Bahá) has lived the greater part of his life in 'Akká, Syria, yet there are millions of people—in Persia, India, Europe and America—who follow him and respect him to the point of worship and adoration. Whosoever associates with him, finds him a man who has information upon all subjects of human interest; his words are eloquent and attract the hearts, and enkindle the souls. His teachings and conversation revolve around the center of the greatest of the world's problems: To remove entirely, religious, racial and patriotic prejudices and lays the foundation of a brotherhood and unity that will last throughout the ages and eternity."

Such is the statement of the leading newspaper printed in Arabic, while the editor of an influential Persian newspaper printed in Cairo writes in a personal letter that he was summoned by 'Abdu'l-Bahá to his presence, and although a few weeks before, he wrote and published an article against the Cause of Bahá'u'lláh, he accepted the invitation and left Cairo for Alexandria. He met 'Abdu'l-Bahá and became a changed man. He went a stranger and an avowed antagonist; he returned a friend, and will write an article in favor of the Cause. He writes: "Indeed, I was very much benefited in meeting 'Abdu'l-Bahá. The Arabic newspapers are now anxiously waiting to read my comment upon the matter. You shall read my paper No. 20 and believe you will prize it very highly. There is no doubt that some people will slander and accuse me of being bought, but I do not care. I have seen the Truth, and I will write the truth, no matter what may happen."

Many others, who have been the enemies of the Cause, have gone, either through curiosity or honest investigation, to visit 'Abdu'l-Bahá—the Servant of God and man—and have returned with the Glory of Truth in their faces.

What is the key to this irresistible spiritual power that thus opens the locked doors of the hearts of men? Those who are familiar with his Teachings, answer that it is his practice of them. He says: "Be ye kind to the human world as be ye compassionate to the race of man. Deal with the stranger as you deal with the friends. Be ye gentle toward the outsiders as you are toward the beloved ones. Know ye the enemy as the friend. Look upon the satan as upon the angel and receive the unjust with the utmost love like unto a faithful one."

Truly, as of old, great miracles are transpiring on the banks of the river Nile, and the ancient land of the Pharaohs!

The following also appeared in the same issue:

News from the Orient.

Egypt, Port Said.—News of the progress of the Cause in Persia, India, Turkey, Arabia and the West, is received weekly and forwarded to 'Abdu'l-Bahá in Alexandria. Pilgrims arriving from various parts of the world go to Alexandria. Thus, for the present, the eyes of all the Bahá'ís are turned toward that city, seeking enlightenment, wisdom and divine love.

Bahai News, Vol. 1, Chicago (December 12, 1910) Masa'il, No. 15

Third of a series of special news items pertinent to the sojourn of 'Abdu'l-Bahá in Egypt.

Special to the *Bahai News*:
> You have asked for an account of 'Abdu'l-Bahá's departure to the land of Egypt. 'Abdu'l-Bahá did not inform anyone that he was going to leave Haifa. The day he left he visited the Holy Tomb of the Báb on Mt. Carmel, and when he came down

from the mountain of the Lord, he went direct to the steamer. This was the first anyone knew about the matter. Within two days he summoned to his presence, Mírzá Núri'd-Dín,[3] Shoghi Effendi, Khusraw[4] and this servant. The only persons who accompanied 'Abdu'l-Bahá to Egypt were Mirzá Munír Zayn and 'Abdu'l-Husayn, one of the pilgrims who was leaving at that time. When Mírzá Núri'd-Dín arrived in Port Said, his brother Mírzá Munír returned to Haifa.

For nearly one month 'Abdu'l-Bahá remained in Port Said and the friends of God came from Cairo, in turn, to visit him. One day he called me to accompany him when taking a walk in the streets of the city. He said: "Do you realize now the meaning of my statement when I was telling the friends that there was a wisdom in my indisposition?" I answered, "Yes, I do remember very well." He continued, "Well, the wisdom was that I must always move according to the requirements of the Cause. Whatever the Cause requires for its promulgation, I will not delay in its accomplishment for one moment! Now, the Cause did require that I travel to these parts, and had I divulged my intention at that time, many difficulties would have arisen."

The day that he left for Alexandria he did not mention the matter to anyone; nor did this servant know the time of his departure. However, when I heard that he had left, I hurried to the steamer and there met him with two pilgrims from 'Ishqabad. He said: "Tell the friends, how, under severe circumstances of bodily weakness, I have accepted the hardships of traveling to promote the Word of God, to spread the Cause of God and to diffuse the Fragrances of God! I have left behind friends, relatives, and home for the sake of the Cause!" By this he meant that the believers of God must follow in his

---

3. Mírzá Núri'd-Dín Zayn was a son of Zaynu'l-Muqarrabin, who had been an apostle of Bahá'u'lláh and had transcribed many of His Tablets. Mírzá Núri'd-Dín served as a secretary to both 'Abdu'l-Bahá and later to Shoghi Effendi.
4. Khusraw was an attendant of 'Abdu'l-Bahá of Burmese origin.

footsteps and illumine the East and the West with the lights of knowledge, peace, and brotherhood.

While in Alexandria many mooted persons, formerly enemies of the Cause for years have met him and after being in his presence are changed entirely. Also, distinguished editors of Arabic and Persian newspapers, such as Moaid and Tchehre Neina, have talked with him and afterward wrote and published columns of praise and commendation on his Teachings and greatness. Thus the newspapers have given great publicity to the Movement. In regard to the Moaid article, 'Abdu'l-Bahá says: "A clipping from the newspaper of Moaid, which is the first newspaper of Egypt and its editor well known throughout the world for his learning, is enclosed. Formerly, this person, through the instigation of some influential resident Persians, wrote many articles against the Cause and called the Bahá'ís infidels. But when 'Abdu'l-Bahá arrived in this country, with one interview he was completely changed and contradicted all his former articles with this one. This is the type of the just man!"

There is no doubt that this trip is fraught with wonderful results for the Cause and many people will become awakened. In one of these interviews 'Abdu'l-Bahá stated he may go to Cairo and pass the remainder of the winter in that city. The Egyptian winter weather is ideal, temperate and agrees with him. Since he has arrived in Egypt his health is much improved, and should he decide to go to America it will not be before the springtime.

With great love and greeting to all the friends in the West, I am always

Your co-worker in the Cause,
[Sayyid] Asadu'lláh Qumí[5]

Bahai News, Vol. 1, Chicago (January 19, 1911) Sultan, No. 17

Fourth of a series of special news items pertaining to the sojourn of 'Abdu'l-Bahá in Egypt.

---

5. He was 'Abdu'l-Bahá's attendant during His journey to the West.

A Call to the American Bahá'ís
From Muhammad Yazdí

Praise be to God! that 'Abdu'l-Bahá has left the gloomy city of imprisonment for the freedom of the world. His only aim is to teach and raise the Standard of the Cause. When he was under the surveillance of the authorities in 'Akká and confined to a limited prison life, he created the spirit of happiness and joy in every heart, and never complained, neither did he show distress or sadness on account of that imprisonment. When freedom was proclaimed in Turkey, a constitution declared, the prisoners set free, and a new era of brotherhood and good fellowship ushered in among the various sects, 'Abdu'l-Bahá, while happy for the freedom of the people, longed for his own imprisonment. His opinion was that under all circumstances he ought to serve the world of humanity, and while living in 'Akká he served it effectively, even though a prisoner; but being freed, nothing was left for him to do in 'Akká, and, like a bird released from its cage, he soared to other climes and countries.

'Abdu'l-Bahá in all the divine characteristics is intensely human and keenly alive to the joys and sorrows of existence. There is no one who feels more acutely the sufferings of humanity than he and no one loves his fellow-men more than he. Here, in Alexandria, he lives exactly like other men; he goes into the stores, into the mosques, into the prisons. He converses just as kindly and amiably with the humblest man in the street as with the highest in the land. His matchless and magnetic kindness attracts all, whether ignorant or wise, rich or poor; he is no respecter of persons and in some instances, after a half-hour's conversation, his bitterest enemy has become his staunchest friend.

His coming to Egypt has added great enthusiasm and zeal to the hearts of the friends. He has uplifted them from a state of comparative oblivion to a world-wide celebrity. He is no more a possible myth or a fable; he is there, standing "powerful, mighty, and supreme!" The sun of his presence radiates the light of love and compassion; people see him, feel the wonderful influence of his presence, talk with him, walk with him as did the men of old walking with Jesus of Nazareth along the shores of Galilee. They can no longer doubt him and his Teachings.

When he first arrived in Egypt, a great cry and clamor was raised by the representatives of the people (the newspapers). All were expressing opinions of 'Abdu'l-Bahá. No one could form a just and impartial view of him. Facts were exaggerated and misrepresentations abounded in every paper.

One writer expressed the opinion that 'Abdu'l-Bahá hates all religions, that his followers throughout the world are very few, and that his teachings are destructive to the well-being and prosperity of human society.

Such were the conditions when 'Abdu'l-Bahá with his might and his glory, his meekness and humility, entered the land of Pharaoh. But lo! after a short time the clouds of misrepresentation were dispelled and the light of reality shone forth with great splendor. So much so, that at present there is not one dissenting voice in the land of Egypt about the greatness of 'Abdu'l-Bahá. Muqaddam, one of the most influential Arabic newspapers, in a long article of November 28, 1910, comes out valiantly and defends in most eloquent terms the Teachings of 'Abdu'l-Bahá. Not being satisfied with this, the editor quotes from the Book of Aqdas wherein Bahá'u'lláh commands all despotic rulers to lay aside their absolutism and accept the constitution and establish in their kingdoms the Houses of Justice. He even upbraids in the strongest terms the other newspaper writers, calling attention to the responsibilities and duties of their positions—that is, to mirror forth facts and realities and not falsehoods and accusations. He says that every writer has been reveling in a riotous feast of exaggeration and derision; that they have gone beyond the limit of politeness and courtesy, which attributes differentiate man from beast. Now, if we compare such articles with what first appeared concerning 'Abdu'l-Bahá, we will find them as different as day from night.

Some people have expressed anxieties and fears because of 'Abdu'l-Bahá's possible visit to America; they think that the newspapers will write sensational articles and ridicule the Cause. Such people are very short-sighted. They have not realized deeply, or superficially, the force of 'Abdu'l-Bahá's presence. Neither have they dreamed of the magnetic influence of his Highness (rather his Kindness, ah, me!). He is a man whose very appearance will solve all the perplexed anxieties of the visionaries of disaster. We as Bahá'ís have nothing to be afraid of. We are the spiritual physicians of the world; we are the torch-bearers of the ideal civilization; we are the teachers of the Kingdom of Abhá. Should we be afraid to receive the One who is the source of all our inspiration and all our light; America must raise a gladsome voice of spiritual beatitude, spread a heavenly banquet, and be prepared, for "he shall come as a thief in the night."

Future historians will record the coming of 'Abdu'l-Bahá to America as a great and momentous event. Broaden your vision and look into the future, when the nations of America shall celebrate, from one end of the continent to the other, the anniversary of the day when 'Abdu'l-Bahá set foot upon "the land of the brave and the free!" Future generations will sing in anthems and songs the resplendent glory of such a day. Children will be taught to respect and love that day. America is on the threshold of a great spiritual awakening, and it must arise to fulfill the responsibilities of such a wonderful and glowing promise.

'Abdu'l-Bahá has written to you in several Tablets that he will come as soon as the friends in that country are united as bands of steel or a golden chain of life. Now it depends upon you. You must show to the world that you are united, that you are worthy to receive him in your midst. Let not this opportunity slip from your grasp. Arise, work, band together, and remove the difficulties from his path. This day is not for fretting and discontentment, nor imagining the possibility of ridicule by the masses. Have you not faith in him? Has he not grappled with and solved the greatest problems for the past sixty years!

Has he not conversed with the wisest men of the age? Again we say, prepare the way for his coming! Let not your minds be troubled with outside questions. He is able to change the ridicule into praise, the enmity into friendship and the derision into exaltation. When he arrived in Alexandria we were not prepared to receive him. There is no need of preparing houses and establishments for his reception; the probability is that he will take a place for himself when he arrives. The first thing that he did when he arrived in Alexandria was to take a house, and all the friends from far and near flocked around him He does not want your houses and palaces, but your hearts. Prepare your hearts, purify your hearts, cleanse your hearts, that he may find a place therein!

The life of 'Abdu'l-Bahá is simple; his attitude is humble; his needs are very few. You think that if he should come to America you must have a house prepared and surround him with luxuries of modern civilization. Far from it! With love, unity, and harmony, shining like stars of heaven in your midst, a little cottage is greater than the imperial palace of kings. All through his life his sole purpose and aim has been to spread the fragrances of God, to serve the Kingdom of Abhá, and to sacrifice himself for the good of the world. He has done all these; nay, rather, his services to man cannot be measured by any criterion. His life, like unto a tempestuous sea, is ever in motion, casting pearls of significance and truth upon its shore. Humanity owes to him a debt that can never be paid with money or gratitude. Notwithstanding all he has done for the world, hearken to what he says in a recent Tablet:

The invisible hand has opened the doors, and wisdom requires that 'Abdu'l-Bahá hasten to the country of Egypt; for he is infinitely ashamed and chagrined that he has not yet been assisted in servitude. Perchance, through traveling in this land, he may be assisted in the future to some small service. Now we are living in the country of Canaan and are supplicating day and night at the Threshold of Mercifulness and beg confirmation and assistance for the friends of God, so that all of us may participate and become partners in the servitude of the Holy Threshold and be aided in accomplishing one service.

(Signed) Muhammad Yazdí

The following appeared in the same issue:

From Sydney Sprague.

At present, I am in Alexandria with 'Abdu'l-Bahá, who has given me the many supplications from America to translate; also Mrs. Ford's new book, The Oriental Rose, which I am translating with Mírzá Mahmúd of India. The book is finely written and ought to be of great help in attracting people to the Cause. I notice Mrs. Ford gives the number of oriental Bahá'ís as twelve millions. A movement which is growing every day cannot have statistics. No one knows how many there are, and to make a statement that there are many millions only opens us to criticism. If we are asked the number of Bahá'ís in the world, is it not better to reply that it is impossible to know, and that we care much more about the quality of the believers than the quantity? This is the policy of 'Abdu'l-Bahá, as the following incident will show:

Two nights ago, an American journalist, Mr. William Ellis, representing The Continent, came especially to Alexandria to interview 'Abdu'l-Bahá. It was my privilege to be the translator on this occasion. One of the first questions Mr. Ellis asked was: "How many followers have you?" The answer was: "We have no statistics and we do not consider these things important. It is the quality of the believers we care for. If a few were characterized with the attributes of God and live according to the divine Teachings, it is praiseworthy. Five diamonds are worth more than five million stones." Again the journalist asked: "Have you not many followers in America?" "I have a few friends in different cities who love me," was the reply. "Is it not true that half of Persia is Bahá'í?" persisted the journalist. "No; it is not," replied 'Abdu'l-Bahá, "but many there who are not Bahá'ís, are influenced by our Teachings." "Are there not many followers in the Turkish Empire?" "No," and again 'Abdu'l-Bahá reiterated the non-importance of numbers. The journalist seemed very much taken aback. He evidently expected 'Abdu'l-Bahá to boast of a large following. What an example 'Abdu'l-Bahá has set us!

Then Mr. Ellis asked briefly: "What are the Teachings of the Bahá'í Revelation and in what does it differ from other religions?" 'Abdu'l-Bahá replied: "While all the other religions are hating and denouncing each other, the Bahá'ís are the friends of all religions and the lovers of all peoples, and their aim is to unite and harmonize all." There were many other questions which drew forth wonderful, illuminating explanations from 'Abdu'l-Bahá. I have not the time to write them now, but be on the lookout for an account of this interview in The Continent. Mr. Ellis is on his way to Persia to write articles about that country, so he may write of the Cause there.

There are two interesting English persons here, a Mr. and Mrs. Atwood, at one time prominent spiritualists in London. As Mr. Atwood is slightly paralyzed, 'Abdu'l-Bahá went to see them, much to their great joy. They are now eager to serve the Cause.

There are pilgrims here from Persia, Russia, India and England, and every night we meet in 'Abdu'l-Bahá's house and our cups are filled to overflowing. His health is good. When Mr. Ellis asked him if he was benefited by the change of air, he replied: "Certainly, one who has been a prisoner for forty years must be benefited to breathe another air." I thought to myself, can we Bahá'ís realize what those forty years mean? The Christians think so much of the forty days Jesus fasted in the wilderness and observe a penitential season to commemorate this; but forty years for every day a year!

(signed) Sydney Sprague

The following also appeared in the same issue:

News from the Orient.
Egypt, Port Said.—Many pilgrims from different parts of the world are arriving and leaving here for Alexandria to meet 'Abdu'l-Bahá.

Letters received here from various parts give glowing descriptions of the progress and advancement of the Cause everywhere.

Bahai News, Vol. I, Chicago (February 7, 1911), No. 18

A Wonderful Movement in the East.
A visit to 'Abdu'l-Bahá in Alexandria.

To most of us the world consists of modern Europe, North America, South Africa, Australia, and since the Russo Japanese war, in a lesser degree, Japan. Our daily newspapers keep us informed, more or less accurately, of social, political, and religious movements that occur within those lands, but of the rest of the world we are for the most part ignorant. In this there is a danger that we may fail to read the signs of the times, not because we are necessarily lacking in wisdom, but because we do not behold the signs. The Bahá'í movement is a good illustration of this. Not one Englishman in a thousand has heard of this religious and social uprising in the East, yet its adherents are estimated to number millions, and its power and influence are growing week by week! In order that our readers may be informed about this remarkable outpouring of the divine spirit, a representative of The Christian Commonwealth recently called upon Mr. Wellesley Tudor Pole, who has just returned from the East, where he has been studying the movement at first hand.

"How did you come to be interested in the Bahá'í movement?" he said.

"I first heard of the movement when on a visit to Constantinople prior to the Turkish revolution in 1908, and I was very much impressed by the fact that 'Abdu'l-Bahá could exert such an influence from within prison walls. When I returned to London I found that very little was known of the movement, and I determined to visit 'Abdu'l-Bahá, known to the outside world by the name of 'Abbás Effendi, on the first available opportunity and discover for myself the secret of his power."

"And it is most extraordinary," Mr. Pole continued, "that so little should be known of this movement in England. There are said to be between two and three million Bahá'ís at least in Persia alone, and many more in India, the Middle East, America, France, Russia, and elsewhere. There is no religious freedom in Persia; if there were it would be found that very great numbers of men would declare themselves disciples. No less than thirty thousand men and women in Persia alone are reported to have sacrificed everything for the movement. I met an old Persian Bahá'í in Alexandria his name was Shaykh Muhammad who joined the movement when he was a young man, and he was publicly flogged and all his property was taken from him. He and his whole household were sent out into the mountains in the heart of winter without food or money. Many times he has been imprisoned, and it has been a miracle how he has escaped with his life. In many towns and villages he has been stoned and brutally treated. Hundreds of men and women have proved themselves ready to endure such treatment, to leave home and country, for the sake of their great ideal."

"What is the ideal which has inspired such heroism?"

"The fundamental principle of what has come to be called the Bahá'í Revelation is a belief in the underlying unity of religions and peoples. It stands for the harmony of all spiritual truths and all faiths, for international peace and goodwill. It asserts the equality of the sexes, the duty of everyone to serve the community, and the duty of the community to give opportunity for such service. It desires a social order where the brotherhood of man shall be expressed in all the relationships of life, and where the community shall be responsible for the sick, the aged, the infirm, and all who cannot obtain their own livelihood."

"What gave birth to this movement?"

"It arose in 1844, when a young Persian, Mírzá 'Alí-Muhammad, went about Eastern Europe prophesying that a great teacher would follow him. He called himself the Báb (the Gate) and stood as the John the Baptist of the new movement. He affirmed that the coming teacher would not only fulfill the prophecies of the Qur'an, but also of the sacred scriptures of the Hindu and Hebrew peoples. Mírzá 'Alí-Muhammad was bitterly persecuted, and finally shot in 1850. By this time the movement had spread all over Persia, and in the early fifties Bahá'u'lláh, the son of a noble Persian family, came forward and proclaimed himself the teacher who had been promised."

"Bahá'u'lláh, by the way, had never met the Báb. In 1863, by an arrangement between the Persian and Turkish Governments, spurred on by the mullás, who were alarmed by the spread of the new teaching, Bahá'u'lláh and his family were first sent to Constantinople, then banished to Adrianople, and finally, in 1868, exiled to 'Akká, a fortified Turkish town on the Syrian coast, where Bahá'u'lláh was kept in more or less close confinement until his death, at the age of seventy five, in 1892. At times he was treated in the most brutal way chained to other men by the neck and subjected to torture. In spite of the imprisonment of the leader, the movement spread with tremendous rapidity throughout the Middle East. Pilgrims came from India and other distant parts to receive the blessing of Bahá'u'lláh at the prison bars."

"What happened when he died?"

"He left a book of laws and many other works, and instructed his followers to look to his eldest son, 'Abdu'l-Bahá, to carry on his work and to expound his writings. 'Abdu'l-Bahá, which means the 'Servant of God,' was kept in prison at 'Akká until the time of the Turkish Revolution in 1908, when, along with all political prisoners, he was released. He went to live near Haifa, close to Mt. Carmel, but about two months ago he started on a journey, and is now in Egypt. That is a bare outline of the progress of the movement, but it gives no idea of the extraordinary power that lies behind it."

"Did you meet 'Abdu'l-Bahá on your recent visit to the East?"

"Yes, I met 'Abdu'l-Bahá near Alexandria, where he was staying with some of his followers. Let me try to give you a word picture of him. He is sixty five years of age, of medium height and of commanding presence; he has long silver gray beard and hair, blue grey eyes, a fine forehead, a wonderful carriage, and a sweet but powerful voice. He was dressed when I saw him, in cream white robes and a white Persian headdress. You feel at once that here is a master of men and a marvelous spiritual personality. He seemed to me to focus in a truly divine manner the spiritual ideal of the coming age. When one has come in contact with 'Abdu'l-Bahá's power, or rather the power behind him, one has no doubt that this movement will vitally affect the religious and social evolution of the whole world. At his table I met pilgrims who had come to receive his blessing from many parts of the world, and representing almost every faith the world knows. Jews, Mohammedans Hindus, Zoroastrians and Christians sat around one table, all holding this one great belief that God has again sent one of his messengers to earth, and that the great call that was focused in Bahá'u'lláh is the call for the unity of nations, the brotherhood of man, the peace of the whole world, and the realization of those fundamental truths that lie behind all faiths. Bahá'u'lláh did not say to the Christian, 'Come out of your religious order,' nor did he say to the Mohammedan 'Turn your back on your faith.' He said to every man, 'Go and live out your faith in unity and brotherhood with all mankind, and thus show that behind all expressions of religion there is one religion and one God.'"

The following appeared in the same issue:

Extracts from a letter from Mr. Wellesley Tudor Pole to *Bahai News*:

You may be interested in hearing of my recent visit to 'Abdu'l-Bahá at Ramleh, near Alexandria. I spent nine days at Alexandria and Cairo during the second half of November, 1910. 'Abdu'l-Bahá's health had very greatly improved since his arrival from Port Said. He was looking strong and vigorous in every way. He spoke much of the work in America, to which he undoubtedly is giving considerable thought. He also spoke a good deal about the work that is going forward in different European centers as well as in London, and he expects great things from England during the coming year. It may interest you to know, however, that the Bahá'í Movement is beginning to take a more serious hold on public attention in this country, and that during the next few weeks a number of meetings are to be held in London, Bristol and in the North, which are likely to produce far reaching results. A Bahá'í paper is to be read at the Universal Races Congress in London next July.

Yours faithfully,
[Major] Wellesley Tudor Pole.

Bahai News, Vol. I, Chicago (March 2, 1911), No. 19

Fifth of a series of special news items pertaining to the sojourn of 'Abdu'l-Bahá in Egypt.

Special. Word has been received from Cairo, dated February 21, that 'Abdu'l-Bahá will not journey to America this year.

The following article concerning 'Abdu'l-Bahá, ('Abbás Effendi) appeared in the January 19th issue of El-Ahram (The Pyramids) an Arabic newspaper printed in Cairo:

> *'Abbás Effendi the Leader of the Bahá'ís.*
> *Statements Regarding His Morals and Religion.*

Continually, the greatness of the Leader of the Bahá'ís, 'Abbás Effendi, is the topic of conversation, among the men of affairs and statesmen. The wise men of Alexandria and the nobility of that city are paying him great respect and homage. Lately he has received many letters from his numerous followers in the United States, requesting him to travel to those parts so that they may meet him. They have prepared a great house in New York in accord with his station and position amongst them. However, it is probable that he will not respond to their invitation, on account of the remoteness of the country and the length of the trip.

We have received a letter from the celebrated scholar, Shawkry Effendi, who has just arrived from Syria, in which he praises 'Abbás Effendi, explains his religion and produces certain arguments in his favor.

He says: "The wisdom of 'Abbás Effendi, our respected guest, descends from a family which was noble in lineage and descent in the Kingdom of Persia. He is the son of the 'Dweller of Paradise, Bahá'u'lláh, the founder of the Bahá'í Movement, and he is the successor of his Father. In regard to his morality and character, he is the pattern of dignity and perfection. He is gracious, generous, noble minded, philanthropic, charitable and full of benevolence. He is very kind to the poor and patient to the indigent. He does not make any difference between the followers of any religion, whether they be Christians, Jews, Mohammedans or Brahmans. To him all are the same; he looks upon them as part of the same family of humanity and not their particular religion. The aim of his movement is the unity of religions in the world and their equality among the children of men. He thinks that the differences of religions are impeding the progress of the world and he believes that the removal of these differences will benefit mankind."

"This religion has spread greatly and is carried to Europe and America so much so that today the number of Bahá'ís has reached the number of fifteen million, men, women and children included. Many of these Bahá'ís are in New York, Chicago and India, Persia, Egypt and Syria, and it is continually growing and spreading."

"The Tomb of Bahá'u'lláh is in 'Akká, called Bahjí and every year the Bahá'ís come from all parts of the world to visit it."

"Twice I have called upon 'Abbás Effendi while in Ramleh and have seen the poor and indigent gathered around his house waiting for him to come out and when he appears, they beg alms and he gives to them. This is just a short sketch of his generous qualities and I confess my inability to do it justice. His physical appearance is medium size, white hair, penetrating eyes, smiling face and wonderful countenance, courteous, and his manner, simplicity itself, disliking any ostentation and show. He is a wise man, a philosopher and his knowledge of the Turkish, Persian and Arabic is unsurpassed."

"He knows the history of nations and understands the causes of their rise and fall."

"He is sixty years old and on account of certain nervous ailments he has come to Egypt for change of air. He personally reads all the articles and letters sent him from all parts of the world, and answers the most important of them in his Persian handwriting which is famous for its beauty. Many of the great men of this country and delegates from other nations have met him and he gives a personal interview to each one of them. No one has visited him without leaving him impressed by his presence and praising his qualities and wondering at his magnanimity and his astonishing mind."

"Concerning the reports of his leaving 'Akká and the statement that he is against the Constitution, this was without foundation and the proof of this is his endeavor to unite the religions in the world and establish equality among nations. If such were his qualities, working against religions and constitution, and on the other hand trying to bring union and harmony amongst them, how can we reconcile the two? This is indeed far from him, for he is a man who advocated the Constitution from the very beginning and before the Turkish people received their Constitution. But the real object of his coming to Egypt is for the change of air and his physical condition. This is the real truth we are proclaiming at the top of our voice and if there is any virtue in it, it requires no praise or blame."

Star of the West

Star of the West, Vol. 2, Chicago (April 28, 1911), No. 3

Egypt, Alexandria.—A daily newspaper, The Valley of the Nile, in its issue of March 22nd presents a full page concerning the life and teachings of 'Abdu'l-Bahá. It is a noteworthy fact that all the prominent people of Egypt are beginning to feel his spiritual presence and call upon him to receive instruction. The news of the looking forward of the American Bahá'ís to the coming of 'Abdu'l-Bahá to that country has reached here and it is hoped that all the friends may attain to this blessing and that the Center of the Covenant may travel to the West. Not only are the American Bahá'ís anxious to have 'Abdu'l-Bahá in their midst, but the friends of every country are supplicating him to visit them. Now that he is free the believers are not satisfied with Tablets as Messages, but they long to have him personally.

Star of the West, Vol. 2, Chicago (September 8, 1911), No. 10

Impressions of 'Abdu'l-Bahá while in Ramleh.
By Mr. Louis G. Gregory.

I am asked by the Star of the West for impressions gathered during a recent pilgrimage to 'Abdu'l-Bahá at Ramleh and the Holy City. Now I can respond but briefly; but later I hope that a full account may be given to the friends of the Cause of all the valuable lessons received from the Perfect Man.

It is the will of 'Abdu'l-Bahá that all the friends should be united and happy in the light of the Kingdom. On one occasion Bahá'u'lláh said, "Heaven is happiness and peace. Hell is the hearts of those who deny and oppose." Today the happiness and peace of the Glory of God (Bahá'u'lláh) are reflected in the clear Mirror of 'Abdu'l-Bahá. Thus by meeting him one meets all the Prophets and Manifestations of cycles and ages past. It is difficult for one to realize at the time, or for a long time afterwards, the true honor of such a meeting. To one who realizes even faintly who this Servant of God is and what powers he represents, such a meeting is high above all honors of earth. But no soul can give adequate testimony of what 'Abdu'l-Bahá may be to any other soul. With mental and spiritual horizon more or less limited, each pilgrim discerns according to his capacity the Majesty and Power that radiate from the Center of God's Covenant.

At Ramleh, 'Abbás Effendi† might at times be seen walking about the streets. Oft times he would ride upon the electric tramway, making change and paying his fare in the most democratic fashion. His reception room was open to believers and non believers alike. Upon a visit to some unfortunates one day I asked if they knew him. "O yes," they responded, "he has been in this house." Thus in one way or another, thousands of Persians had opportunity to see 'Abbás Effendi; but among these how few perceived 'Abdu'l-Bahá.

Viewed with the outer eye, he is about the medium height, with symmetrical features. His lineaments indicate meekness and gentleness, as well as power and strength. His color is about that of parchment. His hands are shapely, with the nails well manicured. His forehead is high and well rounded. His nose is slightly aquiline; his eyes light blue and penetrating; his hair is silvery, and long enough to touch the shoulders; his beard is white. His dress was the Oriental robes, graceful in their simplicity. On his head rested a light tar bush, surrounded by a white, turban. His voice is powerful, but capable of producing infinite pathos and tenderness. His carriage is erect and altogether so majestic and beautiful that it is passing strange that anyone seeing him would not be moved to say:

"This truly is the King of men!"

On the rational plane his wisdom is incomparable. During the time of my visit, persons were present from different parts of the world. But people of acquired learning are but as children to 'Abdu'l-Bahá. They were reverent in their attitude

---

† The name by which 'Abdu'l-Bahá is known among those not believers.

toward him and one of them, an Oxford man, praised his wisdom with much enthusiasm. They sought his advice and found it of the highest value in application to life.

'Abdu'l-Bahá has the power to make his friends very happy. What music and harmony, joy and peace, may enter into the lives of those who attain this meeting! He has a balm for every wound and feeds hungry souls with the Manna of his Perfect Love. One of the friends at Cairo, a noted worker in the Cause, exclaimed, "If I could only see 'Abdu'l-Bahá once a week!" At 'Akká and Haifa were to be found those who had spent most of their lives with him. But they were all longing for his Presence. Among the letters received by him at Ramleh was one from the daughter of a king, expressing as her utmost desire a visit at the threshold of his door. This is the Power of the Spirit.

Thus the friends of the Cause may catch a glimpse of what is in store for them if he visits America. Nor should we spare any pains or hesitate at any sacrifices to ensure his coming. The Reality of 'Abdu'l-Bahá, the supreme joy of the Kingdom, is found by promoting that which tends to unity and harmony among the friends of God and the whole human family. "Son of Man: Lift up thy heart with delight, that thou mayest be prepared to meet Me and to mirror forth My Beauty."

The following appeared in the same issue:

News Items

'Abdu'l-Bahá, after staying nearly three months in Cairo—during which time he was interviewed by many prominent people—returned again to Ramleh, the delightful suburb of Alexandria in July. He was accompanied by Mírzá Asadu'lláh, Mírzá Munír, Mírzá Mahmúd and Áqá Khusraw. On August 11th, 'Abdu'l-Bahá departed for Europe; arriving first in Marseilles, France.

Star of the West, Vol. 9, Chicago (April 28, 1918), No. 3

The Power of the Holy Spirit
Words of 'Abdu'l-Bahá: From Diary of Mírzá Ahmad Sohrab, June, 1913

In Tiberius the missionaries have built a modern hospital and pharmacy. The doctor has been serving there for thirty-two years. At least every year one thousand Jews enter the hospital and go out healed, but none of them ever becomes a Christian. The doctor used to tell me: "I am at my wit's end in thinking out the reason of the success of the Bahá'ís in the propagation of their teaching. Without any means at hand they succeed in making these Jews Bahá'ís, but with all these hospitals and schools and charities we do not succeed. How is this?" I replied: "Think for one moment of this singular fact. The Jews who became Christians in apostolic and post-apostolic times were not attracted to the Christian doctrine by hospitals, etc. On the contrary they were beaten, persecuted, and killed. Notwithstanding these things they accepted Christianity. Why is this? Those early teachers possessed the heavenly power and with that power they were able to carry the gospel into distant lands. Now, in this day the Bahá'ís are teaching people with the same divine power. They are baptized with the power of the Holy Spirit. They have forgotten the ego and are soaring toward the Kingdom of sanctity. The most efficient capital of the Bahá'í teacher is the divine power. With that alone he may conquer the cities of the hearts."

Abdul Baha in Egypt

by Mírzá Ahmad Sohrab

Originally published by J. H. Sears & Co. Inc.
for the New History Foundation, 1929

Approved by the Publishing Committee of the
National Spiritual Assembly of the Bahais
of the United States and Canada

The text for the following section of this compilation was originally published in 1929. The English translations of the Tablets of 'Abdu'l-Bahá included here are the same ones in the original book. While the Tablets are authentic, the translations have not been updated by the Bahá'í World Center. They should be considered, therefore, early and unauthorized translations.

The utterances of 'Abdu'l-Bahá published in what follows are important and precious records of his words. However, this record only reflects the sayings of 'Abdu'l-Bahá as they were remembered by the author. They should be regarded as pilgrim notes and not as the authorized text of Bahá'í scripture.

Port Said circa 1913

PORT SAID, EGYPT, JULY 1, 1913

1. *To Look Back and Survey the Activities of the Month*

I believe it would be a good practice if, on the first of every month, we would survey the collective activities of the days just past, to see whether we have accomplished anything either beneficial or harmful to our fellow men; if we find the former, we should make these actions stepping-stones for greater things; if the latter, we should try to turn into the right pathway. For those who have just accepted the Bahá'í Revelation there is nothing more useful than retrospection. In this day the Highway of the Lord of Mankind is plain. Many of the past obstacles are removed, and the hollow places and marshy grounds are filled. If we start walking in His path we shall surely reach our destination, behold the Countenance of the Beloved, receive His benediction and ever afterward commune with the Holy Ones.

2. *The Bahá'í Path and Its Pilgrims*

The Bahá'í path is one which leads us to the Kingdom of Eternity. God has illumined it with the Light of His face. Hundreds and thousands are joining those who have begun their pilgrimage upon the Highway of Abhá. As they go along, they raise their clarion voices in thankfulness and praise. They sing the songs of Peace and Spiritual brotherhood. They know that theirs is the victory of attainment. What a happy band of pilgrims they are! Their faith is superhuman, their energy extraordinary, their faces illumined, their feet untiring, their conviction contagious, their love unselfish, their hope transcendent, their sincerity unquestioned, their integrity unimpeachable and their devotion to the Cause attested! My friends! Let us join this holy band of pilgrims!

Last night 'Abdu'l-Bahá told me to come to him in the morning with a number of petitions just received; so I was there quite early. While He was dictating Tablets he carried on different lines of conversations with a stream of callers and pilgrims. Tablets were revealed for a large number of friends in Europe and America, and a wonderful article for the "Theosophy" of Scotland in Edinburgh, the Editor of which is Mr. Graham Pole.

3. Tablet of 'Abdu'l-Bahá to the Theosophy in Scotland in Regard to Divine Civilization and Man's Illumination

To the Secretary of the Theosophical Society and the Editor of Scotland Theosophy, Edinburgh, Scotland.

He is God!

O thou beloved and respected friend:

Your letter written to Áqá Mírzá Ahmad was received. I likewise read it. Its contents imparted happiness, for it was an indication of the magnanimity of your effort and of your philanthropic intention. The Articles which you have published in the Theosophical magazine bear testimony to your lofty aim.

A wise and sagacious writer pens such articles—the results of which are eternal, and its benefits universal; thus the world of humanity may advance toward the kingdom of Mercifulness and divine susceptibilities may shine and gleam like unto radiant lamps from the reality of man.

Today humanity is in need of heavenly teachings, which are the spirit of this age and the light of this cycle. Material, physical civilization has made extraordinary progress, but Divine Civilization is totally forgotten. In truth, Divine Civilization is like unto the light, whereas material civilization is similar to the glass. The glass without the light will be dark.

Therefore, great effort must be made so that the heavenly lamp may become ignited, the world of morality illumined and the inexhaustible virtues which are the decorations of the reality of mankind revealed as glowing stars.

The world of nature is the arena of the animal kingdom. Look thou upon any one of the animals and thou will realize that the virtues of the world of nature are fully manifest in it with the utmost perfection—to an extent that it would be impossible for man to attain. Consider thou a sweet singing bird, beautiful and harmonious, that builds its nest on the topmost branch of a tree growing on the slope of a mountain! In reality this nest is preferable to the palace of the king. The weather is of the utmost delicacy, the panorama indeed entrancing, the water most salubrious, the mountains green and verdant, and the harvest in the valley and on the plain is the wealth of the bird! It has no trouble, no hardship, no thought, no scheme, no sorrow, no grief, no remorse and no regret. Day and night this bird lives with the utmost joy and happiness in its own royal nest! It becomes evident that the virtues of the world of nature are most complete in the animal kingdom.

But look at the condition of the poor man! Now he is exiled, again he is sick, then helpless or perhaps a prisoner, now he is afflicted with poverty and penury, and then thrown amid dangers. Day and night he is striving, so that he may gain his livelihood through toil and turmoil. With your own reason compare the difference between the life of man and that of the animal! These things demonstrate that the virtues of the world of nature are more apparent in the animal kingdom.

On the other hand, although man does not seem to enjoy a complete share or inexhaustible portion of these natural bounties, he is, in the Divine World, the center of infinite Bestowals, the lamp of the light of Reality, the shining mirror of the Beauty of God, the manifestor of human perfection, the dawning place of celestial rays and the possessor of the "holy power" which penetrates into and surrounds the essence of all phenomena.

Man discovers the reality of things, and governing the world of nature, brings its secrets out of the world of the invisible into the realm of existence. Now, like a bird, he soars through the air and again he swims on the surface of the ocean; he travels hither and thither, then dives under the sea with great power. Thus he causes the revelation of all the laws of nature out of the unseen into the seen realm.

For this reason, he is endowed with a higher power to make use of this knowledge to benefit the world and stimulate its progress. This "power" is reserved for man, and by it he is distinguished from the animal.

Inasmuch as man is endowed with such a power, he must become the manifestation of divine civilization, the dawning-place of the light of reality, the founder of heavenly perfections, the spreader of spiritual teachings and the servant of the world of morality. He must rejoice the spirits through the Divine Glad-tidings, free them from discouragement and grant them the hope of Everlasting life.

This is the excellence and glory of the human world! This is the Everlasting Prosperity.

(Signed) 'Abdu'l-Bahá 'Abbás.

4. Article in the Egyptian Gazette about Bahá'í Pilgrims

An article published in the Egyptian Gazette, dated Friday, June 27th, on page three, entitled:

'Abdu'l-Bahá in Egypt.
Wonderful Scenes in Port Said.
Eastern Bahá'ís Assembled in Force.

The description of the Persian believers "who are curiously dressed in great lambskin hats and long divided skirts with enormous pleats" was especially graphic. Here is a quotation giving another sidelight of the manner in which these "Converts" lived:

"At Port Said the pilgrims have erected a huge tent on the roof of a native hotel and there they gather and sing with touching devotion."

5. Home of Bahá'u'lláh and Its Keeper

Mírzá Núru'lláh Vakíl is an old believer from Baghdad. He has been in Haifa and Alexandria for ten months awaiting the arrival of the Beloved. He is a patient, true Bahá'í, ever ready to fulfill the desire of the Lord. He is the keeper of the House in which Bahá'u'lláh and his family lived for eleven years. This house, owing to lack of attention, has fallen into ruin, and for the present there are no means at hand to either rebuild or to repair it. In speaking with him upon this matter he said that with a sum of 500 pounds sterling the house could be suitably repaired. The above answer was given through my own solicitation; but I believe it would cost at least 1,000 pounds sterling to reconstruct the house upon its old plan without any architectural innovation, thus keeping the original form of the time of Bahá'u'lláh. 'Abdu'l-Bahá spoke to Mírzá Núru'lláh and to a number of Bahá'ís from Baghdad. He made it plain that he has great love for the believers of Baghdad, and that they are ever in his heart. Let them not be sad owing to the present ruin of the house. The time for its building will come very soon. It may have to be destroyed and rebuilt but its first form must not undergo any change. Let them rest assured that it will be constructed most solidly. This is a Blessed House; do they not realize it was the home of Bahá'u'lláh? All that quarter in which the House is situated will be destroyed and then transformed into wonderful parks and gardens. It will become most heavenly. The Holy Sepulcher of Christ was for three hundred years a place for dumping all kinds of rubbish, then St. Helena came, cleared the ground and built over it a most wonderful church. However, these times are different, and the Places wherein the Blessed Perfection has lived will be fully preserved.

Today two pilgrims arrived, Mírzá Fadlu'lláh,[6] the son of the oldest brother of Bahá'u'lláh from Persia, and a young Bahá'í from Damascus.

Upon hearing of the arrival of the son of his uncle, 'Abdu'l-Bahá called him into his presence and showered much love upon him. I was not there to witness the scene and to hear his words. But 'Alí-Akbar told me that the Master spoke about his childhood days. Things that I should like to have heard.

---

6. Áqá Mírzá Fadlu'lláh, the Nizámu'l-Mamálik, is the author of *Táríkh Amrí Núr*, published at: http://www.h-net.org/~bahai/arabic/vol5/nur/nur.htm

6. 'Abdu'l-Bahá's Talk to the Pilgrims on the Evidences of the Cause

In the afternoon we were all invited to the Master's house for tea. We waited a few moments downstairs, and as soon as we heard his footsteps everybody arose. He sat on a chair in front of the window and spoke feelingly.

He stated that the majority of the inhabitants of Persia are yet asleep, although God has demonstrated His Cause to them in so many ways.... If this Cause had appeared in Europe or America, those regions would by this time have become illumined and countless souls awakened. So many were martyred in Persia, so much blood has been spilt! If one of these events had transpired in another country, the effect would have been marvelous! Nevertheless there were many people in Persia who became illumined and celestial, and cried out in order to awaken their fellow men!.... An infinite number of these believers of God have been examples of severance, incarnations of devotion, and flaming candles; they have embodied in the world of humanity the Teachings of God, and have become demonstrations, showing how man could be pure, sanctified, attracted, enkindled and honest! The evidences of God they wrote with their own blood upon the earth.

Then he went out to take a walk, telling us to follow him. As the Greatest Holy Leaf ('Abdu'l-Bahá's sister) will arrive from Haifa to be with the Master, and as the present house is small and rather unfurnished, another apartment consisting of four rooms and a kitchen is rented for us. "Us" means Mírzá Mahmúd,[7] Sayyid Asadu'lláh [Qumí], Mírzá Munír [Zayn] and Ahmad Sohrab. The Master therefore walked to this apartment to see if it was ready. On the way he told us two stories of his childhood, one about the Muslim clergy and the "big paradise," another about a bare-headed Mullá before a large crowd of people, the sudden shower of hail upon his head and his precipitated flight.

---

7. Mírzá Mahmúd Zarqání was a devoted secretary and companion of 'Abdu'l-Bahá. His two-volume *Kitáb Badáyi'u'l-Áthár* (Bombay: Vol I, 1914: Vol. II, 1921) chronicles 'Abdu'l-Bahá's travels to North America and Europe.

7. Experiences of a Pilgrim and How He was Robbed on the Way

Coming out of the apartment, 'Abdu'l-Bahá ordered a carriage and with Mirzá Fadlu'lláh they were driven away. We returned to the hotel and had an interesting conversation with a young Bahá'í from Damascus. Having been in Tehran during the Parliamentary period, he gave us a thrilling account of the victory of the Nationalist Cause, and of his journey from Tehran toward Shiraz, and how a large Caravan which included himself was attacked and robbed. He and his friend had to walk six days through mountains and uninhabited places, bedraggled and with large blisters on the soles of their feet before they reached their destination. Although he had suffered much, yet he was very cheerful and happy because today he was privileged to look upon the face of 'Abdu'l-Bahá—the lover of humanity.

PORT SAID, EGYPT, JULY 2, 1913

1. Talk of 'Abdu'l-Bahá on Spiritual Cultivation and Teaching

Toward the end of a wonderful talk given this afternoon to the Persian Pilgrims, 'Abdu'l-Bahá stated that it was not his duty to command particular persons to teach the Cause. Whosoever arises to spread the Word and to perform this service, will behold the Doors of Confirmation open wide before his face. This is the time for teaching and therefore results will be achieved. In every season a particular service will be productive. If, during the seed-sowing time we want to gather the harvest we shall be unsuccessful, if at the period of irrigation we desire to do something else, failure will be the result. Now this is the divine season of seed-sowing. Every Bahá'í must become a heavenly Cultivator, or at the appointed hour the prayers of all the past and future ages, will yield no fruit. In his long trip throughout Europe and America, 'Abdu'l-Bahá's primal object was to show the friends of God by deeds that now is the hour for teaching the Cause. Although 'Akká and Haifa are the headquarters of this movement and he had many reasons to stay there, and from that center administer the affairs of the Cause, yet, he left everything and traveled throughout the earth to herald the coming of the Kingdom of Abhá. Any person desiring to be surrounded by the Confirmations of the Blessed Perfection, must arise and teach the Cause. This is the path.

2. Departure of the Pilgrims, and Remarks of 'Abdu'l-Bahá on Music

Seven more pilgrims left for Haifa and Alexandria. Except one Zoroastrian who will depart for Bombay on the 5th, no one is left of the large number of pilgrims. Today two fine young Bahá'í students arrived from Beirut. They are the advance guard of the rest of the students who will be here soon. These two are very polite and speak English fluently. One of them is the son of Muhammad-Taqí Isfahání of Cairo; his name is 'Abdu'l-Husayn. He has a fine voice and chants the Bahá'í Communes most effectively. He chanted tonight for the Beloved who was very pleased with him.

'Abdu'l-Bahá wishes the believers to cultivate their voices so that they may sing the Bahá'í songs and chant with effect the Prayers of the Blessed Perfection; for Prayer is the food of the spirit.

3. Quiet Association with 'Abdu'l-Bahá

In the evening, at the end of a long walk, the Master came to our hotel. He walked down the veranda where I was sitting alone, opened the door and entered one of the rooms. Little by little the friends gathered around him. Down in the street a motley crowd of Arabs were passing along; above our heads, the stars shone with utmost brilliancy, while at our left the Mediterranean lay smiling. We were all very happy in the Presence of the Master of Illumination. In the darkness his face irradiated like an orb of light, and his tongue uttered such words of guidance and truth as the "Man of Sorrows" spoke 1900 years ago on the Mount of Olives.

4. Progress of the Bahá'í Cause in Germany and Letters from That Country

In the morning we drank tea in 'Abdu'l-Bahá's presence. He sent for us very early. It seemed that he had slept last night in Ahmad Yazdí's apartment, so we all went there. After our arrival he spoke about the progress of the Cause in Germany. He had some letters from Mírzá 'Alí-Akbar and Mírzá Lulfu'lláh Hakím giving the description of the meetings in Stuttgart during their one week's stay there. He read the former aloud and gave me the latter to read to the friends.

There were also letters from the German friends and these he gave me to translate and send to the Star of the West, for publication, which was done on the same day. Then he spoke very enthusiastically about the German believers, their firmness, and their devotion. For more than one hour he talked about Bahá'u'lláh and about the enemies of the Cause, who had at every turn tried to stop its influence, but who had all failed. And he also related several historical incidents of the early days of Baghdad.

5. *Appearance of Truth*

In concluding his remarks he told us that along with the appearance of Truth, the point of opposition raises its head. The former gains signal victory, the other goes into crushing defeat; the first upraises the standard of guidance, the other unfurls the banner of error; one is divine revelation, another is satanic suggestion; the first leads us into the paradise of Peace, the second hurls us headlong into the hell of war.

PORT SAID, EGYPT, JULY 3, 1913

1. The Bahá'í Cause Is in Need of Earnest Workers Who Will Defy All Opposition

We are living in the days in which the Spirit of the Lord is manifest, and the rays of the Sun of Reality evident. The divine Jerusalem has descended from heaven and the Glorious Glad-tidings are proclaimed. We must fashion our lives according to the heavenly teachings, live in a state of internal contentment, peruse the Holy Writings and practice that which will be conducive to our own and to the world's prosperity. The Bahá'í Cause is much in need of real, earnest workers—workers who will defy all opposition, meeting their antagonists with smiling faces and standing as firm rocks before the blowing of the winds of tests and of the storms of trials. How many old trees are uprooted by one wind and how many ships have been wrecked by one storm! There are many lands athirst for the water of life, let the friends of God irrigate them with vernal showers from the Kingdom of Abhá. There are many persons hungry for the heavenly bread; we must invite them to the Banquet of the Lord. The lethargic must become active, the sleepy awakened; the deprived must receive a share of the inexhaustible Favors, and the sweet music of the Supreme Concourse must be heard. We should be up and doing some kind of service no matter how slight it is. Praise be to God that the orb of the Center of Covenant is shining and that His Mercy is all-encompassing. He is teaching and gently and lovingly guiding us in the Right Path. We all desire to serve him in some way and win his good pleasure by sincerely walking in his footsteps; we hope to become the signs of his compassion and the humble followers of his eternal law!

2. Life in Port Said, and Fleas but No Mosquitoes

All this morning and part of the afternoon we were left to ourselves. The Master was busy in other directions and could not call us to his presence. Meanwhile we found time to pack our trunks and move from the hotel into our new apartment. It is unfurnished but as we do not know how long we will stay in Port Said, it is not necessary to purchase many things. I have one large black kitchen table on which I do my writing, a chair and a bed. The apartment is airy and has a wonderful side view of the Mediterranean. It is in the Arab quarter and rented for nine dollars a month. Port Said is famous for its fleas. They bother us to death all night. Those who have mosquito nets escape the attacks of the fleas and sleep comfortably, but I happen not to have any and have to carry on an offensive and defensive war with the swarming army. Several years ago when I lived here, there were many mosquitoes—not as bad as New Jersey ones—but quite ferocious. However, the Egyptian Government organized a Sanitary Commission who undertook the filling of the marshy grounds and thus exterminated the breeding of mosquitoes. During the spring and summer there is not a drop of rain. All that we see is an occasional patch of cloud aimlessly rambling in the sky. Our apartment being very near the Mediterranean, we enjoy a fresh, vitalizing breeze all the time, especially in the evenings. Many people sleep on the roofs which are flat and paved like the floor of a room.

3. Husayn Rúhí and His Bahá'í School in Cairo

About 5 o'clock Khusraw, 'Abdu'l-Bahá's attendant, brought the good news that we were called by the Master to the new house. The believers with others just arrived from Cairo, were already assembled when we entered. Husayn Rúhí who years ago was in America with Khurásání,[8] was present with his three sons. He is a short man and knows English and Arabic very well. He keeps a private school in Egypt, the pupils numbering about a hundred and sixty children; the majority being orphans. The school is named "Abbás" and the master's photograph is hung in a prominent place in every classroom. Husayn Ruhí is an active young man, and I believe that he is doing much good.

4. Palace of Bahá'u'lláh in Nur, Persia

The Master asked Mírzá Fadlu'lláh—the son of his great uncle—to draw the design of the house of Bahá'u'lláh in Nur. Therefore, he, with the assistance of Mírzá 'Alí-Akbar, was busy all day making this plan which was completed this afternoon. It must have been a palatial residence according to the architectural conception of the East. The Master, holding the various papers in his hands, described the different parts of the house as though he had left it yesterday. Then with his matchless power, he contrasted this palace of luxury and worldly comfort with the barren and ruined barrack of 'Akká.

---

8. Hájí Mírzá Hasan Khurásání was a resident of Egypt, who in 1900 was sent by 'Abdu'l-Bahá to America to bring Dr. Khayru'lláh to his sense and discourage him from rebellion against the Faith.

5. Talk of 'Abdu'l-Bahá on His and Bahá'u'lláh's Imprisonment in the Prison of 'Akká, and on Real Happiness

'Abdu'l-Bahá spoke on happiness, saying that the soul of man must be happy, no matter where he is. He must attain to that condition of inward beatitude and peace, where outward circumstances can not alter his spiritual calm and joyousness. No one can imagine a worse place than the barracks of 'Akká. The climate was bad, the water no better, the surroundings filthy and dirty, and the deportment of the officials unbearable, while he and his family were looked upon as enemies of religion and destroyers of morals. The Government had given orders that no one should address them during their stay in 'Akká and that they should not be allowed to converse with each other.

Upon their arrival, the officials found that there were not enough rooms in the barracks to imprison them separately, so all were put into two bare rooms. The court had a most gloomy aspect. It contained three or four fig trees, in the branches of which several ominous owls screeched all night. Everyone became ill and there were neither provisions nor medicines.

At the entrance to the barrack there was an undertaker's room. It was a horrible looking place, yet 'Abdu'l-Bahá lived there for two years with the utmost happiness. Up to that period he had had no opportunity to read the Qur'an from cover to cover, but here he found ample time and used to study this Holy Book with fervor and enthusiasm, going over the incidents and events of the lives of former prophets and finding how parallel they were with the events of these latter days. Thus he was consoled and encouraged. He would read, for instance, the following verse: "How thoughtless are the people! Whenever a prophet is sent unto them they either ridicule him or persecute him."

And then he read this verse: "Verily our host is victorious over them."

He was very happy, because he was a free man. Shut off in that room his spirit traveled throughout the immensity of space. At night he went up on the roof and communed with the countless brilliant stars. What a divine feast! What a heavenly procession! What spiritual freedom! What beatific bliss! What celestial Sovereignty!

6. Remarks on War Waged between Greece and Bulgaria

Then he spoke in detail about the present war between Greece and Bulgaria, and the utter folly of shedding the blood of innocent people. There is no benefit in this human butchery, this spoilation, this destruction! Mankind must learn the lesson of Peace; they must be instructed in the school of love. What is this insanity? What is this fratricide? What is this ruthlessness? Away with the nightmare of war! Banish the thought of strife and sedition! Are we not brothers? Are we not the sheep of one shepherd? How long shall this blindness continue; how long this military lunacy? Then he spoke about the restlessness of kings and rulers and gave us the instance of one Muslim Caliph who, although he had many countries under his dominion, yet could not be happy.

Divine happiness, he said, is obtained through servitude at the Threshold of God, through evanescence, detachment, sincerity and severance from all else save Him.

7. Story about Bahá'u'lláh's Shepherd

Before he left us, he recalled to his mind the name of the head-shepherd of Bahá'u'lláh and related many stories about him. He asked Mírzá Fadlu'lláh whether he were still alive and received the answer: "He is dead, but his daughter is living."

One day this head-shepherd came to the Blessed Perfection and said: "My Lord! I have one piece of advice to give unto you."

"What is it?" Bahá'u'lláh asked.

"Never trust the 'ulamá."

Bahá'u'lláh loved this man because of his simplicity and faithfulness. We were then given permission to retire.

8. A Joke with Husayn Rúhí

'Abdu'l-Bahá asked Husayn Rúhí how many pupils he had in his school. "One hundred and sixty." 'Abdu'l-Bahá said laughingly that Husayn Rúhí was rich and that his hands were certainly full! He himself did not have one pupil. Could Husayn Rúhí find some students for 'Abdu'l-Bahá?

PORT SAID, EGYPT, JULY 4, 1913

1. *Story of Hájí 'Abdu'lláh and His Conversation with 'Abdu'l-Bahá*

Hájí 'Abdu'lláh is a Bahá'í of eighty years of age. He has lived fifty years in Egypt and has ever been a devoted Bahá'í; and a sincere believer. He is dressed in Eastern robes and has a long gray beard. Although advanced in age, he is vigorous and in good health. He has seen Egypt become most prosperous through the opening of the Suez Canal. He lives in one of the small towns in the interior of the country and having heard about the arrival of the Master has come to see him. Today he received permission to return to his work. He had a conversation with 'Abdu'l-Bahá.

'Abdu'l-Bahá asked him how old he was.

He said he was over eighty years old.

Well! He had lived a good long life and now he looked younger than 'Abdu'l-Bahá!

It was through the Favor of Bahá'u'lláh, voiced the old veteran.

It was true! 'Abdu'l-Bahá told him, and wished to know whether he desired to live much longer.

Hájí 'Abdu'lláh gave an affirmative answer.

'Abdu'l-Bahá was surprised.

What? Was this life so sweet to the old man's taste for him to long for an extension of it? Why was this? As to 'Abdu'l-Bahá he was ready to leave this ephemeral world. It contained no attraction for him. 'Abdu'l-Bahá likened himself to a man who has heard that he must travel twenty days before reaching his destination. Having traveled already fifteen days, he is eager to hasten his trip and arrive at his goal. He is anticipating the eternal union with the Beloved at the end of his journey; therefore he is impatient!

The old man was deeply moved and spoke in a tremulous voice. He did not want to live for himself. Looking back at the map of his life, he saw many barren years stretching before his eyes, for he had not been confirmed in the service of the Cause. Therefore he desired to do something. He was hoping against hope that he might yet be enabled to render a great service to the Cause. He knew that he was very old, but his hope was young, and his eyes were filled with tears.

2. 'Abdu'l-Bahá Dictates Tablets for Many Bahá'ís.

This morning the Master received in private many of the Egyptian friends who had just arrived to meet him for one day. Meanwhile he found time to dictate Tablets to many of the friends in America and England and an important one to the International Congress of Free Christians, and other Religious Liberals, holding its Congress in Paris from July 16th to 22nd. Let me share with you the contents of the last.

3. Tablet to the International Congress of Free Christians

To the Secretary of the Sixth International Congress of Free and Progressive Christians, and other Religious Liberals, held in Paris, France, July, 1913.

He is God

Beloved and respected friend:

Your letter was received. Its contents became conducive to happiness of conscience, for it indicated that a group of the well-wishers of the world of humanity have displayed an effort to bring about a Congress of Religions, so that this may become the means of establishing affiliation among those religions, in order that the reality and the foundation of the Divine Religion be disclosed, and the causes of misunderstandings be removed. This is indeed an exalted intention; it is a service to the world of humanity and is conducive to the unveiling of merciful susceptibilities.

I hope that that Congress may be confirmed in affiliating the hearts of the people of the world, and be the means of the creation of peace between religions, so that the darkness of estrangement may be dispelled from amongst mankind and the followers of all religions may be ushered into the world of Unity—that is, accept the principles of the Oneness of the word of humanity.

It has been my greatest longing to be present at that International Gathering, but now I live in Egypt, my physical constitution is weakened, and other infirmities of age prevent me from attending the Congress. Therefore, begging your pardon for this shortcoming, I write a few lines on this subject: It is well known and evident to the wise men of humanity—the wooers of Truth—that the aim of the appearance of the Holy Divine Manifestations, the revelation of the Book and the establishment of the Spiritual Religion, has been no other than to create affinity amongst the children of men, and to found the law of Love between the individuals of the world of humanity. Religion is the basis of spiritual Unity; it is the oneness of thoughts; the oneness of susceptibilities; the oneness of morality; and the necessary connection between all the people of the world—so that minds and souls may grow and develop through divine Education, in order that they may investigate reality, ascend to the lofty heights of human perfection and found on this terrestrial globe a Divine Civilization.

In the world of existence there are two kinds of Civilizations: a natural and material civilization which serves the physical world; and a divine and heavenly civilization which renders service to the world of morality. The founders of natural civilization are the scientists and philosophers of the earth. The establishers of divine civilization are the celestial Manifestations of God. Religion is the basis of Divine Civilization. Natural civilization is like unto the body. Divine Civilization is like unto the spirit. A Body without spirit is dead, although it may be in the utmost beauty and comeliness. In short, by religion we mean those necessary bonds which unify the world of humanity. This has ever been the bestowal of God. This is the object of Divine teaching and law. This is the light of everlasting life. But alas, a thousand times alas! for this solid foundation is abandoned and forgotten; the leaders of religion have fabricated a set of blind dogmas and rituals which are at complete variance with the foundation of divine religion. As these dogmas differ from each other, they cause differences; differences breed strife, and strife ends in war and bloodshed; the blood of innocent people is spilled, their possessions are ransacked and pillaged, and their children become captives and orphans. Thus religion, which was designed to become the cause of friendship, has become the cause of enmity. Religion, which was meant to be sweet honey, is changed into bitter poison. Religion, whose function was to be the illumination of the world of humanity, has become the factory of obscurantism and gloom. Religion, which was meant to confer everlasting life, has become the fiendish instrument of death. Consequently, as long as these blind dogmas are in human hands, and these nets of dissimulation and hypocrisy in their fingers, religion will be but a harmful agency in the world of humanity. Hence these superannuated and tattered dogmas which are current among present day religions must be totally abolished, and, thus, freed from past traditions, mankind will be able to investigate the real objects of divine religion; for inasmuch as the foundation of the religion of God is One, and that One is absolute reality, and reality is indivisible and not amenable to multiplicity, therefore complete unity and amity between all religions shall be instituted and the true religion of God shall become unveiled with the utmost beauty and sublimity in the assemblage of the world of humanity.

Thence, it is the duty of this honorable Congress to rend asunder these veils of imitations, to remove these non-essentials and to disperse these dark clouds that the Sun of Truth may dawn from the Everlasting Horizon with the utmost brilliancy.

Praise be to God, that this century is the century of success! This Cycle is the Cycle of Reality! Minds have developed, thoughts have taken a wider range of vision; intellects have become keen; emotions are sensitized; inventions have transformed the face of the earth and this age has acquired a glorious capacity for the majestic revelation of the oneness of the world of humanity.

Should this honorable Congress display an extraordinary effort in the promotion of altruistic aims, and remove these dogmas which are in the hands of the religionists—such dogmas as are in opposition to the Divine Ideals—this world will become another world, the physical earth will be changed into the universe of the Kingdom, the world of humanity will become an arena for the revealing of the mysteries of Truth; the rays of the Sun of the Divine Firmament will shine upon it; East and West will become illumined; North and South will embrace each other like unto two beloved ones; the followers of all the religions will become investigators and champions of Reality, new eternal Institutes will be founded in the human world and the Palace of the oneness of the realm of humanity raised higher and higher, day by day.

These are the hopes of this Wanderer. I beg of God confirmation and assistance for you—so that you may be inspired with such a spiritual vision: the appearance of which is looked upon as impossible and unrealizable from the very foundation of the world; but which in this glorious Cycle will become manifest in the utmost beauty and perfection.

Upon you be greeting and praise.

(Signed) 'Abdu'l-Bahá 'Abbás.[9]

Although at this time the Master was not feeling well, he continued to dictate Tablets and when he was thus occupied, he entered into a spiritual state, and his bodily weariness completely disappeared, and for the time his health was absolutely restored.

For the last few days he has been complaining about the weather and he may shortly leave for Ismailia, which is the summer resort of Egypt. The Port Said weather at this season is most humid. I don't think he will keep all of us with him, but he may

---

9. For a different translation of this Tablet see, 'Abdu'l-Bahá, *Divine Philosophy*, pp. 159-162.

take one or two; probably Mírzá Munír. In the afternoon, while the believers were sitting in his presence, he dictated many Tablets and they listened most carefully. To them, this is more significant than a talk, because they consider it the greatest privilege of their lives to be present while the holy Tablets are revealed. After an hour or so he said it was enough, and for nearly thirty minutes he related many stories about the futility of studying Islamic theology which is nothing more than traditions and prejudiced dogmas.

4. Poem by Mr. Chase Read to 'Abdu'l-Bahá

The poem of Mr. Chase written on August 9, 1912, San Francisco, California, was read to the Master and he gave his permission to publish it in the Star of the West. It was composed just before his death, begging the Beloved to go to California. The first line of it is:

"O Thou David of the Promised Kingdom of God."

5. Story about Abraham's Hospitality

Another interesting story about Abraham was sent from San Francisco by Miss Bijou Strawn[10] who is preparing a book of the Master's addresses for publication. She desires to include this story as a footnote. It was read to the Master. He gave the source whence the story came. First, I will copy here the story as reported in M. K. Schermerhorn's book, and then I will give the version as the Beloved told it:

> Abraham would scarce break His Fast for one week, lest some hungry traveler should pass who might need his store. Ever he looked out upon the desert, and one day he beheld an aged man, with hair white as snow, tottering toward his door. 'Guest of mine eyes!' exclaimed Abraham, 'enter thou with welcome, and be pleased to share my bread and salt!' The stranger complied and the place of honor was given to him. When the family gathered round the board, each one of them said: 'In the name

---

10. Usually spelled, Bijou Straun.

of God!'—but the aged guest uttered no word. Abraham said: 'Good man! when thou eatest food, is it not right to repeat the name of God?' The stranger replied, 'My custom is that of the Fire Worshipers!' Then Abraham arose in wrath, and drove the aged man from his house, but even as he did so, a swift-winged Spirit stood before the patriarch and said: 'Abraham, for a hundred years hath the divine bounty flowed out to this man in sunshine and rain, in bread and life. Is it fit for thee to withhold thy hand from him, because his worship is not thine?'

According to 'Abdu'l-Bahá, this story is recorded in Rúmí's Mathnaví. It is related that an aged and decrepit man visited His Holiness Abraham and was received with the utmost hospitality and courtesy. When dinner was served, His Holiness Abraham uttered the name of God and then began to eat. His guest, on the other hand, pronounced the name of an idol and also began to eat. His Holiness was grieved, and arose in wrath rebuking his guest most severely; but even as he did so, God's revelation descended upon him:

> "O Abraham! For a hundred years this man has been an idol worshiper and I have been patient with him; I have nurtured him; I have protected him; I have taken care of him; I have trained him; I have showed him with many bounties and have been kind and loving to him; but thou wert not able to endure his society even for one night!"

His Holiness Abraham was deeply touched by this address and begged his aged guest to pardon him.

When we left the Master's presence, he kept Mírzá Fadlu'lláh and later on, as they were walking together in the avenue, the Editor of "Peesah Akbar," an important Indian newspaper, met him. This journalist happens to know a great deal about the Cause through the American press notices which were sent to him by Mírzá Mahmúd who met him while traveling and teaching in India. He has already written several articles about the Cause in his own journal.

PORT SAID, EGYPT, JULY 5, 1913

1. World Conflict and Its Remedy

Whether we live in the East or in the West, the invisible Power of God is unifying our scattered forces and training us for the service of His Kingdom—the Kingdom of Universal Love and inter-racial Amity. Today, more than at any other time, the world of humanity is in need of this Power. The keen competition which is carried on by the captains of industry and finance, the rumbling discontent and social unrest of the laboring class, the bigotry and fanaticism of some of the religions, the heat and bitterness with which fanatic controversies are upheld between the sectarians, the spirit of superiority with which some nations look upon others, the lust of conquest, and the desire for the extension of territory, the social and political rivalries between nations and governments and the hatred and enmity existing between antagonistic races—all these forces clashing against each other, apparently aggravate the situation and make confusion more confounded. But the Power of the spiritual conscience has come to stay, bringing healing under its wide-outstretched wings. 'Abdu'l-Bahá believes that this power alone is the solvent for all these puzzling problems. Here and there may be found some medicine to give temporary relief, but the lasting and permanent cure is the spiritual Power of Love which unites all people and sets at naught their seeming differences. This Power alone transforms hearts, inspires spirits, uplifts minds, reveals the secrets of Truth and unfurls the Banner of divine brotherhood.

2. The Departure of a Zoroastrian Bahá'í for Bombay, and 'Abdu'l-Bahá's Tablet About His Western Trip.

Our last pilgrim, the Zoroastrian from Bombay—Mihraban—has left today for his home. He was an old man with a bushy round, gray beard. He spoke very little, but his eyes were fresh springs of love and gentleness. The Master has been especially kind to him and often praised his race for their uprightness and charity. He called him, this morning, to his presence, and after a few words of farewell, gave him a short Tablet written with his own hand, the translation of which is as follows:

> O thou Mihraban! Praise be to God that through the Protection and Favor of the Omnipotent God thou didst reach the Illumined spot, have kissed the Threshold of the Kind Friend, and have become confirmed and assisted in that which is the highest desire of the angels of the Universe of heaven. Now thou hast for several days been my associate and my companion, therefore return to India and convey the greeting of this Friend to each and all the believers and say:
>
> 'This indigent one does not enjoy one moment of peace. In the evening he is restless, by day he is full of acclamation. He undertook the long trip to Europe and America and cried out over the mountains and on the plains. Now the time has come when the friends may raise their mighty voices and fill the world with the melody of the Kingdom of Abhá. They must show an effort, render some kind of service, create a whirlwind of ecstasy and appear with manifest signs and power, so that 'Abdu'l-Bahá may obtain peace of mind and of spirit....'

3. 'Abdu'l-Bahá's Interview with an Indian Editor

This morning the Beloved sent for Mírzá Munír and dictated several Tablets to the Persian believers, many of them having long or brief accounts of his western journey. Later in the day, Mírzá Mahmúd called on Moulavi Mahboud Alam, the Indian Editor, and together they visited the Master. As he was a Muslim, the discussion dealt purely with the Muslim world and made an exposition of the means through which the different sects might be brought closer together. The journalist was much impressed by the talk of the Beloved and took notes so that he might write a few articles on the Cause.

About six o'clock we gathered in front of the hotel to bid farewell to our Zoroastrian brother. Then we accompanied him to the pier and while he was leaving in the little boat to be conveyed to the steamer, I looked up, and there in the heavens, beheld the most luminous crescent that I had ever seen! It was small, semi-circular, silvery, and so delicate! For a long time I looked at it, and the hunger of my eyes could not be satisfied. It was the silvery bow of the angels of God, the arrows of which are meteors of Truth to disperse the hosts of ignorance and intolerance. Returning to the hotel, we sat around the table and looked into one another's faces. For the first time we were only five, and not only did we miss our many pilgrims, but also the beloved friends beyond the seas in Europe and America!

PORT SAID, EGYPT, JULY 6, 1913

1. The Bahá'í Heart Is a Cool Fountain

The heart of a Bahá'í is a cool spring from which eternally gushes forth the pure water of divine knowledge and heavenly wisdom. This water irrigates the soil of humanity which is parched through the heat of dogmas and the fire of superstitions. Immediately after the distribution of this water, the flowers and anemones of love and affection become manifest and the nostrils of those who are remote and near are perfumed. Barren ground is changed into a luxuriant garden, sterile soil is made productive, bare trees are clad with verdant garments, the silent nightingales break forth into songs of gladness, the frost of the winter is transformed into winsome spring, and the stillness of death is changed into the buoyancy of life!

The Bahá'í heart is a garden. Its gardener is 'Abdu'l-Bahá. With his tender hands he plants roses and violets, carnations and tulips, chrysanthemums and lilies of the valley. The beauty of these ideal flowers is in their imperishableness and in the sweetness of their fragrance. Day and night he sows the seeds from his never-ending store. To him, the ground of every human heart is susceptible to Divine Cultivation. That is why he has so many gardens. He is the most successful spiritual gardener that the world has ever seen! He knows the composition of the soil and the chemical ingredients of every part, and he applies his indisputable knowledge with real success. Give to him the most barren, sterile patch of ground, and before long it is a mass of flowers and an orchard of fruitful trees.

2. Another Interview with the Indian Editor, and 'Abdu'l-Bahá's Talk on Education

This morning the Beloved had a most interesting interview with the Editor of "Peeseh Akbar." The Editor propounded many questions concerning the return of the old glory of Islam, the education of the Eastern women, the matter of the veil for women, etc., to each one of which the Master gave detailed answer. The Editor was carried away with enthusiasm, because he found all his difficulties removed with such simple, yet eloquent expressions. He wrote down all the Master told him. He understands Persian quite well and is a progressive and intelligent journalist. He has been out of India for nearly seven months and expects to go to Tunis, Europe and New York before returning to his native land. The Master has given him an introduction to the Persian Chargé d'Affaires in Washington, D.C., so that he may be shown all due respect and proper hospitality.

Toward the end of his talk to him, 'Abdu'l-Bahá stated that we must ever think of the education of the public and try our utmost to improve the conditions of the submerged classes and to lay a solid foundation for the erection of the Temple of human happiness. For the realization of this hope, divine Education is essential, and the inculcation of the idea of the oneness of the world of humanity is necessary. We must deal with all with loving kindness and be the real well-wishers of mankind. They are the sheep of God and God is the Universal Shepherd. He is compassionate to every member of His flock. He trains all, He feeds all. He protects all. We must free them from the old prejudices. We must confer upon them a new life, which is cordial love, good-fellowship, amity and unity, amongst the children of men. Our behavior and conduct must be an example to them. We must abandon all forms of prejudice, religious, racial, sectarian, and national. The object of all the religions has been the moral progress of the race. Only by walking in this path can the illumination of the world be assured, and the prosperity of mankind obtained.

3. The Bahá'í Cause in Paris and Tablets for the Friends

'Abdu'l-Bahá dictated several beautiful Tablets for Miss Sanderson, Mons. et Madame Richard, Mons. et Madame Bernard and Mr. and Mrs. Scott of Paris. He expressed hope for the future illumination of Paris and exhorted these friends to continue the spreading of the message.

PORT SAID, EGYPT, JULY 7, 1913

1. Importance of Correspondence between the Friends

Often a letter from a far-off friend gives one good cheer and encouragement. This is part of that invisible chain which unites all mankind; more especially this is the case with those who are working for a common Cause. Thousands of miles, oceans and lands may divide them, but when the word comes, the hearts are united, space and time annihilated and they live as though in one room, talking and conversing together and creating an atmosphere of uplift. This in itself is a sufficient reason why the Bahá'ís from various countries and out-of-the-way places should correspond one with the other and keep themselves informed, not only of the progress of the Cause, which, is of course, the most important thing, but of other current events which would be of interest.

2. 'Abdu'l-Bahá's Talk on the Enemies of the Cause

This morning I was summoned to 'Abdu'l-Bahá's presence. Mírzá Fadlu'lláh was there. Packages of letters were all around the Master. He was writing, and now and then he raised his head and spoke, evidently following the thread of a long conversation. When I arrived he was saying that the Cause has many enemies! The Bahá'ís must be very happy. The priests and the 'ulamá, the Rabbis and the Mobeds are attacking the Cause right and left, but their attacks make it stronger and more powerful. We are invulnerable. We know no defeat. We are fighters to the very last. There are no deserters in the Grand Army of Abhá! They are all good fighters!

One of the missionaries in Beirut in his sermon cried out in wrath and hopeless anger: "We always thought that the Bahá'ís would be a good, wholesome influence for civilizing Islam alone, now they have started to civilize us and are trying to teach us by demonstrating a plan of propaganda, the like of which has never been seen since the time of Christ and His Apostles!" Ah, me! We have many enemies, bitter, dangerous and revengeful! But we defeat them through the Power of Love! This is our only weapon. The Ocean of the Cause is limitless, shoreless, depthless. One wave and all these foams will be scattered to the four corners of the sea. 'Abdu'l-Bahá did not look at the present disturbed conditions of the ocean. His heart was assured and confident as to the future of the Cause. No person, no matter how powerful, can shake the foundation of the Bahá'í Faith. It rests upon the Eternal Rock of Ages. After the departure of His Holiness Christ, there were only eleven disciples. These were of the humble class, deprived of any social distinction and yet their faith was often shaken, but behold the result of their work! Now after the departure of the Blessed Perfection there were more than one million Bahá'ís scattered all over the earth, each one faithful, sincere and self-sacrificing. Praise be to God, that singly and alone, without any helper or assistant, we are attacking the trained army of darkness and have come out of the field victorious!

Such is the sublime faith of 'Abdu'l-Bahá that must animate and quicken all the Bahá'ís throughout the world.

3. Arrival of Hájí Niyáz, the Old Patriarch

In the afternoon we were called again. Hájí Niyáz had just arrived from Cairo. He has been many times in the presence of Bahá'u'lláh. He is a venerable Bahá'í, about eighty years old, and has lived in Egypt for the last thirty-five years. He is tall, has a long white beard and wears a turban like the Master. He has a gentle personality, and all the American Bahá'ís who have passed through Cairo, have made it a point to see Hájí Niyáz. The Master loves him very much and welcomed him with open arms. He talked with him about the believers in Cairo. Then the Master dictated several Tablets, including a long one on "Universal Peace" for the Christian Commonwealth. From this time on the Beloved may write more Articles for the Western press to be read by many thousands of people who cannot be reached otherwise.

4. Tablet to the Editor of "The Christian Commonwealth" on Universal Peace

O thou esteemed and kind friends:

After journeying throughout the United States of America and the great capitals of Europe, I have returned to the East. I am most pleased and well satisfied with the result of this journey—because I met noble people and associated with worthy souls, who are the cause of honor and glory to the world of humanity. They are learned and wise, well informed about the realities of events, well-wishers of the human world, especially they are advocates of Universal Peace.

In these days, the world of humanity is afflicted with a chronic disease. It is one of bloodshed, of the destruction of the divine edifice, of the demolition of cities and villages, of the slaughter of the noble youths of the world of humanity making children become orphans and women homeless. What calamity is greater than this? What crime is more heinous than this, what disease more dangerous, what folly more direful?

Consider that in former days there were only religious wars, but now there are racial and political wars, fought at staggering expense and sacrifice. A thousand times alas for this ignorance, for this bloodthirstiness and ferocity!

I am pleased and grateful to the Societies which are organized in the west for the promotion of universal peace, with whose presidents, officers and members I have frequently conversed. I hope that the sphere of their activities may from day to day, become enlarged, so that the lights of higher ideals may illumine all regions, the oneness of the world of humanity be proclaimed in the East and in the West, and men attain composure and well-being. These revered souls who are the servants and the promoters of the cause of universal peace shall ere long shine like brilliant stars upon the horizon of mankind, flooding all regions with their glorious lights. In the past century freedom was proclaimed and the foundations of liberty were laid in all the western countries. Praise be to God that the sun of justice has shone forth and the darkness of despotism and tyranny has disappeared.

Now in this radiant century in which the world of humanity is being matured, it is assured that the flag of universal Peace shall become unfurled, waving over all the regions of the globe. This is the most great principle of Bahá'u'lláh, for the promotion of which all the Bahá'ís are ready to sacrifice their possessions and their lives.

Notwithstanding my bodily weakness and infirmity, I have traveled East and West for the last three years. In many temples I have cried out, and before many audiences raised my voice for the enlistment of their sympathy. I have declared the evils of war and explained the benefits of Universal Peace. I have elucidated the causes which lead to the honor and glory of the world of humanity and told of the ferocity and bloodthirstiness of the animal kingdom; I showed the defects of the world of nature and made an exposition of the means whereby the illumination of the world of humanity can fully be realized. I unfolded and disclosed the foundations of divine religion and proclaimed the teachings of His Holiness Bahá'u'lláh. I demonstrated the existence of God by irrefutable, rational proofs, and proved the reality of all the prophets of God. I gave utterance to my inmost conviction that the verity of the religion of God is the cause of the life of the world of humanity; it is divine civilization and pure enlightenment.

In giving the explanation of these principles, my object has been no other than the desire to promote Universal Peace. Praise be to God, I have found hearing ears, observed seeing eyes, and discovered informed hearts. Therefore I am well pleased with this journey.

But on the other hand the well-wishers of the world of humanity and the advocates of Universal Peace must make an extraordinary forward step, organize important international congresses and invite as delegates progressive and influential souls from all parts of the world—so that through their wise counsels and deliberations this ideal of Universal Peace may leap out of the world of words into the arena of actual and practical demonstration. This question is of paramount importance and will not be easily realized, but we must take hold of every means until the desired result is obtained.

Fifty years ago, whosoever talked about Universal Peace was not only ridiculed, but called visionary and utopian. Now, praise be to God, it has assumed such importance that everyone acknowledges that this question of Universal Peace is the light and spirit of the age.

I hope the noble leaders of the world of humanity who are the divine bestowals among the people, and the means of pacification among the nations, will arise with the utmost effort and with whole-hearted resolution extinguish this world-raging conflagration, especially now that the blood of innocent people and the cries of orphans are reaching to the very gate of heaven, while the harrowing sorrow of mothers penetrates souls with the irresistible force of human tragedy. Thus through the endeavors of these guardians of the rights of mankind, the world of creation may enjoy the repose of conciliation, the banner of Universal Peace be unfurled, the tabernacle of the oneness of the world of humanity be pitched, all mankind be gathered under its protecting shade and the shining star of eternal felicity and happiness of the world of humanity will dawn with the utmost brilliancy from the horizon of international comity, while the luminous arks of spiritual brotherhood of all races and tongues will illumine the united gathering of mankind with the ineffable lights of God throughout countless ages and cycles.

(Signed) 'Abdu'l-Bahá 'Abbás.[11]

---

11. This Tablet was published in *Star of the West*, Vol. 5, (August 1, 1914), Asma, No. 8, p. 70.

PORT SAID, EGYPT, JULY 8, 1913

1. What is the Function of Real Religion?

Pure religion, free from dogmas, contributes to the happiness and progress of a people, suffering them to attain to the highest summit of democracy and brotherhood. Religion, hampered by the chains of fossilized traditions will keep mankind within limits of intolerance and prejudice. Religion must be as pure as the breeze of the early morn, as bright as the stars of heaven, as fragrant as the sweet flowers of spring, as clear as the limpid and cooling water of the fountain, as verdant as the delectable paradise, and as universal as the rays and the heat of the sun.

Therefore, when religion does not perform these functions, it is not fulfilling its mission. In this connection 'Abdu'l-Bahá, in a Tablet just revealed to the Sixth International Congress of Free and Progressive Christians and other Religious Liberals to be held in Paris, July 16-22, 1913, says:

> Thus religion, which was destined to become the cause of friendship, has become the cause of enmity. Religion, which was meant to be sweet honey, is changed into bitter poison. Religion, whose function was to be the illumination of the world of humanity, has become the factor of obscurantism and gloom. Religion, which was to confer Everlasting Life has become the instrument of death.[12]

The duty of every one of us is, therefore, to spread the principles of Pure religion, in accordance with the needs of this age.

2. 'Abdu'l-Bahá's Perennial Cordiality and Courtesy

When one enters the presence of the Beloved, even if it is for the thousandth time, one feels quickened by the spirit of reverence, humility, and evanescence. When this morning I found myself, standing before him and heard his rich vibrant voice greeting me: "You are welcome! You are welcome!" I felt as though this was my

---

12. See *Divine Philosophy*, p. 161, for a slightly different translation.

first visit to him. He always receives everyone, even his servants, with heavenly cordiality, a sweet smile, divine courtesy, and inimitable friendship, making them feel as though they were his own sons and daughters.

3. The Joy of Serving 'Abdu'l-Bahá

With his discourse, his remarks, and his teachings, he uplifts one's heart and makes one long to sacrifice everything in his path. Really to be with him for one hour is more glorious than a long association with all great men of the world; and to render service to him is better than serving kings. To win his good pleasure is a source of eternal joy; to upraise the flag of his truth is more wonderful than all the wealth of this earth! May we all remain faithful to him and live and act in such a manner as to win his approval! If we continue to be firm in the Cause and pray every morn and eve for this pearl of great price our brows will be crowned with the diadem of God's Bestowals! The Cause of humanity must become a glowing fire in our hearts and not a flickering flame in our minds. It must become a flowing fountain, ever gushing forth from the innermost part of our beings! No obstacle must seem to us insurmountable and no difficulty discouraging. We must face all the problems, try to solve them and encourage others through deeds and sympathy! What if the whole world be against us! We may be in the minority—the Christ and His Apostles were in the minority 1900 years ago—but whenever God is on the side of the minority it will become the majority.

4. There Is a Power in This Cause

After dictating several wonderful Tablets 'Abdu'l-Bahá laid stress upon the fact of the great power existing in this Cause, a mysterious power, far, far, beyond the ken of men and angels. That invisible power is the source of all these outward activities. It moves hearts. It rends mountains. It administers the complicated affairs of the Cause. It inspires the friends. It dashes into a thousand pieces all the forces of opposition. It creates new spiritual worlds. This is a mystery of the Kingdom of Abhá.

The Tablets were for Mrs. Harriet C. Cline, and Mrs. Mabel Rice-Wray of Los Angeles, Calif.; Miss Harriet Magee of New York, Mrs. Dixon of Washington, D. C., Miss Dorothy Hodgson of Paris and Miss General Jack of London.

5. Hájí Niyáz and the Story of the King and Ayáz

Leaving the Beloved to his divine contemplation, I went to the hotel and there had a talk with Hájí Niyáz. I knew him before my trip to America several years ago. Through him I had received my first Tablet from the Master and because of this I love him very much. In fact everybody loves him. He is a veteran in the Cause. He related in his rich language, the story of a king and his ministers and courtiers.

> Once upon a time the king went out to hunt with the members of his Cabinet, the Diplomatic Corps, the officials of the Court and a large number of important personages, especially invited for this occasion. As the king intended to stay in the country, he ordered the Master of Ceremonies to take the Imperial Tent which was a wonderful work of art. On important occasions he had in past seasons caused the inner walls and ceiling of this royal tent to be decorated with hundreds of precious jewels. This year he also asked the Minister of Finance to take with him the casket of jewels. After many days of preparation, the Imperial Caravan, which was more than a mile long, set forth. The King headed the procession. After him came the Cabinet Ministers, the Diplomatic Corps, the courtiers and the guests. They had to travel six days before they could reach the hunting ground. After four days it so happened that the horse carrying the box of jewels lagged at the end of the Caravan. Three hours march, and the king looked around, when to his apparent surprise, he found no one with him except Ayáz, and observed the Caravan more than a half mile away, surrounded with dust and great confusion.
>
> "What is this?" asked the king.
>
> "Half an hour ago," Ayáz humbly and serenely answered,

"the casket of jewels fell from the back of the horse, and all of the precious stones were scattered on the ground, and in the wild scramble that followed, everyone forgot his duty, and tried to seize the jewels."

The king did not move or speak to show that an extraordinary event had happened.

But after a few moments of reflection, he said "Ayáz!"

"Yes, my Lord."

"Why didst thou not join them to get a portion of the spoil? Are they not precious jewels?"

"Yes, my Lord. These jewels are good for them, but I preferred to remain with thee. Thou art the greatest Jewel of my life!"

PORT SAID, EGYPT, JULY 9, 1913

1. Our Life in Port Said

My room has two doors which open on to the veranda and at night there is always a cool breeze from the Mediterranean which is not more than a thousand feet away. At midnight I get up and go out and listen to the music of the waves, played for the bright stars. Tonight, the moon is shining. The voices of the Arabs chanting their Qur'an come to my ears. It is a weird, monotonous sound, but very soothing. My table is covered with papers and letters; Mírzá Mahmúd, a few steps further, is writing and copying Tablets. My light consists of a dear little lamp. I am indeed happy.

2. The Death of a Bahá'í Child and the Ceremony of Her Burial

We have just returned from a memorial meeting, held on account of the death of Mírzá Jalál Afshár's little daughter, he is one of the Port Said Bahá'ís. We were invited at 5 P. M. to go to the funeral. Mírzá Mahmúd chanted one of the prayers of Bahá'u'lláh then the little body was washed, wrapped in silk, and as there was no ring for her finger, the prayer was written on a piece of paper and put in the palm of her hand. The second ceremony, the Muslim one, consisted of the coming of the Mullá, and the chanting of prayers and then they carried her body by hand to the nearby Mosque. All those who entered the Mosque left their shoes at the door. The body was laid on the floor, the tall Mullá before it. We stood behind the Mullá. He began then to read the prayer for the dead with the rapidity of lightning, and from time to time raised his two hands to his face and ears, which exercise was copied by us automatically, according to custom. All this, however, did not take more than five minutes. Several carriages were ready at the door of the Mosque, and as soon as we came out, Mírzá Jalál, his brother, the Mullá, carrying with both hands the body of the child, and another relative got into one carriage, and we followed in the others. We were driven posthaste toward the cemetery, situated in the west of the city. The Mediterranean was on our right and always very near. On the way we observed many little hills of soft silk-like sand, formed by the winds. Often one observed the extremely soft sand trickling down from the upper part of the little hills exactly like the flowing of a tiny rivulet. It was a strange sight, and reminded one of the passing of our own lives.

3. The Christian and Muslim Cemeteries

First we drove by the Christian Cemetery, surrounded by a wall. We saw the cross in all forms—large and small—defying the crescent of the Muslim burying-place. I had to stand up in the carriage to see the Christian Cemetery. It was not as beautiful and flowery as the Cemeteries of America—because it is most difficult, in this land of sand, to raise trees and flowers—but it was fairly clean, and one could see patches of green and there were flowers here and there. Finally, we reached the Muslim cemetery! It was very unclean. Shrieking Arab men and women were in evidence. The tombstones are made of wooden boxes, and I believe a spark of fire would burn the whole place. The dead girl was interred beside her grandfather, buried here a few years ago. The poor father was weeping and quite inconsolable. Hájí Niyáz, being the oldest man, tried to comfort him.

4. Visiting Taqí Manshádí's Tomb in the Cemetery

Probably many of the American friends remember the faithful Taqí Manshádí through whom the East and the West carried on a large and voluminous correspondence with 'Abdu'l-Bahá. He died a few years ago and his body is buried in this cemetery. I met him during my first visit to 'Akká, and from that time till the day of his death corresponded with him. I expressed a desire to visit his tomb. Yúsuf directed us to it, and we offered a prayer. Unless one knows the place, it is not possible to find it, for there is no tombstone, a piece of wood without an inscription is its only mark. Hájí Niyáz knew Taqí Manshádí well. The brief outline of his life is as follows:

5. Outline of Taqí Manshádí's Life and His Services to the Bahá'í Cause

He was from Manshad, a little village near Yazd. In his early youth he had accepted the revelation, but had found the people of his own village extremely fanatical and dogmatic, and as the rabble threatened to kill him, finally left the place and moved to the city of Kerman. There he began to teach the Cause but when the 'ulamá received news of his presence, they sent word to him that he must leave the city immediately or they would take the law into their own hands. So with much difficulty and privation he came at last to the city of Shiraz. After some time, with the object of visiting Bahá'u'lláh, he made a pilgrimage to Mecca, and thus acquired the much-respected title of Hájí. From Mecca he went to Alexandria. It was before the 'Urábí Revolution.[13] Here, with a number of other Persians, he engaged in business, but not being constitutionally fitted for that kind of work, and having always the hope of serving the Cause, and of beholding the Face

---

13. The Urábí Revolution was a nationalist uprising in Egypt from 1879 to 1882. It was led by Colonel Ahmed 'Urábí and sought to depose the Khedive Tewfiq Pasha and end British and French influence over the country. The uprising was ended by an Anglo-Egyptian War and takeover of the country by the British which lasted until 1954.

of the Blessed Perfection, he one day left everything and went to 'Akká. After attaining the supreme desire of his heart, he made 'Akká his final home and there tried to seek congenial occupation. Little by little, his eagerness to serve the Cause, and his longing to devote his whole time to the Movement, was demonstrated, and Bahá'u'lláh from time to time gave him a packet of Tablets to mail to different parts of the Orient. When the believers from all over the world observed that they received their Tablets through him, they began directing their petitions in his care so that he might give them personally to Bahá'u'lláh and intercede for them Thus, without any ceremonies or formalities, Taqí Manshádí became the most well-known and talked of Bahá'í. Everyone was eager to receive his letters. It has often been stated by those believers who are familiar with both Persian and English writings that Taqí Manshádí and Mr. Charles Mason Remey were brothers in calligraphy, only Taqí Manshádí was an older brother.

6. Manshádí's Epistolary Style and His Peculiarities

Manshádí's letters are well preserved by all the Persians. Hájí Niyáz tells me that he has 500 of them. I may have two hundred or more. These letters are masterpieces of news writing. He had a sense for bare facts and news, and he knew that no one expected philosophy from him or the literary style of Oriental compliments. He had done away with all this form. It was really a radical departure from the established rule and many young people, seeing the wisdom of his course, followed his epistolary innovations. The letters generally opened with a few sentences about the Master's health and his family. This to the Bahá'í world, was considered the most important part. Then the record of the arrival and departure of the pilgrims, their names, the events in 'Akká, a general outline of the progress of the Cause in other parts of the world, etc. They were indeed "newsy letters." After the ascension of Bahá'u'lláh the activities of the Cause increased a hundredfold, the number of the believers became considerably larger, the movement spread in America and Europe and the matter of correspondence with all these heterogeneous elements became of the utmost importance. The Master looked about for an efficient experienced man who could hold in his hand the helm of the ship of correspondence, and who with a cool head and infinite patience, could direct it through the tempestuous seas of difficulties. In the whole Bahá'í world, there was no one more fitting than Taqí Manshádí, and he was selected for the position. For many years he worked untiringly, unceasingly, ever receiving assistance from the Supreme Concourse. In his early days at 'Akká and Haifa, his room became a general meeting-place for all the Bahá'ís. "I will see you tonight at Manshádí's home at such and such an hour," was an oft quoted expression. The door was open to everyone. All pilgrims were welcome. He was always the first to go to the steamer to greet the newcomers or say farewell to those who were returning, laden with the spiritual gifts from the Presence of Bahá'u'lláh. Hájí Niyáz says:

"Taqí Manshádí was well known amongst all the Bahá'ís for his fidelity, simplicity, loving disposition, truthfulness, sincerity and above all, for his ability to serve everyone with gentleness, courtesy, and marvelous patience. His room was furnished with simplicity. He always sat on the floor, surrounded with a pile of letters. He was often literally buried in them. He smoked a 'water-pipe' all the time, and an over-indulgence in this, finally caused his death."

When Sultan 'Abdu'l-Hamíd sent several commissioners to 'Akká and conditions became intolerable, the Beloved sent Taqí Manshádí to Port Said—so that from this place he might carry on his work, It was in this town that he passed away at the age of sixty, serene and happy. The Master was much grieved when he heard the news, and after a while appointed Sayyid Asadu'lláh in his place, this position he has filled with credit to the Cause and to himself. I hear however, that Sayyid Asadu'lláh is going to leave for Russia tomorrow to teach the Cause. After the wonderful trip through America and Europe he will no doubt be confirmed in attracting many souls to the Kingdom of Abhá! The Master, before long, will appoint another person to carry on his work.

7. How to Conduct Bahá'í Meetings, and the Importance of Public Speaking

This morning, I called on the Beloved. He had received packages of letters, some from America. There is one point which has been brought to his attention of late. It is this:—In certain Assemblies in America a number of the believers desire to exclude all public speaking and to confine themselves to the reading of Tablets, etc. This is positively not in accordance with the Bahá'í Plan of teaching, nor with the instructions of 'Abdu'l-Bahá. To read Tablets, and the Holy Writings is only half of the aspect of the question; the other aspect is the delivery of eloquent addresses and fluent talks elucidating the spirit of the Cause. The Master's wish is always to encourage the believers to speak at the meetings. This I know is his will. When today the subject was again presented to him in a letter from America, he told me that he had written in many Tablets that the friends must speak at the meetings. We must encourage public-speaking, especially in those who have this talent. The Cause must be spread through eloquent, sincere addresses. We must unloose the tongue, spread the Fragrances of God and diffuse the words of God. We must present to the public the proofs and evidences of this Cause with a language of fire—so that souls may be exhilarated, and minds become full of tumult and of acclamation. With words of Love and illumination we must set the hearts aglow with this Fire of Divine Truth and enkindle the spirits with this Power of the Kingdom. We must explain the Teachings orally, so that the consciousness of men may be stirred; then invisible inspirations will descend. Bounties from the Holy Spirit will be revealed, rays from the Sun of Reality will shine forth, Breezes from the Paradise of Abhá will waft abroad and the Glad-tidings of the Kingdom spread throughout the world.

8. Tablet by 'Abdu'l-Bahá Regarding the Delivery of Eloquent Speeches

Then he revealed a Tablet on this subject and may issue others before long:

Thou hast written concerning the spiritual meeting. The spiritual meeting must be in the utmost state of ecstasy and tumult. Prayers may be recited, Tablets and verses read, eloquent speeches delivered and divine proofs explained. Then the audience may be encouraged and incited to enter the Kingdom of God, news received from different countries may be imparted and at the end they may repeat collectively a supplication.

PORT SAID, EGYPT, JULY 10, 1913

1. Sayyid Asadu'lláh Departs for Russia to Spread the Message

Our traveling companion, and fellow-worker, Sayyid Asadu'lláh Qumí, who has been with Bahá'u'lláh and the Master for many years and traveled with the latter throughout America and Europe, left today for the Caucasus to teach the Cause. We will miss him. He has been like a father to us during our wanderings and although Mírzá Mahmúd wrote the official report of the trip of the Beloved, yet Sayyid Asadu'lláh corresponded with the friends in small assemblies all over the East. They could not receive any direct news, were he not traveling with us. Now, detached from all else save God, alone, at the age of seventy-six, he faces the world. Carrying in his hand the Ideal Banner of the Cause, he leaves port Said with a firm confidence and trust in 'Abdu'l-Bahá.

After the ascension of Bahá'u'lláh he made a trip through Persia, taught many souls, and was bitterly persecuted for his glorious faith. Last night and this morning he went to 'Abdu'l-Bahá and no doubt received his orders and heavenly benediction. Today at one o'clock we were all gathered at the station, to bid him farewell. He goes first to Alexandria to meet Mírzá Abú'l-Fadl and then taking a ship, will sail for Constantinople.

2. Sayyid Asadu'lláh's Talk with 'Abdu'l-Bahá and His Glowing Resolution

I confess that nothing has so deeply stirred me in my whole Bahá'í career as the heavenly resolution of this old man to go alone into the world and teach the Cause! He himself went to the Master and begged for his permission. He said: "I have heard thy glorious proclamation from pulpits and platforms. I have seen wondrous scenes of the Majesty of Our Lord. I have hearkened to the divine words falling from thy blessed lips. My Lord! My cup is full to overflowing. I am an old man. I question if I can accomplish anything in thy Cause, but I supplicate thee to let me try. I can contain myself no longer. I do not wish to flicker out on the couch of rest, but long to end on the battlefield. I would love to die as a soldier, fighting the good fight to the very last moment, and not as a pensioner."

And so he went! With such a superhuman example of deeds and self-sacrifices does anybody wonder why the Bahá'í Cause has such stupendous power? All the friends in America and Europe who have met our dear brother Sayyid Asadu'lláh love him, and I know that from the depth of their hearts they will pray that the Lord may keep him and protect him many years yet for the service of His Cause, and as a witness to His Power.

3. Farewell to Sayyid Asadu'lláh

My beloved Sayyid Asadu'lláh farewell! You have been a loving companion and a faithful attendant to our Beloved! Your cheerful face and disposition shall never be forgotten! Your memory will shine in our inmost hearts as a radiant star! Your faith will be a glorious example for all the younger generations. During the years of your life you have served your God to the best of your ability! You have suffered and accepted much persecution in the Path of Baha! And now, although a veteran of many wars, you are again enlisted in the ranks of active work and are entering on a new campaign! Farewell!

4. 'Abdu'l-Bahá's Expectation to Go to Ismailia

For a few minutes we were privileged to see the Master in the morning. He said that the weather in Port Said had not agreed with him, and that he expected to leave tomorrow for Ismailia, a town about one hour and fifteen minutes from this city. He is going there for two or three days and if all goes well, he will send for us. Ahmad Yazdí and Khusraw will accompany him.

5. Poems of Mr. Moxey Read to 'Abdu'l-Bahá

In the afternoon Mírzá Abú'l-Qásim Isfahání and Mírzá Mahmúd, two merchant Bahá'ís from Cairo arrived with their wives to see the Master. They accompanied me into his holy presence. He was dressed in spotless white and looked very beautiful. A large envelope containing the poems of Mr. Frank K. Moxey of 575 Riverside Drive, New York City, had just been received. The Master gave them to me to read. After looking over the title of each, I told him about them. He then asked me to translate the poem on the Báb, which I did immediately. He was most pleased and praised it very highly. The poem is very eloquent and shows true inspiration. It is hoped that he will continue to write upon such soul-stirring ideals. A Bahá'í poet is needed in America There are many in Persia.

6. 'Abdu'l-Bahá Speaks about the "Star of the West"

Then the Master took from the table the "Star of the West," No. 5, and showed all those who were present the photograph of the Mashriqu'l-Adhkár Convention in New York City. He was very happy, saying: "Look at this photograph and wonder at the penetrating influence of the Bahá'í Cause."

He expressed the hope that the "Star of the West" would, little by little, widen its field and become a power for good in the Cause and in humanitarian activities. Its Persian section is eagerly read by all the Bahá'ís.

7. Talk on His Tour to America

Then, referring to his arduous tour through the United States, he mentioned that the confirmation and assistance of the Blessed Perfection were his companions; otherwise his body could never have stood all the difficulties of the voyage. He did not feel well, yet he worked. He traveled. He went there. He came here. He did not give any importance to his body. The wisdom of this was that the believers might see with their own eyes that he was rising above hardships, vicissitudes, sickness and troubles so that the Cause might prosper. Except for the diffusion of the Fragrances of God, he desired nothing. Except for service at the Threshold of Abhá, he cared for nothing. His hope was to teach the Cause, to proclaim the Glad-tidings of the appearance of the Kingdom of Abhá, and to advance the Cause of International peace and human brotherhood.

PORT SAID, EGYPT, JULY 11, 1913

1. 'Abdu'l-Bahá's Departure for Ismailia

Knowing that the beloved departs today for the city of Ismailia, we called on him about 6:30 A. M. The train leaves at eight, so we had ample time to have our last meeting. There were several pilgrims, who had just arrived, and to them he expressed his regrets. He will stay there two or three days. If the weather agrees with him, he will rent a house and send for us. If not, he will return, and go either to Alexandria or Ramleh.

2. He Praises the American Bahá'ís

He spoke about the innumerable meetings he had attended in America, and how he found in the believers a true spiritual sense, and a divine and heavenly attraction which made them strive upward; how the paeans of their glad praises were raised to the supreme Concourse; how they were making great efforts to bring into being the spiritual consciousness of mankind; how they were servants of the oneness of the world of humanity, the promoters of universal Peace and the standard-bearers of the spiritual brotherhood of man.

3. He Tells the Persians about Fred Mortenson Who Traveled from Minneapolis to Green Acre in Order to See Him

Then he told the Persian friends about Fred Mortenson, a young Bahá'í from Minneapolis, who had been so anxious to meet the Master that he risked his life by concealing himself under the train till he reached Green Acre, Maine.

Praising the courage of this fine clean fellow 'Abdu'l-Bahá said that when he passed through Minneapolis he had again met him and his wife. Such events could not happen by the effort of any human being, but they are the confirmations of the Holy Spirit and the marvelous signs of this Dispensation!

About 7:45 the carriage was ready, the two small satchels of the Beloved were brought down, and after saying farewell to each one of us, he was taken to the station, Ahmad Yazdí and Khusraw accompanying him.

4. The Absence of 'Abdu'l-Bahá Is Noticed Everywhere

We returned home saddened because we could not go with the master, but were consoled by looking forward to our reunion, which would not be long.

A young Persian Bahá'í, by the name of Áqá Jamál, arrived yesterday from Haifa, and he will cook for us in our own apartment as long as we are here. He is a tall, quiet man, very willing to serve and to please everybody.

Mírzá 'Alí-Akbar, Hájí Niyáz and Mírzá Fadlu'lláh live in the hotel, but for their board and tea they come to us. Hájí Niyáz is a good conversationalist and knows many anecdotes and stories. While I was writing in my room, they had gathered around him on the veranda and he spoke to them about many things of interest.

At noon we received a telephone message from Ahmad Yazdí assuring us of the master's safe arrival and that he is stopping at the Hotel Vaseteef. He is pleased with the place and is well.

In the afternoon we were again gathered on the veranda, drinking tea and talking about the Cause; Hájí Niyáz described his meetings with Prof. E. G. Browne of Cambridge University, when he was in Egypt, when the latter was invited to the house of Khurásání, where all day one of the Bahá'í teachers discussed with him aspects of the Cause referring to rational and scriptural proofs.

Let me translate for you a few extracts from recent Tablets:

5. Tablet on 'Abdu'l-Bahá's Trip in America

Less than a year, 'Abdu'l-Bahá raised the cry of 'Yá Bahá'u'l-Abhá' from his heart and soul as he crossed the mountains and deserts of that continent! In churches and meetings he imparted the Glad-tidings of the appearance of the Kingdom of God. With a resonant voice he announced the dawn of the Sun of Reality and explained divine proofs and evidences. With a heart and spirit overflowing with the Love of God he raised the New Wonderful Melody. Undoubtedly it will have great effect. Consider that the soul-imparting Melody of His Holiness Christ, (may my life be a sacrifice to him!) became effective and world-conquering after three hundred years, but in a short space of time the Song of the Kingdom of Abhá has quickened the East and the West!

The future of the Cause in Stuttgart:

> I hope that the Ensigns of Divine Verses may be upraised in Stuttgart; the Fire of the Love of God be so enkindled as to set all those parts aglow, and that each one of those blessed souls may become as a bright candle, shedding the light of guidance in every direction.

6. The Power of the Bahá'í Cause

The Glad-tidings of the Kingdom of Abhá can overcome hard stones and resuscitate dried bones. Like unto the down-pouring of the vernal shower, they cause the growth of roses and hyacinths, jasmine and jonquils to come forth out of black soil! Likewise if the inhabitants of a city are submerged in the sea of materialism, it may take some time to awaken them, yet the Melody of the Kingdom of Abhá shall finally quicken them; the cup of the Love of God will become full to overflowing, imparting a wonderful exhilaration to allay the thirst of the thirsty ones.

PORT SAID, EGYPT, JULY 12, 1913

1. Telephone Message from Ismailia about 'Abdu'l-Bahá

Today at noon we received a telephone message from Ismailia giving us news of the master's improved health and wishing us to give his greeting to each one of the friends. Two Bahá'ís arrived from Cairo, not knowing that the Master was not here. We entertained them to the best of our ability with stories of the spiritual Conquest of the Beloved in the West. As one of them had only two days leave from his work, we got the Master's consent by telephone that he might be permitted to see him in Ismailia.

Everybody was here as usual talking about the Cause; Hájí Niyáz told us about some incidents in the life of Bahá'u'lláh. Toward evening we walked to the quay where the Casino Palace Hotel, the small municipal garden and DeLessep's statue are situated. We observed great preparations for festivities and upon inquiry were told that the French were celebrating their Independence Day, 14th of the month.

As there is a strong element of French in the Canal Company, they seem desirous to impress the Egyptians with their patriotism, and they are making very elaborate preparations. In Cairo they celebrate this Feast on a much larger scale.

2. Mírzá Mahmúd Prepares Three Volumes on the Tour of 'Abdu'l-Bahá Throughout Europe and America

The last few days Mírzá Mahmúd is preparing 'Abdu'l-Bahá's addresses from the time he sailed from Alexandria to America. These addresses will form the first volume; the second will be his diary in Persian of the journey, and the third the translation of the articles which appeared in the principal papers and magazines of America and Europe. Once these books are published and circulated in the Orient, they will have great effect in furthering the Cause of the Kingdom of Abhá!

3. Translation of a Tablet to the Believers in Kerman, Persia

The following is a Tablet to the believers of Kerman, Persia:

O ye kind friends! A letter was received from Kerman giving you utmost praise and saying, the friends of God are like unto flames of fire and radiant lamps of the Kingdom; they are as fire-temples of spirituality and brilliant stars of heaven. This letter has become the cause of happiness to my heart, for praise be to God, the Fire of the Love of God is set aglow in Kerman, the veils which have covered their eyes are burned away; the believers are attracted and stirred into gladness, and the friends are in a state of supplication and invocation. Therefore, I prayed and implored at the Divine Threshold and wished for the beloved ones a cup overflowing with the Grace of God, so that, in Kerman, the day of resurrection may be set up, the hearts become exhilarated, the city moved by the resounding voice, and the world stirred with the power of the Holy Spirit!

Praise be to God! The Eastern horizon is luminous and the nostrils of the people of the West are perfumed. The splendor of the luminary of the East has cast a reflection upon the West which has illumined it. The Voice of the Almighty is raised in these regions and the Pure Religion of God is being promoted. Ere long it shall yield important results and the ensign of Yá Bahá'u'l-Abhá shall be lifted so high as to wave over all the continents.

4. How to Deliver Bahá'í Public Addresses

The basis of this divine call (teaching and delivering addresses) must be the oneness of the world of humanity; so that religious fanaticism, sectarian bias, racial prejudice and political rivalry may be removed, so that all mankind may enter under the uni-colored tent of the oneness of the world of humanity, and hearts may affiliate with each other, souls be attracted and East and West embrace each other. This must be the basis of your addresses in public meetings.

5. How Great Movements Have Advanced

All great movements have advanced through altruism, selflessness, and self-sacrifice and not merely through an interchange of public opinions. It is my hope that all may arise with the greatest power to serve this most important Cause (Universal Peace) and become the means of the welfare of the world of humanity.

6. About 'Abdu'l-Bahá's American Tour to a Persian Bahá'í

It is nearly two years and a half since I have been a wanderer over mountains and deserts and a traveler over seas and lands. The journey was extended to many climes.... The penetrative power of the Holy Cause has stirred the columns of the world. In many cities of America the Divine Call was raised. Likewise in the countries of Europe. In numerous churches, clubs, groups and Universities of America the Glad-tidings of the Kingdom of Abhá were explained precisely with resonant voice, and no one arose to make opposition. They listened most attentively and afterwards expressed their pleasure. Ere long this Call shall yield glorious results and will fill the world with its fruits.

PORT SAID, EGYPT, JULY 13, 1913

One of the believers, Mírzá Abú'l-Qásim Isfahání coming from Cairo a few days ago brought with him a package belonging to Sayyid Asadu'lláh. This package among other things contained three precious volumes of Tablets from the pen of 'Abdu'l-Bahá. They are copies of very old letters, some of them addressed to the believers in America. Herein I will translate a few. The following may have been revealed to one of the American Assemblies and probably is sixteen years old:

1. Tablet of 'Abdu'l-Bahá on Progress

He is El Abhá!

O ye friends of the Blessed Perfection!

This century is the century of attraction. This Cycle is the Cycle of His Highness the Lord of Lords. The East and West are in commotion and acclamation and the North and South in ecstasy and tumult. The world is progressing with marvelous acceleration and the realm of existence is growing and developing with an eternal velocity and at geometric ratio. Mankind, like unto a suckling babe is being trained in the Arms of Providence, and humanity like unto a newly planted tree in the ground of the world, is waxing in stature and size, becoming more beautiful and lovely through the downpour of the rain of Grace. The greater the exertion, the more the descent of the divine Bestowal. The more we ascend heavenward, the greater will be the realization of universal progress from all directions.

Therefore, O ye friends of the Ancient Beauty and ye beloved ones of the Most Great Name! Make an effort, so that in all the grades of Human existence, whether spiritual or material, ye may make extraordinary advancement. The Mercy and Favor of His Highness, the One is with us!

(Signed) 'Abdu'l-Bahá 'Abbás.[14]

Here is another Tablet which was revealed probably thirteen years ago to (Mrs. Helen G. Goodall), a believer in San Francisco, California, the contents of which shows how the Master's prayers are fulfilled in her behalf:

2. A Tablet by 'Abdu'l-Bahá on Personal Illumination and Guiding Others to the Truth

O thou spiritual pearl and leaf stirred by the wafting of the Breeze of God! Verily with a heart overflowing with love and affection I perused thy letter which was an eloquent expression of thy praise for the love of God, of thy firmness in the Covenant of God, thy gladness through the Fragrances of God and thy great exertion in the guidance of the servants of God!

Verily I supplicate God to confirm thee with the Breaths of the Holy Spirit, to dilate thy breast with the Zephyrs wafting from the direction of the Paradise of Abhá and to suffer thee to become a light from which radiates the rays of supplication, invocation and prayers toward the Kingdom of God:—so that

---

14. An authorized translation of this Tablet is provided in *Selections from the Writings of 'Abdu'l-Bahá*, pp. 66-67.

thou mayest become a Cause of the awakening, mindfulness and quickening of the servants and maid servants of God, and a means of giving them of the wine of knowledge and of summoning them to the Kingdom of the Merciful with evidences and proofs. . . .

I will close this day by the translation of another wonderful Tablet:

3. The Day of the Glorious Bounties of the Invisible Kingdom of Abhá

He is El Abhá!

O ye real friends!

This day is the day of the Glorious Bounties of the Invisible Kingdom of Abhá and of the tumultuous waving of the seas of the Inexhaustible Bestowals of the Supreme Countenance. The rays of his effulgences have dawned from all directions and the breezes of His generosity and compassion are wafting from all parts. The doors of His kingdom are flung wide and the verses of His Omnipotence are spread abroad. His ancient Grace like a mighty torrent is flowing with great impetuosity, and His manifest light is apparent from the horizon of Certainty like unto a shining moon.

But these servants must appreciate the value of this Eminent Grace and consider this sublime generosity as the most great Bounty—so that we may become its signs and be illumined with its rays. When vernal showers descend upon good and pure soil, flowers will grow therein and the black earth will become a delectable Paradise.

4. Mrs. Stannard May Go to India and Teach the Bahá'í Cause

Mrs. J. Stannard, an English Bahá'í, is back in Port Said and may stay with us for several days. I had a most pleasant conversation with her about the progress of the Cause in Germany and England. The Master may send her to India. She is a very active and energetic worker and no doubt will be able to spread the Bahá'í movement very effectively.

PORT SAID, EGYPT, JULY 14, 1913

1. *The French Day of Independence in Port Said*

The European part of Port Said is decorated with thousands of Japanese lanterns, the French flag is seen everywhere, and everybody seems to enter into the spirit of celebration on this National Feast of the Republic of France. After sunset the principal avenues, the French Consulate, the Banks, firms and buildings are lighted up by electricity. The street in which the Eastern Exchange, Continental and Casino Palace Hotels are built, is a riot of music promenaders, Arabs, Greeks, Italians, English, German, and French. Everybody is out to have a good time and to see the sights. The avenue from one end to the other is wired, and a roof is constructed of Japanese lanterns. The trees also bear such luminous fruits. During the day there have been many public functions and receptions in the Consulate, in the government house and in the Canal Company headquarters. Last night there was a grand Ball in the Casino Palace Hotel. About eight o'clock we left home, our destination being the Municipal Park. The Casino Palace Hotel is so built that it fronts the Mediterranean and on the other side faces the Park. The hotel was illumined from top to bottom with electric festoons and it was indeed a glorious sight to thousands of Arabs, men, women and children—who had come to see what wonders these - "strangers" have wrought! The weather was cool, a brisk breeze was wafting from the sea. The heaven was clear and the soft silver rays of the Queen of night streamed down upon a merry-making population. The searchlight, built upon a high pillar to guide ships into the harbor, revolved round and round, sending its powerful rays into the remote distances of the sea. At nine o'clock a cannon boomed forth, and the display of fireworks was started. More than twenty coal barges were tied together at the wharf. People crowded near the harbor. The fireworks were on these barges and hundreds of rockets ascended to the skies displaying many colors. Some strange, fantastic contrivances, were displayed on the water, which ran hither and thither like lizards. For one hour and a half the display of pyrotechnics continued, showing all the original devices and magical works that a French mind can invent.

As soon as the fireworks started, three ships illuminated from top to bottom, came into view from the other side of the port. These were followed by more than one hundred boats in an orderly line, all brilliantly lighted with electricity. It was really a very imposing naval procession, fairy-like, picturesque and beautiful. Beside these boats there were several hundred others belonging to the merry-makers, afloat on the calm sea. Now and then the air brought to our ears the sweet notes of a mandolin or guitar. . . . It was half past eleven when we returned home!

2. Abdu'l-Bahá's Life in Ismailia

This morning Ahmad Yazdí returned from Ismailia and brought good news of the Beloved. The first two days he had not felt well, but now he is resting better. While there he had met an old friend of his, a famous doctor who had prescribed a regime of rest and diet to be followed strictly. The Master has decided to remain a week; if the weather agrees with him, he will send for all of us, if not, he will return and then may go to Ramleh. He has sent for Mírzá Fadlu'lláh to go to him as soon as possible. So he left at seven P.M., and will be in Ismailia at 8:15 P.M.

Today I will translate another Tablet to an American Bahá'í:

3. What Constitutes Everlasting Fame

O thou who are attracted by the light shining from the Kingdom of God!

Verily I have read thy eloquent letter and wonderful epistle expressing thy excessive joy through the divine Gladtidings, and reflecting the susceptibilities of thy conscious and spiritual emotions through the Bestowals of His Majesty the Lord of mankind. Blessed art thou for this Bounty! Gladness be unto thee for this Gift! Rejoicing be thine for this confirmation. Happiness be unto thee for this assistance. Ere long thou shalt behold with eyes of beatitude the signs of success and prosperity because of thy firmness in the Love of God, thy steadfastness in the Covenant of God, thy superlative attraction to God, thy unwavering perseverance in the diffusion of the Fragrance of God and thy source of joyousness through the Glad-tidings of God!

Know thou, verily I say unto thee that the condition of this mortal world, even if it is the kingship of the whole expanse of the Globe, is ephemeral. It is an illusion. It ends in nothing, neither does it contain any results nor in the estimation of God is it equal to the win of a mosquito. Where are the kings and the queens? Where are the palaces and the empresses? Where are the imperial thrones and jeweled crowns? Where are the mighty rulers of Persia, Greece and Rome? Verily their palaces are in ruin and desolation, their thrones destroyed, and their crowns cast in the dust. But any one of the maid-servants of God who has arisen in the diffusion of the Fragrances of God, serving the Kingdom of God, summoning the people to the Word of God, eternally her signs shall be widely spread and handed down through centuries and cycles; her dawn shall ever be luminous; her star always shining; her flag continually flying; her station divinely glorified; her crown scintillating; her message living; her fame immortal; her voice resonant; her spirit in the apex of the Kingdom; and her effulgence in the horizon of the Realm of Might I beg of God to make thee one of these maid-servants.

PORT SAID, EGYPT, JULY 15, 1913

In the Persian notes of our brother Mírzá Mahmúd, I find a glorious message to the Unitarians of America which I am sure was not translated at the time: It is the second day after the Beloved's departure from Alexandria, March 26 or 27th, 1912. An American woman expresses her interest in the Cause, saying that she is a Unitarian and requesting the Master to send a message to them in the United States. Then 'Abdu'l-Bahá utters the following words:

1. *The Message of 'Abdu'l-Bahá to the Unitarians*

Convey to the Unitarians my loving greetings and say: The most exalted aim in this world is the promotion of the Love of God and the establishment of good fellowship and unity between the people. This is the signal distinction between man and beast. When thou reachest America, announce to the Unitarians:

Glad-tidings! Glad-tidings! The Sun of Universal Love hath dawned;

Glad-tidings! Glad-tidings! The Banquet of friendship and divine association is spread.

Glad-tidings! Glad-tidings! The Banner of the Kingdom of God is unfurled!

Glad-tidings! Glad-tidings! The heavenly Spring hath appeared.

Glad-tidings! Glad-tidings! The Cloud of spiritual Grace is pouring down!

Glad-tidings! Glad-tidings! The trees of the orchard of humanity are verdant and abloom.

Glad-tidings! Glad-tidings! The Herald of the Kingdom hath become manifest.

Glad-tidings! Glad-tidings! The prophecies of the holy Books have been fulfilled.

Glad-tidings! Glad-tidings! The age of human brotherhood is dawning upon mankind!

Glad-tidings! Glad-tidings! The Century of Light and Universal Peace hath come!

As I read these vital words it seemed to me that they were a most significant prelude to the enthusiastic reception given to him by the Unitarians of America at their Convention in Boston, in the Tremont Temple.

Another beautiful talk that I may be permitted to translate here from the Persian notes is the Beloved's words to Bishop Birch of New York, who came to call on him at the Hotel Ansonia on the sixth day of his arrival. After a preliminary conversation he said:

2. 'Abdu'l-Bahá's Conversation with Bishop Birch of New York City

Praise be to God that stupendous material developments are obtained in this country; but material civilization alone does not safeguard the progress of a nation; because through material civilization, dynamite, Krupp guns, projectiles and Mauser's rifles are invented: thus the infernal instruments of human fratricide are multiplied and constantly perfected. Therefore, natural civilization fosters both good and evil. All this warfare and bloodshed, and all this feverish multiplication of military armaments are the results of material civilization. When material civilization joins hands with spiritual civilization, then it will be perfect. In former times a wooden box may have protected your objects from the thief, but now safes with their complicated keys and signs do not daunt the robbers. Consequently just as 'good' is advanced through material civilization, 'evil' has taken the same pace. Earthly civilization must become the handmaid of heavenly civilization. Natural civilization is like unto the body of man. If the body is animated by the spirit, it is alive, otherwise it is a corpse which in time will become decomposed."

The Bishop expressed his pleasure and delight at hearing the above words of truth. The Master replied:

3. Some Churches are Free from Prejudices

I am likewise very grateful to you. Praise be to God that your churches are free from prejudice. They are not so creed-bound as to be unable to breathe. Many Christian Churches in Europe are as yet extremely dogmatic, but I have already spoken in churches belonging to your denomination. The congregations consisted of most delightful and intelligent people. This is a great distinction. I love you with all my heart and soul. My chief aim is to remove the present misunderstanding between the nations of the East and the West—so that we may express love toward each other and promote the essentials of heavenly civilization. I hope that such a confirmation may be vouchsafed, so that we may become united.

The Bishop said:

Up to this time no one has come from the East to the West with such power, such lucid teachings and such exalted aims. Therefore I am very grateful to you and most pleased to have met you.

The third contribution for today is going to be a part of a touching Tablet revealed by the Beloved to a friend in 'Akká, on the fourth of this month. He says in part:

4. 'Abdu'l-Bahá Expresses Desire to Visit the Shrine of His Father in 'Akká

Truly I say, the extreme desire of my heart and soul is to be present at the Court of Bahá'u'lláh, so that I may perfume my face and my locks with the dust of the Holy Threshold.

It is now three years since 'Abdu'l-Bahá has been deprived of this Favor and has remained too far to become the recipient of the dawning lights of that brilliant spot. Day and night he has suffered from regret and deprivation. It is hoped from His Highness the Desired One, that this weak body which through the effect of the long journey has come to the verge of complete disintegration, may before the cessation of breath, become so assisted as to throw itself upon the Dust of the Holy Threshold. May this servant attain to a new life, illumine his eyes, and transform his heart and spirit into a rose garden and meadow, start on his journey to reach the Abode of the Friend and haste from this to another world.

5. 'Abdu'l-Bahá Praises the Faith of German Bahá'ís

In a Tablet revealed on the same date to Mírzá 'Alí-Akbar he says about Germany:

In short, Germany shall become illuminated; because its inhabitants are religious and not submerged in the sea of materialism. Those souls who travel along the path of nature are like unto dead people; the breath of life does not play upon them to any effect. Praise be to God that you have become assisted in service and that you have ignited the candle of guidance before the eyes of all. It is hoped that most weighty results may become apparent. The German believers are in a state of real enkindlement; firm and steadfast in the Cause of God; therefore their influence will be very great.

Today a letter was received from Mírzá Munír who is in Ismailia, giving the news of the well-being of the Master, and saying that he will soon send for us; he is looking for a house large enough to accommodate all. In the morning we called on Ahmad Yazdí at his store; in the afternoon Madame Stannard came to see us and we talked a great deal about the probability of the Beloved's trip to India. She has lived in that country for a long time and is thoroughly familiar with the situation.

Today several letters arrived from America imparting cheer and happiness. Through the golden chain of correspondence hearts are united even if seas and lands separate them.

PORT SAID, EGYPT, JULY 16, 1913

1. The Scope of 'Abdu'l-Bahá's Talks in California

Now that we are temporarily separated from the Beloved, we occupy our time with the past, working upon the notes of his American tour. I am copying all the Master's public and private talks given in California, so that when I am with him, he may correct them for future publication. The Master's talks in California reached the high water mark of his trip, showing the wonderful versatility of his divine mind. During those days, a flood of teachings was poured from his tongue, irrigating the soil of hearts.

2. The Program of a Day's Activity in Port Said

Mírzá Mahmúd is busy writing the diary of 'Abdu'l-Bahá's tour in America. Mírzá 'Alí-Akbar copies the Tablets and addresses of the Beloved. He is eager to have these heavenly words to read in the Bahá'í meetings which he will attend on his way to Persia. For the present our group consists of only these three persons. We live very quietly. Seldom anything or anybody disturbs the peacefulness of our abode. I get up at five o'clock and after reading a few prayers, go out on the veranda and look at the Mediterranean, sometimes perfectly calm, and again rough. Then I work for an hour or two, till my friends are awake. Mírzá Jamal, our Bahá'í cook, has by this time prepared our breakfast, which consists of tea, bread and cheese. Then we work again till noon, and now and then one of us may go upon some errand or to visit Ahmad Yazdí's store to receive the news. For lunch, often we have bread, cheese, cantaloupe or watermelon, and if not these, "ábgúsht" or "Persian stew." Our friends take a nap. I work. At four we have tea. At six we take a walk and call on Madame Stannard at the Eastern Exchange Hotel. Generally we are back by eight. Between nine and ten we have our supper, sometimes rice or meat. Then we sit on the veranda for about an hour, speaking about the Cause, and enjoying the moonlit night, then we return to our room to work until eleven or twelve o'clock, after which we retire. This is the program of our life for the present. A great contrast to our strenuous activities in the West.

3. Permission Comes to Visit 'Abdu'l-Bahá in Ismailia

This morning Mírzá Fadlu'lláh returned from Ismailia with a package of Tablets from the Beloved for me to translate. On the envelope the Master writes with his own hand: "Translate these Tablets immediately. We hope soon to rent a house. As soon as it is prepared, we will send for you."

This message danced before my eyes and I started on my translations. Our happiness was complete when Mírzá 'Alí-Akbar brought us permission to leave for Ismailia tomorrow, to spend the day. The anticipation of meeting the Master gave us a new vigor and all day and night we walked on a cloud of joy and happiness.... Mírzá Fadlu'lláh has received permission to leave tomorrow for Persia.

The following is the translation of a Tablet revealed for the Persian believers on July 4th, which may be of interest:

4. What Is Real Friendship

O ye friends of 'Abdu'l-Bahá! Material friendship is not permanent; for every kind of love which is not purely for the sake of God is ended in hatred. Amity which is not for the sake of the Lord, changeth into enmity. But the divine friends are the faithful ones. They are the consolation of the heart and the peace of my spirit. They are spirit embodied, love personified, sincerity incarnated, loyal friends and staunch lovers. Therefore they are the cause of the happiness of the heart and the soul.

5. Prayer for the Friends

During this long journey, whenever the memory of the friends crossed my mind, hardships were forgotten, inconceivable joys were realized, and vicissitudes and inconveniences changed into composure and tranquility. Then I supplicated toward the Kingdom of Glory, saying:

"O thou kind Beloved! Be thou the associate of the hearts and the souls of the friends; send them at every moment dew from the sea of thy bestowals; exhilarate them every second with new wine and cause them to become intoxicated with thy cup; so that they may take the divine goblet in their hands, give the choice wine to the seekers and confer the exhilaration of the wine of 'Am I not your Lord?' upon the wooers!"

6. For Me to Be Silent, For You to Be Singing

In short, during this trip you were all with me and were visible before my sight. In my wanderings, the Melody of this divine bird reached the apex of heaven, and the cry of Yá Bahá'u'l-Abhá was heard by the people of the world. Now it is the turn of the believers of God. I will be silent and they must sing with acclamation and joy—so that they may awaken the heedless ones.

(Signed) 'Abdu'l-Bahá 'Abbás.

PORT SAID, EGYPT, JULY 17, 1913

To begin this day with thanksgiving on my lips and in my heart, I will translate a Tablet revealed by the Master many years ago to the Persian believers. It is from one of the books of Sayyid Asadu'lláh.

1. A Prayer of Illumination

I praise Thee, O Thou Remover of Sorrows, Overlooker of faults, Rejoicer of hearts and Illuminator of faces! Verily to the beloved ones at the door of Thy oneness, the worthiest amongst Thy people, the noble ones amongst Thy creatures and the righteous ones in the congregation of Thy servants, are evidences of the manifestation of Thy singleness. Verily Thou hast chosen Thy believers for the sake of Thy Love, elected them for Thy Knowledge, appointed them as the custodians of Thy Mysteries and exalted them above all Thy other servants, under all circumstances, and conditions.

O Lord! O Lord! Illumine their eyes with the beholding of Thy Lights, refine their consciences with the appearance of Thy Mysteries and enlighten their hearts with the traces of Thy Names! Suffer them to become the signs of Thy Unity, and the Banners of Thy singleness, the stars of Thy Graces and the candles of Thy Assemblages; so that they may arise to serve Thee and be steadfast in Thy worship. Verily Thou art the Merciful, the Giver, the Mighty and the Generous.

2. The Dawn of the Sun of Reality

O ye kind friends of 'Abdu'l-Bahá! It is night. The impenetrable darkness hath covered all regions, but the hearts of the yearning ones are illumined and enlightened by the rays of the Bestowal of the Clement. The effulgence of the Morn of guidance is manifest and clear and the brilliant rays of the Sun of Reality are diffused throughout all Continents. The verses of the divine Majesty of the Most Great Name are read by all the people in all tongues; and through explanations, the evidences and proofs of the Blessed Perfection are demonstrated.

The Melody of Holiness ascends to the ethereal sphere and the songs of Unity descend from the Kingdom of Singleness. The Breezes of the most eminent Guidance confer life, and the sweet Fragrances of the Paradise of Abhá perfume this world and the world beyond.

3. People Are Heedless

Notwithstanding this effulgence and this diffusion of the Fragrance of the Rose garden of the Covenant, innumerable souls are yet afflicted with the sleep of negligence. Their eyes are veiled and their nostrils do not inhale its fragrant perfume. What negligence, what inadvertence, what ignorance and what heedlessness is this! Verily this is the condition of the deprived ones in this Most Great Dispensation!

4. The Duty of the Followers of Truth

But as regards you, turn your faces toward the Kingdom of Abhá and join your voices in anthems of thanksgiving and glorification—that, praise be to God, the Sun of Unity hath so illumined the hearts of the righteous ones as to cause them to become the envy of the dawning-places of light and this is only through His all-comprehending Mercy and special Favor! Its source is—'He chooseth for His Grace whomsoever he willeth,' and its mainspring is—'This is through the Bounty of your Lord, He bestoweth on whomsoever He desireth.' Therefore, appreciate the value of the Most Great Bestowal of this ineffable Grace, and of this manifest Favor and Bounty which has been given to all the inhabitants of the world; so that by this appreciation and thankfulness the Mercy of the Peerless Lord may be increased, the Ancient Grace be revealed in the hearts and souls and spiritual outpouring be vouchsafed.
Upon ye be greeting and praise!

(Signed) 'Abdu'l-Bahá 'Abbás.

5. Our Journey to Ismailia

As we were leaving this morning for Ismailia we arose early. The train left at eight o'clock. In our company there were several other

Bahá'ís with their families who planned to stop over at Ismailia, to meet the Master and then continue upon their journey to Cairo. All along the road the mighty Canal joining the two seas was visible, and now and then great ships passed before our eyes. On the other side was the barren desert with its lack of vegetation. We also passed by a great salt lake, the whiteness of which dazzled us in the light of the sun. The train stopped at many stations, allowing passengers to get on or off as the case might be. By ten o'clock we reached Ismailia. It has a small, up-to-date station. As it is practically inhabited only by Europeans, it is one of the cleanest spots in Egypt. It has, of course, an Arab quarter, but in comparison with other Arab quarters I have seen this one is quite clean. Ismailia is a new town.

6. Visit to 'Abdu'l-Bahá in the Hotel Room

As soon as we reached the station we hurried to the hotel of J. Bosta. The first persons we met were Mírzá Munír and Khusraw, who have been fortunate enough to be with the Master. One of them conducted us to room 13 where the Beloved was living. When we entered we found 'Abdu'l-Bahá in bed in a weakened condition He welcomed us and inquired about our health. One of us had brought a package of letters and after a few minutes it was delivered to him. For a while he read them. There was one from an American believer (Miss A. Boylan) announcing the sad news of the death of her mother; another from India welcoming him to Egypt and inviting him to visit the former country. There were many more letters and cablegrams which for the present were left unread.

7. Formation of Habits

He raised himself and sat up in bed. He complained of the hardness of the cushions, saying, that when he was in Paris one of the believers had brought him a soft cushion and had urged him to put it under his head. He had become accustomed to it, and as there was none in the present hotel his neck consequently suffered pain all night. He said it was very bad to become the slave of habit, and that when he was young he often had a brick or a piece of rock to rest upon and slept soundly.

Hájí Niyáz said he had a soft pillow with him and begged to be allowed to go out and bring it. 'Abdu'l-Bahá would not have it, because he wished to get accustomed again to his old habits. One must never habituate himself to anything the absence of which may affect one's comfort.

8. Bahá'u'lláh's Life in the Persian Barrack of 'Akká

Then he related the story of Bahá'u'lláh's cruel incarceration in the barracks of 'Akká, substantially as follows:

When two years had passed, a regiment of soldiers was assigned to 'Akká. Of course there was only one place for them to live and that was the barracks. Therefore they had no alternative other than to turn out the Bahá'í prisoners. At the time there was an inn in 'Akká which was inhabited by different people. In after years this inn became a hospice for the pilgrims. 'Abdu'l-Bahá went to the innkeeper, stating, that inasmuch as the Bahá'ís were numerous and included several families, he desired to rent the inn and if it were possible for the present inmates to lodge themselves elsewhere.

The innkeeper agreed to accept this offer, but when after a few days he came back to draw up the papers and to sign the document, the Master observed that one of the rooms was still inhabited.

"Who is here?" he asked.

"It is the German Consul," the innkeeper replied.

"He must leave the premises; otherwise I will not rent the place. It is impossible for an outsider to live here."

The innkeeper looked at him with ridicule and contempt.

"Ha, ha!" he laughed. "And they say you are a prisoner! You talk to me as though you are my lord and master. What do you think, Mr. Prisoner! Do you expect to get an exclusive palace in this prison town? Not much, not much. This man is the German Consul. I cannot drive him out." To which 'Abdu'l-Bahá replied:

"There are many palaces in the outside world! If a prisoner

can find a palace in a prison town, he has indeed accomplished something."

9. 'Abdu'l-Bahá's Room in Prison

Finally the German Consul left of his own accord, only requesting the use of the room for two hours a day so that he might attend to his official duties, to which proposition 'Abdu'l-Bahá consented cheerfully. Then the Bahá'ís began to repair the rooms, but one of them had to be left untouched because their funds were exhausted. The rooms were then assigned to the various families and friends, and 'Abdu'l-Bahá chose the unrepaired one for himself. This room was so damp that grass had grown on the walls and there were several cracks in the ceiling which gave free admittance to the rain. The floor consisted of humid earth and was a breeding place for fleas.

10. The Fleas of 'Akká

'Abdu'l-Bahá had a mat and a long Persian fur coat. The latter was his garment by day and his blanket by night. When he covered himself with it, an army of fleas, hiding in the ambuscade of fur, attacked him and did their best to defeat him, but he outwitted them by turning the coat and by using its other side. Then for an hour he slept, until the wily, indomitable fleas would find their way again to the inner side. Every night he had recourse to this maneuvering eight or ten times, yet notwithstanding this, he was by far happier and more joyful then than at this time, sleeping on a fine bed in the hotel.

11. 'Abdu'l-Bahá Leaves for Alexandria

Then to our surprise he informed us that he would leave today for Ramleh and stay there for one week. If the weather agreed with him, he would send for us; if not, he would return to Port Said and together we would all go to Haifa. Therefore at 2:30 P.M., accompanied by Mírzá Munír and Khusraw, he left for Alexandria and Ramleh. The station master was a European, and when the Beloved reached the station a few minutes before time, he was conducted by him to his private office to rest. When the train arrived, this station master followed him very politely to the first class compartment. This sign of distinction was great enough in the eyes of the natives and officials of the railroad to excite their wonder and curiosity. Then as the train pulled out from the station we were once more separated from the Master. Our train leaves for Port Said at half-past nine, and therefore we have several hours on our hands.

12. Ismailia Is a Clean City

In order to pass the time profitably we took in the sights. There is a beautiful large park, lovely buildings, clean avenues and many electric lights. I was quite surprised at the size of the park with its big pine trees and flowers. We saw also the native quarter. The goats, the hens, the donkeys and the other animals live in the same room with the Arabs, making a peaceful family.

When we set our feet in the Port Said station, familiar faces greeted us. Ahmad Yazdí, Ibrahim Effendi and Áqá Jamál. They were, of course, surprised to hear that the Master had left Ismailia, but they said quietly: "He doeth whatsoever he willeth."

PORT SAID, EGYPT, JULY 18, 1913

1. 'Abdu'l-Bahá's Bust, Made in Vienna, Is Sent to Port Said

I have no news to write. We did not hear anything from Ramleh. It was a hot day, so we stayed at home and worked until 7 o'clock P.M. Then we paid a call on Madame Stannard and returned by way of Ahmad Yazdí's store. He had received the Master's little bust from Stuttgart. Mr. Herrigel has sent one to Mírzá Mahmúd and one to me. At present, mine is on my writing table and is a reminder of his wondrous personality and heavenly Love. "His spiritual face" is printed on the Tablets of our hearts. We think of him and work or him, for his spiritual face" is the Love of God, is the Knowledge of God, is the Breath of the Holy Spirit S the Divine Inspiration and love for all mankind.

2. A Prayer for the Success of the Bahá'ís

The following is a prayer revealed from the tongue of the Beloved many years ago:

> He is Glory, the Most Glorious!
>
> O God! O God! Behold Thou these radiant faces made joyous through the Fragrances of the flowers of Thy Kingdom, El Abhá, and illumined with the lights of Thy Supreme Concourse. Verily Thou seest that the temples of the believers are stirred by the fresh breezes of the Morning of Eternity and that the hearts of the pure ones are attracted by the signs of the Sacred Mysteries!
>
> O Lord! Fill for them the cups of joy; enlighten their faces by the rays emanating from the lamp of divine prosperity; cause them to hear the sweet songs of the birds of Holiness in the rose garden of Spiritual success; gladden them by allowing them to listen to the melodies of the Doves of light in the delectable heavenly fields, and suffer them to enter into the Paradise of Abhá, Thy Celestial Garden.
>
> O My Lord! O My Lord! Intoxicate them with the Wine of Knowledge, sweeten their taste with the delicacies of prayer in the early morn and eve; gather them together into one congregation; confer upon them a shelter; protect them in the cause of Thy Covenant and Testament; shield them from doubts and from the evil suggestions of the waverers,; make them Mines of Knowledge, of Wisdom and of Assurance, cause their feet to be firm and steady in the Straight Path, and grant unto them prosperity in whatever country they call the people to Thy Name! Verily, Thou art the Lord of the Cause and Thou art Powerful to do whatsoever Thou desirest!
>
> (Signed) 'Abdu'l-Bahá 'Abbás.

Here is another prayer. It may have been revealed for the American believers.

3. Prayer for Illumination

He is El Abhá!

O Thou Incomparable God! Make Thou these hearts intimate with Thy Mystery; suffer them to be detached from the known and from the unknown; cause them to drink from the overflowing cup of the morn of Unity and intoxicate them with the wine of 'Am I not your Lord?'

O Lord! These servants are captivated by Thee. These longing ones are attracted and enthralled by Thy Beauty. They are wanderers about Thy abode; lovers of Thy Countenance, and the flocks of gazelles of Thy meadow.

O Lord! We are stumbling in the desert of remoteness and are scattered in the valley of deprivation! Send Thou to us the Messenger of Providence and the Angel of Guidance—so that the Fragrance of Thy Garden may reach unto our nostrils, the refulgent light of Thy Countenance illumine the 'house of sorrows' of these grief-stricken people; the darkness of night be changed into the sunlight of day and the thorny place of regret transformed into the garden of hope. Verily Thou art the Mighty, the Seer and the Hearer!

O ye believers of God! Rejoice in the Most Eminent Bounty of your Lord! Be happy; for the Favors of the Glad-tidings of the King of the Kingdom are unlimited. Be ye prepared for the down-pouring of the Cloud of Mercy. Upon you be the Bestowals of your Lord, the Ancient! Dilate your breasts, increase your fervor, exalt your ambition, add to your yearning, and be rejoiced in heart, for God hath chosen you from amongst His creatures, for the sake of His Love. Verily He is Merciful and Clement to you.

(Signed) 'Abdu'l-Bahá 'Abbás.

I bring this day to a close by translating another Tablet revealed to an American Bahá'í several years ago:

4. The Covenant Is a Lamp

O thou spiritual leaf, which is verdant and fresh through the down-pouring of the Kingdom of God!

Verily I pray at the Threshold of God, the Mighty the Powerful, that He may illumine thy heart with the light emanating from the height of the kingdom, cause thy tongue to speak the praise of the Living, Self-subsistent, Eternal Lord, and suffer thee to become a light shining with the rays of Knowledge, so that thou mayst enlighten those vast cities and great states.

Verily, Verily, I say unto thee, the Covenant of God and His Testament is a lamp with world-illuminating rays which from the Supreme Concourse enlightens the horizons of the earth and heaven. Whosoever stations himself before this divine light, will be illumined with Manifest Glory, his speech will become effective in the hearts and spirits, and God will reinforce him with a power which will penetrate through the realities of all things. Upon thee be Bahá'í!

(Signed) 'Abdu'l-Bahá 'Abbás.

PORT SAID, EGYPT, JULY 19, 1913

1. Arrival of 'Abdu'l-Bahá in Ramleh

This morning we received a short note from Mírzá Munír telling us about the safe arrival of the Master in Ramleh where he has taken rooms in the Hotel Victoria. Unfortunately owing to the fatigue of the journey and to the recurrence of fever, he had not been sleeping well at night. On the way they had met Sayyid Jalál who was also going to Ismailia to meet the Beloved.[15]

Toward evening I called on Mrs. Stannard. She read me a letter, just received from Miss Hiscock of New York, who has been living in Ramleh for two or three years. She spoke of her happiness on hearing of the arrival of the Master. Mírzá Abú'l-Fadl has already called on him and she and other friends intend to avail themselves of the first opportunity to do the same.

The Master has sent one of the Bahá'ís, Sayyid Yahyá, to Haifa to accompany his daughter, Rúhá Khánum, back to Alexandria....

---

15. Siyyid Jalál, or at times referred to as Mírzá Jalál Síná in these pages, was a son of the renowned Bahá'í teacher and poet, Síná, who lived in Tehran.

A house will be rented in Ramleh, and in a few days we will be on our way to join the Spiritual Caravan.

2. *The Presence of 'Abdu'l-Bahá Holds the People Together*

When the Master leaves a place all the different elements which have been holding together are seemingly scattered; the collected individualities regain their entities each person follows his own inclination; one feels that something is lacking, for the touchstone of life has gone the great social leveler has disappeared. The "I" and the "MY" stalk abroad. Futile conversation and bickering, sneak around the corner and if encouraged, step boldly into the courtyard and to the private chamber. We must ever gaze toward the sun of Universal Fellowship, otherwise we will dissipate our forces.

This morning I was reading the diary of the Master's voyage on the steamer Cedric from Alexandria to New York. Omitting the usual details and descriptions of the trip, I have chosen a few selections from his talks with different travelers which have a general bearing upon his expected arrival in America.

3. *Brahma, Krishna and Buddha Taught the Oneness of God*

It is the third day of the trip. An American, after hearing the Master's teachings on reincarnation, goes to his cabin and carries to him an idol worshiped in China and Japan. The Master holds it in his hand and remarks:

"What vast difference exists between the souls of mankind! One retrogrades to such a low level as to worship statues and stone idols: forms which are devoid of spirit and reason, while God hath conferred upon him reason and adorned his shoulders with the mantle of spiritual attributes! Another soars to such a high summit of perfection and perspicacity as to become the Sign of God and the Instructor of humanity. Brahma, Krishna and Buddha never advocated polytheism. They were eminent teachers of monotheism as were all the other prophets of God; but succeeding generations misconstrued their words and in order to further their own selfish interests fabricated these false doctrines."

4. The Law of Change is Universal

On the sixth day he spoke to a group of passengers as follows:

> All created phenomena are subject to the law of change and transmutation. Youth is followed by old age; a tender plant grows into an aged tree; dynasties are born, wax strong, reach to the zenith of glory and then totter to the ground. Likewise everyone of the world religions has been a cause of progress and advancement in its own time, but now they have become as very old trees, and do not yield any more luscious fruits. Some people persist in the unscientific belief that these very old trees will again become young and push forth leaves, blossoms and fruits. This is impossible. This age needs a young sapling with universal growing capacity. Are you informed of such a plant?

5. In the Bahá'í Cause No One Holds Religious Offices, Titles and Ceremonies

On the eighth day, he speaks to the Persians—The Blessed Perfection has torn up the root of the tree of superstition and religious offices. In the past the ignorance and the retrogression of nations. In this Cause there is no religious title, no ceremony of ordination. One is not respected simply because one wears a peculiar dress or has been given a religious title or has inherited one from Patriarchs of the Church. No! These are not marks of distinction.

6. Who Are the Sanctified Souls?

"On the other hand, there are holy souls, the signs of whose divine sanctity and spirituality become apparent in the hearts of others. People are unconsciously attracted to them through their pure morality, their justice and loving kindness. Everyone is drawn to them on account of their praiseworthy attributes and pleasing qualities and all faces are illumined by the light of their virtue and integrity. In this Movement there is no title to be given to anyone, and no position to be inherited. 'The hands of the Cause' are the hands of Truth. Therefore whosoever is the promoter and the servant of the Word of God, is the hand of Truth. By 'the hands of God' certain definite spiritual meanings are conveyed. It is not only a verbal expression. The more a man is humble in the Cause of God, the more he is confirmed; and the more he is evanescent, the more he is favored."

PORT SAID, EGYPT, JULY 20, 1913

1. Who is 'Abdu'l-Bahá?

The heart of 'Abdu'l-Bahá is the fountain of life out of which flows the Water of Truth. Are you thirsty? His Universal Teaching is divine Food descending from the exalted heaven of the Will of God. Are you hungry? His utterances are the roses and anemones of the garden of Abhá. Do you love flowers? His words are the brilliant stars of the firmament of spiritual Glory. Are not the stars beautiful? His presence inspires confidence, manhood, loyalty and uprightness. Should you not characterize yourselves with these attributes? His Ideals are fresh breezes heralding the approaching dawn of the springtime of human regeneration. Are you stirred into gladsome life? His message is the sweet melody of the Kingdom of Abhá. Do you listen to the soul-enrapturing strains? His pathway is the pathway, leading the traveler to the ultimate reality. Are you ready to walk in it?

2. A Catholic Procession in the Streets of Port Said

Today the French inhabitants had a gorgeous religious procession which started from their church. All the streets through which it passed were adorned with flags, bunting and Japanese lanterns. The priests were dressed in their pompous surplices of red, gold and silver. There were long lines of young girls dressed as angels, also a company of choir boys. The procession was brought to an end by a large statue of the Virgin Mary, holding the child, Jesus, in her arms. Of course thousands of Arabs left their work to gaze at this very spectacular sight of what they called "idol worship," and not understanding the sacredness of these symbols, they poked fun and laughed in their sleeves. How sad is the ignorance of humanity!

I will continue to translate a few more sayings of the Beloved when on the steamer Cedric.

3. First Journey of the Persians to America

Ninth day—"Formerly it was most difficult to cross the Atlantic and up to this time few travelers with our aims and intentions have gone from Persia to America. There are some who have visited the United States, but it has been either for personal affairs or for the transaction of business. One can therefore say, that this is the first disinterested journey of a group of Persians to America. Our great hope is in the divine Confirmations through which all doors will be opened to us. Today the nations of the world can be conquered by divine Power, and this divine Power revolves around the servants of the Blessed Perfection. All personal interests must disappear beside this wondrous Aim."

Eleventh day—'I go to America on account of the invitations of the American Peace Societies and the urgent appeals of my friends, because the objects of this Cause are universal Peace, the oneness of the world of humanity and perfect equality between all mankind. As this century is the century of light and the cycle of the revelation of Mysteries, undoubtedly these glorious aims will be fully established, and the influence of this great Cause will encircle the East and the West."

4. Material and Spiritual Food

Twelfth day—At the table the Master speaks about simple diet: how much better it is for one's constitution to eat one or two courses. One of the American Bahá'ís asks Him if he will not prescribe a simple recipe of dieting for the believers upon His arrival in America. He laughs heartily and says:

"We do not interfere with their material food, but we will give them a simple recipe of spiritual food. This is our work."

5. Steam a Marvelous Energy

Sixteenth day: "We will be only one more day on the steamer. In reality steam is a marvelous energy. Were it not for this power, how could we cross the Atlantic Ocean? What a wonderful means of transportation God has prepared for us and how the Blessed Perfection has confirmed us! Otherwise what relation between America and Persia!"

6. 'Abdu'l-Bahá's Welcome to New York

Seventeenth day—Great skyscrapers are visible in the distance. The Goddess of Liberty holds aloft her lamp. The Master walks up on the deck watching with great interest the shifting scenes; hundreds of Bahá'ís are impatiently waiting on the pier. He talks with the Persians:

"When we embarked on the steamer in Alexandria no one dreamed that we should reach America in such safety and cross the Atlantic with such ease."

Now the steamer docks in its berth; the Bahá'ís on the pier wave their handkerchiefs and hats; The Desire of their hearts is not seen from the dock; he is in his cabin surrounded by a number of newspapermen. Patiently 'Abdu'l-Bahá gives interviews to each, answering ever question and satisfying all. Here I will translate one of the many beautiful interviews. It is the shortest.

7. Interview with the newspapermen on the Steamer Deck

"What are your aims?" the reporter asks.

"Our aims," he answers, "are Universal Peace and the Oneness of the world of humanity. Last year I visited London and Paris. This year I have come to America to meet the lovers of Peace, perchance we may find a basis for co-operation. It is my hope that the American Peace Societies may consolidate their forces, and thus, shoulder to shoulder, may render an effective service to humankind.

"How will Universal Peace be established?"

"By educating the public with the sentiments of Peace. Today the full realization of Universal Peace is a panacea for every social disease."

"What are these diseases?"

"One of the diseases is the poverty of the middle classes through the unbearable burden of war taxation. This craze for militarism has reached its height and shall soon recede. The income of the farmer and of others is taken by the power of a military government and foolishly expended upon useless implements of destruction. The prospect becomes gloomier every year because the war budget of every nation is being increased without any regard to the feverish signs of social unrest and industrial upheaval. The people are seething with ideas of insurrection and agitation. Their burden has become too heavy and their patience is exhausted. They groan under this load, and grope in the darkness, seeking the light of Peace. Their pitiful cries ascend to the throne of the Almighty. Lo, lo! He has listened to them; He has answered their prayers. The dawn of Peace has appeared, the lights of brotherhood are breaking through the foul clouds of human prejudices. Lovers of Peace! Rejoice! Rejoice! O ye who are heavy laden, be happy, be happy! Weep no more, for your burden will be taken away from you.

"This military and naval expenditure is a great disease. Look at the result of the war between Italy and Turkey! How dreadful! There exists a reign of Terror. Fathers weep for their sons; sons weep for their fathers. How many peaceful villages are laid waste! How the wealth of the nations is exhausted! The remedy for this disease is through Universal Peace. This will ensure public security! Today that which is the cause of dispersion is war. If the nations enter into a faithful agreement to at once lay armaments aside, they shall secure for themselves and their posterity eternal welfare; they shall become freed from every difficulty and from international confusion. This end must be attained through the development of minds and hearts and by inculcation of peaceful ideals in all the institutions of modern civilization."

PORT SAID, EGYPT, JULY 21, 1913

1. There Is No Diary of Bahá'u'lláh's and 'Abdu'l-Bahá's Words During the Long Years of Incarceration

Aside from the impression that the Beloved will stay in Ramleh and not go to Haifa, there is no news. We are anxiously waiting to receive the word for our departure. Not only do I miss the glory of his presence, but so much of his wonderful words of light and guidance are lost because there is no one to report them. The art of diary writing is comparatively unknown in the East. The believers have not been accustomed to it. For example, throughout the life of Bahá'u'lláh and during that of 'Abdu'l-Bahá until the present no one dreamed of reporting their sayings. I have not yet seen a book or pamphlet, biographic in tone and diary-like in construction. The recent Persian pilgrims, learning this from the West would whenever they were summoned to the presence of the Beloved, beg either Mírzá Mahmúd or myself to go with them and report the Master's words. We were really stenographers, and our services were much in demand. Had the Master lived in America for the last forty years, there would besides his Tablets have been volumes of memoirs and diaries written by those who were fortunate enough to be near him.

While we are waiting patiently to receive his command, we are not idle. The calmness and sweetness of the Peace which passeth all understanding wafts over our minds and hearts, and in this temporary separation we have experienced that deeper spiritual union which will more and more be realized as time goes on.

2. Teaching the Cause Is the Most Important of All Services

Just as the Master has sacrificed everything in his life in order to spread the Fragrances of the Paradise of Abhá, just as the Spirit of Bahá'u'lláh is his guardian and protector, so likewise must we forget all other thoughts and occupy ourselves with those matters which pertain to the exaltation of the word of God among mankind, and be confident that the Blessed Perfection, under all circumstances, will sustain and reinforce us. At the present time the promulgation of the Teachings is of paramount importance because the Power of the Supreme Concourse is behind it.

In a Tablet revealed by the Beloved many years ago, to the Persian friends, He says:

> O ye believers of God! Supplicate and entreat at the Threshold of the Almighty that He may confirm you in the diffusion of the Fragrances of Holiness which are wafting from the direction of the Garden of God. Blow ye over all creation like the Breezes of the early morn and impart ye a freshness and verdancy through the Power of Truth upon the flowers, the sweet hyacinths and the roses of the garden of existence. This is the quintessence of the meeting and the superlative degree of success and prosperity, for it causes the attainment of man unto the kingdom of Abhá, attracts him to the Sacred Court of His Highness the Almighty and suffers him to reach the Sublime Presence of the Powerful, the Omnipotent Lord.

The translation of another dynamic Tablet to the Persian believers, revealed likewise many years ago, may be of interest:

3. It Is the Day of Action and Happiness

O ye merciful friends of 'Abdu'l-Bahá! Although it is night, yet it is the morn of the dawn of the divine Kingdom. Lights are shining and faces are radiant. The Ancient Bestowal of the Beauty of Abba is the Companion of every pure heart and the Effulgence of the Manifestation of the Mount of Sinai is the associate of every firm and steadfast one. The soul-entrancing Melody of the Blessed Perfection is heard from the Invisible World by every upright and righteous person, and His Glad-tidings and gospels of joy bestow undeniable Favor. The Fame of His greatness hath filled all regions and the songs of the birds of the meadow of His Reality confer spirit upon all the inhabitants of the globe.

Consequently, we must send forth a joy-cry and through the Power of God infuse a mighty thrill of spiritual emotion through the pillars of this mortal world. Eternal Life must be revealed in this mundane existence heavenly Grace must become apparent and the Everlasting Bounty of the Paradise of Abhá must adorn this earth. How long this silence! How long this speechlessness! How long this lukewarmness! The flaming torch of the burning Fire of God is set aglow on the apex of the world and the lighted candle of guidance is a witness in the gatherings. If we are not enkindled with the heat of this divine flame, with what heart-burning fire will we then be lighted! If we are not intoxicated with this Wine of God, what kind of wine, then, will exhilarate us! If in the Assemblage of Transfiguration we do not forget ourselves, becoming joyous and enraptured, then in what gathering will we make tumult and acclamation. O ye divine friends! The Call is the Call of the Beauty of Abba, streaming down from the Invisible Kingdom! The Melody is the Melody of the Supreme Concourse, be ye happy, be ye joyous, be ye exultant, be ye glad!

Upon ye be greetings and praises.

(Signed) 'Abdu'l-Bahá 'Abbás.

PORT SAID, EGYPT, JULY 22, 1913

1. The Spiritual Lesson Drawn from the Material Progress of Port Said and the Suez Canal

The material progress of Port Said is a great lesson for all the Bahá'ís. Forty years ago there were only a handful of dingy hovels with half-naked Arabs. There was no trade, there were no houses, and no communication existed with the outside world. Almost all the area on which the present up-to-date city with its 60,000 busy inhabitants is built, is land reclaimed from the sea. When the Suez Canal joined the two mighty oceans together, Port Said became an international port, and from that date the magical progress of the city continued uninterruptedly. Just as God inspired the heart and mind of DeLesseps with this most wonderful thought of joining the two seas, in like manner, Our Beloved, as a spiritual Engineer, is appointed by Bahá'u'lláh to unite the East and the West. The concerted efforts of thousands of laborers made possible the realization of the

Suez Canal, and thus the greatest engineering feat up to that time was accomplished. Similarly the united zeal and endeavor of all the Bahá'ís are needed to join together the mighty seas of humanity. This is not child's play. This is a stupendous undertaking. Could the laborers complete the Canal if they sat around and criticized one another? Let us be faithful in our enterprise, and work to the end; let no harsh words discourage us, let us leave behind fruitless discussions, and engage in that whereby the Word of God may be promoted and the Fragrances of the Cause diffused. Thus we may bring happiness to the heart of 'Abdu'l-Bahá. Let us look forward, and not backward; heavenward and not earthward. Bahá'u'lláh will assist us. The Canal will be completed and there will be witnessed the Confluence of the seas. Then the two mighty oceans of the human families—East and West—which are being stirred at the present time by the contrary winds of conflicting prejudices, shall be joined together. There will be millions of laborers in the future; but we must hold the breach honorably until they arrive! God does not need our services, but we are in need of His continued Graces. He is the most Potent! He can wait. A thousand years in His sight, is as one day. If through our negligence and inadvertence, we retard His work, we are the losers. He will raise other generations to fulfill His command. He will inspire other hearts to proclaim His words. He will illumine other minds to grasp His ultimate plan. He will reinforce other armies to achieve His triumph. He will instruct other nations to magnify His name. We must not let this matchless opportunity escape us! The tool is his who can handle it.

About six o'clock we left our apartment in search of news. The headquarters of news is Ahmad Yazdí's store, so thither our feet directed us. There to our surprise and delight we found Hájí Sayyid Javád and Rúhí Effendi, just arrived from Haifa at the bidding of the Master. The former is an old Bahá'í of the time of Bahá'u'lláh and has an interesting history as a background; the latter is the grandson of the Master. He is about 13 years old, the son of Mírzá Muhsin.

PORT SAID, EGYPT, JULY 23, 1913

1. Possible Departure for Ramleh Makes Us Happy

I feel that the Beloved will call us to him before the end of this month. I have heard that two houses are rented, one for himself and his family; the other for the secretaries, etc. The houses are near each other. This has indeed lifted our spirits, and has made us decidedly cheerful; now we sing as we work. Mírzá 'Alí-Akbar whistles Russian songs; Mírzá Mahmúd chants Persian poems, and my choice, strange to say, falls to American music. We do not refer to this great change—but as we look at each other, the joy in our eyes speaks volumes. After all, environment plays a large part in shaping our thoughts and aspirations. However, the Master is teaching us to live above environment, and not to let our minds be colored by the changing film of events.

This morning Hájí Sayyid Javád and Rúhí Effendi came to call, and we welcomed them with Bahá'í cordiality. Hájí Javád gave me a short account of his trips to 'Akká to see Bahá'u'lláh during the early days of His imprisonment. Javád is an old gentleman, he is tall, with a short white beard, and has a fund of reminiscences of the days of the Blessed Perfection.

2. Arrival of Mrs. Getsinger

After five o'clock we sauntered out toward Ahmad Yazdí's store, and it was with genuine satisfaction that we met Mrs. Getsinger, who had landed two hours before. She was well and happy, and overflowing with the joyful anticipation of meeting the Master. Strange enough a telegram was received from the Master within an hour, giving her permission to leave the next morning for Ramleh.

3. Translation of an Interview between 'Abdu'l-Bahá and the Reporter of the "San Francisco Examiner"

I would now like to translate from my Persian notes a most interesting interview between a correspondent of the Examiner and the Master in San Francisco. The date is October 3rd, 1912. The hour is about eight P.M. This fine interview appeared the next day in a most crude form, almost unrecognizable:

Correspondent: "Are you pleased with the United States?"

'Abdu'l-Bahá: "The Continent of America is most progressive. The means of instruction are prepared; the educational institutions are thoroughly equipped and the pupils are being systematically trained and educated. Its wealth is on an upward tendency. Its government is democratic. Its advancement unceasing. Its nation hospitable. Its people loyal, energetic and noble. Its inhabitants free and lovers of liberty. Its men civilized and its women cultured, refined and idealistic. On the other hand, all these advantages are on the objective plane and I observe that the majority of the people are submerged in a sea of materialism and agnosticism. Its material civilization is well nigh perfect, but it is in need of the civilization of heaven divine civilization."

Correspondent: "What do you mean by divine civilization?"

'Abdu'l-Bahá: "Divine Civilization is the light. Material civilization is the lamp. Material civilization is the body; In itself it is not sufficient, and humanity, from every point of view, stands in need of divine civilization. Natural civilization produces material welfare and prosperity; divine civilization develops man's ideal virtues. Natural civilization serves the physical world; Divine Civilization serves the world of morality. Divine Civilization is a symposium of the perfections of the world of humanity. Divine Civilization is the improvement of the ethical life of a nation. Divine Civilization is the discovery of the Reality of phenomena. Divine Civilization is spiritual philosophy. Divine Civilization is Knowledge of God with rational and intellectual evidences. Divine Civilization is Eternal Life. Divine Civilization is the immortality of the soul. Divine Civilization is the breath of the Holy Spirit. Divine Civilization is heavenly wisdom. Divine Civilization is the Reality of the Teachings of all the ancient prophets. Divine Civilization is Universal Peace and the Oneness of the world of humanity. The Holy Manifestations of God have been the founders of Divine Civilization, the first teachers of mankind and the spreaders of the fragrances of holiness and sanctity amongst the children of men.

Correspondent: "Are you satisfied with the American people?"

'Abdu'l-Bahá: "The Americans are a kind and affectionate people. All nations are welcomed in their midst. They give to everyone the right of living and allow each to seek happiness in his own way. Here no one feels a foreigner. I am most pleased with them."

Correspondent: "I have heard that you advocate the complete equality of men and women. This radical teaching coming from an Oriental thinker, is of great interest and supreme significance. Just at this juncture the Californian women are clamoring for the right to vote for all National and State officials and your opinion on this important question would be greatly appreciated by the people."

'Abdu'l-Bahá: "The question of equality between men and women has made greater advancement in America than anywhere else, and day by day it is assuming more importance and coming nearer to its full realization. However, so long as complete equality does not exist between men and women, the world of humanity will not make extraordinary progress. The woman is an essential column, while the man is also an essential column. If we aim to have a lasting building, the foundations of both columns must be laid very deep. Women are the first teachers of the children. They instruct them and inculcate morality in their minds and hearts. Later these children attend schools and universities for higher education and specialization. Now if the teacher or instructor is deficient, how can the scholar be properly trained? Therefore, it is proven that the culture and development of men will be intensified and will attain perfect fruition when women have equal opportunities with them. Consequently, the women must enjoy all the learning they are able to assimilate, so that they may reach to the level of men. The same privileges and opportunities must be conferred upon both; so that, just as they share life and its responsibilities, they may also share the same virtues of the world of humanity. Undoubtedly partnership in education and culture presupposes equality in rights. The world of humanity has two wings, one the male, the other the female. Both wings have to become strong so that mankind may soar to the empyrean of its destined perfection; for if one wing is left weak, the upward flight must from necessity be slow. God has created both human. They enjoy in common all the faculties No one is endowed with special privileges. How can we make a distinction which is unknown in the sight of God? We must follow the policy of God. Moreover, there are male and female in the vegetable kingdom. They are on equal footing. Inherently they enjoy suffrage and there is no distinction between them. Likewise in the animal kingdom, the right of suffrage and equality is enjoyed without any feeling of superiority or privilege. Therefore it is admitted that there is no distinction of gender in the vegetable and animal kingdoms, although they are deprived of reasonableness and have not the distinguishing faculties. But we, who are confirmed with the bestowal of reason, and who enjoy all the characteristics which distinguish man from the animal, how can we act in this manner, and build these false barriers? Many women have appeared who have won for themselves fame and name by the versatility of their thoughts. Amongst the Bahá'í women a number have shown remarkable talent for literature, science and art, and have rendered distinct services in all the departments of life.

"In history many capable women have displayed special genius for government and political administration, like Semiramis; Zenobia,[16] Queen of Palmyra, and Queen Victoria of England. In the religious world the Israelites wandered for forty years in the wilderness and could not conquer the Holy Land. Finally a woman achieved this signal victory. In the dispensation of Christ, the apostles became confused; even Peter denied Him thrice, but Mary of Magdalene became the cause of their firmness and steadfastness In the religion of Bahá'u'lláh. Qurratu'l-'Ayn,[17] and many other Persian women, demonstrated their knowledge and

---

16. Zenubia was the queen of Palymra, also known as Tadmor. She was the wife of Odeinats, the governor of Athens, and on passing of her husband in 266 AD, assumed leadership and bravely defended her land. 'Abdu'l-Bahá often spoke of her, see, *Eight Years Near 'Abdu'l-Bahá: Diary of Dr. Habib Mu'ayyad*, chap 10.
17. Táhirih, the seventeenth Letter of the Living.

wisdom to such an extent that even the men were astonished and listened with deference to their advice and counsel.

Correspondent: "What is your object in coming to America?"

'Abdu'l-Bahá: "I have come to America to promote the ideal of Universal Peace and the solidarity of the human race. I have not come for pleasure, or as a tourist."

Correspondent: "What do you think about woman's fashions?"

'Abdu'l-Bahá: "We do not look upon the dresses of women, whether they are of the latest mode. We are not the judge of fashion. We consider rather the wearer of the dress. If she is chaste, if she is pure, if she is cultured, if she is characterized with heavenly morality and if she is favored at the Threshold of God, she is honored and respected by us, no matter what manner of dress she wears. We have nothing to do with the ever-changing world of mode and picture hats."

Correspondent: "What is the greatest thing you have seen in America?"

'Abdu'l-Bahá: "The greatest thing I have seen in America is its Freedom. In reality this is a free nation and a democratic government."

Correspondent: "What is your opinion about Turkey and the Balkan war?"

'Abdu'l-Bahá: "We have nothing to do with war. We are advocates of Peace. Speak to us about the conditions of Peace. Go to the diplomatists and militarists and ask their opinions about this war. But as regards Peace: In the world of humanity there is no more important affair, no weightier cause. It is conducive to the well-being of the world of creation; the means of the prosperity of nations, the reason of eternal friendship between peoples, the cause of solidarity between the East and the West, the promoter of real freedom and the most eminent Favor of His Highness the Almighty. We must all strive to upraise the Flag of International Peace, the Oneness of the world of humanity, and the spiritual brotherhood of mankind."

The correspondent tried to ask a few more questions but

'Abdu'l-Bahá interrupted him by this final statement, while putting his hand on his shoulder and kissing his face:

"Consider how much I love thee and to what extent I respect Mr. Hearst that, notwithstanding the fatigue coming over me as the result of a very busy day, I have answered all thy questions."

Thus the young man left the presence of 'Abdu'l-Bahá with a sense of awe and respect that one feels only when one is saturated with the holy atmosphere which is created wherever he is—the Center of Spirituality and heavenliness.

PORT SAID. EGYPT, JULY 24, 1913

1. *Our Departure for Ramleh*

The Port Said believers have gone to the station to say goodbye to Hájí Sayyid Javád, Rúhí Effendi and Mrs. Getsinger who are leaving today for Ramleh to be honored with the blessing of the Beloved's presence. I am with them too. The train leaves at eight A.M. They are very happy. The train pulls out of the station, and we return home in the heat of the sun to spend another day in quiet work and uninterrupted solitude. I sit at my table, Mírzá Mahmúd at his and Mírzá 'Alí-Akbar in his room is copying the addresses of 'Abdu'l-Bahá, when the door opens and Áqá Azíz enters. He looks at me and smiles. Like a flash of lightning his thought is transferred to me. I get up from my seat:

"Have you any news for us from the Master?" I ask.

"Yes," he quietly answers. "Ahmad Yazdí has just now received a telegram giving you permission to leave for Ramleh."

We are very happy. We must leave by the one o'clock train. In half an hour all our baggage is prepared. What spiritual ecstasy! What divine beatitude! We go to Ahmad Yazdí's store to thank him personally for this good news. Returning home we finish our work and at a quarter after twelve start for the station. There, to our surprise, we find Ahmad Yazdí who has come to say goodbye to us.

2. *Thinking over Meeting 'Abdu'l-Bahá*

Finally everything is ready; the first and second bell rings, and the train starts. In our hearts the birds of joy sing; behind us the pleasant memories of more than a month, all about the sandy, quiet desert—the garden of Allah; ahead of us union—with whom? With the Beloved of our hearts. As I sat in our compartment contemplating the love of the Master, my eyes were filled with tears of joy and I realized more than ever—and no doubt thousands have had this same experience—that 'Abdu'l-Bahá is our Beloved, our Hope, our Desire, the sum-total of all our longings. If one has 'Abdu'l-Bahá for his Beloved, his happiness is not dimmed; his peace is not broken; his faith can move mountains and all his aspirations are fulfilled! O Joy of Joy! O Heavenly Light! O Love Divine! Art Thou not the most beautiful, the most satisfying, the most ennobling, the most rapturous! Would I not gladly dedicate my whole life to treasure Thee in the secret chamber of my heart? Thou art the Poet of transmutation. Thou art the Philosopher's stone. Thou art the remedy for all sorrows! O Love! O God! O Unchanging Lord! Sustain us, feed us with thy ambrosial food; suffer us to drink from thy diamond cup of pure affection. We feel throughout our whole body the spiritual thrills of thy compassion and mercy.

3. Scenes Along the Railroad

By this time we reach Ismailia, the small clean town, blessed by the presence of our Beloved. After a few minutes, the train starts again. The country is fresh and green from the unfailing blessing of the Nile; the palm trees are laden with bunches of green dates, the cotton belt is extensive and the reports are that this year's crop is excellent. As the train passes on we see hundreds of men and women working in the fields, camels are grazing, and there are many cows and sheep. Rice also is cultivated in this part of the country. At 4.30 P.M. we reach Benha where we have to change trains, and after thirty minutes we are again on our way. It is 7:30 when we enter the station of Sidi Gaber, and here Hájí Khurásání and Mírzá Munír are present to welcome and guide us to our new quarters. On the way our train had crossed the noble Nile. It is spanned by a most excellent iron bridge. Toward sunset, the men and women farmers—Fellaheen—showing their religious spirit, leave their work and perform their ablutions and prayers wherever they happen to be. It is a most divine picture to see these simple people praying to their Maker under the open sky. Another lovely scene which is truly Biblical, is the procession of women with jars on their heads, leaving their curious mud-built villages to fill them at the spring.

4. 'Abdu'l-Bahá Calls on Us

Ramleh is a modern Egyptian town with all the conveniences of western civilization. It is a summer resort for the most important European officials in the service of the Egyptian Government, and also for the native Pashas. There are lovely parks, all kinds of hotels and splendid houses. We have a nice furnished apartment about two hundred yards from the residence of the Beloved. At eight o'clock he came to welcome us and our joy at again looking upon his benign face, knew no bounds.

He had just returned from calling upon Mírzá Abú'l-Fadl. He inquired about our health, and after a few more questions, left us, but the happiness of those minutes will remain in our hearts. During the last days while the Beloved was living in the Victoria Hotel, many English officials, native Pashas, and Arab Shaykhs have called upon him, and on many occasions more than twenty of these important men would gather in the salon to listen to his talks. None of these are preserved. There is a weekly meeting at the house of Hájí Khurásání and the Master attended it. At present Túbá Khánum, the Master's daughter, with her son Rúhí and Mrs. Getsinger, are staying in the house of the Beloved.

I will end this letter by the translation of two quotations from Tablets:

5. Real Love Attracts Divine Confirmations

If thou desirest to be confirmed in the service of the Kingdom of God, live in accord with the Teachings of Bahá'u'lláh, and that is: real love for the world of humanity, and the utmost of kindness for the believers of God. This real love, like unto magnetic power, attracts divine Confirmations.

6. Teach the Cause Through Deeds

If a soul calls the people to the Kingdom of God according to the Principles of Bahá'u'lláh, there will be many listeners. First, one may teach by deeds, then speak the word. First, one must become thirsty, then the salubrious water may be offered. No matter how delicious the water is, one who is not thirsty will not enjoy it. Therefore, make ye an effort, so that the people may become thirsty; then enable them to quaff from this divine Chalice.

RAMLEH, EGYPT, JULY 25, 1913

1. A Call on Mírzá Abú'l-Fadl

This morning the Beloved visited our apartment and sat on the Veranda. He is trying to find a house in Ramleh for Mírzá Abú'l-Fadl, so that he may be near us. After a few moments he went out with Hájí Muhammad to look for one. We learned later that a house has been found almost adjacent so that we shall have the privilege of seeing Mírzá Abú'l-Fadl quite often.

In the afternoon Hájí Khurásání came and expressed a wish to call on Mírzá Abú'l-Fadl. Mírzá 'Alí-Akbar and myself begged him to take us, too. It is about one hour's ride to reach the place, and then one must walk several blocks. We knocked at the door. After a minute it was opened and Mírzá Abú'l-Fadl welcomed us. He looked much older than when I used to serve him in America. He still has the same desire to be left alone. He loves to wait on his guests personally. After greeting us, he inquired about many of the believers in America. I was glad to convey to him their messages of love and respect and to tell him how he is remembered and honored by all the friends. He recalled his pleasant summers spent in Green Acre, and wished that place a great future. He asked about the health of Miss Farmer. He inquired about the publication of his recent book, the "Brilliant Proof" and requested that a copy be forwarded to the Rev. Easton. He deplored his inability to travel caused by his physical weakness.

"If I were strong enough, I would never stay in one place more than a month. I would travel constantly and have advised the Bahá'í teachers, that this is the best way to spread this universal message. They must fly from one bush to another and sing the songs of the Kingdom—the Kingdom of Abhá."

Then he served us with tea prepared by his own hands and Mírzá 'Alí-Akbar related some of the incidents during the trip of the Beloved in America.

2. Alexandria is a Progressive City

We were on our way home when we met Áqá Muhammad-Báqir. The Master has appointed him to attend to the occasional needs of Mírzá Abú'l-Fadl. He lives near him. He told us that 'Abdu'l-Bahá sent him to accompany Mírzá Abú'l-Fadl to Ramleh.

Alexandria to all intents and purposes is like a progressive American city. Its tall buildings, its large department stores, its clean avenues, its double-decked electric cars, its delightful parks, its electrically lighted boulevards and streets, its fine promenades around the seaport, are all signs of a wonderful prosperous spirit. As I passed along the streets it seemed as though I was walking on an avenue in New York, and I wondered at the magical transformations which had taken place since this city was burned to the ground during the 'Urabi revolution thirty-one years ago. The inhabitants of all nations, Greeks, Italians, French, Jews, English, Arabs, Persians, live here and associate with one another in perfect harmony.

3. 'Abdu'l-Bahá Talks with the Persian Followers

When we reached home it was nine o'clock and the Master was sitting on the veranda with a number of believers. I learned to my regret that I had missed a large gathering of friends.

"What did he speak of?" I asked. The answer was given; about America, his addresses in churches and temples, the unity of mankind and the beauty and holiness of the spiritual life.

4. Abú'l-Fadl: A Great Bahá'í Teacher

Mírzá Abú'l-Fadl was there and the Master asked him to inspect the house which he is going to rent for him. When he returned, he said that he was very satisfied with the place and in a few days we will have him with us. I shall ever be indebted to Mírzá Abú'l-Fadl who bestowed so much kindness upon me during my first years in America. He is today the greatest teacher in the Bahá'í world, and through his writings he is beloved by friends and respected by foes. May he live many years longer! How the Master loves him, considers his comfort and tries to prepare all means of happiness for him.

In talking with Mírzá Abú'l-Fadl, 'Abdu'l-Bahá said when he will come to Ramleh he would be his physician, and take good care of him. Abú'l-Fadl is coming and like a wise mentor he will guide and instruct us as long as we are in Ramleh.

RAMLEH, EGYPT, JULY 26, 1913

Before chronicling the daily events, I would like to share with you the wonderful contents of a very great Tablet revealed for the believers of God in Adharbayjan.

1. The Fragrances of God and Their Marvelous Results

O ye spiritual friends of 'Abdu'l-Bahá!

The faithful envoy has arrived and in the spiritual world has conveyed the message to the believers of God. This blessed happy messenger is no other than the Fragrance of attraction and the soul-refreshing breeze of the Love of God. These stir hearts into cheerfulness and make the spirits the treasures of joy and gladness. The effulgence of Divine Unity has cast such splendor over the hearts and spirits and created such tremendous effect as to establish a bond of spiritual communication between each and all, making them throb as one heart and beat as one pulse. Therefore one observes that spiritual reflections and merciful impressions are printed in the utmost beauty and art, upon the Tablets of the hearts and that their delicate forms are transparent and graceful I pray God that, day by day, this spiritual communication may become reinforced and cause more and more the appearance of this Divine Unity in the world of humanity; so that all mankind like unto disciplined soldiers may abide under the shade of the Word of God and under the Flag of the Covenant, striving with all their hearts and souls, that universal conciliation, cordial love and spiritual communication may be firmly established among the hearts of the inhabitants of the world; and that all the children of men through the radiant, new Bestowal, may consort and associate with each other in one loving meeting; that strife and war may vanish from the face of the earth; that the love of the Beauty of the Most Glorious may encompass every atom of Creation; that enmity be changed into amity; differences transformed into good-fellowship; the foundation of animosity destroyed; the basis of hatred demolished; the illumination of Union cause the disappearance of the darkness of limitation and the transcendent light of the Merciful suffer the hearts of humanity to become the mines of the refulgent Love of God.

2. *Now Is the Time of the Union of All Nations and Religions*

O ye friends of God!

Now is the time when you must affiliate with all nations with joy and the utmost kindness—thus may you become the manifestors of the Mercy of His Highness the One. Become ye the spirit of the world and the quintessence of life in the temple of mankind. In this wonderful century in which the Ancient Beauty—the Most Great Name—has dawned from the horizon of the world with infinite Bestowals. The Word of God hath created such dominion and potency over the realities of mankind that the effect and influence of human conditions and environments are neutralized. With a penetrative power He hath gathered all into the Court of Union and addresses them as follows:

"Now is the time when the believers of God must unfurl the Banner of Unity, singing the songs of friendship in the Assemblages of the world and inviting all to the universality and all-inclusiveness of the Grace of God—so that the canopy of Holiness may be pitched on the apex of creation and the nations brought under the shade of the Word of Unity. This bounty shall become unveiled in the Center of the world when the believers of God will live in accord with the Teaching of the Merciful One and occupy their time in the diffusion of the sweet Fragrances of Universal Love."

3. In the Bahá'í Revelation There is No Limitation

In every dispensation the Command of friendship and the law of Love have been revealed, but it has been circumscribed within the circle of believing friends and not with those outside of it. Praise be to God that in this wonderful cycle the laws of God are not confined by any limitations; neither must they be exercised toward a special community to the exclusion of another. He hath commanded the friends to show love, friendship, amity and kindness to all the people of the world.

4. Become Ye As Kind Fathers to the Children of Humanity

Now the believers of God must live in accord with these divine Teachings. They must become kind fathers to the children of humanity; affectionate brothers to the youths of mankind and soul-sacrificing children toward those who are laden with age. The aim is this: You must be in the utmost state of joy and fragrance and show love and kindness to all, even to your enemies. Meet persecution and adversity with trust. Whenever animosity appears, deal with it with forbearance: make your breasts targets for the arrows and spears of opposition. Brave the ridicule, the blame and the rebuke with perfect love: so that all nations may observe the Power of the Most Great Name, and all people acknowledge the Potency of the Blessed Perfection—showing how He hath destroyed the foundations of strangeness, hath guided the inhabitants of the world to unity and love, hath illuminated the realm of man and transformed this terrestrial globe into a delectable Paradise. These people are like unto children, negligent and mindless. One must train them with the utmost love and carry them with infinite tenderness in the arms of Grace so that they may taste the love of the Merciful One, become illumined like unto candles and dissipate the darkness of this world. Thus they may behold clearly and manifestly the glorious crown and brilliant diadem with which the Most Great Name—the Blessed Perfection—may my life be a sacrifice to Him—hath adorned the heads of His Believers; what graces He hath poured upon the hearts of His friends; what love He hath brought into the world of humanity and what friendship He hath caused to appear among the children of men?

O Lord! O Lord! Confirm Thy righteous servants in the practice of love and friendship to all mankind and assist them in the diffusion of the Light of Guidance which is descending from Thy Supreme Concourse upon all the inhabitants of the world. Verily Thou art Powerful, Mighty, Omnipotent, Generous! And, verily, Thou art the Merciful, the Clement, the Compassionate and the Bestower!

(Signed) 'Abdu'l-Bahá 'Abbás.

5. 'Abdu'l-Bahá Ready for the Last Call

This morning the Beloved called me to his presence. He spoke of the weather and of the state of his health saying that he had not been feeling well in Ramleh, but that for the present he would not move to any other place, no matter what might happen. He said, he has finished his work. He has nothing else to do. He is now ready for the last call! How he longs to quaff from that cup! How sweet will be its taste! How delightful will be that hour!

He was surrounded by letters and papers. He handed me a package just received from America to be translated and made ready for his answers. He told me to come back in the afternoon. Before leaving he wished me to go into the reception room and visit Mrs. Getsinger, which I did with great pleasure. We had an interesting conversation about the Movement in the United States, and I read to her the above Tablet and together we hoped that the believers of the Merciful would be inspired to carry out its contents.

6. Letters and News from America

At four o'clock I returned. As I passed along the street in front of the house, I looked up and lo—I saw the Master sitting on the balcony dressed in his beautiful white robe. He saw me and bade me come up. When I entered the room, he welcomed me with genuine hilarity. He felt better this afternoon and asked me to read him the letters. He told me to sit down near the open window, so that I might get the cool breeze, while he walked back and forth. Did you ever think of the great attention which he pays to all his servants? We began to work. Because Mr. Joseph H. Hannen of Washington D.C., was an active worker in the field and a special friend of mine, I often read his reports first—so this time I asked:

"May I read Mr. Hannen's report?"

The Master laughed heartily and said, that if Mr. Hannen was my dear friend, he was at least his son.

He was amused when I read how a clergyman was brought into the Cause by hearing a lecture against it.

7. Eloquent Speeches Must Be Delivered at Public Gatherings

As regards speaking at meetings, he emphasized the fact that he has written many times on this subject. He sent a Tablet only a few days ago, which was meant for all the believers. He wished me to send a copy of it to Mr. Hannen and to write him that at the meetings and gatherings eloquent addresses and inspiring speeches must be delivered, explaining the principles of the Blessed Perfection, and setting the hearts aglow with the Fire of the Love of God.

8. Persian American Educational Society

He also was pleased to hear that $250.00 had been sent to Dr. Moody in Tehran, Persia, and expressed the hope that the activities of the Persian American Educational Society may increase yearly, and may be enabled to wipe out its debt. He often speaks about this Society, its large, disinterested platform and the fame which it has acquired in such a short space of time.

9. Many Tablets Dictated for Believers

He revealed a Tablet for Mrs. Hannen about the Bahá'í Sunday school and to many other believers in different parts of the world. While he was dictating these Tablets he was carrying on a long conversation with an Arab Shaykh. When he had finished he came out, followed by all of us. He took a long walk and about eight o'clock returned to our apartment and stayed for nearly an hour speaking at times and then lapsing into silence.

10. Pray with an Attracted Heart

Here I end with the following quotation from a recent Tablet:

> Thou hast written asking what thou shouldst do and what prayer thou shouldst offer in order to become informed of the Mysteries of God. Pray thou with an attracted heart and supplicate with a spirit stirred by the Glad-tidings of God. Then the doors of the Kingdom of Mysteries shall be opened before thy face and thou shalt comprehend the realities of all things.

RAMLEH, EGYPT, JULY 27, 1913

1. The Effect of Association with 'Abdu'l-Bahá

We are bathed in the sea of 'Abdu'l-Bahá's love; are flying in the atmosphere of his beauty; drinking the wine of his Grandeur; eating the food of his humility; listening to the thrilling music of his divine voice; resting under the ever-spreading tree of his teachings, and watching the light and shade of his countenance. He inspires our hearts with wondrous thoughts of social service and mutual helpfulness. He reveals to our souls the secrets of forgiveness and loving kindness. He teaches us patience and long suffering. If hearts are not stony, these lessons will, in the long run, bear fruit; and I believe they will affect even the most adamant. For behind every heart of stone, there is a warm one of flesh and blood and under many a tattered coat, may live a noble prince. His presence teaches us how insignificant are our endeavors, how narrow our thoughts, how futile our works in comparison with his grand accomplishments, his sweeping, universal conception of mankind, his increasing activities in all directions, and his attention to all details. If we could walk in his footsteps, emulate him in all our lives, serve our fellowmen as he serves them, spread the Glad-tidings of the Kingdom as he spreads them, then we shall have won his good pleasure.

2. 'Abdu'l-Bahá Dictates Tablets for the Persians

This morning 'Abdu'l-Bahá called Mírzá 'Alí-Akbar to his Presence. He felt radiant and most happy. Mírzá 'Alí-Akbar, finding him in some light-giving mood, relates a few funny stories which make him laugh more. Afterwards he sends for Mírzá Munír and dictates to him many Tablets for the Oriental believers, some of which I translate herein because they contain paragraphs concerning his trip to America. From now on there will be a flood of Tablets flowing from his tongue. For more than three years the Eastern believers have been deprived of the traces of his pen. Now it is time to compensate them.

Toward noon he passed by the door of our house, followed by an Arab. We thought that he was coming in and so we prepared to receive him, but he passed on, making the sign of salutation. He was evidently going to fulfill an engagement.

3. Tickets for Charity Bazaar

Later he returned with a letter in his hand and distributed among us several tickets for a charity entertainment, which was to be held in the San Stefano Hotel. A Pasha, who is a patron of the hotel had sent these tickets to him. The fete was for a worthy cause—the erection of a school, called Urvatu'l-Vuthqá [The Sure Handle].

4. Importance of Cleanliness in All Things

After the distribution of these tickets he spoke very emphatically about cleanliness, especially in cooking. He wished our Persian Bahá'í cook to wear a spotless white apron, to wash his hands often with soap, to keep his kitchen as clean as a pearl and to be as tidy and neat in his cooking as the best French chef.

Concluding his remarks he smilingly stated that if he did not see these changes in the cook, he would use the big stick, because some educators believe that one whipping will do more good than a hundred words of advice.

He recalled with much satisfaction a cook who had kept a restaurant in Beirut many years ago, and who was the embodiment of cleanliness. This cook did not touch the meat with his hands, but cut it with a special instrument and cooked it with great taste and delicacy. 'Abdu'l-Bahá stayed in Beirut for a long time and he went often to his kitchen to watch him at his work. As long as the Master lived in that city he remained his customer.

5. Description of a Charity Bazaar in Alexandria

When he left, we hurried along to the fete in the San Stefano Casino. It was a palatial hotel, most splendidly built. Hundreds of carriages and automobiles were waiting in rows. As we entered, we saw a large crowd of people, nearly five thousand, dispersed all over the grounds. Several bands of music were playing at different places. Many other amusements attracted the attention of the people. The wonderful sea with its ebb and flow was shimmering under the sunshine. The crowd was orderly and jovial. Except for the Tarboushes on the heads of the young men, and the thin white veils which covered the lower halves of the faces of women, letting their black eyes and eyelids shine forth, I could not see much difference between this and any American charity affair. By seven o'clock it was almost impossible to move, so dense was the throng. At night there were many moving pictures, and an excellent display of fireworks which evoked general applause. Later, the Master called at the house of Hájí Khurásání, and finding there a number of Arabs, he gave them a talk which was taken down by one of those present. After this meeting he returned to the house, and entertained us with stories which evoked much laughter. He was well and happy today.

RAMLEH, EGYPT, JULY 28, 1913

The following are a few quotations from Tablets revealed yesterday for the Persian believers:

1. First One Must Teach Himself, Then Others

After my return from America and Europe, owing to the difficulties of the long voyage and to the innumerable inconveniences of the journey, a physical reaction set in and I became indisposed. Now, through the Favor and Bounty of the Blessed

Perfection, I am feeling better; therefore, I am engaged in writing this letter, so that thou mayst realize that the friends of God are never forgotten under any circumstances.... Now is the time when the believers of God may imitate the conduct and manner of 'Abdu'l-Bahá. Day and night they must engage in teaching the Cause of God but they must be in the same spiritual state which 'Abdu'l-Bahá manifested while traveling in America. When the teacher delivers an address, his words must first of all have a supreme and powerful effect over himself so that everyone may be in turn affected. His utterances must be like unto flames of fire, burning away the veils of dogmas, passion and desire. Moreover he must be in the utmost state of humility and evanescence—so that others may become mindful. He must have attained to the station of renunciation and annihilation. Then and not until then, will he teach the people with the Melody of the Supreme Concourse.

2. Heralding the Kingdom of God in the Cities of Europe and America

Praise be to God that, through the Bestowal and Grace of the Beauty of Abhá, (from the Continent of Europe) (I have returned to the Continent of Africa.) I have tarried in Egypt for a few days because I was weakened by the fatigue of traveling through the Cities of Europe; by the variable climates of the American mountains and prairies and by the length and hardships of the voyage. While in Europe one day we were in London and another in Edinburgh; now in Paris and anon in Stuttgart; once in Budapest and again in Vienna. We were almost every hour in another place, delivering lengthy speeches and addresses, and notwithstanding the indisposition of the body, day and night I cried and raised my voice in large meetings and important churches.... As there were many obstacles, the door of correspondence was closed; but the faces of the illumined friends were manifest at every hour in the Court of Consciousness, and at all times they were present in my memory. As I have now found a little leisure, I address you this letter so that I may occupy myself with the servitude of the believers of God and become the means of the happiness of the hearts. This is the utmost desire of 'Abdu'l-Bahá.

3. While Encircled by the Whirlwind of Calumnies, Blossom Ye Like a Rose

During this long trip great capacity was created in every clime for listening to the Word of God; even in the vast countries of the Orient the fame of the Cause of God is spreading more and more. Therefore, the friends of God must take as example my behavior and demeanor. They must not rest one moment. They must not seek quietude for one second. At all times they must emanate joy and gladness. They must be occupied in teaching the Cause of God. No event must sadden their hearts. No catastrophe must break their spirit. With divine happiness they must withstand every impending disaster. During the time of peace, security, comfort and the absence of grief, even the monkey will be a jovial fellow. He will be happy, joyful, grateful, patient and overflowing with gladsomeness. But the sincere servant of Bahá'u'lláh, who is firm in the Covenant and steadfast in the Testament, while surrounded by the most great sea of tests, threatened by surging, rocking waves of persecution, encircled by whirlwinds of calumnies and back-biting—will blossom like unto a rose and break into joyous songs and sweet melodies like unto the nightingale.

4. 'Abdu'l-Bahá Sacrificing His Life in the Path of Baha

Your letter was received; but 'Abdu'l-Bahá, owing to the infirmity of the body; the difficulty of voyaging over seas and lands, the lack of rest, the striving and exerting day and night; the delivering of long addresses in different cities; and of answering the varied and intricate questions of the people—has not been able to answer it. His life, his identity, his heart and his body are gladly sacrificed in the Path of Bahá! This is the Bestowal of the Almighty! This is the Inestimable Favor of God! This is the Favor of the Blessed Perfection! These are the Graces of His Highness the One!

5. 'Abdu'l-Bahá Tells of His Early Life

It was about six o'clock in the morning when the door of the house was opened and the Beloved came in. I had Just finished dressing and was about to take my place at my table to translate a few Tablets. The rest were asleep, but they jumped out of bed and were dressed in a few minutes. He was surprised that they were yet asleep and told us he had already read many letters, written several Tablets and attended to various other things before leaving the house. Up to the time he was 32 years old he never slept in bed, preferring always a piece of mat and using for a pillow one or two books. He went to sleep without changing his clothes, fearing that it would take him some time to dress in the morning. But now he cannot do these things. When he lived in 'Akká he generally kept ten secretaries busy; often dictating important letters to three of them at the same time.

6. 'Abdu'l-Bahá Tells the Arabs about His Western Trip

Then he started to correct one of his addresses delivered in San Francisco and made some remarks about the speeches before the open Forum and the Japanese Independent Church. Just as he came suddenly, he left suddenly, and there were many pledges that henceforward everybody will be up before six A.M.

He again came in the afternoon, stayed a long time, and told us stories about three men who were great cowards, but who became courageous and intrepid after accepting the Bahá'í revelation. How graphic, how simple, how matchless he is in his description of such events. Then he called on an important native Pasha and after nine o'clock, returned to our house bringing an Arab with him. After offering him coffee, he described the meetings in the Bowery Mission in New York and spoke of the Salvation Army in London and of other incidents of the wonderful Western trip. When he left the room, we felt the sweet fragrance of the presence of God.

RAMLEH, EGYPT, JULY 29, 1913

1. *Glad-Tidings of the Kingdom of Abhá from Minneapolis*

This morning the Beloved sent for me and within a few minutes I was standing in his holy presence. He dictated several cablegrams and spoke a few minutes on various topics. Then I went to Alexandria to dispatch the cables and attend to other errands. As he handed me one of the corrected addresses of California, he said these talks must be translated into Arabic. Let it be done at once.

A package of newspapers was received from Minneapolis in which the Glad-tidings of the Kingdom of Abhá were printed. These Glad-tidings had been sent to the Master for correction while we were in Paris. I would like to quote them because the Master was pleased with my Persian translations of them.

> Glad-tidings of the Kingdom of Abhá!
>
> We announce to you Glad-tidings of great Joy! Similar words were spoken almost two thousand years ago. Reflect and be not of the heedless. This is the Great Day of God. This is the Day of Universal Peace of Universal Brotherhood, of a Universal language and of the Union of All Religions. This is the Day wherein the Prophecies of the Holy Books of every tongue have been, or are being, fulfilled. This is the Cycle of Bahá'u'lláh!
>
> We announce to you His Holiness, the Bab, the Precursor of 'He whom God shall manifest.'
> We announce to you Bahá'u'lláh, 'He whom God shall manifest.' The one who has broken the Seals of both the Creational and Collective books.
>
> We announce to you 'Abdu'l-Bahá, the Center of the Covenant, the Interpreter of the Holy Books of all peoples and of the Bahá'í Teachings, and the door through which mankind can enter the Kingdom of God in this Day and Dispensation.

For dinner the Beloved ate a special dish prepared by one of the Pashas and left at his house. In turn he sent part of it to us. It was one of those rare delicacies of Arabia, a kind of meat cake with vegetables and pine-nuts.

2. Modern Hospital in Alexandria

I forgot to write that yesterday we called on Sayyid Jalál, the son of a celebrated Bahá'í poet and teacher, living in Tehran.[18] He is in the German hospital. A few days ago he was operated on but now he feels much better. The hospital is a model of elegance and cleanliness. All the floors and walls are built of marble. Really, I am amazed at every turn, at the practical signs of progress in Egypt. It is nothing short of miraculous! Walking through the avenues and the European business districts of Alexandria one thinks that one is living in Europe or America.

3. 'Abdu'l-Bahá Takes the French Bahá'í Doctor for a Drive

In the afternoon I called on the Beloved and in his presence found DeBons, a French Bahá'í dentist practicing in Cairo—now on his way to Switzerland to meet his wife. 'Abdu'l-Bahá is going to take him for a drive through Nozha Park, which is the National Park of Alexandria. I have heard much praise of it but have not yet been there. They say it rivals any park in Europe or America. For nearly two hours 'Abdu'l-Bahá entertained the doctor driving through the park and speaking to him about his spiritual experiences in America. When he returned, he was as fresh as when I saw him in the morning. For the last three or four days his health has been improving and for this great blessing we proffer thanksgiving and praise to the Lord. He walks among us as a divine witness to all men. Every day spent in the neighborhood of his light is equal to an age, the significance and beauty of which cannot be grasped by the mentality of man.

---

18. The poet in Tehran was the renowned Bahá'í teacher, Síná.

Place of Mehemet Ali, Alexandria during the time of 'Abdu'l-Baha's time in Egypt

RAMLEH, EGYPT, JULY 30, 1913

1. The Cause of Bahá'u'lláh Is the Mainspring of Love and Peace

The Cause of Bahá'u'lláh is the Cause of life. Life is the mainspring of material and spiritual activities. One of the active principles is Love, the other is Peace. The life of a Bahá'í is not rounded and developed without the full manifestation of these two active principles. They must become the dominant influence of his whole existence. He must "love" the world and be at "peace" with humanity; so that these two harmonious notes may blend together and assist him to ascend to the highest summit of true greatness and innate spiritual perception. The prophets of God have come to inculcate in the life of every individual these two principles; especially Bahá'u'lláh. "He hath held aloft the banner of love and peace. Whosoever is imbued with the realities of these two principles has life. Love and Peace are the causes which hold together all the different elements of the mineral, vegetable and animal kingdoms. Were it not for the presence of these two divine forces constantly exercising their benign influence, the whole scheme of creation would have been smashed to pieces long ago. The power of gravitation or attraction is no other than one of the signs of these heavenly energies. Whenever the secret power of these two spiritual verities is fully revealed in the world of humanity, impelling mankind to grow greater and greater in its capacity, then the glorious zenith of divine civilization will become visible. It is our duty to cause these two principles more and more to be revealed, among ourselves, toward one another, and among the people of the world. What a lofty privilege! What a divine Bestowal! What a wonderful responsibility! What a radiant glory! What ecstatic joy! What pure happiness!"

2. 'Abdu'l-Bahá Tells about His Health and Work

This morning 'Abdu'l-Bahá sent for me. Joyfully I hastened to his holy house to receive the rays of his love and benediction. He dictated cablegrams to various parts of the world and spoke about the amount of work to be accomplished. He stated that no one can imagine how many different issues must be met, and how many conflicting interests harmonized! He was now advanced in age. The physical reaction of his long journey has had a terrible effect upon his weakened constitution, and he cannot work as vigorously as he used to in his youth. When he reads a letter his eyes grow weary; when he dictates a few Tablets, his mind gets tired, when he walks a few thousand feet he becomes exhausted.

How heart-breaking and joy-imparting is his condition in these days. The barometer of his health never stands on one mark for two days. Like the ebb and flow of the sea, is the condition of his health. We watch him with great solicitude but are unable to do anything to alleviate his pain or to increase his health. One day he told us that the doctor enjoins upon him the dictum, Do not work, Do not speak, Do not write, but God commands him to work, speak and write. Now whose commands should he obey?

3. Oriental Bahá'ís Anxious to Receive the News

A few minutes later I was out in the open, sad at heart because I had seen 'Abdu'l-Bahá so heavy-laden with the burden of the world and there is not a single soul to lighten it. While Sayyid Asadu'lláh was here he carried on a large and profitable correspondence with all parts of the Orient, thus informing the friends of the passing events. They did not receive any Tablets, but his correspondence kept them in touch with the Center and was of course, a great consolation. But now he is gone to be a soldier in the field and up to this date no one has been appointed to fill his place; thus the believers in the Orient are concerned and anxious. Mírzá Mahmúd, upon his arrival on Port Said, discontinued writing weekly letters and is now, day and night, busy compiling his notes. I also am occupied with my own duties. Mírzá Munír takes the dictation of Tablets for the Oriental Bahá'ís which are being revealed almost every day.

4. Mírzá Abú'l-Fadl and His Position in the Bahá'í Cause

When I returned, the Master was in the house, Mírzá Abú'l-Fadl also being present. He recited in detail a resume of his addresses in the Jewish synagogues of America. The respect and utter humility of Mírzá Abú'l-Fadl in the presence of the Beloved is most touching. He hardly raises his voice when he addresses him. Those who have seen and heard Mírzá Abú'l-Fadl, know the extent of his knowledge, the wide range of his learning, and the brilliancy of his services to the Cause of God. Men like him are rarest jewels and therefore they are loved and honored by the Master. He has suffered imprisonment for two years for the sake of his faith and has undergone much persecution.

5. Muslim Mullás and Their Hair-splitting Metaphysical Discussions

In the afternoon the Master came in again and immediately two Muslim Mullás called on him. These Arabs love hair-splitting religious controversies; and therefore one of them tried to start the ball rolling. The Master, with a wonderfully divine attitude, silenced him and gently rebuked him for the utter uselessness of theological discussions which are not productive of any result. They were advised to investigate the Truth, free from any prejudice. Then he spoke about his lecture in Oxford University, his meeting with Mr. Alexander G. Bell, the inventor of the telephone, in Washington, and ended by telling them that his field of activity was in Europe and America. He had come here to rest for a few months.

The Mullás were utterly defeated, begged humbly for his forgiveness of their apparent negligence, and expressed their conviction that they were highly profited by the meeting and hoped that they would never forget the lesson they had learned today.

RAMLEH, EGYPT, JULY 31, 1913

1. *The Progress of the Bahá'í Cause in the Orient*

The progress of the Bahá'í Cause is evident. The signs of awakening are apparent. The beauty of the spiritual life is manifest. The traces of the Sun of Reality are spreading. The mysteries of the Words of God are revealed. The clouds of superstitions are dispelled. The horizon of divine religion is clear. The rose-garden of hearts is adorned. The nightingales of significances are warbling. The flowers of faith are perfuming the nostrils. The Breezes of the Holy Spirit are vivifying the dead. The fountains of eternal life are flowing. The vineyard of the Lord is verdant. The servants are faithful. The gardeners are honest and sincere.

From all parts of the Orient the news of the forward march of the Bahá'í Cause is being received. Men and women are advancing toward the Kingdom of El Abhá! On their lips are new hymns of praises! In their hearts [are] tumultuous voices of glorification. In their ears are the sweet, ravishing melodies of the birds of paradise. The teachers of the Cause are inspired with a new zeal. Their hearts are fired with the unprecedented example of 'Abdu'l-Bahá. Difficulties! There are none. From every corner of the Orient the still small voice grows into volume and force, becoming irresistible in its might, removing every obstacle from its path, and attacking the rank and file of the forces of darkness, putting them into complete rout.

Through the gloomy night of ignorance and fanaticism, the light-bearers of Reality, with torches in their hands are running through the length and breadth of the East, illumining hearts with the effulgence of the Kingdom. Lo! do you hear the songs of the Eastern teachers which are being co-ordinated into one mighty voice:

Let us follow the example of 'Abdu'l-Bahá! He has paved for us the highroad of teaching! Let us follow him! We shall seek no rest, wish for no comfort! We are his soldiers and he is our commander! We must increase the power of our activity! We must travel! We must forget everything else save the promotion of the Cause!

Thus a new spirit is aroused all over the East, impelling the teachers to go forward, to rush onward, to follow 'Abdu'l-Bahá!

2. 'Abdu'l-Bahá Tells About Rasheed Pasha and His System of Extortion

The Beloved called this morning. He was in a happy mood. Mírzá Abul Fazl was there; so the main part of the talk was directed to him. First 'Abdu'l-Bahá spoke of the two Mullás who visited him yesterday, saying that these Arab Shaykhs do not understand what fair discussion means. They love a good fighty argument better than their lives. They do not mean to investigate a given subject, examine its minor and major points and obtain the conclusion. They love to go on, pro and con, ad infinitum.

Then he spoke about Rashíd Pasha, a former Governor of Syria who had called upon him many times in Paris. He said, in part, that this man, according to popular tradition, must have been bad even before Adam and Eve. He extorted money with the flimsiest excuses from the peaceful citizens of Syria. For example, he would send for a wealthy merchant or manufacturer to come to Beirut on urgent business. Then on his arrival he would tell him, "I have received bad reports concerning your character and dealings. You must stay here till I send a committee to investigate these reports and then I will set you free." The man, finding himself helpless in the face of such accusations, stayed one, two, three, four weeks. Meanwhile, there was no one at the head of his business, and alarming reports come to him. Finally he felt constrained to give a few hundred pounds to the governor so that he might get away. Rashíd Pasha was also a favorite spy of the Sultan of Turkey. He would forward the most dreadful reports about the law-abiding citizens, thus filling his pockets with bribery and extortion.

3. The Episode of Rashíd Pasha and Madame Jackson about 'Abdu'l-Bahá's Freedom

It so happened that at one time the secretary of the Turkish Embassy in Paris met Madame Jackson at a reception. Madame Jackson told him about 'Abdu'l-Bahá's incarceration in the town of 'Akká, and of the cruelty and injustice of the Turkish authorities. This secretary, being a relative of Rashíd Pasha, answered Madame Jackson, saying, that there must needs be at least 3000 pounds sterling to bring about 'Abdu'l-Bahá's freedom. Madame Jackson agreed to pay this sum if he succeeded in achieving his liberty. Immediately he reported to Rashíd Pasha that there lived a woman in Paris who was willing to pay a large sum if 'Abdu'l-Bahá could be set free. The governor, who loved money better than his life, cabled back to Paris, "Very well, it will be done."

Meanwhile 'Abdu'l-Bahá heard about the episode in this way: One day, the Mutisarrif of 'Akká, who was the husband of the sister of Ahmad 'Izzat Pasha,[19] came running to him, saying, "God be praised! All the means are prepared!" "How?" 'Abdu'l-Bahá asked. "What has happened?" "Oh! do you not know?" he said. "Soon you will be free. You will go out of this prison. You will travel wherever you wish." Then he told the rest of the story. As soon as he left 'Abdu'l-Bahá's abode, the latter sent a cable to Madame Jackson.

---

19. He was the right-hand man of Sultan 'Abdu'l-Hamíd and fled Turkey for Egypt when the Sultan's fall was imminent.

"Beware! Beware! Lest you pay one cent for my freedom. In prison I am feeling happy!" When the governor heard about 'Abdu'l-Bahá's instructions to Madame Jackson, he was, of course, furious. He had thought it would be so easy to get this sum of money. So he changed his tactics, and 'Abdu'l-Bahá one day received a letter from his secretary saying that the governor was very anxious to see him enjoying the air of freedom. 'Abdu'l-Bahá did not answer. After a week, he received another letter from the same secretary announcing that the governor had instructed him to draw up a petition to his Imperial Majesty, begging for 'Abdu'l-Bahá's liberty. Again 'Abdu'l-Bahá did not answer. Then he wrote that the petition was ready to be mailed. No answer. Again: the governor is going to sign the papers and mail them tomorrow. No answer. Then 'Abdu'l-Bahá received his last letter, saying that the governor had read the petition and had written over the envelope, 'Not to be sent.' No answer. When the governor realized that he had failed in everything, he sent his own son to 'Akká to see 'Abdu'l-Bahá personally, thinking that perchance he might succeed. The son was, of course, lavishly entertained by Mutisarrif. 'Abdu'l-Bahá was invited to meet him. After dinner the son brought up the subject from various points of view. 'Abdu'l-Bahá took the attitude that he knew nothing about the matter. After dinner he followed 'Abdu'l-Bahá to his house and spoke a great deal, but to no effect. "I am sorry to see you in prison," he would say. "Here I am happy," 'Abdu'l-Bahá answered. When in the morning he was leaving, disappointed, he made another effort by saying, "I hope, my Effendi, that I shall see you next time in Haifa." 'Abdu'l-Bahá waved the matter aside. When the governor heard the unsuccessful report of his son, he was crestfallen and angry. At that time he was so powerful that all the inhabitants of Syria trembled through fear of him. His reports to the Sultan were laws. One word from him would bring down the ire of his Majesty on anybody's head, no matter how important and influential they were.

When 'Abdu'l-Bahá realized that they were again at their old tactics, trying to make him say the word "yes" to their extortionate demands, he one day called Mutisarrif to his house and told him defiantly: "Do not make any more intrigues; you shall fail in all your secret machinations. There is a destined period for my imprisonment. Before the coming of that time, even the kings of the earth cannot take me out of this prison, but when the appointed moment arrives, all the emperors of the world cannot hold me a prisoner in 'Akká. I shall then go out. Rest thou assured of this."

When the Mutisarrif heard this emphatic statement, he wrote a letter to the governor, advising him not to make any further move "because 'Abbás Effendi knows the Talisman of Imam 'Alí. He has learned from the position of the heavenly Constellations the time of his freedom and no one can hasten it. It is better for us to give up this idea."

4. *The Infinite Patience of 'Abdu'l-Bahá in Answering the Tribunal Questions Put to Him*

At noon Mírzá Munír brought me a letter to translate into Persian. When this was finished, I called at the Master's house to deliver it. I knocked at the door three or four times before Khusraw answered. As I waited outside, I heard the voice of the Master, dictating Tablets to Mírzá Munír. I was then announced and ushered into the room. The Master welcomed me. He was sitting near the balcony; in front of him was a chair piled high with letters from the East and West. His dress and turban were of snowy white matching his beautiful locks and beard. Across the street there was a tall green acacia tree which attracted his attention. Now and then his eyes closed and again opened revealing infinite pity and love hidden in his eyes. Mírzá Munír was sitting writing down the heavenly words which flowed like a fountain from the tongue of the Beloved. As I watched him, I was struck by the divine beauty of his countenance, soft, tender and most adorable.

The many difficult problems of the Bahá'í world are solved by him. Now he writes to Persia on how to hold an election, then to far-off America on how to rent a hall. One Bahá'í desires to know whether she should cook food for her child; another person asks how to proceed to buy a piece of land. There are some misunderstandings in this assembly to be removed; the feelings of some person are ruffled and must be smoothed down. One man's mother or father is dead, he requests a Tablet of visitation, another desires to have a wife. To one a child is born, she begs for a Bahá'í name; another has taught several souls, he asks for Bahá'í rings for them. This man has had business reverses, he must be encouraged, another has fallen from a ladder, he implores for a speedy recovery. One has quarreled with his wife, and he wants advice on how to be reconciled; another supplicates for blessings upon his marriage. The Master goes over these one by one with infinite patience and with his words of advice, creates order out of chaos. The sorrows of the world troop along in review before him, and as they pass, lo, the transformation happens! The sorrowful becomes joyful, the ill-tempered good-natured, the lazy active, the sleepy one awakened. With magical words he transmutes iron into gold and darkness into light. At last he rises from his seat and for a while walks to and fro, still dictating Tablets to the philosopher and to the simple; soaring toward the empyrean of spirituality, giving us a vision of sanctity, and of the roses of Paradise, and for a while we roam, guided by him, in those delectable gardens of Abhá, intoxicated with the fragrance of God and then we find ourselves in the streets, walking home upborn on the wings of light.

RAMLEH, EGYPT, AUGUST 1, 1913

1. What Can We Do to Spread the Bahá'í Cause?

What can we do to become more fitting instruments, and purer channels, devoted whole-heartedly to the furtherance of the Bahá'í Cause? Is it through the organization of various committees? The discussion of various plans? The reading of Tablets and Words? The delivery of public addresses? The expounding of the Holy Utterances? The holding of Friday or Sunday meetings? The announcement of the Message? The publication and circulation of literature? It may be through any, or all of these, in fact each one of the above methods is important in its own place. But from a larger outlook, it is through the attraction of the heart, the purity of conscience, the spirituality of ideals, the concentration of selflessness, the leaping forth of the fire of the Love of God and the entire renunciation of self.

For the last few days many Tablets have been revealed for the Persian believers, and therefore it is very fitting to translate a few extracts:

2. The Difficulties of the Western Journey Have Left Their Impressions on 'Abdu'l-Bahá

The long journey over sea and land, the innumerable difficulties in the morn and at eve, the lack of rest and sleep, the delivery of detailed addresses in public congregations, the meetings with visitors from sunrise to midnight in America, the answering of countless questions and the withstanding of the hardships of the trip, have made their impression on this earthly constitution, and the result is a great weakness. . . . It is now a few days since I arrived in Ramleh, and feeling somewhat better, I am engaged in writing to you.

Convey infinite longing and love on behalf of 'Abdu'l-Bahá to all the believers of God. Day and night I am remembering the friends, kneeling before the Threshold and begging for them the confirmations of the Kingdom of Abhá. I hope that from now on the broken chain of correspondence will be taken up and that through the protection and preservation of the Blessed Beauty the pen will be set in motion.

3. Now the Importance of the Station of the Believers Is Unknown

The Glances of Divine Providence are always vouchsafed; the infinite Bestowals are continually descending. There are clear evidences that in the service of the Cause of God you are confirmed. Know ye the value of this most great Favor and render ye thanksgiving unto the Threshold of God by day and by night; because you have adorned your heads with such Glorious Crowns and have illumined such a light-giving candle in the assemblage of the world! Now the greatness of this station is hidden and invisible, but ere long it will become evident and manifest.

4. Service of the Believers of God

Thank God that thou are assisted in serving the believers of God. Thou art the enkindled brasier of the Fire of Love and a lamp of the utmost purity through which the Light of God's attraction shines forth. Appreciate the value of this Divine Favor. Be self-sacrificing and give exhilaration and rejoicing to the friends of God and engage in adoration and thanksgiving to the Most Glorious Lord with infinite gladness and happiness.

Today the Beloved came to see us in the morning. He sat on the veranda and asked Mírzá Munír to bring the Tablets which he dictated yesterday to be corrected by him. For half an hour he read them over and made a few corrections here and there. Then he dictated a Tablet to Maharajah of Couch Bahar of India. He also dispatched eight cables to the various cities of Persia giving the believers the good news of his health. Then went out to call on Mírzá Abú'l-Fad̲l.

5. A Bahá'í Meeting in Alexandria

For the first time since my arrival in Ramleh I went to a Bahá'í meeting in the house of Khurásání. There were many Persian and Arabian Bahá'ís present. After our entrance, according to the Eastern custom, rose-water was given us with which to anoint our faces. Then tea was served and conversation started. I told them something about our American trip in which they were greatly interested. We spoke of certain people who rise to a great station in the Cause, then suddenly fall and are forgotten. One of the old believers illustrated this subject as follows:

"If a person scales only a few steps of the ladder and falls, he can arise, shake off the dust, heal his bruises and scale the ladder again. But if he falls from the highest step, it will be most difficult for him to arise."

Then an old man began to chant a prayer of Bahá'u'lláh when some one brought in the news that the Master was arriving. Immediately the man stopped his chanting, all voices were hushed, and everybody was on his feet, awaiting the coming of 'Abdu'l-Bahá. As he entered all heads bowed down and he walked toward the upper part of the room and seated himself on the divan. He spoke in Arabic, for the sake of the Arabian Bahá'ís. The subject was the Pyramids and their antiquity. When he left the room, he called me to go with him and I was very happy. He spoke to me with much gentleness and kindness. He is at all times thinking of the welfare and comfort of his servants.

6. Bahá'í Detachment and Independence

While he walked along the street, he was commenting on the fact that he desired every Bahá'í to be severed and detached. If he passes between two mountains of gold, he must not look to either side. Those souls who have entered under the shade of the Blessed Perfection must display such independence as to astonish the people of the world. If men come to them with money and supplicate them to accept it, they should reject it.

7. Arrival of Members of 'Abdu'l-Bahá's Family

On the way Mírzá 'Alí-Akbar brought the news that the Greatest Holy Leaf, 'Abdu'l-Bahá's sister, his daughter, Shoghi Effendi, and five or six others had arrived from Haifa. The Beloved came to see us, sat for one hour, drank a cup of coffee, and then left us to return to his house to see the newcomers.

In the evening Shoghi Effendi brought me a few letters from America sent by Ahmad Yazdí, and the new book by Mr. Horace Holley, *The Modern Social Religion*, which is just out.

RAMLEH, EGYPT, AUGUST 2, 1913

1. The Greatest Holy Leaf—the Daughter of Bahá'u'lláh

Today the Beloved did not come to see us in the morning because he was entertaining the Greatest Holy Leaf and the rest of the friends who had come with her. In the Bahá'í Cause she is a unique woman. She has devoted all her life to the service of humanity. She is a glorious star set upon the crown of womanhood, and a light-giving personality. Everybody takes her advice because she is a loving mother and sister to every Bahá'í. Her noble life is a glorious epic of self-sacrifice, generosity, and kindness. She radiates joy and ecstasy and is the worthiest representative of her kind. All those who have come within the radius of her calm, spiritual influence and have spoken even a few words with her, bear testimony to the fact that she is a heavenly soul—wonderfully spiritual, highly cultivated, and attuned with the ethereal music of the celestial spheres. Well may all womankind be proud of her sweet life, spent in the path of God, consecrated to the Love of God and dedicated to the service of the Almighty!

Two pilgrims have just arrived from Persia. One is from Yazd, the other from Khurasan, a relative of the Bábu'l-Báb,[20] Mullá Husayn Bushrí'í—the first believer in the Báb.

2. 'Abdu'l-Bahá Talks with Two Pilgrims

I was going to take a walk when I saw the Master, dressed in his pure white garment, slowly coming toward me. I stood aside in a reverent attitude until he arrived, then I followed him. He felt very tired because he had read and written a great deal during the day.

He wished that he could get away and be alone for several weeks and do nothing but rest, but he wondered whether he would be happy! He entered the house and our dear pilgrims wanted to kneel before him and kiss his hands, but he prevented them from doing so. He inquired from each how the Cause was progressing in their respective cities. The one from Yazd answered that the Cause was spreading very rapidly in that part of the world, the teachers were very zealous and active, the meetings very radiant and that every day from ten to fifteen people were instructed in various gatherings. The Master praised their zeal and courage and expressed the hope that they would increase their enthusiasm and their power of teaching.

---

20. Lit., the Gate of the Gate.

3. This Is the Day of Teaching

In talking with these pilgrims the Master emphasized that this is the day of teaching. This is the day of service. This is the day of the illumination of the world of humanity. Nothing else will give permanent result. This is their work.

Then he left us, but our hearts were full with his love, a love which never grows dim, but is light upon light.

4. Mr. Atwood, an Englishman

I went out, walking toward the Hotel Plaisance where Miss Hiscock and Mr. Atwood live. I had a most interesting talk with the latter. He is very cultured and learned and the Master thinks highly of him. He writes articles for Magazines, is well-informed on many subjects and has lived in Ramleh with his wife and two children for nearly four years. From now on I hope to see him as often as I can for I have great admiration for him. He is a man of intelligence and sound mind.

I will end my letter today with the translations of a few extracts from the Tablets.

5. Filial Piety: To a father whose son is a teacher in the Cause.

Every son who does not become a cause of glory for his parents is a manifest loss. How many children turn out to be fruitless and unfaithful! Therefore render thanksgiving unto the Lord that thou hast such a kind and skillful son. He is a servant of the Cause and very efficient. He is favored at the Threshold of the Most Glorious King. His heart and soul are vivified through the Breaths of the Merciful. His eyes are turned toward the horizon of His Highness, the Unconstrained. His tongue is fluent with the divine proofs and evidences, and his nostrils perfumed with the sweet Fragrances of the Clement One.

6. The Future of Persia

The region of Nur is the birthplace of the Speaker on the Mount. Consider to what grandeur, importance, and splendor it shall attain throughout future ages and cycles. It shall become the abode of the Paradise of the Kingdom; the forest for the lions of the Forgiving Lord, the Holy Ground for the people of all nations and the abode of the angels of the Most High, for the Fire of Sinai flamed forth from this region and the Most Great Luminary dawned from this horizon. But a thousand times alas, that the inhabitants of that country are still heedless and unaware. Ere long they shall become awakened and mindful, and they will glorify and magnify the Lord for these privileges.

7. What 'Abdu'l-Bahá Saw and Did on His Western Tour

O ye illumined friends of 'Abdu'l-Bahá:

It is well-nigh three years since, like unto the wind I have been crossing vast deserts and like unto the nestless and shelterless bird, I have day and night been singing over mountains and shores. Now, in the middle of the ocean, I watched the crest of the furious tempest and while traveling I beheld the vastness and the immensity of the wilderness. One moment of rest I enjoyed not; one second of peace I sought not. Throughout many cities of the Occident I delivered the Glad-tidings of the appearance of the Sun of the Orient, in many churches I raised the cry of Yá Bahá'u'l-Abbá, and before innumerable audiences, with resonant voice gave the Gospel of the Kingdom.

Praise be to God that the rays of the Sun of Reality are shining upon the East and the West, changing dark nights into luminous days. From every direction the cry of Yá Bahá'u'l-Abhá is being heard and from every side the voice of 'Oh my Lord the Supreme.' has reached to the zenith of heaven....

In short, after great difficulties, from the West I have returned to the East. I shall tarry in Egypt for a while so that I may gain physical strength and energy; perchance, God willing, I may render a service to the Threshold of God, and at the Court of the Beauty of Abhá, may be confirmed in Thralldom. If the believers of God loosen the tongue of teaching, in a short time, undoubtedly this world will become another world, the rays of the Most Great Luminary shall shine and its darkness be transformed into the illumination of the East and the West.

Ramleh in the early 1900s

RAMLEH, EGYPT, AUGUST 3, 1913

1. Spiritual Sustenance Distribute in the Morning

His Holiness the Báb has said that every day before sunrise the spiritual sustenance of mankind is provided and distributed. Similarly, how appropriate it is to adore the beginning of every letter with the name of the Lord of mankind and with quotations from the Tablets revealed from the tongue of the Beloved! He thus writes to a Persian believer:

2. Spiritual Receptivity

The Cloud of Providence hath poured down the rain of guidance upon the East and the West; the rays of the Sun of Reality has shone forth upon all the inhabitants of the world, but out of the brackish ground nothing will grow except thorns and thistles and the effulgence of the Orb of Truth do not penetrate through the black stone. Therefore, thank God that thy pure heart was the clear mirror reflecting the radiant rays of divine guidance, and that thy mind was fertile soil, because, through the downpour of the rain of Grace there have appeared the flowers, anemones of wisdom. Thank God for this Eminent Bounty, for verily thou art of those who have attained.

3. 'Abdu'l-Bahá Sang a New Song in Every Garden

Thy letter was received. Thou hast lamented and complained because it is some time since thou hast received any letter from 'Abdu'l-Bahá. For forty years 'Abdu'l-Bahá was kept in prison, but his infinite longing was to spread with a resonant voice the word of God throughout all countries and to unloosen his tongue in the exposition of Truth and in teaching the Cause. No sooner was he freed from prison, than he hastened to every clime and country. On every mountain he raised a cry of 'He is God' and in every city he spoke with public-spirited men. In every garden he sang a new melody and like unto the bird of the morning raised the note of Yá Bahá'u'l-Abhá. In every meeting he elucidated the teachings of this divine Cause and while traveling through the Western countries he summoned all to the Kingdom of God. Under such circumstances, there was no time to write, and therefore correspondence was neglected."

4. The Muslim Month of Fasting

This is the first of the month of Ramadan—the month of Muslim fasting. The Beloved made this announcement this morning as he entered the house. He sat down on the veranda and spoke on the subject of fasting. The Muslims are very strict about it. One must eat, drink, and smoke nothing from sunrise until sunset. As the eastern calendar is lunar, the month of fasting falls in different seasons; as a result of this arrangement it is in August this year—a month extremely hot with days exceptionally long. The laborers and farmers suffer very much from thirst during the day, but they do not break the laws of their religion. If by mere chance a Muslim is seen eating in the street, he is punished by the Shaykh. In the evening all good Muslims go to the Mosque to pray, and strictly obey all the ceremonials connected with this holy month. Every person—whether he understands it or not—should read the Qur'an, at least once, from cover to cover. This act is most meritorious.

The Master told Mírzá 'Alí-Akbar to go to Alexandria and bring our two new pilgrims back to live with us. They had taken rooms in a native hotel somewhere downtown. By three o'clock they were here full of joy and delight because they were going to be near the Beloved and see him every day.

5. What Is the Real Object of the Fast?

In the afternoon the Master came and as there were present several Arabian believers, he talked in Arabic on physical and spiritual fasting. Real fasting is to abstain from carnal desires and the promptings of ego. Fasting means to purify the heart from every stain of egotism, replacing material tendencies with spiritual susceptibilities, refining the moral fiber, intensifying the Fire of the Love of God, cleansing the self from the dross of haughtiness, teaching humility and dispelling the darkness of ignorance.

After the Beloved left, the audience scattered, and went out for a brief stroll. In a few minutes I found myself in the Hotel Plaisance talking with Mr. Atwood, Miss Hiscock and a very charming Turkish lady. She spoke French and English quite well besides three or four other languages.

I will conclude today by quoting the translation of another Tablet.

6. 'Abdu'l-Bahá Writes to an Indian Prince

Through Rev. Promotho Loll Sen
To His Highness Prince Maharaj Couch Baha, (Upon him be greeting and praise)

He is God!

O happy starred and noble Prince:
    The gift you have forwarded was very acceptable because it was from your Highness: this exiled one over mountain

and plain, this wanderer over land and sea took that cup as a symbol, signifying: 'I am thirsty for the Water of Reality and longing for intoxication with the Wine of Knowledge.'

Therefore I upraised the hand of supplication toward the Kingdom of the Incomparable One, praying: O Thou Almighty, Deign to fill this Divine Cup with the Wine of Thy Love and let this golden goblet overflow with the nectar of Thy Grace; so that friends and strangers may become exhilarated with the wine of 'Am I not your lord?' and shareless ones become the adorers of the Ideal Wine.

In short I offered the utmost prayer and supplication at the Threshold of the Possessor of Glory that your kind father the leader of the Worthies, the Glorious Amír, may be submerged in the Ocean of divine Grace, become intoxicated with the Wine of Celestial Bestowal and Favor, obtain the Peace of the spirit in the Rose-garden of the Merciful in the midst of the Paradise of Knowledge, and attain to the station of Transfiguration in the Delectable Heaven of God.

May the Almighty confer the happiness of both worlds upon thee, O happy starred Prince, grant eternal joy and felicity never-ending, suffer thee to become the manifestation of confirmation and to inspire thee under all circumstances with a new spirit!

This is the prayer of this wanderer in behalf of that leader of freedman.

Upon thee be greeting and praise!

(Signed) 'Abdu'l-Bahá 'Abbás.

RAMLEH, EGYPT, AUGUST 4, 1913

1. *The Blessings of the Universal Mind*

Praise be to God that the world has heard the message of Reality, listened to the clarion call of Wisdom, quaffed the Water of Eternal Life, hastened toward the arena of Knowledge, embraced the Beloved of Truth, has been quickened by the breaths of the Holy Spirit, stirred by the Glad-Tidings of the Lord of Hosts and rejoiced by the wonderful words of God! May the hearts become as fountains from which the limpid water of divine spirit ever flow! May the minds become as the rose-gardens wherein the flowers of idealism grow and develop! May the spirits become as mines out of which nuggets of love and jewels of friendship are produced! This is the world's heavenly heritage. The inner world, like a beautiful meadow, is carpeted with hyacinths of affection, violets of harmony, anemones of immortal ideals, and lilies of spiritual susceptibilities. No one should hide these tender flowers under a glass. Let the light shine. Sing like unto a nightingale. Gird up the loin of endeavor. Soar heavenward. Step into the arena of activity. Diffuse the radiance of the celestial light. Leap forward. Raise the ringing watchword of Peace and Brotherhood. Do not tarry. Travel on and on in the mystic realms of Guidance. Your helper is God. Your inspirer is the Holy Spirit. Your co-workers are the angels of the Supreme Concourse. Ye have received the Truth, and the Truth hath made you free. What greater blessing is there than this? This is Eternal Glory and everlasting Life.

In order to teach the Cause of Peace, every person must become a clear channel for the expression of God and the manifestation of the attributes of God. We are all His servants, and before His throne we stand with the utmost humility. We must increase our effort, strive in the pathway of righteousness, illumine the world of humanity with the rays of brotherhood and inter-racial feeling and upraise the standard of the solidarity of mankind. This is the world's work! This is the task set for man! With the assistance of God and the co-operation of all public-spirited leaders we will not fail.

2. *'Abdu'l-Bahá and the Family Prayer in the Morning*

Hardly were we out of our beds when Khusraw rang the bell. Hájí Sayyid Javád and myself were summoned by the Beloved. When we arrived at the door of his apartment, Khusraw made a sign to wait. The door was shut and we could see nothing. In a moment I heard a sweet voice of a woman. Oh! She was chanting a prayer and I was all attention. I knew what it was. Like a flash it dawned upon me. It was the family morning prayer offered at the Threshold of Bahá'u'lláh and presided over by the Center of His Covenant. As I waited there, I pictured in my mind a spiritual society, when every home would be a temple of God like unto the home of the Beloved. From these hearths every morning chants of thanksgiving and praise would be sent up to heaven from the lips of those whose hearts were stirred by the spiritual Fragrance, whose spirits were treasuries of the mysteries of God and whose consciences reflect the longing and aspirations of the angels!

The chant continued soaring higher and higher, carrying me away to a glorious world! I thought I was listening to the delectable voices of the Seraphim and Cherubim. Then it ended in a hush of silence, leaving behind the delicate hues and perfumes of the world of God and filling the void with a rare atmosphere of spirituality!

3. 'Abdu'l-Bahá and Shoghi Effendi

Now the door opened and we were bidden to the Master's writing room. As we sat there, we heard Shoghi Effendi chanting with pathos and sweetness. As he ended the prayer suddenly, I heard the voice of the Master. I was on my feet. What marvelous depth of feeling! It causes the stones to dance with joy! He was teaching Shoghi Effendi how to chant and how to control his voice under various expressions.

What a heavenly Feast I have had this morning! Manna from on high! What a great privilege to have even a mental glimpse of this Holy Shrine of the Lord of Mankind where every morning prayers are proffered for the general welfare of all the human race; such prayers as will affect the very foundations of the social consciousness of every man and woman in this world.

Then the Master entered our room and said that, inasmuch as it was the month of Ramadan, he couldn't serve us tea. He had prepared many envelopes containing Tablets to be mailed and he asked Hájí Sayyid Javád to take them to Port Said and there to be registered.

4. The Persians Delighted with the Pictures in American Magazines

While I was in 'Abdu'l-Bahá's presence the mail man brought several letters from America and four big packages of the Magazines, "Travel," kindly sent by Mr. Roy C. Wilhelm. These magazines delighted many. Already several copies are with Shoghi Effendi, some of them are with Mr. Atwood. Everybody is interested in the pictures. I would appreciate it if the friends could send every month some of the current magazines and papers. They would delight the hearts of many friends, especially the illustrated ones.

5. Universal Homage Paid to 'Abdu'l-Bahá

In the afternoon I called on the Master. He was sitting on the balcony. He asked me about the news from America. I read him the letters just received from Miss Thompson, Mrs. Ralston, Miss H. Magee, Mrs. Fraser, and others.

After half an hour's talk about the Cause in America he left the house and I accompanied him. He is shown marked respect by everyone as he walks in the streets. The policeman standing at the corner salutes him, the man sitting on the ground gets up as though compelled to do so by a superior force. He walked toward our house and surprised everyone by his sudden appearance. For nearly an hour he sat on the veranda watching the slow stream of life passing by. Now and then he spoke in monosyllables and then he took his customary walk.

6. Life during the Month of Muslim Fast

During the days of Ramadan life is very interesting just before and after sunset. Before sunset, because everybody is exhausted with hunger and thirst; then restaurants are filled by the people awaiting anxiously the setting of the sun, and the streets present a hustling, motley crowd; after sunset, because once they have satisfied their appetites they go out to the cafes, amusement places and theaters.

7. How Eager Are the Bahá'ís of Persia for Martyrdom

Mírzá Abú'l-Fadl came in the evening and told us a few incidents out of the rich treasury of his life. When he was imprisoned in

Tehran with 18 others, there was an old man among them by the name of Mírzá Muhammad-Ridá. He was well known for three rare qualities: firmness, fearlessness and truthfulness. He defied the prison authorities by his courage; awed the enemies by his firmness and set at naught the intrigues of the foes through his truthfulness.

"Whenever," Mírzá Abú'l-Fadl said, "the Hájibu'd-Dawlih, one of the Ministers of the Court, came to the prison to investigate the condition of some one, Mírzá Muhammad-Ridá would approach him and speak to him with great earnestness. Finally the Hájibu'd-Dawlih would turn to him with a despairing look saying, 'Sir! This is impossible! I cannot do it. Why did you not ask the Prince Náyibu's-Saltanih about this? He can do it. He has the authority.' At last one day we asked him 'What is this which you talk about with the Hájibu'd-Dawlih, whenever he comes to the prison, and why does he refuse you so emphatically?' He said: 'I ask and plead with him to sentence me to death. I tell him: I am an old man; I am of no good to the world. I want to bathe my body in blood for the sake of Bahá'u'lláh. Please, please, I beg you to do something for me. Is this too much of a favor that I ask of you? Are you not kind enough to fulfill this last wish of an old man? Praise be to God that you are an influential person. But he does not listen to me and answers me loudly in the manner you have all heard.'"

8. *'Abdu'l-Bahá Confounds the Mullás in the Mosque*

Mírzá Abú'l-Fadl was giving us a graphic description of another prison scene, and he had just reached its climax when the door opened and the Master entered. Apparently he felt well and in a happy mood. He told us that last Friday he had gone to the Mosque of Sidi Jabar. There were many Mullás present. One of them was chanting verses of the Qur'an, while another was addressing the people. 'Abdu'l-Bahá could hear neither, so he addressed the one who was speaking, 'What art thou doing? Hast thou not heard the saying of Mohammed, that when Qur'an is read everyone must listen?" The man turned red and was ashamed and all the other Mullás looked at each other wonderingly.

9. Story of Mullá Sádiq, the Fanatical Shaykh

Then he related another story: During the early years of his arrival in 'Akká, he was one night invited to a feast, where, for the edification of the guests, the Qur'an was being chanted by a very good singer. The Muslims having forgotten their reverence for Holy things, and overlooking the injunction of Muhammad, smoked and talked on such occasions, and when 'Abdu'l-Bahá arrived, there was a hubbub of confusion, people chatting, smoking and drinking coffee and tea; while in a corner of the room two singers chanted the Qur'an with great feeling. 'Abdu'l-Bahá looked about and saw beside him a very fanatical Shaykh, Mullá Sádiq. 'Abdu'l-Bahá asked him whether this was fitting and if, according to the text of the Qur'an these people should not listen quietly. He answered: "Yes." "Then enjoin the law of God upon them," 'Abdu'l-Bahá told him. Mullá Sádiq arose from his seat: "Be silent," he hurled at them with tremendous fury, and struck at their water-pipes, glasses and cups, breaking them all in his religious zeal. He then harangued them for their lack of religious spirit, their forgetfulness of the Laws of God, and their awful disobedience. The people were astonished and thought that he had become a lunatic; but from that time on, at all the feasts, nothing was served and everybody listened reverently while the Qur'an was chanted.

Although Mullá Sádiq considered the Bahá'ís infidels, yet he used to come every night to 'Abdu'l-Bahá's house; staying for supper and talking until midnight. He was so fanatical that if any person deviated one hair's breadth from the prescribed formulas of the religion, he would consider him an atheist.

10. 'Abdu'l-Bahá's Love-pat

The Beloved continued talking and relating several amusing stories, which made us laugh. When he had finished, he told us that his intention had been to entertain us. Then he arose to leave and as he passed me he looked at me with twinkling eyes—and raising his hand brought it down on my left cheek. It was a hard blow, and everybody enjoyed it, especially myself. It has been some time since I had received a "love-pat" and I was thinking that I was somewhat neglected. A "love-pat" from the Master is worth all the kindnesses of all the people of the world.

RAMLEH, EGYPT, AUGUST 5, 1913

1. 'Abdu'l-Bahá Does Not Rest

Let me share with you another translation of the words of the Beloved revealed to the Persians:

> It has been some time since 'Abdu'l-Bahá has been deprived of correspondence, because he has been engaged in the delivery of public addresses. He has been speaking constantly. He has been crying out at every morn and shunning rest at every eve. On many a night and day he has been giving the Glad-Tidings of the appearance of the Kingdom of Mystery in the temples of both friends and strangers. This delay in correspondence comes from the lack of time and opportunity; otherwise you are always before his sight. It is hoped from the Favor of the Self-Subsistent Lord that your hearts may be flooded with a new effulgence—that is, that you may obtain a new joy and ecstasy and leap high like an inextinguishable flame—so that the light of your love may illumine all regions.

2. The Significance of Spiritual Meetings

The meetings that thou art holding in thy house are the means of strengthening the hearts of the spiritual ones, of guiding the seekers and of awakening the sleepy ones. These meetings are illumined with the splendor of divine Providence, and like unto the rose-garden of Wisdom they are adorned with the flowers of significances and Ideals. I hope that they will make progress.

3. The World Is a Farm and the People are Farmers

O thou who are attracted by the Fragrances of God! Every person is a farmer. One sows the seeds of industry; another scatters the acorns of commerce, and a third farms politics. All various agricultural pursuits culminate in harvests, yet these do not enjoy the blessings of the eternal springtime, neither do they yield inexhaustible benefits. But as the friends of God are scattering seeds in the farms of reality, they will gain an increasing blessing and will collect throughout centuries and cycles thousands of harvests. Now praise be to God that thou art sowing seeds in the ground of Truth and art the farmer of His Highness the Peerless One.

4. Spiritual Guidance

Thank God that a light of guidance has shone in the court of thy heart and soul! Thirsty wert thou, thou didst attain to the fountain of eternal life. Sick wert thou, thou didst receive the Most Great Antidote of the Glorious Lord.

5. Be Seekers of Truth

Your letter was received. I supplicated and entreated at the Threshold of the Kingdom of Abhá to Confer upon you a new Grace and Bounty; so that those souls may ever walk in the straight Path, move in the Ancient Highway of the Lord and be seekers of Truth and speakers of Truth. This is the utmost hope of 'Abdu'l-Bahá.

6. Divine Confirmations

O thou servant at the Threshold of the Blessed Perfection! Offer thou glorification unto the Lord because the radiant morn of the most great Guidance has appeared upon the dawning-places of the heart and spirit the musk-diffusing fragrance of the garden of realities has reached the nostrils; the divine Confirmations have rent the veils asunder; the sight and the insight have beheld the most glorious signs; the dove of the Love of God has returned to the meadow of the Covenant and the moth of attraction has circled around the divine Lamp.

7. Selfish People Are Tied with Iron Bands

Our home was illumined very early this morning by the presence of the Beloved. He walked in with confident strides. His face was beaming with joy and health. And the sun of his countenance irradiated happiness, so we in turn were made glad for our peaceful life depends upon his good health.

As he sat upon a chair, he told us that he had slept soundly the last two nights and today felt very well. I could see the effect on his animated face. It had not any of the former weariness. Then he spoke about fasting and of how it is necessary for the rich to think of the poor during the month of Ramadan. Those souls who prefer themselves to others are tied with selfish iron bands, while those who prefer others to themselves are the benefactors of the human race. Such was the conduct and the life of Bahá'u'lláh.

8. How 'Abdu'l-Bahá Built a Bath for Bahá'u'lláh

The name of Bahá'u'lláh brought to his mind the following incident:

In the military barracks of 'Akká, there was a small primitive bath which the Blessed Perfection used occasionally. After their departure from this place 'Abdu'l-Bahá rented a little house in the town. This house consisted of two stories, two rooms being on the lower floor and four on the upper, all of very modest proportions. Now the family was numerous, and 'Abdu'l-Bahá wondered how all those souls could be accommodated in this small house. Finally thirteen of them agreed to occupy one room, and here they lived and slept and worked together. They kept this house for well-nigh twenty years. It so happened that, although it was small, it yet contained a primitive bath, and the Blessed Perfection could use it as often as he wished. At the end of twenty years, 'Abdu'l-Bahá rented a much larger house, but it had no bath. He went to Bahá'u'lláh and asked permission to build one. The more he begged, the more definitely he was refused. 'Abdu'l-Bahá stated, that a bath could be built for only fifty pounds, but Bahá'u'lláh did not give his consent.

After a month had passed he went to an Arab friend and borrowed from him 250 pounds at two per cent. This money he took to a merchant who was in former times a grain-dealer, but who was now out of work. He told him something to this effect:

"We will enter into a partnership; the capital will be from me, the labor from you. With this fund you will deal in grain for four months. After paying off all the expenses of rent, etc., and receiving your monthly salary, we will divide the profit; one-third for you and two-thirds for me."

This agreement was made and the merchant started the business. After four months they cleared their accounts. The debt was paid back with its two per cent interest; the merchant received his one-third profit; all the other expenses were defrayed, and 30 pounds left in the balance for 'Abdu'l-Bahá. With that sum he built a bath in the house of Bahá'u'lláh. This house is kept intact to the present day.

9. Spiritual Humility and the Story of the King and the Arab

Then the conversation turned upon another subject—how outward circumstances, such as wealth, honor, titles and even spiritual gifts made some people proud.

Concerning this the Master told a story:

> It is said that at one time a king went traveling incognito. He put on a humble suit of clothes and started on his adventures. After a few days journey, during which he had lost his way in the scorching desert, he finally reached the tent of an Arab. The Arab, finding the man exhausted from heat and hunger, dragged him to the shade. When the king was revived, he asked the Arab what he had to eat and drink. "I have a goat-skin of wine and a little goat," the Arab answered. "Very well, bring the wine and let the goat be cooked." The wine was brought. When the king had drunk one cup, he looked at the Arab and said: "Do you know who I am?" "No." "I am a soldier in the king's army." The Arab was glad to entertain a brave man.
>
> He drank another cup. "Do you know who I am?" "Who are you?" "I am a Minister of the King's Council Chamber." "I am delighted to receive such a distinguished statesman." A

third cup was taken. "Do you know who I am?" "Well?" "I am the King himself." The Arab could stand it no longer. He arose from his place and took away the goat-skin of wine. "Why do you do this?" the guest asked, astonished. "Because I believe that if you drink another cup, you will declare yourself to be the prophet of God, and a fifth one may raise you to the station of God himself; so it is better for you to cool down a little."

10. 'Abdu'l-Bahá's Generosity

At five o'clock 'Abdu'l-Bahá returned with Mírzá 'Alí-Akbar and went out to call on Mírzá Abú'l-Fadl. He came back after two hours and complained of fatigue, because he had been speaking with several Arabs who had made an appointment to see him. He said, that from morning until this very moment beggars of all nationalities and religions had knocked at his door, and that even now one was waiting outside, and he gave me some money for him.

His munificence extends to all people. Freely he gives without distinction for race or color. Our duty in life is to follow his glorious example, in taking care of the poor in time of need, and in practicing charity and kindness. I do not see or hear what he does and says during the day, but I know that every minute is spent in the service of others.

How to make the world better, how to improve the conditions of mankind, how to raise the standard of moral consciousness, and how to make the hearts gladder is his hourly preoccupation. Before leaving he told us that the duty of each believer is to be the servant of the other and to attend to his brother's wants. He considered himself the servant of all the friends of God.

RAMLEH, EGYPT, AUGUST 6, 1913

1. God's Favors Measureless

This morning I was musing upon the events of the past two years, the extraordinary occurrences concerning the Cause, the historic tour of 'Abdu'l-Bahá through the United States and Europe and the contrast of our present quiet stay in Ramleh. "What does the future hold for us?" I asked subconsciously. Bahá'u'lláh has caused the descent of divine blessings; he has spread before us a heavenly Table bearing many kinds of spiritual food, he has left amongst us his son, 'Abdu'l-Bahá—to interpret his words and to spread his Universal Message and he has summoned into existence glorious souls all over the world to promulgate His principles. We must let the lamp of hope burn, we must free ourselves from regrets or pessimism. If we fall, we must immediately rise and push forward. The same God who has assisted others will come to our help.

2. Spiritual Relationship

'Abdu'l-Bahá visited us this afternoon and we gathered about him like moths around a candle. Little by little the friends arrived. Then an American Bahá'í came with an Arabian believer—a tall young man. The Master spoke with them on the spiritual union of hearts, irrespective of color and nationality.

This spiritual union is one of the wonders of the age, that an oriental and occidental can meet on common ground. Although there exists between them no racial, no patriotic, no political relationship, yet they are able to enjoy a friendship as though they belong to the same race. This is a spiritual bond. Often two brothers reared in the same household are antagonistic, but on this divine plane others who have no material connections can in reality be more sympathetic than if they were blood relations. Happy are you that you have drunk from this spiritual fountain and have attained to the reality of existence.

Then he spoke about his western trip, mentioning the names of the various cities of America, and of how his time was spent in those places. Although often he had not felt well, he had been happy because he could teach the Cause and spread the Glad-Tidings.

3. A Walk through the Streets and the Radiance of the Star of Hope

At sunset he ordered tea and in the calm atmosphere of a lovely eastern evening we felt his power more than ever. He is the King of our hearts and spirits and our love for him is increasing daily. He left very quietly, followed by the Arab believer. I felt a new ray of hope dawning upon the horizon of my soul. After dinner I wished to be alone so that I might contemplate the divine sweetness of the Beloved. Walking through the streets I looked up and millions of stars were shining in their accustomed glory. The night was beautiful. The Eastern sky was radiant. The stars were the shining lamps of God. At last I sat down on a broken wall and I looked about me. Thinking upon the past, I became confident for the future. God in his bounty has guided the ship of my destiny so far and he will continue to do the same. I returned with a light step. On my way back I met three other believers. They are sincere in their strivings and longing to be of more useful service. How confident they were! How simple! how spiritual! how glorious their faith! they inspired me with a greater faith. In the darkness there arose a light, full of radiance and beauty. I entered the house very happy. My heart was singing. The future was in the hands of God.

RAMLEH, EGYPT, AUGUST 7, 1913

1. The Beauty and Charm of the Palaces of Ramleh

From my room I see the great clock of the New Victoria Hotel wherein the Beloved stayed from time to time. The manager with much pride shows to the guests the various rooms occupied by the Master. He knows something about the Cause, and recognizes the great honor and blessing bestowed upon him and his hotel. When the Master was here the last time, he gave two large feasts just before his departure for America. There are a few other hotels and houses in which the Beloved has lived periodically. The homes of the Pashas are really wonderful specimens of the best Renaissance architecture. They very much resemble the houses and villas I have seen at Nice. Wonderful palaces, furnished with a taste truly magnificent, and are enclosed within gardens, the beauty and charm of which rival the fairy-lands of the artists and the poets. These "villas" are surrounded by walls from two to four yards high. The principal avenues are macadamized and clean and the narrow streets are also very much like the garden paths of Nice. As one walks through them the perfume of the flowers is inhaled, the branches of the trees overhanging the walls give a cool, inviting shade and the climbing vines add to the charming verdancy. A man passing through the streets and observing the houses, sees all the windows tightly shut. The stranger may think that they are not inhabited, but on inquiring about this custom of closing the windows, he is politely informed that as the owner is Muslim, the blinds are drawn, so that no foreign eyes may gaze upon the dark beauties of the women.

2. The Egyptian Pashas are Proud of 'Abdu'l-Bahá and His Philosophy of Religion

Several of the houses of these Pashas are honored by the presence of the Master, for they admire him and appreciate his teachings of tolerance and broad-mindedness. It is very strange that although these men do not believe in the Cause, yet they boast before strangers about the existence of 'Abdu'l-Bahá.

A very prominent Pasha, who was an admirer of 'Abdu'l-Bahá, received from time to time some English periodicals with accounts of the Bahá'í movement, among them was the Christian Commonwealth which contained an article explaining the Cause.

After showing the article to a visiting Englishman, the Pasha said:

"We have produced in the Orient a man such as 'Abbás Effendi, who alone visited Europe and America, and who through the sheer force of his personality and the wonderful soundness and brilliancy of his philosophy, captivated the pulpits and platforms, revolutionized the current of western thoughts, opened before your faces vistas of glorious ideals, and drew to his audiences thousands of men and women who were deeply attracted to his humane and divine wisdom, while the Press of the West from one end to another had but one tongue by which to praise his many virtues and to elucidate his system of religion and philosophy. Yes, we are proud of him. We honor him because he comes from the heart of the Orient. He represents us, he utters our ideals and longings. You have never sent us a man who could travel in the Orient and deliver lectures as 'Abbás Effendi has done in the West."

Thus these people are spreading the principles in a most effective manner, because they are men of great influence, although not "believers" in the Bahá'í Movement.

3. A Call from 'Abdu'l-Bahá and His Encouragement

This morning the Master did not come to our house but passed by, asking for Mírzá 'Alí-Akbar. During the day he came in two or three times, but for only a few minutes. His health has improved much. He seems very busy, for he is out often, paying visits to this or that person.

In the morning I was told many interesting stories of how certain people had become Bahá'ís and the manner in which some of the believers taught. These stories are really worth recording, for they illustrate the peculiar disposition of a people who may be instructed by a line quoted at the right time but refuse to listen to all kinds of logical arguments.

In the evening the Beloved came with a number of friends, tea was prepared according to his directions and served by himself. He stayed for half an hour, speaking now and then about the Cause and encouraging the Pilgrims to teach when they are back again among their associates and relatives.

RAMLEH, EGYPT, AUGUST 8, 1913

1 A Practical Lesson in Cleanliness

Today I played the part of house-cleaner and cook. I spent most of my time in the kitchen cleaning the dishes, washing the utensils, scrubbing the floor and dusting the ceiling and the cupboard. It was an object lesson to our cook, who does not know the simple ways of cleanliness. When I left the kitchen all the Persians came in and admired the spotlessness of everything. The cook was most willing to learn, but there had been no one who would take a day off to demonstrate a method of tidiness to him.

My parents did not teach me any of these things; in fact I did not know them, was the way he explained this lack of knowledge.

Most of the simple, loving folks here have plenty of religion. They are honest, truthful, hospitable, but they lack the knowledge of hygiene and sanitation. Their children are allowed to remain dirty; in many cases they do not dress them well for fear of bringing them to notice and of possibly attracting the "Evil Eye." Woe betide anyone if he praises or admires the beauty of the child of a Muslim! What these people need is a practical knowledge and the inculcation of sanitary laws. Once they learn these, they will forget their superstitions; the outlook of their cramped lives will be expanded, the light of intelligence will shine, and the beauty of holiness appear. The most important thing for them is the supreme knowledge of cleanliness which is next to godliness. The Bahá'í Revelation is in inculcating this lesson, and they are learning as fast as opportunity is offered to them. Bahá'u'lláh has said that cleanliness is the perfume of paradise!

2. The Story of the Dervish and his Resignation

While I was busy with my house-cleaning, the Master was dictating Tablets for the Oriental believers. In the morning he came to see the pilgrims, but most of them were not yet up. However, within a few minutes they were in his presence. He asked the cook what he was going to prepare for us. The cook did not know and 'Abdu'l-Bahá demanded from one after the other what they liked, and finally the decision was made. Then the Master told us the story of a Dervish, as follows: When Bahá'u'lláh with his family were leaving Baghdad, a Dervish begged 'Abdu'l-Bahá's permission to join the party. He was told that the trip would be most difficult, but the Dervish was willing to accept all manner of hardships, so he traveled with the party as far as Constantinople. Then when they left for Adrianople, he stayed behind but joined them later, for having become accustomed to associate with the Bahá'ís, he could not live without them. In Adrianople, he rented a room in an adjoining Mosque with another friend, and for some time they lived together peacefully. One day the Dervish came to Bahá'u'lláh, saying: "My friend attacked me this morning and gave me a sound beating, but I said nothing. I was in a state of utmost resignation. Then after half an hour he returned, kissed my hands and said: 'Verily, you have attained the stage of great merit, you are now a saint.'" Bahá'u'lláh, listening with interest to this story, said laughingly: "if he beats you another time and you demonstrate such resignation, he may believe that you have attained the station of Prophethood."

3. 'Abdu'l-Bahá Amid the Roses

In the afternoon, we met 'Abdu'l-Bahá in a garden walking among the lovely roses. He was talking on the mission of the Manifestation of God.

Before sunset we went to a Bahá'í meeting in the house of Khurásání. They expected 'Abdu'l-Bahá but he did not come, because he was very tired on account of the activities of the day. In the evening a number of Arabs called on him in his own house. One of them had composed an eloquent poem in his honor and read it aloud. They stayed until twelve o'clock and went away impressed with his knowledge and wisdom.

4. 'Abdu'l-Bahá Raises the Call of the Kingdom.

In a Tablet revealed to the Persian believers he says:

> O ye friends of 'Abdu'l-Bahá:—It is now three years that, like unto a nestles and shelterless bird, I have been wandering through mountains and plains and flying over the wilderness and Sahara. I rested not one moment, neither did I tarry long anywhere. Constantly was I moving and traveling. The cry of the Kingdom of Abhá was raised and the Most Great Glad-tidings penetrated throughout those vast and remote regions. The Flag of the Cause of God was unfurled over every hill and waved over every country. As I was occupied day and night, spreading the world-consuming call of the Cause, I failed to correspond with the friends of the heart and the soul, but as soon as I returned to the Orient, notwithstanding my indisposition, I immediately started to correspond. For the utmost desire of my heart and spirit is to remember the believers and to mention the names of the friends, especially those who

have been at all times the objects of tests and who are submerged in the sea of trials; notwithstanding this, with infinite firmness and steadfastness, you withstood the attack of the waves, underwent bravely violent storms, and guided the Ark to the shore of salvation. Therefore I am greatly pleased and most satisfied with the believers of Bushruyih, Khayru'l-Qara and Faran and all those of Khurasan. I hope that in the future their flame of enthusiasm and the fire of their devotion may be enkindled more and more. Upon ye, and upon the maid-servants of the Merciful be Bahá'u'l-Abhá.

RAMLEH, EGYPT, AUGUST 9, 1913

1. The Bounties of God

No matter where we go and what we do, the protecting hand of God overshadows us. We are tenderly and wistfully taken care of by Him who rules the world of Creation. In His mighty grasp He holds the scepter of Guidance and in His hand. He carries the golden crown of the heavenly Glad-tidings. He illumines the hearts of the sincere ones with the light of Providence and summons all the nations to come under the Tent of His Mercy. He quickens the dead with the Breaths of the Holy Spirit and inspires hearts with divine Knowledge. He adorns the heavens with countless scintillating stars and commands the winds to blow from every direction. He causes the water to gush out of the adamantine rock and irrigates the soil with the rain of Reality. He reveals unto man the mysteries of His Kingdom and spreads abroad the vision of Paradise! Glory be unto Him for this Manifest Bestowal. Thanks be unto Him for this Evident Grace! Praise be unto Him for this spiritual outpouring!

His true servants adore Him under all conditions and circumstances. They obey His will and follow His commandments. They lose the self and attain to the station of renunciation. The love of humanity flows through the stream of their lives. They become the spiritual springtime which are followed by no autumns. They become the guardians of the rights of men. They are the angels of the Supreme Concourse, the fruitful trees of the Orchard of the Almighty and the singing nightingales of the meadow of Truth. It is the hope of every lover of humanity to become the center of these merciful qualities, to attract these praiseworthy attributes, to surround himself with these wonderful virtues and to reflect the rays of the sun of righteousness!

2. A Tablet for the Believers of Isfahan, Persia

A Tablet was revealed yesterday for the believers of Isfahan. Isfahan is my native home and I have a secret predilection for that place. The Tablet is through Sayyid Asadu'lláh, a native of that city who is a fine young man amongst the present pilgrims. After having a most memorable visit of many days with the Blessed Master, he leaves tomorrow via Constantinople for his home. Here is the translation of the Tablets:

> O ye friends of 'Abdu'l-Bahá! His Honor Sayyid Asadu'lláh arrived in Alexandria and a meeting was obtained. When he received permission for his departure, he mentioned your names and asked for a Tablet. But 'Abdu'l-Bahá, like unto a bird who has been constantly flying for many days and nights is exhausted. He has not rested for one moment, and is in the utmost fatigue and weariness, to such an extent that he has not the endurance for writing even one word. Notwithstanding this, through the tremendous power of the Love of God and the rising of the waves of affection for the believers of God, I am thus engaged; so you may realize how this heart is attracted toward those blessed souls and is the captive of the memory of the friends.
>
> In short, it has been some time since, like unto a Breeze wafting, I have been traveling in the regions of the West, but under all conditions and circumstances, I have remembered the friends of the East. At every moment, the spirit enjoyed a new exhilaration, and often I regretted the fact that I was far from the opportunity of association with those faithful believers. I did not choose any plane as my shelter. One night I was crossing a mountain and spending the day on the plains and in

the flowerbeds. At one time I was traveling in the midst of the great ocean and at another, landing on the shore of a continent. Day and night I raised my voice and cried out in the name of His Highness the Almighty! Now at last I have reached Alexandria and have looked in the faces of the Oriental believers. Praise be to God that I beheld such pilgrims who are in the utmost of supplication and adoration of God. I have also remembered you. It is hoped that the Sun of Reality may so shine upon the East that the West may become illumined with one of its effulgent rays and that the friends of Persia may be the means of the union of the hearts of the people of other countries and arise for the guidance of the inhabitants of the earth. Praise be to God that the confirmation of the Blessed Perfection descends incessantly like vernal showers and that merciful reinforcements are constantly bringing assistance. Therefore, O ye believers of God, avail yourselves of this opportunity, be ye engaged in the enlightenment of souls and think ye of the unlimited illumination of your hearts. Enlighten the East. Perfume the West and let nostrils inhale the Fragrances.

Upon ye be Bahá'u'l-Abhá.

(Signed) 'Abdu'l-Bahá 'Abbás.

3. *Contrast between the Oriental and Occidental Houses*

This morning the Beloved paid us an early visit. He called each one by name and our hearts glowed with unchangeable love. He said to the pilgrims that it was the wonderful Love of God that gave him the impetus to write so many Tablets to the friends of Persia. Otherwise physically it would have been impossible. Then he said that he could not sleep last night, because he had been submerged in a sea of thought and reflection. He pointed out the contrast between the Oriental and Occidental houses by saying, that all the Oriental houses were enclosed within beautiful courts and gardens. If a person cannot sleep during the night, he can go out in the court, walk around quietly, commune with the stars, and pass the night in the open. But one cannot leave the Occidental houses except to go into the streets.

4. 'Abdu'l-Bahá Gives Money to the Poor

In the afternoon he returned and asked for Mírzá Munír. While he was standing in front of the house, an Arab stopped and begged for money to feed his children, because he was a stranger in the city. I wondered whether he was telling the truth, but the Master gave him one Majidi, which is quite a sum in this part of the world. Then he went into the garden nearby. For more than one hour he sat silently, his eyes half-closed; only now and then opening them to look at the flowers, and thus he remained in the garden until sunset.

RAMLEH, EGYPT, AUGUST 10, 1913

1. How 'Abdu'l-Bahá Dictates Tablets to His Friends in All Parts of the World

This morning I was called into the presence of the Beloved. He was very happy. He asked for the letters which have come from America and Europe. I returned home and brought a full-sized package. As soon as he started to dictate, and the words of wisdom like unto a sparkling stream flowed from his blessed mouth, he was a transfigured person. He sat immovable on the sofa, his eyes most of the time shut, but his heart a waving ocean of revelation. Now he revealed a Tablet to a believer in Constantinople, and again to a friend in Rangoon, India; Stuttgart and Switzerland, London and Paris, New York and Honolulu, Washington and Boston were represented. How wonderful and significant appears to me this golden network of spiritual correspondence, reaching to the different parts of the earth! This correspondence is not based upon any commercial or material scheme. It is the eternal plan of God, to diffuse the fragrance of the spiritual rose and scatter the rays of the Divine Sun! Every day an ideal Congress of religions and nations is held in the rather small room of the Beloved and he presides over the proceedings with a dignity and wisdom that is nothing short of miraculous. Some of the friends who became the recipients of the Tablets are as follows: Miss Beatrice Irwin, Miss Rhoda Nicols, Mrs. Isabel Fraser, Mr. Ch. Remey, Miss A. Boylin,

Miss O. Schwartz, 'Abbás Butt Ally, Mr. Ekstein, Madame d'Ange d'Astre, J. Miller, Dr. Skinner, J. Wieland, Miss Alma Knoblock, etc., etc. Toward the end, the Master was so moved that he got up from his seat and began to walk to and fro while continuing dictation. I tried to keep up with the rapidity of his uttered words. When I mentioned the name of one of the believers, his whole countenance changed, and he was very happy, saying that he loved him, because he was very sincere in the Cause. In the Tablet, addressed to this particular Bahá'í, he said:

> May His Holiness Bahá'u'lláh be thy Confirmer and Helper! May the Effulgence of the Sun of Reality be the light of thy path! May the sea of Divine Confirmation cast its waves over thee! May the cloud of Celestial Grace pour upon thee! May the Breeze of Providence be the cause of the fragrance of thy nostrils! May the treasury of the Kingdom be thy wealth! This is the prayer of 'Abdu'l-Bahá in thy behalf.

What a heavenly prayer! Then he revealed a Tablet, on the sinfulness of back-biting, evil-finding and gossip, which must be spread all over the Bahá'í world. Soaring again toward the spiritual realms of eloquence and pausing for a moment, he said, if these Tablets do not move and stir the hearts out of their sleep and do not spur them into activity, they are harder than stones; because in this condition of weakness, he was writing to them with such love and tenderness.

It was about 11:30 that I left his presence. In the afternoon he went to the rose-garden, and while sitting on the soft grass dictated many more Tablets to the Persian believers.

2. 'Abdu'l-Bahá Speaks on Theosophy

In the evening he came to our house. He sat on the veranda. Many believers were gathered around him. He spoke on the doctrines of the Theosophists, of his interview with Mrs. A. Besant in London and with other prominent Theosophists in the West, about the story of the boy who is being educated in Oxford to become the manifestation of God, and a most instructive exposition of the principles of reincarnation which was greatly beneficial to all. Mírzá Abú l-Fadl said afterward:

"I have read many books on this subject, but have never seen anywhere, such clear and lucid explanations."

RAMLEH, EGYPT, AUGUST 11, 1913

1. *The Spread of the Bahá'í Cause Similar to the Spreading of Early Christianity*

Three of our pilgrims, one from Isfahan another from Yazd and a third from 'Ishqabad, departed for their respective countries, carrying away the Glad-tidings of the Kingdom of Abhá. As they travel along, from country to country, before reaching their native lands, they will cheer many hearts, console many despondent spirits, teach many souls, and diffuse far and wide the fragrances of the Roses of Love and Affection. How exactly parallel is the promotion of this Movement to that of early Christianity! Wholehearted, spiritual, zealous men and women, without the expectation of any salary, are spreading the Cause throughout all the countries of the world! Their only reward is the good-pleasure of the Lord of Mankind. They are affected neither by the praise nor the blame of the people! They work for the sake of God. They are always in good humor, ever teaching their fellowmen the ways of charity and freedom, amity and concord. 'Abdu'l-Bahá sent for the pilgrims early this morning, so that he might speak to them words of blessing and comfort. He praised the steadfastness of the Persian believers before the executioner's sword and under the severest trials; how they danced with joy when they were surrounded by persecution, and how they faced martyrdom with benign faith and smiling countenances!

2. *'Abdu'l-Bahá's Tablets Are the Never-fading Roses of the Kingdom of Abhá*

Early in the morning I went down to the sea, and as I passed the house of the Beloved, I saw him walking in his room and talking to the Pilgrims who were about to leave. At four o'clock he sent for

Mírzá Munír. In the rose-garden nearby many Tablets were dictated for the Eastern and Western Bahá'ís. These Tablets carry with themselves, not only the ideal fragrances of the paradise of Abhá, but the perfume of the flowers before his loving vision. They have a special charm and significance to me and as I translate or read them, the beautiful rose-garden with its luxuriant verdancy and fragrant flowers passes before my sight, and I look upon each one of these Tablets as a spiritual rose, never-fading, imperishable, sent as a divine gift to the friends of God. These roses of the Kingdom of Abhá are being scattered all over the earth, to perfume the nostrils of mankind, not only in these days, but throughout the coming generations. Just think of 'Abdu'l-Bahá, visualize him in your mind! He is walking among the flower-beds, pausing here to pick a rose, there a violet, inhaling them with the sweetness of his spirit and dictating words of knowledge and wisdom!

3. The Most Great Sin Is Back-biting

Herein I translate the important Tablet on back-biting. It is written to Dr. M. G. Skinner of Washington, D.C.

> He is God.
>
> O thou my doctor!
>
> Thy letter was received. Thou hast written regarding thy aims. How blessed are these aims! Especially for the suppression of back-biting (gossip, fault-finding, etc). I hope that you may become confirmed therein; because the worst human quality and the most great sin is back-biting; most especially when it emanates from the tongues of the believers of God. If some means might be devised so that the doors of back-biting could be shut eternally and each one of the believers unsealed his tongue only for praise of the other, then the Teachings of His Holiness Bahá'u'lláh would be spread, hearts illuminated, spirits glorified and the human world attain to Everlasting Felicity.
>
> I hope that the believers of God will shun back-biting completely, (gossip-making and fault-finding) and each one praising the other cordially, and believing that back-biting is the cause

of divine wrath; that if a person back-bites to the extent of one word he may become dishonored amongst all people: because the most hateful characteristic of man is fault-finding. One must expose the praiseworthy qualities of the souls and not their evil attributes. The friends must overlook each other's shortcomings and speak only of their virtues—not of their faults.

It is related that His Holiness Christ—may my life be a sacrifice to Him—one day accompanied by His Apostles, passed by the corpse of a dead animal. One of them remarked: 'How putrid has become this animal!' The other exclaimed: 'How it is deformed!' A third cried out: 'What an odor! How cadaverous looking!' But His Holiness Christ said: 'Look at its teeth! How white they are!' Consider that He did not look at all for the defects of that animal, nay rather, He searched well until He found its beautiful white teeth. He observed the whiteness of the teeth only and entirely overlooked the deformity of its body, the dissolution of its organs and its evil odor!

This should be the attribute of the children of the Kingdom!

This should be the conduct and the manner of the real Bahá'ís!

I hope that all the believers will attain to this lofty station. Upon thee and upon them be Bahá'u'l-Abhá.

(Signed) 'Abdu'l-Bahá 'Abbás.[21]

Toward evening the Beloved called at the apartment of Mírzá Abú'l-Fadl and finding there a few young Arab students, spoke to them on general subjects. For the present Mírzá Abú'l-Fadl is writing a book which when finished may be considered the chief work of his busy and eventful life.[22]

---

21. An edited version of this translation appears in *Star of the West*, Vol. IV, No. 11, p. 192.
22. A reference to *Radáu'l-Ruddud*, which was intended to be a thorough response to various polemics against Mírzá Abú'l-Fadl's earlier masterpiece, *Kitáb Fará'id*. Unfortunately with the author's passing, it remained incomplete and when sent to 'Ishqabad for it to be completed by his nephew, the text was lost. Only the Preface of the book in 18 pages is extant.

RAMLEH, EGYPT, AUGUST 12, 1913

1. The Bahá'ís Must Start a Forward Movement of Teaching

This is the time when the believers must give attention to the spreading of the Teachings among those people who have not yet heard of this Cause. There should be a general forward movement in all the Bahá'í Assemblies. The supreme question of spreading the Lights of the Kingdom of Abhá must gain the upper hand. 'Abdu'l-Bahá desires to see the results of the work of the friends. We must recruit new soldiers for the Army of Abhá. The friends should avail themselves of this great opportunity. They should loosen the tongues of eloquence and invite all men to the heavenly Banquet. They should speak with fire and let the spirit of God inspire their hearts. 'Abdu'l-Bahá is crying: Teach, Speak, Spread the Message! Can we remain indifferent, speechless, and voiceless? No! A thousand times No! Why has God given us tongues? To speak about his Grace, to proclaim His Manifestation, to raise our voices in public meetings and gathering-places, to widen the circle of human thought and to teach His Principles.

Because 'Abdu'l-Bahá traveled throughout America and Europe, the zeal and enthusiasm of the Persian teachers have been increased a hundred times. We have seen him with our own eyes, heard his teachings with our own ears. The slogan of every Bahá'í must be: "Let us teach the people brotherhood and tolerance!"

2. Mrs. Getsinger and Her Forthcoming Trip to India

This morning the Beloved sent for me. He was feeling well. Mrs. Getsinger was called into the room and the plan of her journey to India discussed. Since her arrival she has been living with 'Abdu'l-Bahá's family which is presided over by the Greatest Holy Leaf! Then the Beloved dictated a few Tablets and cablegrams. In the afternoon he passed by the house, followed by Shoghi Effendi, and asked for Mírzá Munír. Many Tablets were revealed in the garden. No one is allowed to go there during these hours unless permitted by him. One of the Tablets is to Mr. Ekstein of Stuttgart. He is a fine Bahá'í and translated the words of the

Master on many occasions during our trip to that city. The Tablet is as follows:

3. 'Abdu'l-Bahá Praises the German Bahá'ís in Tablet

O thou illumined man!

The days that I spent with thee in Stuttgart I shall never forget, for at all times we associated with the Assistance of the Breaths of the Holy Spirit. The power of Confirmation of His Holiness Bahá'u'lláh waved over those meetings, the lights of the kingdom shone forth from the horizon of Abhá, the invincible aids descended successively, the hearts were in the utmost joyousness, the spirits were exhilarated with the Divine Glad-tidings, and each one of the believers like unto a candle. On this account those days will never be forgotten.

Now it is my hope that after my departure; the Fire of the Love of God may flame forth with greater intensity, and that thou mayest sing a heavenly melody in every gathering.... I am most grateful and satisfied with the believers of Stuttgart. Truly I say that they are blessed souls. I will never forget them for one moment. The thought of them makes me very happy....

RAMLEH, EGYPT, AUGUST 13, 1913

1. The Story of the Man Who Made It Appear That He Was a Bahá'í in 1830, while the Movement Began in 1844

This morning the Master came in to inquire about the health of his servants. We responded joyfully to his humorous questions about fasting, eating, etc. After walking a few minutes he sat down and corrected the Tablets which had been dictated during the last two days. Then, in connection with his remarks about those persons who profess to be Bahá'ís because they expect some material reward, he related the following story:

"When the Bahá'ís were living in Baghdad there was a very prominent man who used often to come to see Bahá'u'lláh. He sat in His Presence with the greatest respect and listened attentively to his utterances. One day he tried to express his faith and belief in the Cause with all apparent sincerity and devotion. 'Yes, my Lord!' he concluded his talk, 'I thoroughly believe in this Cause. In the year 1830, one or the great teachers of this Movement passed by our city. I met him and he talked with me for several days and his words convinced me of the validity of this revelation. From that time on I have been a believer.'"

Then 'Abdu'l-Bahá laughed, saying, that this man did not know that the movement was inaugurated only in 1844 and so, in order to convince Bahá'u'lláh of the genuineness of his belief, he had set the time of his acceptance 14 years before the declaration of the Báb!

2. The Story of the Fifteen Robbers of Baghdad

At another time there were fifteen robbers in Baghdad. They raided many houses during the nights. The government and police were unable to find their whereabouts. One night they robbed the stores of several Persian merchants and according to the law of capitulation, the Persian Consul did his best to catch them. This Consul was, however, very greedy and avaricious, and he thought more of his personal profit than of finding the robbers and of giving back to the merchants their stolen goods. One morning 'Abdu'l-Bahá arose early and came out of the house. He saw in the court fifteen uncouth men waiting for him. Their spokesman told him that they were the band of robbers and that in order to escape the wrath of the Consul and his rapacity, they had come to take refuge under the shelter of Bahá'u'lláh and become Bahá'ís. 'Abdu'l-Bahá inquired about their whereabouts, gave them a little advice, and sent them away. Then knowing that if the goods were taken by the Consul, they would never be returned to their owners, he sent one of the believers to the chief of the band, requiring him to return everything, which he did without any protest. The merchants in turn, received quietly all their stolen goods without the mediumship of the Consul. But when the Consul heard of 'Abdu'l-Bahá's part in this affair, he was very wroth, because the matter had been taken out of his jurisdiction. He had expected to fatten his pockets, and not succeeding in this he forever afterward tried to injure the Bahá'ís on every occasion.

Among these robbers there was one by the name of Haydar. As a punishment for his former raids, the government had cut off both his hands. He was, notwithstanding this handicap, the cleverest of them all. One morning, a Bahá'í came to 'Abdu'l-Bahá, saying that last night his money which was sewed in a special pocket of his vest had been stolen. He did not know how, and he wondered who had done the deed. 'Abdu'l-Bahá told him to go and bring his vest, and when it was before him, he observed that the pocket was not ripped with a knife, but chewed to pieces with teeth. He did not say anything but sent for Haydar. When Haydar arrived, 'Abdu'l-Bahá told him: "Thou hast stolen the money of this poor man. Give it back to him." He tried to deny it, but 'Abdu'l-Bahá said: "Look at this vest! Thou hast chewed the pocket with thy teeth; it is not torn with a knife as any other man would have done were he in possession of his hands." No, he would not confess that he had stolen it. Then 'Abdu'l-Bahá ordered the bastinado to be brought in. After receiving a few lashes on the soles of his feet, he brought out of his pocket the small bundle of money and gave it to its owner. Then he was released.

3. 'Abdu'l-Bahá Talks about Helping the Poor and Needy

Before 'Abdu'l-Bahá's departure for America, the poor of all nationalities came to him, Persians and Turks, Arabs and Syrians, Greeks and Europeans, belonging to all religions and faiths. He gladly helped everyone without any distinction for race or color; but this year he could not give to the same extent, because the expenses of his travels in America and Europe had totaled a great sum. Even now he was under a heavy debt. However, although these difficulties existed, he would not send one man away without satisfying him and relieving his immediate needs. The worst condition in life is, when one is in urgent want of the means of livelihood. It is indeed very sad when a person begs for assistance to be unable to lighten his burden, or to contribute anything toward his relief.

4. The Story of the Mullá and the Questioner

Then, changing the mode of his expression, he said:

One day a layman went to a Mullá and asked several questions. The Mullá did not answer him. The man then said: "Have you not read in the Qur'an 'You must not turn away a questioner?'" The Mullá in turn rejoined: "Hast thou not also read the injunction in the same holy book, 'Give thou not thy possessions to the fools.' Now, my possessions are the ideals of knowledge and of Truth. I must protect them from intruders."

Then he interpreted a dream of Mírzá 'Alí-Akbar and left our precincts to attend to the many works of charity which call for his personal attention.

5. Arrival of a New Pilgrim

A new pilgrim arrived today from Beirut. He is an old Bahá'í and has a most interesting history. He has a limited education, but out of the clearness of his heart and the beauty of his faith, he interprets the verses of the Qur'an and can carry on most instructive discussions on spiritual subjects. The Master has expressed a wish that he should interpret in his presence, one Qur'anic verse every day.

6. With 'Abdu'l-Bahá in the Rose-garden

When I returned from Alexandria in the afternoon, I was told that the Master had asked for me. I went immediately to the garden. Seeing me standing near the door, he permitted me to enter and to take a seat. He was walking in the avenue fronting a most charming rose-garden and dictating Tablets to Mírzá Munír. Shoghi Effendi was there also. For nearly three hours, the limpid stream of revelation flowed to irrigate the parched ground of hearts in distant climes! Just as the sun was sinking behind the western horizon, he revealed a most touching prayer. His voice was like the music of the spheres, now chanting in a clear rich voice, now in a low, sweet undertone. The effect made us forgetful of everything. The dusk of the evening, the murmur of the breeze through the roses and trees, the unbroken calmness of the atmosphere, the spiritual beauty of the presence of the Master, and then as we looked up, the twinkling stars all combined to weave around our hearts a garland of spiritual enchantment! We were in reality worshiping the glorious King of Kings in the holiest moment of our lives! The prayer was a supplication to the throne of the Almighty for the purification of souls and the spiritualization of hearts—in order that men might sing the praises of their Lord and cause the ringing cries of Yá Bahá'u'l-Abhá to ascend from their meeting places to the Supreme Concourse.

As we left the garden, I carried with me that wonderful prayer of the Beloved! On the wings of Light it had ascended to the throne of the Almighty and had been accepted by the Ruler of Mankind.

RAMLEH, EGYPT, AUGUST 14, 1913

1. Bahá'í Schools in Kashan and Tehran and Their Examinations

Yesterday afternoon the Master read to us a letter received from Kashan, giving the details of the examinations of the children of the Bahá'í school in that city. He said that there were more than 700 persons present on Commencement Day and that all the pupils examined came out with flying colors. The school has become a credit to the Bahá'í community and everyone speaks about it. Another letter from Tehran was given us by the Master to read. It contained a graphic description of the examinations at the school of Tarbiyat. Thirty students together with the President of the school and the teachers presented themselves before the Board of Examiners, appointed by the government in the College of Dáru'l-Funún. Twenty-one out of the thirty pupils received their diplomas. This shows the earnestness of these students of Tarbiyat and their thorough education. After this examination which lasted several days, the Faculty of the school gave a public reception, to which more than 2000 persons were invited. The school of Tarbiyat is well known throughout Persia as a Bahá'í institution. It ranks high for its educational standard, and its Branch for the girls is headed by Miss Lillian Kappes.

Notwithstanding many stumbling blocks in its path, it has been slowly, but surely forging ahead. Its progress and steady advancement are very dear and near to the heart of 'Abdu'l-Bahá. He hopes that it may become a wonderful influence for culture and refinement throughout Persia; and those friends in America who are assisting it are helping the Cause in an unqualified manner. Not only the American friends have realized the importance of this fact, but also the Indian Bahá'ís in their far-off country.

2. *The Orient-Occident Unity*

In a Tablet revealed two or three days ago to the believers of Rangoon 'Abdu'l-Bahá says:

> Whatever contribution you may send to the school of Tarbiyat is in the estimation of 'Abdu'l-Bahá, most acceptable. In this we observe the aim of God working for the advancement of public education in Persia. The Western friends have rendered a worthy service to the Tarbiyat School through the instrumentality of the Orient-Occident Unity in Washington. It is hoped that this channel of philanthropy will be continually widened, its various interests solidified, its annual scholarships kept up and increased in number, and its wholesome, disinterested influence expanded. Inasmuch as it is a universal undertaking, and every universal undertaking is divine in origin, its activities will continue. God has confirmed this work in many ways and will confirm those who are serving it.

3. *'Abdu'l-Bahá Praises Mrs. Goodall and Mrs. Getsinger*

In the afternoon he passed by the house. He called me to go with him. In reply to a cablegram to Mrs. Goodall, he had received an answer which had made him very happy. He said that she was his beloved, heavenly daughter, that she was the daughter of Bahá'u'lláh, ever serving the Cause with a rare faithfulness and magnanimity. He also spoke very lovingly about Mrs. Getsinger.

He said that if Mrs. Getsinger conducts herself according to his instructions, she shall move India and teach many souls. Her words are endowed with Spiritual efficacy. Severed from all else save God she must go to India, relying upon Bahá'u'lláh for Confirmation.

I gave the Master a list of the names of the Bahá'í Assemblies of America and Europe requesting him to reveal a Tablet for each assembly.

At the gate of the garden, two poor Persians were standing. He told me to bring them in, and finding that he did not have money, he borrowed two English pounds from a believer, and gave one to each.

4. Difference between 'Abdu'l-Bahá and Others

In reference to a certain individual, he said that the difference between himself and many men is that he wishes the welfare of the people for their own sakes, and without any ulterior motive. He desires that every one of the friends may shine like unto the sun. Others may love you, but it may be for some purpose. They may love you because they expect some day or some time to receive a reward from you; but 'Abdu'l-Bahá expects no reward. There are some people who are submerged in mud, yet they believe that they are world-illuminating suns. He wishes to free them from this water and clay, clear their wings from these impediments, but they cry out: "No, No, we are suns and stars; we are not in need of thy education," Notwithstanding this, he must open the way for their freedom.

5. 'Abdu'l-Bahá and Three Roses

Then he walked toward the end of the garden and spoke with the gardener. The latter picked three roses, one white, one pink and one red, and offered them to the Master, a beautiful symbol to those who know the meaning and significance of each color. With these roses in his hand, he faced the setting sun—the horizon was suffused with purple and crimson. For a long time he looked toward the West, as though expecting to see the sun rise from that direction. He was in deep thought. Without a word he left the garden and we followed him.

RAMLEH, EGYPT, AUGUST 15, 1913

1. *How Are You Today? (not that interesting)*

How are you today? Are you happy? Are you glad because you are living in this unparalleled cycle of the Lord? Are you facing the world and its puzzling problems this morning with courage and enthusiasm? Are you going to make another heart happy beside your own? Will you open wide the window of your soul? Is the meadow of your life verdant? Will you continue to be hopeful and optimistic? Will you dedicate yourself anew to the service of your fellow men? Are you feeling the whir and stir of the new dawn? What will you do next to benefit mankind? What kind of thoughts and ideals will you hold in the secret chambers of your minds? Will they be exalted and lofty? Will they be humanitarian and disinterested? Let us on this day make a new resolution. Let us stand up and with a radiant faith proclaim the Cause of God.

2. *Talk on Religion and Atheism by an Illiterate Bahá'í*

This morning our new pilgrim, Hájí Muhammad from Beirut, carried on a long discussion with me.

"Religion and atheism; faith and agnosticism are like two streams which have been flowing from unknown sources since the genesis of mankind. The former is sweet and the latter is bitter. When the stream of religion becomes active, the stream of atheism is dried up; therefore the fresh stream of faith must ever be strong and aromatic, in order to consume the bitter stream of unfaith which is tasteless. In this day Bahá'u'lláh from the inaccessible heights of the mountains of revelation has sent down upon the valley of humanity fresh and sweeping torrents of faith to swell the volume of the stream of religion, and to irrigate the network of the brooks of materialism. Each Bahá'í is a new torrent and must roar with the power of reality. This stream of truth is greater than an ocean. It clears the path from all thorns and thistles and leaves behind it culture and civilization."

To hear from the tongue of a simple man such a dissertation was an extraordinary thing.

3. 'Abdu'l-Bahá Sends His Secretaries to Nouzha Park

At 3 o'clock Bashír told Mírzá Mahmúd and me that according to the wish of 'Abdu'l-Bahá, Shoghi Effendi would take us, this afternoon, to the famous Park of Alexandria. I welcomed this invitation, because I had been looking forward to the day when I could see this public garden. We took the electric car for Alexandria then another one through the city. The park has a fine gate, and as one enters, one finds shady, inviting avenues on every side. There are many animals, and a part of our time was spent in watching them. The flower-beds are laid out very artistically, there is a lake and many small reservoirs of water in which goldfish disport themselves with great abandon. Tall palm trees, at the top of which many clusters of green dates are hanging, lend a charming effect. It was about sunset when we left the Park, having thoroughly enjoyed the scenic beauty and large green vistas. We walked back half the way, and then took the car.

4. Attending a Bahá'í Meeting with New Pilgrims

When we returned, the Master was talking to the friends. He told us to go with the rest of the believers to the weekly meeting in Hájí Khurásání's house. There we saw three other pilgrims from Cairo, Mírzá Abú'l-Qásim, El Yahou and Mírzá Javád. Later on three other Arab believers arrived to meet the Master, and so the gathering was enlivened by the presence of these newcomers. Tea was served, prayers were chanted, and different ones spoke.

5. 'Abdu'l-Bahá and the Khedive of Egypt

During our absence in the afternoon, Osman Pasha, one of the Ministers of the Khedive, called on the Master conveying the loving greetings of the Ruler of Egypt and his longing to meet him. The date was then fixed for the afternoon of August 17th. His Highness the Khedive is now staying in Alexandria. His summer resort is near Ramleh. He lives in one of his palaces fronting the sea called Raas-ottin. The Khedive is friendly to the Bahá'í Movement and has special regard for the Master. It may be that history will record that he is one of the few Oriental Rulers who has received 'Abdu'l-Bahá with due honor.

6. A Sweet Tablet to the Little Darling Mona

While we were walking through the Garden of Nouzha, the Beloved was dictating beautiful Tablets to Mírzá Munír in another garden in Ramleh. One of these Tablets is to the little daughter of Mrs. Theodora de Bons whose husband is a dentist in Cairo. Now all three are on a vacation in Switzerland. Her name is Mona; so in this delightful manner the Master begins the Tablet:

> O thou my darling little Mona! Thy tiny eloquent letter was received and thy sweet dear thoughts became known to me. Rest thou assured that I shall behold thy charming, lovely face, and from thy dainty mouth shall hear a wonderful melody and song in glorification, thanksgiving and praise of the Almighty!
> Upon thee be Bahá'u'l-Abhá.
>
> (Signed) 'Abdu'l-Bahá 'Abbás.

RAMLEH, EGYPT, AUGUST 16, 1923

1. 'Abdu'l-Bahá Writes to a Hindu Bahá'í

May I be permitted to start the day's record with a Tablet revealed to an Indian Bahá'í in Rangoon, who has translated into the Hindustani language the holy books of the Íqán, the Seven Valleys and the Hidden Words? His name is 'Abbás Ally Butt Cashmirce. Mr. Jos. Hannen, of Washington, D. C., had forwarded a copy of a letter written by him to the Master and the following is an answer to it:

> He is God!
>
> O thou 'Abbás of 'Abdu'l-Bahá! O thou namesake of 'Abdu'l-Bahá!
>
> The letter that thou didst write to Mr. Joseph Hannen was forwarded by that beloved person to me. Couldst thou realize what an ecstatic condition was obtained through the reading of thy letter, unquestionably thou wouldst become enkindled

like unto a candle. Like unto the moth thou wouldst burn thy wings and even as the nightingale thou wouldst break forth into songs of thanksgiving and glorification.

I love thee, and my heart and soul obtain the utmost joy and fragrance when I remember thee. I hope that thou wilt become assisted in rendering mighty service.

It is my desire that thou wilt become confirmed and aided in the diffusion of the Fragrance of God and in the spreading of the Tablets and Holy words.

Convey to all the friends the wonderful, Abhá greetings. Upon Thee be Bahá'u'l-Abhá!

(Signed) 'Abdu'l-Bahá 'Abbás.

2 El Yahou Arrives from Cairo

One of the pilgrims—El Yahou, an old man—had brought with him from Cairo a bouquet of fragrant white flowers and six white fezes for the Master. He stayed with us last night and kept our party in a good humor until very late. In the morning he wanted the flowers and fezes to be taken to the Master, which I did with great pleasure. I knocked at the door, and the beloved opened it. He took the bundle out of my hand and told me that he would send for him in a few minutes.

3. 'Abdu'l-Bahá Dictates Tablets in the Garden

In the afternoon after four o'clock the Beloved could be seen in the garden of roses, preparing spiritual bouquets to be forwarded to the Believers of the East and the West. May these heavenly roses perfume the nostrils of all mankind! May they scatter their aroma to all parts of the globe! May they refine the atmosphere of materialism and unbelief! May they dispel the clouds of superstitions and doubts! May they adorn the chambers and halls of the spirits and souls!

4. Walks and Bahá'í Reminiscences

Every night after dinner Mírzá 'Alí-Akbar and I take a long walk as far as Sidi Jaber. Arriving there, we sit in front of a Turkish Cafe facing the broad avenue. Round this cafe there are many palm trees. We watch the long streams of carriages and automobiles driving by from Ramleh to Alexandria, many of them carrying shrouded Turkish and Arab ladies of the social world going to theaters and places of amusement. Then we drink coffee, lemonade or sherbet, all for the sum of five cents. After half an hour's rest we walk back, talking now and then about America and the friends. These lovely walks in the moonlit Egyptian night are most attractive.

5. 'Abdu'l-Bahá Gives Persian Names to Two German and Austrian Bahá'ís Traveling in Persia

A letter from Mashhad stated that two European believers have arrived in that city, a German and an Austrian. The Master in answer wrote:

> Thou hast given the utmost praise to the two believers, German and Austrian. Go to Stuttgart and see with thine own eyes what is there! Those two blessed souls who are living in your midst are the samples of these other friends. Such persons have entered beneath the Tent of Providence in Germany, each one of whom sings like unto an ethereal Angel. Their hearts are attracted by the Love of God and their spirits rejoiced by the Glad-tidings of God! Exercise the utmost kindness and love toward these two holy souls who are with you. Give the name of Husayn to the German and Hassan to the Austrian. In these names there is a wisdom. You will become informed with their purport later.

6. The Believers must Summon the People to the Kingdom

In another Tablet he says:

> All the believers of God and the maid-servants of the Merciful must summon the people to the Kingdom and be the cause of the guidance of the inhabitants of the world. They must live and conduct themselves in such a manner that in sanctity,

prayerfulness and devotion they may become distinguished from the rest of mankind.

7. Acquire Complete Concentration

To the two French Bahá'ís who bade us farewell in Marseilles, 'Abdu'l-Bahá writes:

> Praise be to God that you have not forgotten the time of our meeting and that your hearts and souls are attracted to Bahá'u'lláh. I hope that you will obtain complete concentration of thought; so that you may have no idea and conception save Bahá'u'lláh. Then you shall make extraordinary progress, and the Confirmation of the Kingdom of God shall descend upon you. You shall develop a seeing eye and a heart overflowing with the Love of God. Your breaths shall have influence upon others and your tongues will become the interpreters of the holy Books. Therefore, strive as much as you can to attain to this station.

RAMLEH, EGYPT, AUGUST 17, 1913

1. 'Abdu'l-Bahá and the Khedive of Egypt

This was an important date in the Bahá'í calendar because 'Abdu'l-Bahá and the ruler of Egypt met each other for the second or third time. Beyond this bare announcement I have no other information. The Master may give us, later, an account of the meeting, and thus in our imagination we may construct a picture, or he may not divulge any of the details. None of the believers were with him. For the present it is enough to know that on this day, between three and six p.m., the sovereign of Egypt had the honor and privilege of talking with 'Abdu'l-Bahá.

2. A Traveling Companion for Mrs. Getsinger in Her Approaching Visit to India

I was given the utmost joy of standing in the presence of 'Abdu'l-Bahá this morning. The more you receive his benediction, the greater becomes your hunger.

Mrs. Getsinger was called in and the question of a traveling companion was discussed. Different names were mentioned, but no one measured up to the requirements of the Beloved. Then the name of Mrs. Isabel Fraser was presented. "Yes, yes," he exclaimed delightedly. "She is just the right person." He loves her very much, and he always desires to assist her in serving the Cause. Why did we not think of her sooner? She will be able to render a great service in India. She has no other thought except the Love of Bahá'u'lláh. Then he dictated a cablegram to be sent to her without delay, the contents of which are as follows:

> If possible leave immediately for Port Said. Wish send thee India for service. Cable Yazdí. 'Abbás.

3. Story of the French Ambassador and the Turkish Minister of Foreign Affairs about Christ's Resurrection

Between 6 and 7 the Beloved came to our house and stayed for more than an hour. He spoke of the enmity of the ignorant people in every age and cycle for the manifestations of God. This enmity comes through the accumulation of dogmas and traditions and from blindly following the religious leaders.

Some people, he told us, are like unto the spiders. The more you tear to pieces their cobwebs of imaginations and imitations, the greater will become their zeal to spin again. Once the French Ambassador at the Sublime Porte satirically asked Fu'ád Pasha, the Minister of Foreign Affairs: "How did Mohammed ascend to heaven according to your trustworthy tradition?" Fu'ád Pasha, realizing the scoffing tone of the Ambassador, cheerfully volunteered the answer by saying: "With the same ladder that your Lord Christ ascended to heaven after his resurrection." His Excellency could not say anything. This able answer seemed to silence him and put him "hors de combat."

Then 'Abdu'l-Bahá related several stories of the time of Bahá'u'lláh when he was in Baghdad. These stories entirely lose their beauty and charm if translated into English, because they are in accord only with the Oriental conception, and parts of them are masterful plays on words and their various shades of meanings, which can be enjoyed solely by the Persians. The Master knowing so well their nature, from time to time, supplies the demand and thus makes them more attracted to the Cause by his peerless witticisms. He had just come from his Interview with the Khedive, and as he was in such a delightful humor, I believe the meeting must have been very satisfactory.

I concluded the day with the translation of Tablets to the Persian believers:

4. The Principle upon Which 'Abdu'l-Bahá's Western Trip Was Based

Consider how 'Abdu'l-Bahá forgot every material thought and mention and turned his face toward the countries and empires, cities and villages, mountains and deserts of the West. Day and night he was engaged in teaching the Cause and conveying the message. The principle upon which his trip was based was this:

"O God, make all my ideals and thoughts One Ideal and One Thought, and suffer me to attain to an eternal unchangeable condition in Thy service!"

He sought no rest, neither did he breathe one breath of Comfort Notwithstanding the weakness of his constitution, the infirmity of his body and the nervous fever, every night, he was in a city and every day in a community. Although at times he was hardly able to speak, yet he delivered lengthy addresses. Working in this manner shall bear fruits.

5. America Cannot Be Compared to Europe

In another Tablet, he says:

> Praise be to God that this second journey is happily completed, and that from the West I have returned to the East. But this second voyage cannot be compared with the first European trip, because America cannot be compared with Europe. That country is another world; its inhabitants are another people; their capacities are receptivity of another type; therefore 'Abdu'l-Bahá found a vast arena, and an unlimited expanse and opportunity. In all the conventions and conferences he raised the clamor of Yá Bahá'u'l-Abhá, and caused the clarion of 'O

My Lord the Clement' to reach the Supreme Apex. From the infinite Bestowals of the Blessed Perfection I am anticipating the appearance of the results of this trip. I hope that this conduct of 'Abdu'l-Bahá will become an example for the believers; so that all of them may convey the message accordingly; be wanderers over deserts and mountains; seeking no ease or composure and taking their lives and spirits on the palms of their hands, and sacrificing them to the Blessed Perfection.

RAMLEH, EGYPT, AUGUST 18, 1913

1. 'Abdu'l-Bahá and His Attitude toward Humanity

The most significant Personality living in this age and generation is the Personality of 'Abdu'l-Bahá. Few souls in the history of mankind have been so successful in combining the harmonizing influence of the East and the West. Day and night he wields the scepter of spiritual powers. His gentle, loving Presence is felt in the remote corners of the earth. His unerring judgment reads the secret longings of the hearts. His knowledge spiritualizes the lives of men. His love ennobles every being. His sublime consciousness embraces each race and nation of the earth. His universal conceptions enkindle the fire of brotherhood; his divine mind grasps the plan of creation and its ultimate fruition. In his dealings with the people he is merciful. In his treatment of the poor he is generous. In his association with men he is helpful. In his intercourse with society he is democratic. In his contact with his enemies he is forgiving. In his attitude toward mankind he is a father. He loves all; He showers his mercy upon all; He exercises kindness toward all. 'Abdu'l-Bahá is the mystery of love but an open mystery. God in his wisdom is daily revealing the secret of this Love; so that we may learn more and more of its ineffable sweetness and thoughtful tenderness. His life is a living book of love in all its heights and depths; its ink has been the blood of the martyrs, its chapters the tragic lives of glorious souls; it is written with a pen made of precious stones on the pages of universal history. Who can measure the glorious possibilities of a life so complete as the life of 'Abdu'l-Bahá! He stands in the center of immensity. He voices the mysteries of eternity; he upholds the heavens of justice; he paves the path of the kingdom of God; he ushers in the dawn of the new era; he breathes a new spirit into dead bodies; he begems the firmament of the Cause with the radiant stars of praiseworthy virtues; he breaks the seals of the heavenly books; he fires hearts with the Flame of the Love of God; he sings the songs of the coming age; he calls all the inhabitants of the globe to spiritual solidarity and he spreads far and wide the Fragrance of the rose-garden of Abhá!

2. 'Abdu'l-Bahá and 'Abdu'l-Hudá, a Favorite of the Sultan

This morning 'Abdu'l-Bahá came to see us and stayed a long time. He spoke about a great Shaykh who lived in Constantinople and was a favorite of 'Abdu'l-Hamíd. His name was 'Abdu'l-Hudá. He tried his utmost to intrigue against the Master but failed to accomplish his purpose. After the declaration of the Constitution in Turkey the enemies of the Shaykh confiscated his property and reduced him to wretched poverty. This sudden change in fortune so deranged his mind that he died a year later. This man had thought that Sultan 'Abdu'l-Hamíd desired to send for the Master to come to Constantinople to fill a high position in the government, so he worked hard to poison the mind of the Sultan against the Beloved. The Master sent him a message to the effect that he could rest assured that 'Abdu'l-Bahá would not come to Constantinople, even if he were sent for. He was a humble servant of God. What connection between him and royalty? He loved God and could worship Him better in the solitude of his prison than amid royal splendor; nay rather, the latter would separate him from the Threshold of the Almighty.

In the afternoon while passing by the door of the House he called for Mírzá Munír to go to the garden and take down the dictation of holy Tablets. In the evening a number of the newly arrived pilgrims received permission to see him.

RAMLEH, EGYPT, AUGUST 19, 1913

1. The Coming of Isabel Fraser to Egypt

"Coming immediately, Fraser." The words danced before my eyes as the Beloved handed me the cable. In my heart there was gladness, on my face a smile of contentment. I looked up into the Countenance of the Master and saw that my elation was but a reflection of his own satisfaction. Such a Bahá'í is priceless. Well done good and faithful maid servant, you have made the heart of the Beloved very happy! You have won the ball of victory from the field of spiritual Glory! In the presence of the Master you have received a new baptism of fire and spirit. He will put in your hand the torch of guidance; on your lips the words of light; in your heart the symbol of life and he shall send you off with a new power, a new dedication, a new vision. May the Hand of God protect you throughout your voyage and bring you safely into the land of Egypt wherein the ideal Joseph lives! We are all gladness because you are coming and look forward to the day when we will again talk of holy and divine things as we were wont to do in London and Edinburgh, Bristol and Paris. You will be a welcome guest in the holy household. You shall have much to write for the Bahá'í world.

2. 'Abdu'l-Bahá Attends to His Mail

I stayed only a few moments in the presence of the Master this morning. He had sent for me to give me the above news. I took to him a big package of Tablets with their translations for the friends in America, and Europe. He himself attends to the final dispatching of the rather voluminous mail to all parts of the world. For the last few days his health has been very good and his food, although simple, is regularly served. He takes long walks either at early morning or in the late afternoon, and at such times he is always alone. Outwardly he is walking, but in reality he is thinking and communing with our Maker.

3. Thou Must Be Firm and Unshakable in Thy Power

In the afternoon I had again the good fortune of being summoned into 'Abdu'l-Bahá's room. A cable has been received from Doctor Getsinger saying that he was willing to obey the call and to come. Mrs. Getsinger was sent for and in the course of conversation the Beloved told her that she must be firm and unshakable in her purpose and never, never let any outward circumstances worry her. He was sending her to India to bring about certain definite results. She must enter that country with a never-failing spirituality; a radiant faith, an eternal enthusiasm, an inextinguishable fire, and a solid conviction—in order that she might achieve those services which were required of her. Let not her heart be troubled. If she goes away with this unchanging condition of invariability of the inner state, she shall see the doors of confirmation open before her face, her life will be a crown of heavenly roses and she shall find herself in the highest station of triumph. She should strive day and night to attain to this exalted state! Let her look at 'Abdu'l-Bahá! She does not know a thousandth part of the difficulties and seemingly insurmountable obstacles which daily arise before his eyes. He does not heed them. He is walking in his chosen highway. He knows his destination. Hundreds of storms and tempests may rage furiously about his head, hundreds of Titanic may sink to the bottom of the sea, mad waves may rise to the roofs of the heavens: all these will not change his purpose, will not disturb him in the least. He will not look either to the left or to the right. He is looking ahead. Far, far, away, piercing the impenetrable darkness of the night, past the howling winds, and the raging storms, he sees the glorious light beckoning to him. The balmy weather is coming, and the voyager shall land safely. Qurratu'l-'Ayn had attained to this supreme state when they brought to her the terrible news of the martyrdom of the Bábís. She did not waver; she also had chosen her path; she knew her goal. And when they imparted to her the news of her impending death, no one could see any trace of sorrow in her face; rather she was happier. Although she had never cared for dress, she wore on her supreme day her best white silk robe and most precious jewels and perfumed herself with the fragrant attar of rose. She hailed the chamber of death as a happy bride entering the nuptial bower of the bridegroom.

Then, turning his face to Mrs. Getsinger, he ended his talk by saying that she must attain to this lofty summit of unchanging Purpose. Like Qurratu'l-'Ayn nothing must shake her firm faith.

4. 'Abdu'l-Bahá and His Talk with Miss Hiscock

Miss Hiscock, who was with the Holy Family, was called in. The Master told her that he was well pleased with her. Her aim was to serve the Cause and the day was coming when he should command her to teach. She said:

"I have no other hope save this Cause and the love of 'Abdu'l-Bahá."

The Beloved answered that he knew, he knew.

Afterward he told me that Miss Hiscock's heart was very pure. She was very sincere.

Late in the afternoon he called on Mírzá Abú'l-Fadl and stayed with him for nearly one hour. He passed by our house but did not stay for tea. His spiritual figure saluting us remained with me all night as a heavenly picture of a divine being descended from on high.

RAMLEH, EGYPT, AUGUST 20th, 1913

1. Strange Customs in Different Countries Are Not Tokens of the Inferiority of the People

Instead of giving you extracts from the daily talks of 'Abdu'l-Bahá, often I am obliged to substitute them with extracts from Tablets, for only when I am called into his presence, or when he comes to see us am I able to give an account of what is passing. The rules of social intercourse are so different from those in America that we see 'Abdu'l-Bahá much more seldom than when we were traveling with him. We know well that no nation can ever claim to be perfect, but that each one according to its capacity and environment, has, and is contributing something to the upbuilding of a universal civilization.

2. On Divine Guidance from a Tablet of 'Abdu'l-Bahá

O ye blessed souls! In the world of existence no bounty remains eternal and permanent and no gift continues to be immutable save the Bestowal of 'Divine Guidance'! This is the everlasting Grace! Praise be to God that you have attained thereunto. Should you live thousands of years and unloose thousands of tongues in thanksgiving for this Grace, you would be unable to render adequate praise; for praise is limited but this Grace is unlimited. How many souls have longed to live in this Day, yet their hope was unrealized and how many thousands of people have undergone severe discipline, yet were deprived of the Day of the Promised One.

Consider what a Bounty God has conferred upon you! Without undergoing any hardships you have reached the goal and without traversing vast Saharas you have drunk from the ocean of sweet waters. Without any suffering you have tasted of the fountain of guidance! This is the great Bestowal if man can appreciate its value: otherwise in the estimation of the ignorant, Guidance and error are practically the same. A person who is not thirsty is unaware of the delicacy of sweet waters, likewise the salty ground does not absorb the outpourings of the vernal showers and the withered tree is unresponsive to the call of the rain from the cloud of spring.

Therefore thank ye God that you have received a goodly portion and have become the confidents of the mysteries of the Kingdom.

3. Lack of Trustworthiness

In a Tablet he says:

Untrustworthiness is a poisonous arrow which mortally wounds the heart, the soul and the spirit of 'Abdu'l-Bahá.

4. Persecutions in the Path of God

In a Tablet he says:

Praise be to God that you are soaring in the Divine rose-garden, have found your way to the Kingdom of Mysteries and have become the recipients of the Favors of His Highness the Incomparable One! On the other hand you have endured the ridicule of the ill-wishers; you have suffered sorely and have tasted the poison of the tyrannical serpents, but as this was in the path of the Glorious Lord, the venom became honey and the pain health. Look at the outcome of such events. These ordeals result in Divine Gifts. This blame and derision will be followed by praise, glorification and adoration. Ere long it will become evident and manifest.

5. Teaching the Cause

In a Tablet on Teaching the Cause of God, he says:

Be thou in a state of utmost joy and fragrance and render thanks unto the Forgiving Lord, that praise be to God, thou art victorious and triumphant and art speaking for the Glorification of His Highness the King of Mankind and that in conveying the message thou art striving and putting forth praiseworthy efforts. Know thou of a certainty that the authoritative Firman [royal mandate of the Ottoman sultán] is today revealed from the Kingdom of Abhá for those who teach the Cause. I hope that thou mayst become assisted in this and be a means for the guidance of innumerable people! This is the Divine Bestowal! This is the Eternal Honor! This is the Everlasting Life!

6. Faithfulness at the Holy Threshold

He writes:

I supplicate and entreat at the Threshold of the Blessed Perfection and beg for the Divine Friends infinite Bestowal and Grace: so that they may become confirmed in loyalty at the sanctified Threshold. May they remember His Bounties and Favors sacrifice their lives in His path and freely resign their possessions in the Highway of the Merciful One.

7. Arrival of a New Pilgrim

Today we welcomed another pilgrim from Tabriz His name is Hájí 'Abbás. He is a Turkish poet and does not speak Persian very well.

He is an old Bahá'í and has served the Cause for many years. He will stay for nine days. Generally all the pilgrims have permission to stay nine days after which they return to their native land.

We have heard from Haifa that Mrs. Stannard has arrived there from Port Said. In order to regain her health she may spend the rest of the summer. The Master was very anxious to know where and how she is, and the other day he sent her a loving message of inquiry through Miss Hiscock.

8. 'Abdu'l-Bahá's Photograph in Constantinople

Our new pilgrim told us that while he was walking through the streets of Constantinople he saw a photograph of the Master surrounded by a group of Western Bahá'ís, which was exhibited for sale in the window of a photographer. In the picture the believers held aloft the Greatest Name in their hands. Many people were buying copies. This is very significant, considering that in the same city lived the despot who imprisoned 'Abdu'l-Bahá in the fortress of 'Akká for more than forty years.

9. 'Abdu'l-Bahá Talks on His Meeting and Conversation with a Persian General in Paris

In the afternoon 'Abdu'l-Bahá walked in the garden and two of the friends who had just arrived from Cairo went there to see him. As I was returning from the Post Office, I passed by and observed him talking with much animation. Immediately afterward I was called into his presence.

After supper while I was sitting in my room, writing, the door opened and 'Abdu'l-Bahá came in I had neither my Tarboush [felt headdress] nor coat on and I jumped up from my seat confusedly. He walked toward the veranda and asked:

"Is there any one here?"

It was a typical Oriental night, very quiet and enchanting. In a little while the friends gathered around him. He asked questions about the believers of Cairo, and Mírzá Abú'l-Qásim of Shiraz answered them. In the course of his talk 'Abdu'l-Bahá said that in this day the greatness of the Bahá'í Cause is acknowledged by all people, even by outsiders. A few months ago in Paris one of the Sardars [noblemen] of Persia came to call on him. He told 'Abdu'l-Bahá the following story: When he was in London he was invited by one of the English Peers to a reception. There he met many members of the English Nobility with their wives and daughters. He was introduced to all and when they heard that he was a Persian, many came forward expressing the utmost delight in meeting a person who belonged to a race which had given 'Abdu'l-Bahá to the world. They asked him "Do you know 'Abdu'l-Bahá? Have you met him?" He noticed that the wife of his host instead of wearing precious stones on her fingers like the other women wore a solitary simple ring. He was a little surprised. He approached her, saying: "What is this stone?" She answered: "This is agate. Do you not know it?" He rejoined: "Yes, but why do you wear it?" "Upon this stone," she answered proudly, "is impressed the name of Bahá'u'lláh." The Persian General was ignorant of the teachings of this Cause and could not understand the significance of "Revelation." He could not comprehend how a man communicates with God. These subjects were beyond his mental capacity; neither should anyone try to teach him these things, because he had made up his mind not to understand them. However, he knew, because he had witnessed it with his own eyes that this Cause has become the means of the honor and glory of Persia throughout the civilized world. To this he would bear testimony to the end of his life!

The teachings of the Blessed Perfection are so humanitarian, 'Abdu'l-Bahá continued, that even the enemy testifies that they are the spirit of this age. For example, Bahá'u'lláh says: "O ye people of the world! Ye are the fruits of one tree and the leaves of one branch! Consort with the followers of all religions with joy and fragrance."[23] Throughout many cities of America and Europe, in

---

23. This exhortation appears in different forms in Bahá'u'lláh's writings and one instance it reads, "The utterance of God is a lamp, whose light is these words: Ye are the fruits of one tree, and the leaves of one branch. Deal ye one with another with the utmost love and harmony, with friendliness

churches and meetings, he declared these Teachings with a loud voice and there was not a single soul to contradict them. Then he gave a detailed account of the meetings in Washington, New York and San Francisco and ended his talk by saying, that this Blessed Cause has such great power that it shall, ere long, vanquish all opposition. We must live and act in such manner as not to lower the station of the Cause, but rather try by day and by night to raise its banner higher. The Blessed Perfection has given us wares which are eagerly sought on the marketplace of the world.

After a few moments of silence he departed but left us happy.

RAMLEH, EGYPT, AUGUST 21, 1913

This morning Shoghi Effendi came and told me that the Master was ready to receive me. Within a moment I was standing in his presence. He inquired about my health and asked how I was getting along with my fast. Yet eleven days remain to the month of Ramadan, after which the Muslim world will hold a natural Fete. Then he called in Lua Getsinger and inquired concerning the Cause in America. A cablegram has been received from Chicago about the re-election of the House of Spirituality. He said that there was no need for re-election at present. He told us that in the election of the members of the House of Spirituality no political tactics should enter. They must be free from self, nor anxious to further their own personal ambitions. The existence of the Spiritual Assembly is for no other purpose than to discuss those means which call further the promotion of the Cause; otherwise its non-existence is better than its existence. The members must not be opinionated but must devote their attention to the services of the people. The promotion of the principles of the Cause must be the uppermost idea in their minds. Nothing else will yield fruit. No secret canvassing will add to the luster of any

---

and fellowship;" (Bahá'u'lláh, *Epistle to the Son of the Wolf*, p. 14) one with another with the utmost love and harmony, with friendliness and fellowship" (Bahá'u'lláh, *Epistle to the Son of the Wolf*, p. 14).

person. The people must be free and untrammeled to choose whomsoever they want. As soon as political plans are introduced in the Cause, the spirit is killed. The apostles of Christ never devised any political schemes whereby to win the majority vote. They went out into the world and taught the gospel of light to all mankind. The result is that whenever we mention the names of John, or Peter or Matthew, a wonderful spirituality is obtained, hearts are inspired, and souls rejoiced. These disciples were not politicians; they were the harbingers of the Glad-tidings of the Kingdom. They did not know anything about elections, votes, initiative and referendum. They were filled with Christ. They knew Him only. Similarly this Cause is pure Spirituality. It deals with the moral aspect of humankind. The hearts of the believers must be fountains of the Love of Bahá'u'lláh. Freeing themselves from all withering restrictions, they should occupy their time with the promulgation of the word. They must love each other and banish all phantasms of suspicion and doubt.

Then he left the room and for a few moments I had time to speak with Mrs. Getsinger. She is most happy in her spiritual nest and is learning to chant many prayers of Bahá'u'lláh in the original.

In the afternoon for nearly two hours 'Abdu'l-Bahá dictated Tablets to Mírzá Munír in the garden, and when he passed by our house, he carried in his hand a bouquet of yellow roses.

In the evening some Arab friends called on him and he entertained them until midnight. When they left he was very tired but well. How glad we are when he is in good health.

RAMLEH, EGYPT, AUGUST 22, 1913

1. Story of the Woodcutter and His Wife

'Abdu'l-Bahá told us three stories about Baktashis who belong to a religious sect in Turkey. I am inclined to report them as the Master has in each case been a direct factor in them.

When the Bahá'ís were staying in Adrianople there was a Baktashi who lived close by them. Professionally he was a wood-chopper, socially he was a wit. Once he became severely ill and was on the eve of departure from this world. Becoming acquainted with this fact, 'Abdu'l-Bahá called on him. He was lying on a low, uncomfortable cot, and his old wife was sitting beside it with the marks of solicitude and care on her wrinkled face. Suddenly she started to speak, addressing her husband: "Thou art going to get well very soon. This sickness shall pass away and thou wilt be strong. Oh, my beloved! I am praying to Allah for thy speedy recovery. May Allah hear my prayers!" The sick man, as though pulling himself out of a heavy drowsiness, half-opened his eyes and said: "What can I do even if I get well? I am tired of the world and want to leave it, my dear. Oh! I am so weary, so weary." And he closed his eyes. The wife, with much agitation declared: "Oh no, no! May Allah never bring that black day! My darling! Thou wilt gain back thy health. Together we will go into the garden and there eat all kinds of fruits. Hand in hand we will walk through the woods and listen to the songs of the birds. Yes, yes, I will nurse thee back to health, oh thou, the apple of my eye!" The sick man, without opening his eyes, and seemingly with much struggle, answered her back—"Oh my wife, be silent! Nothing shall happen if I get well, only this: I have to chop ten or twenty or thirty more loads of wood. That's all. Have I not cut enough already? Oh, let me die!" In this world we are all more or less wood-choppers. If we are attacked by illness and survive it, we have to work a little longer, chop a few more loads of wood, and the world will go on as before.

2. Story of the Sinner and the Mullá

There was another Baktaski who, in his younger days, was an officer in the Turkish government. This man became very sick, and the members of his family had summoned a Mullá to his bed. Then 'Abdu'l-Bahá called on him and they asked the Mullá to pray that God might forgive his past sins before his death. After the performance of many ceremonials, the Mullá, in his most solemn voice, told the patient to repeat the formula: "Oh, God! I have sinned much. Confer upon me thy forgiveness." The sick man did not answer. The Mullá repeated the formula over and over, but to no effect. Finally the patient, getting tired with this repetition, turned his eyes to the Mullá and said with earnestness: "Man! for many years I have sinned against God and his servants. I have ransacked houses, orphaned children, burned hearts and committed all kinds of iniquities. Is the government of God so childlike as to forgive all my past sins by the repetition of a mere formula? Is God's system of dispensing justice so loose? Be gone, thou ignorant Mullá! Thou art telling me all these things to get ten Piasters as thy fee. Come, come, my friends, give him some money and let him depart quickly from my presence. He is a Satan and a tempter!" Then the Mullá left the room in haste, and when 'Abdu'l-Bahá was alone with him, the man fell on his knees, and from the depths of his heart, cried out: "Oh Lord! Oh Lord! I am a real sinner and thou art the just God! beg Thy Mercy! I have committed many sins. I have not done that which Thou hast commanded me and have practised those things which Thou hast made unlawful. With humility and contrition I am standing in Thy Presence. Do with me whatsoever Thou willest!" 'Abdu'l-Bahá was much affected by this outpouring of sincerity and departed, praying that his supplication might become acceptable at the Threshold of the Almighty.

3. Story of Baktashi and of His Strange Death amid the Laughter of His Friends

Facing the house of 'Abdu'l-Bahá in Adrianople there was a cafe. Here every day sat a retired officer of the Turkish Army belonging to the Baktashi's sect. The Baktashis are always on good terms with the Bahá'ís. They are a peaceful people. This retired soldier received a pension of 5 Piasters (25 cents) a day from the government. Every morning he would come and take a chair in front of the cafe, and order a cup of coffee. Then the people would gather around him and listen with delight and laughter to his stories until noon. At that hour he would call the waiter and give him five cents to buy him two loaves of bread, two rolls of roast-meat and a dish of salad. Then he would ask for a clean table and use his neat handkerchief as a tablecloth. Every day he invited one of the habitués of the cafe to lunch with him.

"Come here, my friend!" he would say placing a chair on the other side of the table, and leaving before it a loaf of bread, with one of the roast-meats. "Come and be my guest today!" Then he would commence to eat. Every mouthful that was taken was followed by the short sentence, "Oh God! I thank Thee! How delicious is this lunch!" till it was finished. Then again, he would start his conversation, always tempered with sharp wit and the joy of living.

From time to time he would come to the Mosque of Sultan Suleiman where the Governor and the officers would gather about him to pass a pleasant hour. He would keep them roaring with laughter over his stories. One day, when 'Abdu'l-Bahá was also present, the Baktashi entered with a mat under his arm. Laughingly he saluted every one and said, "Today I am going to start on a long journey; therefore, I beg you to forgive all my past shortcomings!" "Art thou going to Baghdad?" one asked. "Further! much further!" "Surely to China?" "Very much further." Then no doubt to Australia?" 'Still further." All this time everybody laughed because they thought that he had a joke up his sleeve. "Please, please," he pleaded, "I beg you to forgive me. Say that you do!" In order to humor him, they said: "All right, we forgive thee!" Then he said: "I am now happy. I will also forgive you, my good friends!" Then he walked toward the court of the Mosque; spread on the ground half of his mat, laid himself down and covered his body with the other half. The spectators, thinking that they had reached the climax of the joke, laughed uproariously. Five minutes passed—no movement; ten, fifteen minutes, half an hour, no sign of life. The time grew heavy and strained. They looked at each other, with wonder in their eyes. Then laughing and shrugging their shoulders, they left their places and gathered around the mat. One of them, on tiptoe, cautiously lifted one corner. Wonder of wonders! The Baktashi had breathed his last. Then these men carried him on their shoulders laughing and singing, took him to the undertaker laughing, washed his body laughing and buried him with roars and thunders of laughter. It was a most phenomenal event! This Baktashi used to call on 'Abdu'l-Bahá. He had heard about Bahá'u'lláh and knew something concerning the Cause. The believers asked him several times to call on the Blessed perfection, but he always refused, saying: "How can I, the essence of sin, stand in the Presence of the Essence of Holiness! I am not worthy of this privilege. Whenever I find that I have deserved such an honor, I will go; but not now, not now!" Thus this good man lived and died in happiness.

4. 'Abdu'l-Bahá Goes to the Mosque and Gives Money to the Poor

It was about noon when the Master passed by our house and called for Mírzá 'Alí-Akbar to follow him. When Mírzá 'Alí-Akbar returned he told us that as there was a great festival at the Mosque of Sidi Jaber, the Master had been invited to be present. The Mosque was most beautifully decorated with flags and draperies. The Khedive was there. After the ceremonies, 'Abdu'l-Bahá came out and all the poor—men, women and children—gathered around him with their tattered garments and dusty appearances. He placed money in their hands, patting each on the shoulder and cheering everyone with his loving glances.

About four o'clock he went to the garden, but this time all alone.

Today I received letters from our American friends. I read them with much pleasure, and their contents will be presented to the Master at the first opportunity! May this link of spiritual correspondence bring the East and the West closer together!

RAMLEH, EGYPT, AUGUST 23, 1913

1. The Bahá'ís Must Embody Their Teachings in Their Lives

The Bahá'í Movement has come into the world principally as a Cause of Love, Spirituality, Unification, Reformation, Reconciliation, Universal Peace, Idealism, International Language, Unity of Religions, General Education, Brotherhood and Celestial attributes which will contribute toward the Union of the Orient and the Occident. The inevitable conclusion is that those who call themselves Bahá'ís must embody these principles in their lives; so that mankind may discern with their own eyes the concrete, spiritual results of the Bahá'í teachings and arise to spread them more universally. We all desire to see our ideals realized in a human being. If we admire courage, we would like to see this quality in a hero. If we love, we consider it a high privilege to behold this attribute manifested in a person. In brief, we are hungering for results.

2. The Story of the Man Who Did Not Know the Window in His Own Room

The other day Mírzá Munír told us a story which will illustrate this point. There was a young man in Beirut who worked as a waiter in a restaurant. For some time he had lived in a small room on the top of a house. He worked all day and returned to his room at night. One day he met an old friend of his on the street, who had just arrived from his native town. "Where are you going to live?" he inquired.

"I am at this very moment looking for a hotel."

"Oh, no! Don't go to a hotel. Come and be my guest."

After some insistence the invitation was accepted.

"Here is the key to my room. Take it. The address is at such and such a place. Go there now and rest. I will come after work, about nine o'clock."

The man took the key and found the place. As soon as he had unlocked the door, a stuffy odor struck him. He waited outside for a few minutes, and then with much difficulty, entered. He found the room dark and dirty and all the furniture covered with several layers of dust. As he was accustomed to cleanliness, he began to sweep the floor and to dust the objects. In carrying the furniture and boxes from one corner to the other, he uncovered the rusty shutters of a window, apparently untouched for a long time. He opened it with much effort and a flood of light poured into the room. Then, he sat down and waited for his friend till night came, then he went out and bought a candle. He lighted it and began to read a book. Nine o'clock, and his friend did not arrive; ten o'clock and there was no sign of him; at eleven o'clock he got up from his seat and went out to see what had become of him. He saw a man walking to and fro on the veranda.

"Who art thou?" he asked in the darkness.

"I am . . . and it seems that I have lost my room."

Realizing that this was his friend he told him that this was his own house. The friend walked in and looked about with evident astonishment:

"I have lived in this room for a long time," he said, "and never knew that it had a window. I have never lighted a candle. I enter the room by night and feel my way to the bed. I take off my clothes and sleep. Before sunrise, I dress and go out. Thus I have never been here in the daytime. Now, when I came tonight, I looked at the room and saw an open window; so I thought that it surely was not mine, and for more than two hours I have been pacing outside wondering what I should do."

Now God and His generosity have given us many things, but we have to find them; he has revealed many precepts, but we have to live by them. If we close the shutters of our hearts, the light will not come in, the spiritual atmosphere will not become purified, dormant powers will not be awakened, divine susceptibilities will not be obtained; intellectual faculties will not become active; heavenly illumination will not be realized; Celestial Love will not be revealed; results will not be produced, and moral civilization will not raise its standard.

3. No Power on Earth Can Withstand the Cause of God

'Abdu'l-Bahá passed by our house before noon and called for Mírzá 'Alí-Akbar. He sent him to Alexandria to attend to an errand and to personally call on an important personage. Then he spent the afternoon in the garden dictating Tablets for the Oriental Bahá'ís. About sunset he came to us. Many believers were here, and he spoke now in Arabic and again in Persian.

He told us that the stories of the prophets recorded in the Qur'an were not mere historical writings. They were warnings to future generations after Mohammed; so that they might know how former people treated the Messengers of God. Although they opposed the Cause, yet they were defeated in their purpose. Who can stand before the Will of the Almighty? Let me give you an example. His Holiness Christ, after his crucifixion, had only eleven disciples. One of these had betrayed him; another had denied him thrice, and the rest had deserted him. On the crucial night of his life, he was left all alone, friendless and helpless; yet in future years the combined forces of the Roman and Greek emperors and philosophers could not stamp out His Power. Like a mighty torrent everything was swept before it. Now after the departure of Bahá'u'lláh, at least five hundred thousand men and women believed in Him; thousands having already testified with their blood, and the rest, ready at any moment to give up their lives. If we reflect for one moment and compare the immediate results of the two Movements, we will logically conclude that no power on earth can stand in the path of the progress of the Bahá'í Cause, which is the Cause of humanity.

Then he spoke of some of the incidents which had occurred during the stirring days of 'Akká, when, the Investigating Committee at the instigation of his enemies had arrived to send him to Feyzan. The events of those years, 1906-1907 if collected and written, would form one of the most dramatic chapters in the Master's epic life. They illustrate more than anything else his divine courage, endurance, patience and spiritual control over great difficulties.

RAMLEH, EGYPT, AUGUST 24, 1913

1. *How Tablets to the American Friends Are Spread All Over Persia*

The other day I observed one of the pilgrims from a faraway town of Persia holding a book in his hand. He was reading it with great attention. Approaching him I looked at the top of the page. To my surprise I read the name of Mr. William Hoar of New York. It was a copy of a Tablet revealed for him by the Master on the eve of his departure from 'Akká many years ago.

"Do you know whose Tablet you are reading?" I asked.

"Of course I do. It belongs to one of our American brothers," he said with pride.

"How did you come to get a copy of it?" I asked.

"Oh! It is spread all over Persia," he rejoined. "By the way," he said, as though remembering something, "tell me about this Mr. Hoar. When I go away, I would like to tell the story to my friends, because we used to read this Tablet at every meeting."

"Very well. Then ask the others to gather together in the room and I will talk to you about him." Having told them all I knew about Mr. Hoar, and of what a splendid and upright Bahá'í he was, I got a copy of the Tablet, and I will share its contents with you; the original is in eloquent Arabic.

2. An Eloquent Tablet to Mr. William Hoar of New York

To Mr. William Hoar, (Upon him be Bahá'u'lláh)

He is God!

O thou visitor to the Blessed Tabernacle!

Verily the Messenger of Confirmation and the Commander of Assistance invited thee and brought thee safely to this radiant Holy Land. Verily thou hast crossed the seas and passed through the cities until thou didst reach to this Center of Lights, this Origin of divine Traces and this Dawning-place of the inspiration of thy Lord, the Mighty, the Master of Destiny! Verily, Verily, I say unto thee, this is a Bestowal through whose mention the Unitarians are rejoiced and for whose attainment the sincere ones are longing. This is a food for the spirit, a sustenance from heaven, a Grace through which the hearts are resuscitated and a favor by which the souls are re-vitalized. Render thou thanksgiving unto the Lord for His Generosity and Liberality. Appreciate thou its value and guard its preciousness.

I declare by the True One, that if a faithful believer in God, while turning his face toward His Kingdom, the Supreme, arrives at this White Land—the Luminous Spot—and perfumes his nostrils through the Fragrance of Holiness, which is being diffused to all parts of the world—the most dynamic Power shall aid him, the Glorious Giver shall reinforce him with His Love and Good-pleasure and confirm him in the accomplishment of a matter which shall have no parallel in the realm of existence and no similarity in the World of Visibility.

But as to thee, gird up the loins of endeavor and return to that distant continent which is thy home and give the Glad-tidings of the Kingdom of God to the people, the Kingdom whose doors are opened before the faces of all that who live upon the earth and in the heavens; a kingdom for the attainment of which the chosen ones from amongst the dwellers of the cities of the Almighty have longed, but have not attained. Verily the capability for the receiving of this uninterrupted Down-pouring, is a grace from the Graces of God and a most glorious gift; and verily the Generosity of Thy Lord is not limited.

Declare thou unto the people: Verily at this time the Sun is shining, the orbs are gleaming, the stars are sparkling, the lamps are ignited, the fire of the Love of God is flaming high, the heavens are expanding, the seas are becoming tempestuous, the breezes are wafting, the rain is pouring down; the earth is adorned, the Tabernacle of the Lord is lifted up, the rose gardens are embellished, the orchards are in luxuriant growth, the birds are singing, the flowers are blossoming, while Fragrance scatters and the zephyrs blow!

How long, how long will ye remain asleep in your tombs, and rest upon the beds of negligence! Will ye not awaken from your slumbers, cleanse your ears, respond to the call of your Lord, the Omniscient and become the objects of the Favor of your God, the Clement; reading the verses of His Mercy and worshiping the Adored Countenance in this Manifest Day? Hasten ye, Hasten ye, O ye sincere ones! Hasten ye! Hasten ye, O ye attracted ones! Hasten ye, Hasten ye! O ye expectant ones! Hasten ye, Hasten ye, O ye longing ones! Ere long ye shall behold the Banners of Guidance waving from the summit of the highest mountains; the Knowledge of God encircling this terrestrial globe and the signs of the Bounties of your Lord manifesting in all directions as the appearance of the sun in midday. On that day the faithful ones shall break into songs of gladness, the people of Unity shall rejoice and the hearts which are filled with the Love of the Living, the Self-Subsistent will become dilated, the heedless ones will be in loss, the violators of the Covenant will regret and the rebellious ones be in degradation.

O ye servants of God! Avail yourselves of the opportunity which is offered to you through these Favors, and do not ye forget that which was promised you in all the holy writings. This day is the day of attraction! This day is the day of enkindlement! This day is the day of soaring toward the ethereal atmosphere of the Merciful! This day is the day of the Call! This day is the day of Grace! This day is the day of the Most eminent Bestowal! This day is the day of the discovery of the most valuable treasure! Oh ye servants of God! Deprive not yourselves of the Ocean of Favor, and shut not your eyes to the vision of the signs of your Lord, the Omnipotent. Approach ye toward the Kingdom of Abhá, the Supreme Heaven, the Loftiest station with radiant faces, with hearts overflowing with the mention of God and breasts dilated by the verses of God: so that you may attain to that which was longed for by the righteous ones—the station coveted by the saints and prayed for by the holy souls. Verily this is that which causes astonishment to the people of intelligence.

Convey my greetings and praise to all the believers of God in that vast and spacious continent and say unto them from the tongue of 'Abdu'l-Bahá: 'O ye believers of God! It is incumbent upon you to work mightily (in the Cause), and to strive nobly to declare the Bounties of God; be ye engaged in the Commemoration of the name of God; be ye severed from all else save God; take a firm hold of the rope of virtue, shun obedience to the dictates of self and passion; practice kindness toward all the people of the world; serve the Cause of Universal Peace and show ye love to all the nations of the earth.'

Upon ye be greetings and praise!

(Signed) 'Abdu'l-Bahá 'Abbás.

3. *The Minute Questions Asked of 'Abdu'l-Bahá*

I did not see the Master this morning. Having received large packages of letters from the various countries of the East, he was busy reading them. Like simple children they come to him for advice to solve their problems.

4. 'Abdu'l-Bahá Jokes and Beats His Secretary

At four o'clock I found myself at the door of the Master's house. He was coming down with firm strides. The carriage was waiting. He had promised to take Mr. Atwood for a drive, and this was the day of fulfillment. In my hand I had a package of letters to be read to him. Looking at the rather thick package, he laughed and taking it out of my hand, showed it to the upper windows (apparently some of the members of the holy family were looking down) saying:

"Look what an amount of work Mírzá Ahmad has brought for me. Does he not deserve a sound beating?" and with the umbrella's handle he gently struck me twice on my back. Then he entered the carriage, after him Shoghi Effendi and next myself. Before reaching the Hotel Plaisance to call for Mr. Atwood, he talked with much humor, laughing all the time.

5. 'Abdu'l-Bahá Says That If People Wish to Sneeze They Ask Him about It

On the way he told us that matters had reached such a point that if the friends wanted to cough or sneeze they wrote to him to do it for them. He has repeatedly written that any realizable plan which has for its aim the spread of the Cause is acceptable. Each one wishes 'Abdu'l-Bahá to free him from his perplexities and to lighten his work; but no one yet has asked to come and be of service to him; and help to lighten his load.

6. A Talk by 'Abdu'l-Bahá on Creation

Finally we reached the hotel, picked up Mr. Atwood, and started again. Mr. Atwood has written two articles on the Bahá'í Cause. The first has appeared in the Christian Commonwealth, the second will be published in another English paper. On the way he asked two questions, one on creation and its apparent incongruities and anomalies; the other on free will and determination.

'Abdu'l-Bahá answered as follows: If we look upon creation from a remote outlook, we see symmetry and harmony; the apparent differences and anomalies blending into one harmonious whole; but if we study the world of genesis from a partial standpoint, these freaks of nature come to our notice at every turn. All parts, kinds and species of the creational life are interrelated. There is an invisible chain binding all into one mass of homogeneity. Those anomalies of creation which we call freaks are not freaks at all; but are made by a definite wisdom. As soon as we learn the purpose of their creation, they are no longer freaks, but parts of a whole. For example, we know the wisdom of the existence of the eyes, the ears, the teeth, the hands and the feet, but we may wonder why a single hair is grown on the top of somebody's nose. This also has a purpose were we to become cognizant of it. The law of composition and decomposition, amalgamation and dissolution, construction and destruction, protection and danger are two basic principles of creation. An organism—whether living or inanimate—must be decomposed at a stated time; so that through its scattered atoms, elements of other organisms may be composed and created. Creation therefore, is based upon the activities of these two fundamental laws. On the other hand, there is the law of the eater and of the eaten. The higher forms of life feed upon the lower species of genesis. The grass takes its nourishment from the soil, and every day grows taller and taller like unto this (extending his hand toward the tall grass waving in the field). The animal in turn (showing a cow grazing in the field) eats the grass and is sustained by it. After a while man appears, kills the cow and eats it. Thus we observe that the various kingdoms of Life feed upon each other; but they have no conscious knowledge of the other's existence. Hence the inferior degree is entirely out of touch with the superior degree, but the upper can look down upon the lower and help it. Therefore, while we are living in this world, we are not informed of the existence of the Spiritual world, but the dwellers of the spiritual world know about us and can assist and help us.

7. Explanation of Free Will

As regards free will. There are two distinct kinds of affairs, the first dominated by man, the second which is beyond his control; the first voluntary, the second involuntary. I am a free man so far as walking is concerned, but I am not free to soar in the air, unless I build an aeroplane.

8. 'Abdu'l-Bahá Talks to Shaykhs and Young Egyptians of His Trip to the West

While the carriage was rolling on past fields of cotton, palm groves, and primitive hamlets, the Master continued speaking on the above two subjects. We returned about 7 o'clock. Mr. Atwood enjoyed the ride and thanked him for it. At 8:30, 'Abdu'l-Bahá came to our house. There were some Arab Shaykhs waiting. After indulging in some poetry and philosophic jargons to which the Master listened patiently, one of them ended with the announcement that his wife and children were sick and he had no money. The Master gave him five Majidis (5 dollars) and he left the house happy. Afterwards six young Egyptian nobles arrived. For more than two hours 'Abdu'l-Bahá spoke to them about the virtues of the English and American people, of their scientific achievement, and of his travels throughout those distant countries, so full of wonders. Then he gave a resume of his lecture in the Jewish Synagogues of America. He was very lively in his descriptions and laughed throughout this interesting talk. The young Egyptians were all attention.

Today the Master was very happy and well. And his words created joy and spread sunshine. When he laughed the waves of his mirth rippled over the sea of our lives; creating wider and wider circles of the joy of living.

RAMLEH, EGYPT, AUGUST 25, 1913

1. International Bahá'í Correspondence Conducive to Unity

Most important of all is the establishment of a line of correspondence between the East and the West. Not that it may go on for a year or two only, but that it may continue without interruption.

The success of every affair depends upon one's firmness in following it up. Of no less importance is correspondence between the various Bahá'í Assemblies; for each assembly thus becomes informed of the status of the other and gives its moral support. It would be well to designate certain active centers in America—Chicago, Washington, New York, San Francisco, Boston, etc.—to correspond regularly with European and Oriental Assemblies and in turn disseminate the news they receive to smaller centers; that the future Bahá'í conventions may give one or more sessions to the consideration of this important subject; that the secretaries may report on what they have done during the year and how many letters they have written and received.

As a confirmation to the foregoing statement, I translate the following Tablet, and am sure, that after reading it, the Bahá'ís will do their utmost to carry out its contents:

> The correspondence of the believers of God with all parts of America and from America to all directions is very acceptable . . . . It will be the means of drawing hearts together. Display the utmost effort in this matter. The friends of God must be like bouquets of roses, disseminating their sweet fragrances one to another. They should assist each other, so that, through the powers of the Kingdom, cooperation and reciprocity may be obtained. Correspondence and communication are the two greatest means for solidarity.
>
> It is said that correspondence is equal to half-meeting. Forward a copy of this Tablet to all parts, so that the friends of God in every city may correspond in a representative way, with other cities; especially with America. This will be the cause of enkindlement and the means of attraction. The souls will become exhilarated, the spirits gladdened, the hearts stirred into cheerfulness, and the breasts dilated.

2. The Weather in Ramleh

The days and nights of Ramleh are without rain. In the shade it is always cool. The sky is as blue as the bluest turquoise. At night the heavens are illumined with radiant stars. During the winter there is no snow, and the weather is balmy.

3. Receipt of Bahá'í Reports from America

Today, at about half past three, 'Abdu'l-Bahá, passing by the house, called out my name, and in a second, I was following after him. He told me to bring the letters with me. I was glad for this. Reaching the gate of the garden, I knocked at the door, and the gardener opened it. The Master entered, took off his black coat and yellow 'Abá, and placed them on the branch of a fig tree. He was now all in white. For a few minutes he walked along the avenues and I could see his wonderful stature through the branches stirred by the wafting of the breeze.

He told me that when the weather was good his constitution responded to it and that he felt like a different person.

Then he started to dictate Tablets.

The third monthly report of Mr. Joseph H. Hannen, from Washington, D.C., was read. As he listened, his face brightened, and recalling different names mentioned in the letter, he exclaimed "Bravo Mrs. Belmont," "Bravo So and So." He directed me to send copies of this report to Cairo and Tehran; so that they might spread it to other Bahá'í Centers, and to keep the original for him. In the evening he told the believers that a good report had been received from Washington which made him very happy. They should read it.

4. The Story of Fu'ád Pasha, the Grand Vazir of Turkey

After two hours of dictation he left the garden to see a house which he desired to rent for the coming pilgrims from India and Persia. On the way we met the son of the former Consul of Damascus, Háshim Khan, with the Secretary of the Consulate of Alexandria. They had come to pay their respects to 'Abdu'l-Bahá. After seeing the house, the Master took his guests to the apartment of Mírzá Abú'l-Fadl, and there, on the veranda, he conversed with them. As the son of the Consul—a pleasant, polite young man—had just arrived from Constantinople, the conversation naturally turned in the direction of the late war and its dreadful consequences.

'Abdu'l-Bahá said that the thoughts of the statesmen of the East are atrophied, and their hearts devoid of desire for the progress of the nation. Their ideas are petty, not sublime; selfish, not disinterested; local, not general. They think more of the advancement of their own interests, than of those of the country. They are not far-seeing patriots, but inexperienced tyros. They sell the resources of their country, if they think that by so doing they can fill their own pockets. Except in two instances, the Muslim countries of the East have not produced any real statesmen for the last 200 years. When he was in Constantinople, he heard on every side the praise of Fu'ád Pasha, the then Grand Vazir. At that time 'Abdu'l-Bahá was about seventeen or eighteen years old. One day he was in the house of Kamál Pasha, the former Ambassador of Turkey to Persia. The latter spoke Persian fluently, and as 'Abdu'l-Bahá had known him when he was an official in Tehran, he called on him during his short stay in Constantinople, and 'Abdu'l-Bahá returned the visit. While they were engaged in conversation, Fu'ád Pasha was announced. 'Abdu'l-Bahá thought to himself: "Now I shall have the opportunity of meeting this celebrated statesman, and of hearing words of political wisdom from his lips." As soon as Fu'ád Pasha entered, his first word was addressed to Kamál Pasha. "I could not sleep last night." A statesman who cannot sleep all night must of necessity be thinking out the vast plan of some administrative reform, or public or civic welfare. "I did not enjoy one wink of slumber till this morning: the result being the composition of two blank verses," he said. "Do you want me to read them to you?" 'Abdu'l-Bahá was astonished at this state of affairs that the Grand Minister of an Empire does not sleep all night for the writing of two blank verses. The lines were some poetical exaggeration about the beauty and tresses of his Beloved. When he left the room 'Abdu'l-Bahá asked Kamál Pasha: "Why did you praise so volubly those vapid verses?" He said: "Why, we can't do otherwise."

5. Qá'im-Maqám, the Persian Statesman

Then 'Abdu'l-Bahá told us another story about this man. He had ordered the killing of several hundred persons, exiled two or three thousand innocent men, and paid a large indemnity of eight million to one of the European powers, to satisfy their demands based upon certain occurrences which had transpired in Syria. But in Persia, during the Ministry of the Great Qá'im-Maqám, the Legation of one of the Foreign Nations was burned down and seventy-two people were killed by the populace, yet that far-sighted and astute Persian Minister so dexterously satisfied that foreign Power without paying an indemnity or killing or banishing anyone, that this one act alone became the greatest political feat of that Persian statesman, Qá'im-Maqám.

6. The Story of the Sick Soldier and the Watchman

While 'Abdu'l-Bahá was in Adrianople, Khurshíd Pasha, the Válí, one day asked him about the future of the Turkish Empire.

"Do you want me to give you my frank opinion?" 'Abdu'l-Bahá said.

"Yes, of course," he answered.

Then, let me illustrate your position by a story. During the war against a foreign nation, one of the soldiers was stricken with a severe sickness. The military doctor, observing his case, recommended him to the watchman, saying: "This man must not sleep tonight. It is the crisis of his illness, but tomorrow morning he will feel much better. Nurse him very carefully and watch over him." The doctor left, and about sunset the watchman came around to look after the sick man. After an hour or two he saw that he was getting worse and was moaning and lamenting loudly. In order to alleviate his pain, the watchman gave him an opium pill, as a result of which he slept soundly all night. In the morning, the doctor called and saw that the condition of the patient was worse than the day before. Not being able to understand this relapse, he sent for the watchman. "What did you do for him last night?" "Oh, he was in such a frantic condition that I gave him a pill of opium, after which he slept soundly." "Did you not think that I, who am a doctor, knew this remedy just a well as you, but I did not give it to him because I knew that it would make him worse?" "What do I care? I wanted to sleep and this patient disturbed me. I gave him an opium pill, and it served its purpose. Tonight there will be another watchman. If the patient is getting worse, it does not trouble me in the least."

Now, 'Abdu'l-Bahá told the Governor, it is your watch-time. You are not doing anything to improve the condition of the sick country. You are putting it to sleep by giving it narcotics, and when you leave your position, what do you care whether the patient will live or die? You have had your night's sleep. Instead of watching the patient solicitously, and pulling him through, you prefer your own rest and comfort.

RAMLEH, EGYPT, AUGUST 26, 1913

1. The Bahá'ís Must Raise a New Voice

Last night Hájí Muhammad, the brother of Ahmad Yazdí, arrived from Port Said, and brought us our mail. I had a few letters from America, the contents of which gave much pleasure to 'Abdu'l-Bahá. The breeze of good news must ever waft from the direction of the West to gladden the heart of the Center of the Covenant. May the believers of God, during the coming years plant new seeds in the gardens of hearts, educate new souls in the divine school, adorn with new stars the heaven of Reality, upraise new banners in the army of the Kingdom, cultivate new flowers in the Paradise of Abhá, issue a new voice through the pillars of the earth, herald the new message with a new enthusiasm, break through the rank and file of indifference with a new impetuosity, invite new guests to sit around the heavenly table, ask new thirsty ones to drink from the spring of life, create a new motion in the spiritual spheres, throw a new stir in the world of ideals, and pave new highways leading to the Supreme Concourse.

In the morning I went to Alexandria and having dispatched some letters and attended to duties entrusted to me by the Master, returned. All day our house was an interesting center for the coming and going of the believers and pilgrims. Hájí 'Abbás, received permission to return to his home via Constantinople and Russia.

2. The Article of Arthur Brisbane on Science, Translated and Published in Arabic Daily and Discussed by Students

In the afternoon I called at the apartment of Mírzá Abú'l-Fadl. There were several young Arab Bahá'ís present, and to my pleasant surprise, the subject of discussion was an article by Arthur Brisbane, feature writer of Mr. Hearst's papers in the United States. The article dealt with the wonders of science and the discoveries of this age. It was translated into Arabic by an Egyptian daily and published in the current issue. Mírzá Abú'l-Fadl could not agree with certain statements made by Arthur Brisbane. After much discussion pro and con, he directed Husayn Rúhí to write an answer and to forward it to the Editor of the paper. As I sat there, I thought how small the world was! What would Arthur Brisbane say or think did he know that his article, written thousands of miles away, in a new world, surrounded by a complex civilization, was being discussed and criticized by a number of Arabian students, supervised by a Persian philosopher, in a summer resort of Ancient Egypt. Truly the world is becoming one!

I may conclude with extracts from some Tablets which I have gathered out of the manuscript book of one of the pilgrims. They reflect the Bahá'í qualities and spirit.

3. This World Is Dark, It Must Be Changed into a Universe of Light

O ye friends of God and assistants of 'Abdu'l-Bahá!

What can I write, and what can I say? That which is in the heart can be neither translated into words nor written on paper, and that which can be molded into phrases cannot express the susceptibilities of the heart and conscience; therefore, I address you, O ye real friends: Turn the mirrors of your hearts toward mine. Unquestionably the mysteries of this heart shall become reflected upon yours, and the emotions of this longing one will become evident and manifest in all regions.

The world is black; the Divine Bestowal is Radiant. This blackness must be changed into light, and this narrow, dark sphere be transformed into a vast, illimitable universe of illumination. The body of the world is a dead corpse, it must be resuscitated; it is withered. it must be made fresh and blooming; it is extinct, it must be enkindled; it is the arena for the expression of animosity, it must be made the dawning-place of love and good fellowship; it is the origin of the emanation of contention, we must make it the axis around which revolves unity; it is the exposition for the baser qualities which lead to eternal disgrace, we must make it the rising-point for the refulgent rays of the Everlasting Glory. The stranger must be instructed in the lesson of neighborliness; the heedless ones be made aware; the enemies must be loved and the hateful ones be shown kindness. We must become flaming torches and burning Fires of God. We must move the world and illuminate the dark globe. All this depends upon the effort of the friends and the sacrifice of the beloved ones.

4. Attraction Is Not Realized Save through Teaching the Cause of God

O thou servant of the Almighty! Beg of God that in this world, which is groaning with pains and troubles, thou mayst aspire to a breath of rest and that in this sorrow-begirdled globe, thou mayst obtain happiness. This Bestowal will not become unveiled and this Grace will not adorn the Assemblage of the heart except through severance from all else save God and by complete concentration upon the kingdom of Abhá. This severance and attention will not be obtained save by attraction to the Fragrances of God, and by enkindlement with the Fire of the Love of God. This attraction and enkindlement will not be realized except through teaching the Cause of God and by firmness and steadfastness in the Covenant and Testament of God. Upon thee be Abhá, and upon everyone who is severed, attentive, attracted and enkindled; conveying the message while he is firm and steadfast. . . .

5. Confer upon Every One Spiritual Joy

O thou who art exhilarated with the Cup of the True One:

Thou hast the desire to render a great service at the Threshold of the Almighty. Happy art thou that thou art confirmed with this bounteous aim. Today, ecstasy and yearning at the Threshold of God, enkindlement with the Fire of the Love of God, attraction with the Fragrance of God and the Song and melody of the Supreme Concourse, are true service. Be thou an ignited torch and cast upon all people the reflection of its rays Enkindle the Fire of Love and burn away all veils Confer upon everyone spiritual joy and gladness and manifest a merciful nature and disposition. Deliver men from prison and lead them to the Court of Guidance.

6. A Poetic Tablet, Like a Bouquet of Fragrant Flowers

O ye who are intoxicated with the Wine of God!

The Breeze of the Merciful is wafting from the rose-garden of Eternity, the luminous Morn hath dawned from the horizon of significances; the clarion Call reaches to the ears from the Kingdom of Abba; the melody of the wisdom of the nightingale of the meadow of sanctity is raised; the Paradise of unity and the orchard of Abstraction are opened and luxuriant; the roses of idealism, and the flowers of the merciful verities are laughing and blooming; the hyacinths and anemones are fresh and full of fragrance: the trees of the divine Garden are fruitful, their roots firm in the ground; the rivers of life are flowing; the fountain of unending Grace is gushing forth, leaping playfully on and on; the liberty-loving Cypress has raised its branches toward the sky; the longing dove is cooing; the real Leila with a rosy-cheeked Countenance is manifest; the Majnún of Consciousness with burning heart is evident."

RAMLEH, EGYPT, AUGUST 27, 1913

1. This Is the Seed-sowing Time

Teaching the Word of God—spreading the Glad-tidings of the Kingdom—conveying the Message of Unity and raising the Flag of International Peace hold the foremost ground in the Bahá'í Cause. When we receive certain heavenly privileges and spiritual distinctions, we must share them with the rest of our fellow men.

The very fact that we have received, connotes the idea of giving. By teaching, our own knowledge will be increased. When the water is not constantly flowing, it will stagnate, no matter how crystalline and pure. If you have a handful of seeds, you must sew them during the season, so that you may gather a goodly crop at the harvest. Now this is the seed-sowing time of the Kingdom of Brotherhood. This and this alone will yield fruit. We must, like wise farmers, get up early in the morning, and go about our business with no other thought in our minds except sowing the seeds. We must sow all the seeds that God has given us, and if we have scattered all our stock, he stands ready to replenish it from his invisible storehouse. Once the seeds are sown; the sun of Providence will shine forth, the Breeze of Mercy will waft, the rain of clemency will pour down, causing the growing of the field, waving with a soft, beautiful verdancy and soon attaining to the stage of fruition—the sheaves laden with golden corns. Then is the time of rejoicing for the farmer, because the result of his labor and industry is spread before his eyes.

2. *This Is the Day in Which to Lay the Foundations of the House*

Before everything else we must lay the foundation. Then go out and gather mortar, stones, bricks, lime, hauling machinery and laborers to build the house. What benefit will accrue to us if we buy the furniture or utensils before the house is ready? How can we build the roof before the structural framework is put together? A wise builder lays a good basis for his house, collects all the necessary material, and then goes on, step by step, in its construction. 'Abdu'l-Bahá has shown through his life, and deeds how this is the most important work of the Cause. The autumn and winter seasons will come in due time. Our supreme duty now is to arise unanimously for the awakening of souls! Should we follow the example of the Divine Farmer, we will reap a great crop in the harvest season, we will see the reflections of our contented faces in the mirror of the Kingdom, and will observe our names inscribed upon the scroll of time with the pen of light. The friends all over the world are longing to serve the Cause. Praise be to God that their aims are humanitarian, their ideas are lofty, their love for the Truth manifest, their eagerness to diffuse the lights of the Sun of Reality evident and their spiritual susceptibilities warm and glowing. They are servants of the world of humanity, and heralds of the Kingdom of Light. May they become confirmed to teach the Cause with a new fervor and inspiration!

In a Tablet written by 'Abdu'l-Bahá several years ago, he says:

3. Our Efforts Must Be Centralized About the Spreading of the Cause

The believers with the utmost steadfastness and firmness must engage in the teaching of the Cause. They must become united and agreed. They are all the drops of one river, waves of one sea, breezes of one garden, streams flowing from one fountain, birds soaring toward one apex, hyacinths adorning one Park, intoxicated with one wine and their hearts ravished with one melody. . . . It is hoped that the friends may become sanctified and holy above all earthly conditions and in concord and harmony, in unity of identity, unity of quality, unity of opinion and unity of thought, set an example for all the believers of other countries and become the spiritual leaders in this arena. Now all aims must verge toward one spring, and all efforts be centralized in one object, and that is: the diffusion of the Fragrances of the Merciful, and the promulgation of the Word of the Almighty. The time of systematization and crystallization shall come. It has not yet arrived. The aim of all the friends must be this: the diffusion of the Fragrances of Holiness. When a man's efforts are concentrated on this one object, he will undoubtedly reflect the confirmation of the Manifest Light. Except for the guidance of souls, no other cause is equally confirmed. If any person entertains other thoughts than this, he will unquestionably regret them.

During the season of seed-sowing you cannot gather a crop and at the time of irrigation, harvesting is unthinkable. The soul who, during the summer season, engages in planting trees, will not reap any reward, for that is the season of fruit-gathering, and not that of tree-planting. In short, the purpose is this: During the season of the Divine Spring we must occupy all our time in seed-sowing and irrigation, and not in harvesting and crop-collecting.

This morning 'Abdu'l-Bahá called on Mírzá Abú'l-Fadl and spoke with him for half an hour on the importance of teaching the Cause in this day, and of the subservience of all other ideas to the idea of promoting the word of God. In the evening he entertained a Russian Prince and a number of Arab Shaykhs at his home.

4. Hope for the Reunion of the East and the West

Letters and cablegrams are pouring in from all parts of the world. The Master is daily growing stronger and is attending to all the innumerable duties which are laid on his shoulders.

RAMLEH, EGYPT, AUGUST 28, 1913

1. The Life of the East and the West and of How the Bahá'í Movement Unites Them

The spiritual life of the East is calm and uplifting. It has a celestial outlook. It purifies one's aims. It ennobles the character. It changes the Satan into the angel. There is a subtle influence in this life which works like magic over the hearts of men. It steadies the nerves, confers equipoise, intensifies spiritual feelings, and bestows mental calmness and serenity. The realization of the power of faith and prayer dawns upon the mind; the divine Presence is felt as never before, and the holy light breaks upon the dark chambers of the heart. Those who have lived in the East and have experienced this feeling cannot describe it in words. It is a fire the flame of which sets aglow many hearts, and which inspires the imagination with pictures of heavenly attributes.

While the life of the East on the one hand is sweetly contemplative, the life of the West is energetically active; the former is a calm river, the latter a rushing cyclone. One interprets life subjectively, the other elucidates it objectively. The Bahá'í Movement establishes a balance between the two poles. The materialism of the occident is imbued with spirit and the unproductive mysticism of the Orient is discountenanced when work is constituted as worship. Thus the Bahá'í Cause is in a position to help both hemispheres with its new spiritual philosophy. 'Abdu'l-Bahá is daily working for the consummation of this object.

2. *'Abdu'l-Bahá Writes on the Future Condition of Women*

This morning we got glimpses of 'Abdu'l-Bahá as he passed by our house two or three times. He was busy all day. In the evening, the correspondent of the Agdam, published in Cairo, called on him and had a long interview. These days, the Master is devoting much of his time to writing Tablets for the Persian believers. He is fulfilling his promise, that after his return from America and Europe, he would answer all their petitions. I produce herein the translation of one of these Tablets on the "Feminist Question,"—one that is very opportune. It is as follows:

> O thou my beloved daughter! Thy eloquent and fluent letter was perused in a garden, under the cool shade of a tree, while the gentle breeze was wafting. The means of physical enjoyment was spread before the eyes and thy letter became the cause of spiritual enjoyment. Truly, I say, it was not a letter, but a rose-garden adorned with hyacinths and flowers. It contained the sweet Fragrances of Paradise and the Zephyr of Divine Love blew from its roseate words.
>
> As I have not ample time at my disposal, I will give herein a brief answer. It is as follows: In the revelation of Bahá'u'lláh, men and women stand shoulder to shoulder. In no instance will the women be left behind. Their rights with men are in equal degree. They will enter into all the administrative branches of the body politic. They will attain to such a high plane that they will be honored in the very highest station of the world of humanity and will take part in all affairs. Rest ye assured of this! Do not look upon present conditions; in the not distant future the world of women will become all-refulgent and all-glorious. For His Holiness Bahá'u'lláh hath willed it so. At the time of elections the right to vote is

the inalienable prerogative of women, and their admittance to all the departments of life an irrefutable and incontestable right. No soul can retard or prevent it. But there are certain matters, participation in which, is not worthy of woman. For example, at the time when the community is taking up vigorous defensive measures against the attack of foes, the women are exempt from military engagements. It may so happen that at a given time, warlike and savage tribes may furiously attack the body politic with the intention of carrying on a wholesale slaughter of its members; under such circumstances defense is necessary; and it is the duty of the men and not of the women to organize and execute such defensive measures, because the women's hearts are tender, and cannot endure the sight of horror and carnage, even if it is for the sake of defense. For such, and similar undertakings, the women are exempt.

As regards the Constitution of the House of Justice, Bahá'u'lláh, in the Book of the Aqdas, addressed the men, saying: 'O ye men of the House of Justice!' but (when the members are being elected) the right which belongs to women, so far as their voting and their voice is concerned, is indisputable. When women attain to the ultimate degree of progress, then, according to the exigencies of time and place, and of their capacity, they shall obtain extraordinary privileges. Be ye confident on this account. His Holiness Bahá'u'lláh has greatly strengthened the Cause of women and their rights and privileges are the special principles of 'Abdu'l-Bahá. Rest ye assured! Ere long the day will come when the men, addressing the women will say: Blessed are ye! Blessed are ye! Verily ye are worthy of every gift and deserve to adorn your heads with the Crown of Everlasting Glory; because in sciences and arts, in virtues and perfections, ye have become equal to men and as regards the tenderness of heart and the abundance of mercy and sympathy, ye are superior.

I received several letters from England, France and America, each containing cheering news of the steady growth of the beloved Cause.

RAMLEH, EGYPT, AUGUST 29, 1913

1. The College Life and Its Expected Results

One of the Persian poets says: "All the means are prepared for thee, and yet thou art sitting idle."

The outcome of school and college years must be a useful life for the community. If a child is possessed of happy surroundings, if fortune has smiled upon him, he must avail himself of these opportunities and daily prepare himself, so that when he leaves college, he may enter upon the stage of life, ready to act his part with confidence.

In a spiritual way we are all the children of the Heavenly Father. He has prepared for us the means of advancement. He has placed within our reach the instruments whereby we may obtain an ideal education and fit ourselves for the service of humanity. He has given us lessons in many ways. He has encouraged us with words of wisdom and has pointed out the glorious goal. Yet some of us play truant, do not learn our lessons, and at the time of examination fail. Do you not think the Father will feel sad and keenly disappointed, when he finds that His years of solicitude have brought no results? Let us, therefore, be the studious children of Truth; avail ourselves of all the opportunities prepared for us, so that throughout our lives we may give happiness to others and fulfill the expectation of the Great Teacher.

2. A Talk by an Old Bahá'í on the Sins of Backbiting

El Yahou is an old Bahá'í. In years gone by he was a Jew before becoming a Bahá'í, he is well conversant with prophesies of the Old Testament. He has a sweet nature and loves 'Abdu'l-Bahá more than words can express. In the course of conversation he told us that the Cause of the Blessed Perfection is the reality of Love and the means of unity and concord amongst the children of men; so that all of them may become the waves of one sea, the radiant stars studded in one illimitable sphere, the brilliant pearls of the shell of unity and the sparkling gems of the mine of singleness; thus may they serve each other from their hearts; praise and commend each other; unloose their tongues in manifesting the good qualities of each, and thank the Lord for His Graces and Gifts. They must look toward the horizon of everlasting Glory and as they attribute themselves to Bahá'u'lláh, they must see no evil, and never speak of the faults of others. They must shut their ears to all gossip and backbiting. They must be spiritual beings, with spiritual qualities. A number of souls are walking in this straight path, and, praise be to God, are assisted and confirmed in all countries; but others have not yet reached this exalted, and supreme station, and are not fully established in this Divine Principle. This is a cause of great grief to the heart of 'Abdu'l-Bahá. There is no greater obstacle to the Cause of God than faultfinding and no greater handicap for the word of God. The friends of God must become the essences of union and accord, enter under the unicolored tent of the Almighty, the expression of one great Ideal, walk in one road, forget conflicting opinions, and leave behind them their divergent views. Then 'Abdu'l-Bahá will be pleased with them, because he sees that they have dedicated all their thoughts and energies to the promotion of Love and affection, throwing into the corner of oblivion their differences, and growing in the image and likeness of the Creator.

Thus El Yahou spoke from the depth of his heart.

3. Permission Given to Persian Bahá'í Students to Come to Ramleh

Today we did not see 'Abdu'l-Bahá, but he sent me several cablegrams to be forwarded to various parts of the world. One of these was to Haifa giving permission to half of the Bahá'í students to come to Ramleh. There are about thirty young Persian Bahá'ís who are students in the American College in Beirut. As this is vacation time, they are spending their summer on Mount Carmel. In a few days, half of them will arrive; the other half will come later. Tonight we had a meeting at the House of Khurásání. Mírzá Mahmúd spoke on the trip of 'Abdu'l-Bahá to Edinburgh. There were many Bahá'ís of different nationalities.

4. 'Abdu'l-Bahá Praises Mrs. Besant, President of the Theosophical Society

An interesting Tablet was sent to Mr. Graham Pole, the Editor of the 'Scotland Theosophy' in Edinburgh, in which 'Abdu'l-Bahá refers to Mrs. Besant, the President of the Theosophical Society. As he has spoken before many of their societies in various cities, both in the United States and Europe, it will not be out of place to quote it herein, so that the friends may become informed of its contents:

O thou my beloved friend!

Thy letter was received from India. From its contents it became evident that thou art occupied, and art spending thy days in the company of that respected lady, Mrs. Besant. I hope thou mayst be ever happy, serene, confirmed and assisted; so that thou mayst become able to render a signal service to the respected lady, Mrs. Besant. The ideal of Mrs. Besant, I say truly is very lofty. She is working and laboring most valiantly, and her utmost hope is to render a service to the world of humanity, and to be the means of the establishment of good-fellowship and love between all the communities of the earth. At all times I am praying in her behalf, so that the Confirmations of the Kingdom may surround her, that she may sow the seed of service in pure, productive soil; and that she may gather many, many harvests; then the heavenly benediction Will be obtained, the outpourings of the Holy Spirit realized, and her services, troubles and hardships crowned with eternal results. I desire this station for her.

Consider how many important women have come into this world! How many queens have lived upon this earth! How many distinguished ladies have become the presidents of Societies! But neither have their names nor any great account of their deeds been left behind! Yet Mary Magdalene, who was only a peasant woman, because she became inspired to serve the Kingdom of Christ and to scatter his seeds in productive ground—what a great crop she gathered! And through the blessing of that harvest, they are even now building churches in her name! In all the Churches the people glorify and praise her and now, after 1900 years, 'Abdu'l-Bahá is speaking of her lofty station! He testifies to the fact, that, in the Kingdom of Christ she served more than all the apostles She even became the cause of the firmness and steadfastness of the Apostles, for, accordingly to the Text of the Gospels, their faith wavered after the crucifixion, but Mary Magdalene inspired them with resolution, and certainly. Consider what a service she rendered to the Kingdom of Christ! That is why, like unto a star, she is shining from the horizon of Eternity.

Convey my most respectful greeting to the revered Lady, Mrs. Besant.

Upon thee be greeting and praise.

(Signed) 'Abdu'l-Bahá 'Abbás.

While in America and Europe 'Abdu'l-Bahá often stated that the Bahá'ís must associate with the Theosophists because they were nearer to this Cause than many other groups.

RAMLEH, EGYPT, AUGUST 30, 1913

1. Spread of Bahá'í Cause in the Interior of Turkey

'Abdu'l-Bahá received a letter from the interior of Turkey, the city of Antab where the Bahá'í Cause is being spread. He read to us a portion of it which describes a lecture given by an Armenian before an audience of five hundred people. The lecturer dwelt upon the trip of the Master of Europe and America and gave a synopsis of the Teachings. What interested the audience more than anything else was the principle of the Conformity of Science and Religion, philosophy and faith. Science and religion, he told them, have always been in accord, but the despicable, accursed, satans ('ulamá) have always sown seed of discord between them. The Master laughed heartily when he read the above conclusion.

2. Let the American Friends Wait

Then he gave each of us the letters just received in our names and while we were sitting in his presence, he wrote several Tablets with his own hand. At last he told us that he was trying to make amends for the past and was devoting all his time to the Oriental friends. Before leaving for America, he wrote that the Bahá'ís must excuse him from any letter-writing, but that after his return he would correspond with them as of old, and now he was fulfilling his promise.

When we left, I ventured to say that many petitions from America and Europe were accumulating and solicited his attention. He answered me in a humorous fashion; wait, wait a little longer. Let him now attend to the Persian believers, and the turn of my American friends would come soon.

When we left his house, we were all intoxicated with his divine Love. During our interview the Master spoke a great deal with Mírzá Jalál, because one of the Princes of Persia taught by him had written him a letter.

3. Story of How a Bahá'í Feast Was Given in Baghdad

Mírzá Jamál, our cook, told us a story about a feast in Baghdad.

"The Bahá'ís in Baghdad," he said, "were not rich, but were firm and filled with fervor. They kept the nineteen day feast. One morning they sent word to one of the friends that the Feast would be held in his house. He touched his pockets and there was no money. What should he do? He had a watch which he had bought for ten majidis. He took it out of his pocket and sent it to the bazaar to be sold at auction. Accidentally one of the Bahá'ís passed by and recognized the watch. He stopped and saw that it was going to be sold for two majidis. He raised the price half a dollar and bought it. Quietly he carried it home. When night came, he went to the meeting, and after the refreshments were served, he approached the host and, taking the watch out of his pocket offered it to him as a present. The host was very much surprised, but delighted. All the friends were pleased when they heard the story.

4. 'Abdu'l-Bahá Writes on the Nineteen-day Feast

I may now conclude by quoting from a Tablet, which 'Abdu'l-Bahá writes to Mr. Jos. Hannen:

O thou who art firm in the Covenant!

Thy third report was received and its contents imparted the utmost exhilaration. The 19-day Feast was the Lord's Supper, and its results are eternalized. Although physically 'Abdu'l-Bahá was far away, he was present in that meeting with heart and soul. Truly I say, it was a glorious feast, perfect in every way. Do not ye look upon the present, nay rather, look into the future. The Lord's Supper during the lifetime of that divine Light, had no importance in the estimation of the public; but consider how the rays of that sun of Reality illumined that meeting afterward. . . . O thou my kind, Mr. Hannen! I am most pleased with thy service, and I hope that these services of thine shall make thee a standard in the Divine Kingdom. Announce the utmost kindness to Mrs. Hannen. If Mrs. Hannen can undertake to spread broadcast the diary letters which are forwarded to you from the East concerning the travel and sojourn of 'Abdu'l-Bahá, it is very acceptable. . . .

5. *The Muslim Month of Fasting Comes to an End*

In two days the month of Ramadan will come to a close and all restrictions will be taken away. There will be general feasting and five holidays. To the Muslims, this is one of the most important occasions for joy-making and for calling on each other. Already the air is full of expectation for the coming feast!

RAMLEH, EGYPT, AUGUST 31, 1913

1. *The Story of the Blind Man and the Serpent*

"When I was in Sisan," said Mírzá Jalál Síná, "the friends of God brought to me a very old man with a patriarchal beard and wished me to speak to him about the Cause. They had often told him of the teachings, but with no evident result. He was simple, yet fanatical, tender-hearted, yet full of religious superstitions. At heart a child, in body a Hercules. He had the strength of a lion, yet his firm belief in dogmas, inspired him with apprehension as to his future. With rough and uncouth gestures he entered the room and squatting on the floor cried out: 'Tell me now, what have you to say? I have no patience to sit through a long sermon!' Immediately I got, as in a flash of lightning, how I must handle this overgrown child of nature. I told him, 'My friend! I have really nothing to tell you but with your permission I shall relate a story. Will you give me your ears?' 'Forsooth I shall. I do love to hear a good story with a moral to it,' he said, his face already brightening with interest. 'All right, then listen with attention:

Once upon a time there was a man of good position and fortune. As a public servant he ranked high in the estimation of the members of society. He had a palatial residence, and his servants were innumerable. His stable, stocked with Arabian and Persian horses was the pride of the neighborhood. Many famous men sat at his table and ate of his bounteous food. He dispensed hospitality like a prince and received people of all ranks with royal courtesy and lavish splendor. As time rolled on the heaven of his fortune became beclouded, and like the thunders of the sky, successive reverses overtook him, breaking the mountain of his wealth into a thousand pieces. Soon he found himself in complete poverty. By this time all his old friends had left him, and in the hour of destitution, no one would condescend to so much as recognize him. From height of opulence, he was thrown headlong into the depth of despair and indigence. As though these humiliations were not enough, the Fates visited him again and made him totally blind. Now indeed, the cup of his sorrow was full to overflowing, and all doors were closed forever before his face. He was considered an outcast, and no one would associate with him. Finally through this chain of circumstances, he was forced to become a beggar in the public square.

One cold morning in the winter, he left his dirty hovel and went to his accustomed place. While he was walking, his feet stumbled against something. He knelt down and searched for it. He felt a long sinewy thing in his hand and thought it was a silk whip of some special value. He took hold of it and he walked along unconcerned. A passer-by, frightened by the sight of the object being carried by the blind beggar, cried out: 'Man! Man! Dost thou not see what thou art holding in thy hands? It is a serpent, it will bite thee. It will kill thee. Throw it away quickly.' 'No, indeed. No indeed!' the blind man retorted angrily. 'This is a silk whip which costs at least five majidis. Feel it with thy fingers, how soft it is. No! I shall not listen to thee. Thou art a covetous, greedy beggar and want me to throw it away so that thou may take it up and sell it.' 'Really, my friend! This is a poisonous serpent, but the cold weather has benumbed it, and soon the rays of the sun will bring it to life.' 'No! No! Don't talk to me like that. I will not throw it away. If thou art very anxious to have it, I will sell it to thee for four instead of five majidis.' By and by a large crowd gathered, each one calling upon him to throw away the seemingly dead serpent, but he, having lost all confidence in humanity, persisted in believing that it was a whip. In order to show his utter contempt of public opinion, he folded the serpent and placed it near to his skin, standing erect in the already rising sun, in the horrified sight of the spectators. 'What art thou doing? Art thou thine own enemy? The serpent will sting thee with its venomous fangs. Cast it away while there is yet time.' No! the more they insisted, the closer he hugged it to his breast. The serpent, warming up under the downpour of the rays of the star of the day, started to move slowly up and down the body of the beggar, stinging him several times. He shrieked and cried with pain, then fell to the ground in terrible agony. The deadly poison working up rapidly through his body caused his death.

"Now, my old friend, thou art in the position of that blind beggar, because thou art hugging to thy heart the old, superannuated symbols of a decayed and dying religion which will not benefit thee in the least. That serpent, however, caused the death of only the body; this serpent causes the death of the spirit. During the past years all these friends of thine have testified that the old form of religion will not be conducive to thy salvation, but like the old beggar, blindly, thou art in thine obstinacy persisting in that this is the silk whip—my religion is good enough for me—and not a serpent. The serpent of superstition, ignorance and dogma is next to thy skin, and these men cry out to thee to cast it away; so that thy spiritual life may be saved, but no, thou wilt have none of their advice. I portrayed his inner condition so vividly that he commenced to shake and weep. From that time on he became a dweller in the kingdom of Abhá, and a most progressive member of the community."

'Abdu'l-Bahá went to Alexandria this morning and in order to have some papers signed by the judge, he presented himself to the court.

During the evening he came to our house for half an hour, and the talk was on the coming national Fete of Ramadan.

RAMLEH, EGYPT, SEPTEMBER 1, 1913

1. *The Watermelons of 'Akká*

We have received fine watermelons from 'Akká. Abú'l-Qásim sent ten big ones for the Master and he forwarded six of them to our house. If we cannot go to 'Akká now, at least the watermelons of 'Akká come to us. While we were enjoying them, I said that I wished that I could send one of them to America to show the friends how big and juicy are the watermelons of 'Akká. Mírzá Mahmúd laughingly said: "Thou wouldst have sent it if thou didst know how!"

2. *'Abdu'l-Bahá, and the Story of the Policemen of Ramleh*

Arising early this morning Khusraw entertained us with some sidelights on the current events. He sleeps in this house and goes to the Master's home a little after sunrise to begin his work. This morning he delayed his departure, and explained the reason as follows:

"All the policemen in this quarter have received generous gifts of money and presents from the Master. There is one who stands in Khusraw's way every morning and tells him a long story, so that he may repeat it to the Master who may give him some money. 'I have three children. My salary is not sufficient and since the Pasha, His Excellency ('Abdu'l-Bahá) has come here, a new hope has dawned from the horizon of my heart. One of my children goes to school, and for him I have bought a pair of new shoes for the coming feast. The other two who are only a few years old, left stealthily their small beds last night and came to me without any noise. They woke me gently and said: "Papa, papa, we are the Furies. If thou dost not buy two other pairs of shoes for us, we may strangle thee right now." I laughed and hugged them to my breast and sent them back to their beds with a promise that if they are good, behave well and obey their mother, then probably the new "Pasha" may give them the shoes. Now, please, Khusraw Effendi, tell this to "Pasha." Other policemen whose duties are patrolling in other quarters come to Khusraw and ask him: "How long is the new 'Pasha' going to live here?" He says: "Probably one month!" "Good, good! Because after two weeks this quarter will be assigned to us and then the 'Pasha' may be as generous toward us as he has been to others."

3. 'Abdu'l-Bahá Talks on the Power of Imagination

Hájí Niyáz arrived this afternoon from Cairo and brought us the good wishes of the believers. He is the same happy old man with a nature of sunshine and good will toward all. About 6 o'clock 'Abdu'l-Bahá passed by and called on Mírzá Abú'l-Fadl. After a few moments Shoghi Effendi returned and brought me the good news that I was summoned by the Master. I stood before him on the veranda. He was speaking to Mírzá Abú'l-Fadl on "imagination," quoting the epigram of an Oriental Philosopher: "Imagination is the greatest ruler in the human world." No matter how scientific a man may be, yet at time, "imagination" gains an ascendancy over his mind. For example, while a man is alive he is able to strike, to beat, to kill, yet you sleep with him in the same room. When he is dead, science teaches us that his body returns to the mineral kingdom. He can neither strike, nor kill. The body lies there like a piece of stone, inanimate. But you would not sleep with it in the same room. What is the reason of this? It is the power of imagination. It grips you with its imperial energy and overwhelms you with invisible force. All the convincing proofs of science will not induce you to live in the same room with a corpse.

Then he related a dramatic story to further illustrate the subject, but as soon as he finished it, he turned to me and said: "Don't write this." He could see in my face how deeply interested I was! Ere long, he fell into a deep heavenly silence, and the beautiful atmosphere was permeated with a languorous quietness and peace. The brilliant hosts of the sky were arrayed in shining armor of white light, fighting bravely against the deepening darkness. With the ears of the spirit we could hear them chanting and praising, because the face of the earth was illumined by the Face of its Lord.

4. Oriental Bahá'ís Portray "Natural Spirituality"

Returning home, I found a number of the friends engaged in conversation. How happy, how carefree, how detached these people seem to me! They are beings created and fashioned in other worlds. Their happiness, their joy, their detachment are all so natural, so unconscious, so outflowing from the springs of their hearts. There is no affectation, no sanctimony, no religiosity. They do not try to be spiritual. It is not through the exercise of the will. How well 'Abdu'l-Bahá echoes the secrets of their inmost hearts when he writes in a recent Tablet:

> The days of human existence are like vanishing shadows. With the utmost rapidity they are brought to a close. From amongst mankind those who live a heedless life are at the end, afflicted with manifest loss. For the days of their lives will come to a sudden close, leaving no leaves, no blossoms and no fruit. They shall remain in the lowest degree, and no mention of them will be left behind. From kings to servants all walk in this path and live in this circle, except those souls who are freed from all ties. They are not greedy after comfort, nor are they seeking fleeting pleasures. They are not longing for honor, neither are they chasing phantasmal pictures of glory and wealth. They are the devotees (or veterans) of the Blessed Perfection and are in the utmost state of renunciation and evanescence. They are wanderers over mountains and deserts. They call the people to the kingdom of God and are the cause of the guidance of souls.

Like unto candles they are ignited with all the virtues of the world of humanity. This is Everlasting Glory! This is Eternal Life! This is the divine sublimity of the Creation of God!

Daily the cord of correspondence between the East and the West is becoming stronger, and the interchange of ideas more common. Each one of us must do our humble part, no matter where we are; so that the millennium for the coming of which we pray, may soon be established between all peoples and nations and tongues.

RAMLEH, EGYPT, SEPTEMBER 2, 1913

1. Moving Picture Theatres in Egypt

This is the second greatest feast in the Muslim world, the feast celebrating the passing of the month of Ramadan. In a way it fills the place of the New Year in America. It is called the Feast of "Beyram" [ed. Feast of Sacrifice] and is a national holiday. All the government departments, offices and stores are closed for from one to five days. The older people pay visits to each other, and the younger generation dressed in bright colors, receive gifts and presents, and eat much candy to their great delight. Although the thin air of sadness broods over many hearts owing to the Balkan wars, yet the general impression is that of happiness, gaiety and fun. Life to a simple-hearted Arab is like a moving picture gallery, and he loves to see the scenes of creation unfolding before his eyes without leaving his seat; to this we may attribute the springing up of many nickelodeons and cheap show-places all over Egypt who advertise their pictures in a lurid and sensational manner. These show-places attract a large clientele of heterogeneous elements. On a day such as this, the managers, mostly Italians, Greeks and Levantines, reap a golden harvest.

2. The Feast of Ramadan and Its Spirit of Joy

On the other hand, the religious spirit of the people finds expression in the gorgeous decorations of the mosques and in long hours of prayers and preaching.

Last night Mírzá 'Alí-Akbar brought three kinds of candies

for the callers today, so this morning they were put on different plates ready to be served. The Samovar was boiling and the tea brewing. I was dressed and walking on the veranda, when I saw 'Abdu'l-Bahá coming toward our house. I was glad to look into his face on this Fete day, and my heart sang the songs of joy. What else really do we want except his good pleasure? Is there anything more worth while? Do we not live and move and have our being in him? Is he not the supreme object of our lives? The sun of his unalloyed peace shines upon all and everybody is contented.

How thoughtful and beautiful of the Master to call on Mírzá Abú'l-Fadl before anybody else! Is it not just like him?

By the time he returned to us a number of believers and outsiders had gathered on the veranda. He greeted them with affability, and afterwards he wished them a happy and blessed "Beyram." Then tea and candy were served in turn. He beamed on the friends with heavenly joy and cabled to the Bahá'í world the glad news: "My health is perfect."

3. Talk on Education and the Story of a Selfish Mother

The subject of his talk was "Education" and the duty of mothers toward their children, a most appropriate message to go out to the world of motherhood.

He stated that fathers and especially mothers must always think how best they should educate their children, not how to fondle and embrace them too much and thus spoil them. By every means at their disposal, they must knead onto their growing bodies, souls, minds and spirits the basic principles of sincerity, love, trustfulness, obedience, true democracy and kindness toward all races; thus, hereafter the world-civilization may flow in one mighty current and the children of future generations may secure the foundation of human solidarity and good-will. From tenderest childhood, the children must be taught by their mothers the love of God, and the love of humanity; not the love of humanity of Asia nor the humanity of Europe, nor the humanity of America, but the "humanity of humanity".

There are some mothers who have a strange, inexplicable love for their children. One may call it the inversion of love, or as we call it in Persia, "Bearish love". This kind of love does more injury to the child than good. When 'Abdu'l-Bahá was in 'Akká, during the life of the Blessed Perfection, he entrusted the son of one of the believers to a German carpenter. After a month the mother went to Bahá'u'lláh and lamented and bemoaned that she wanted her son, because he was unhappy with the carpenter, who cursed his religion. Bahá'u'lláh told her to consult with Áqá ('Abdu'l-Bahá) and abide by his decision. She went to 'Abdu'l-Bahá and after telling her side of the story, he said to her: 'The Germans do not curse anyone. They are not accustomed to it.' She went away and after a month called again with another complaint, saying that this carpenter had forced her son to carry a load of wheat on his back. Again 'Abdu'l-Bahá told her that if the carpenter had done this, it was for her son's discipline.

Outwardly 'Abdu'l-Bahá satisfied her, but she was murmuring inwardly. A few months rolled by and she returned with another set of complaints, frankly confessing that she did not want her son to be away from her, for he was the apple of her eye. Realizing how selfish her love was, 'Abdu'l-Bahá told her at last that he would not take her son away, but that he must stay with the carpenter for eight years, until his apprenticeship was over. She yielded to the inevitable. After eight years of study the son left his master, and his mother was very proud of him, because his work was in demand on all sides. In short, mothers must not think of themselves, but of the progress of their children, because upon the children of today depends the molding of the civilization of tomorrow.

All day telegrams poured in from the leaders and important men of Turkey, Egypt, Arabia, etc., congratulating 'Abdu'l-Bahá on this Fete and wishing him a happy "Beyram"!

4. Story of the Theologian and the Sea Captain

There was a caller on 'Abdu'l-Bahá, a theological student of the College of Al-Azhar, and the discussion turned upon the utter futility of Islamic theology and metaphysics, and of how some young men wasted their lives on the study of this one branch for twenty or thirty years. Once there was a theologian who took a sea trip. While he was pacing the deck and watching the calm sea, the captain passed by and inquired about his health. Our friend was so full of his theology that he asked the captain: "Dost thou know theology? He answered "No." "Then," the student declared with much pompous dignity, "half thy life is lost." The captain did not answer him but continued his walk. Next day the sea became very stormy, and the ship was in danger of being wrecked. The captain called on the theologian and found him prostrated with sickness. "Dost thou know how to swim?" he asked. 'No.' "Then all thy life is lost," the captain thundered at him. And you should have heard the Master laugh. Then he quoted several of their metaphysical, hair-splitting axioms over each one of which the theologians wrangle and dispute days and nights.

5. Story of a Metaphysician and the Correction of His Book by a Teacher

Another time, a theological poet, after several years of hardship and privation, finished a book and took it to a learned man to be read and corrected. He read the book and found that the contents were very much like the cobwebs of a spider, or the phantasmal imaginings of a sickly brain. Therefore he marked the first and the last pages, thus conveying the fact that the book was not worth correcting.

In the afternoon the Master sent all of us to the garden of Nozha. We had a pleasant time and on our return we heard that he had been entertaining many Arabs, first at our house and then at that of Mírzá Abú'l-Fadl.

6. Study of Science and True Religion Must Be Combined

At noon 'Abdu'l-Bahá told us that he did not mean that religious study must be neglected, but that practical sciences should be learned, so that the lives of the students might become useful. In the future, the theological seminaries must discard all their dogmas which are contradictory to science and reason, and lay a basic foundation, not to be destroyed by the fretting tooth of time. We hope that they will accomplish this task.

RAMLEH, EGYPT, SEPTEMBER 3, 1913

1. Persian Bahá'í Students of American College Arrive

Last night eleven young Bahá'ís arrived from Haifa. They are students in the American College at Beirut and have been passing their summer vacation on Mount Carmel, waiting impatiently for permission to visit the Master. These are not all of them. When the present party leaves for Haifa, another one composed of an equal or larger number, will come. They are all young boys from 8 to 18 years, studying in various branches of science, and equipping themselves to become useful members of the body politic. Morally pure, intellectually keen, spiritually susceptible, mentally alive, they combine with these qualities rare power of reserve, simplicity, naturalness and dignity of character, seldom to be witnessed in other youths of the same age. Everyone knows by memory many communes and supplications, and this morning after drinking tea, they sat around and chanted Tablets. The American spirit of freedom and activity is in their constitutions. They will become fine and progressive citizens of Persia, when they return to that country. Although their names may sound unfamiliar to our American friends across the ocean, yet they may be of interest. They are as follows: Mírzá 'Azízu'lláh Khán, Mírzá 'Alí-Muhammad Khán, Mírzá 'Abdu'l-Husayn Khán, Mírzá Mahmúd Khán, Mírzá 'Abdu'l-Hasan Khán, all of Shiraz; Mírzá Aflátún of Hamadan, Mírzá 'Alí Áqá of Rasht, Mírzá Mahmúd Khán of Isfahan, Qudsí Effendi of Haifa and Áqá Sayyid Qásim of Sabzivar.

'Abdu'l-Bahá sent for me and after a few minutes talk told me to go and bring the students. I conducted them to the house and they were ushered into the reception room. Hardly a minute had passed when the Master appeared. They all rose to their feet and although he told them not to do it, yet one after another knelt before him and kissed the hem of his garment, his hands or his feet. This is the highest sign of respect, nay rather adoration, and flows from the depth of their hearts. It is spontaneous and natural, full of sweetness and attachment. It is neither dictated by custom nor ceremony.

2. Persian Students in Paris and London

He told them that they were very welcome! He had been longing to see them, but up to this time the way was not open. Was their vacation spent pleasantly in Haifa on Mount Carmel? The College of Beirut was very good. They could not realize how some of the Persian students spent their time in profitless pursuits in London and Paris. Not only did the Europeans look down upon them, as members of an inferior race and half-civilized, but they (the students) confirm them in this opinion by indulging in the questionable pleasures and vices of the European lower society. They hardly do any study. The major part of their time is spent in the gratification of the appetites, such as sensuality, attending dance halls and theaters, wine drinking, association with undesirable members of the community in which they live, and leading an insipid and voluptuous life, ruinous to themselves and the Persian nation alike. . . . Praise be to God that the faces of these Bahá'í students were radiant; the rays of the love of God were shining from their countenances. He was most pleased to have met them. It is very strange that when a face is not illumined with the light of the Love of God, it is dark, and when you look into it, the traces of the divine Glad-tidings are not manifest, but when the light of God shines upon it, it becomes bright and enlightened, as it is said: "In their faces you shall see the verdancy of Paradise and in their countenances there is the sign of worship."

3. 'Abdu'l-Bahá Tells the Students How to Study

Afterward the Master left the house to call on Uthmán Pasha, and in his company, a visit was paid to the Khedive who celebrated the feast yesterday in Cairo, and today in Alexandria. Before noon, the Master came to our house to meet the students. He told them that it was his hope that they would make extraordinary progress along spiritual lines as well as in science and art; so that each one might become a brilliant lamp in the world of modern

4. The Students Read 'Abdu'l-Bahá's Talks in America

In the hands of the students there were copies of 'Abdu'l-Bahá's address given before the Forum Club of San Francisco. He asked one of them what he was holding in his hand? The student presented it to him and he read the last portion concerning the philosophers and the cows, and how the modern materialists should go to the cow to learn the principles of materialism. After speaking on some other subjects, he left us. The students are all eager to take down every word which he says to them and they are writing to their parents and friends the incidents of their trip ad of their experiences.

Before he left, he told Mírzá 'Alí-Akbar to accompany all the students to the Persian Consulate at 4 P.M. As we are quite numerous, both dinner and supper are served in turn; first the students sit around the table, and afterwards the rest of us.

5. 'Abdu'l-Bahá Calls on the Persian Consul

At 4 o'clock, we found ourselves in the large reception room of the Persian Consulate General in Alexandria. For the first half hour we were entertained by the Consul, and then the Master came and spoke with him in Turkish. The Consul is a genial old man and loves the Master very deeply.

When we returned home, the Master had arrived ahead of us, and was talking with a number of prominent callers. At night we had an unusual gathering, full of interest, many of the Bahá'ís related the story of how they first embraced the Cause of God.

RAMLEH, EGYPT, SEPTEMBER 4, 1913

1. The Story of the Royal Bird Qidam

The Eastern mind is a treasure-house of mystic stories, each one fraught with significant lessons. One of these beautiful stories was related to me the other day by Mírzá Jalál Síná, and fore-shadows the coming of the Manifestation of God into this world. I report it here without its interpretation, knowing that my readers will supply it by their own imagination:

Far, far away in a jungle, inaccessible to man, beyond the Indian Ocean, there lived a bird of royal birth, majesty and beauty. Her name was Qidam. Her song was endowed by the Creator of Mankind with incomparable beauty, richness, sweetness, and charm. The strains of her natural melodies belonged to other than this material world, which is full of the cawing of crows, the cackling of geese and the twittering of sparrows. Whenever Qidam began to sing, she raised her melody to such a lofty height as to silence all the other birds, who were ashamed of their own weak, discordant voices noises. Thus were they discomfited and filled with envy and regret, and wondered what they could do to bring about the end of Qidam. Finally they arranged a large meeting in which they might deliberate as to how they should heap vengeance upon her unsuspecting head and cause her death.

After much consultation, they agreed upon the plan of destroying the eggs of Qidam whenever and wherever she laid them; so that her descendants might not increase. In order to carry out this plan with vigilance, they appointed a committee to execute the decree. They agreed amongst themselves that they would continue to break the eggs of Qidam till the time came when she would grow old and die, thus protecting themselves from the power of such a rival. For a number of years Qidam patiently endured the persecution of these little birds who were exulting over the success of their plan in thus systematically destroying her eggs and not letting her progeny increase. Qidam never said anything nor manifested any trace of concern. Then at a time when the birds were away from their nests, she laid one egg in each and flew away, perching on the loftiest branch and singing her own entrancing melody. The other birds, not knowing exactly what had happened, sat as usual on their eggs, and after a while the little ones stepped out of their narrow world into open space. Tenderly and with much solicitude and devotion were they taken care of, and from the mother birds' beaks the little ones were fed.

Soon their dear growing wings were covered with soft feathers like unto velvet, and the parents were delighted to see their darling offspring developing into the size of birdhood. Qidam from the loftiest branch was watching, how day after day, her children were nurtured by these different birds with a wistful tenderness and sympathy as though they were their own. Then, when she observed that they had reached the flying stage, she perched on the highest green branch, filling the empty void with her wonderful music, which vibrated, and rocked through the atmosphere.

The little birds who were her real children, heard the clear, resonant melody and finding its exact similarity to their own, and realizing from the depth of their hearts, their true kinship with the invisible singer, suddenly fluttered their wings, and up they soared to join their Mother. Out of every nest a number of birds such as doves, partridges, sparrows, crows, nightingales, blue-birds, etc. who had become accustomed to the harmonious companionship of the children of Qidam, joined them in their flight. Although they were of various forms, colors and species, voices and kinds, they soared together with love and sweet fellowship, toward the azure height and there composed a divine company, circling and circling around their beloved mother, as the songs of thanksgiving and gratitude with soft appealing notes flowed like a clear stream from their hearts.

2. Purity and Chastity the Foundation of Spiritual Life

While the students and other pilgrims were drinking tea, the Master entered the house. He walked through the rooms and inquired about the health of each. Then he went to the veranda and sat down. The first thing that he said showed his interest in the welfare of the students. He asked Mírzá 'Alí-Akbar to take them to Nozha Park. Then, introducing them to an Arab Bahá'í, he remarked, that these students were doing well with their studies and that in reality they were the cause of his happiness.

He also gave a most interesting talk on what the students should study while in Europe, and what they should shun. After giving a minute account of the social customs of the Western people, he told us that chastity and purity are two divine standards of the spiritual and moral law. The greater the aims of a man the nobler his deeds; man must ever be thoughtful of others and polite and courteous toward his fellow beings. This will win for him the good-pleasure of the Lord and the satisfaction of the general public. One's sitting and rising, conduct and manner, speech and conversation, social intercourse and communication, must be based upon a firm foundation and be conducive to the Glory of the world of humanity.

3. The Brother of the Khedive Calls on 'Abdu'l-Bahá

In the afternoon Prince Muhammad-'Alí, the brother of the Khedive, called on 'Abdu'l-Bahá. The Prince arrived in his automobile at the door of our house, and hearing that the Master lived close by in another one, said that he would walk to it. Mírzá Munír was about to go on ahead to notify 'Abdu'l-Bahá, when he appeared in his long, loose, cream-colored coat from the other side of the street. Thus, in the middle of the road, the Master and the Prince met, each offering to the other courtesies designated for the most distinguished men. Everyone looking at this strange scene wondered, while trying to imagine what had brought a royal Prince of Egypt to the Threshold of 'Abbás Effendi. The Master was walking ahead and the Prince a few feet behind, and while they were talking in the most animated manner, they disappeared from our view.

4. American Ice Cream for Students—Their Visit to the National Park

Late in the afternoon 'Abdu'l-Bahá came to visit the pilgrims and after a few minutes went to see Mírzá Abú'l-Fadl, from which place he returned home to rest.

Before the students left for Nozha Garden, Khusraw brought a jar of American ice cream, prepared for them by Mrs. Getsinger. It was very good, and everybody enjoyed it.

5. The Student's Love for the Bahá'í Cause

All day there were different groups here and there, each speaking about the Cause and putting forth arguments to prove the Dawn of the Sun of Reality. It seems to me that these young men are very devoted to the Movement, and free, and ready to receive and assimilate all kinds of useful information. I have no doubt that from amongst them a number of most capable teachers will arise.

RAMLEH, EGYPT, SEPTEMBER 5, 1913

1. Who Is 'Abdu'l-Bahá and What Is He Doing?

'Abdu'l-Bahá is eloquent in his silence and speaks with the tongue of the angels in the congregation of the elect. His heavenly songs, stream down from unknown heights. Like unto the bird of Paradise, he raises his voice and humanity hears it. His heart is a variegated rose-garden whose fragrant narcissuses of knowledge, gentle violets of wisdom, and sweet anemones of love and graceful hyacinths of sympathy spread their perfume. The heaven of his mind is begemmed with orbs of reality, dispelling the darkness of doubt. The grandeur of his spirit, the sublimity of his ideals and the epic events of his life are the noblest examples set before the eyes of man. To the wanderer he is a refuge; to the thirsty he is a cooling spring, to the poor he is a treasury of wealth; to the despondent he is a source of inspiration; to the orphan he is a kind father; to the sick he is a physician; to the weak, he is a power-house of energy; to the hungry he is a divine table.

2. The Persian Students and Prayers

Every morning presents to my view a happy scene of worship, because all the students pray before sunrise. They attract to themselves a moral force, infusing into their lives that quality of Faith which changes hate into love, strangeness into friendship, and enmity into amity. Through prayer their minds are polished and their hearts purified with the fire of the Love of God. They attain to the station of confidence, realize the divinity of holiness, are drawn unto God, and become clear mirrors in which the ideal images of the Kingdom are reflected. They put forth green leaves of hope and blossoms of radiant acquiescence. With prayer, they learn their lessons; with prayer they take their examinations; with prayer they make intellectual progress and with prayer on their lips they rise in the early morning ad go to sleep at night.

Today I was speaking about the servants of the Cause and Mírzá Jalál Síná told me the following story.

3. The Story of a Man Who Was Hired to Build a Wall around a Garden

A man hired a mason to build a wall around his garden. The next morning the mason came to start his work. The foundations were already laid by other laborers, and an assistant was hired to pass him the bricks. At the moment when the first one was handed to him a friend of his passed by and was hailed to come near, and they engaged in a lively conversation. The mason forgot all about the building of the wall, and the time slipped by until noon. He had yet the first brick in his hand when the hour of twelve struck. At that time the owner of the garden arrived on the scene, and seeing the work not even started, dismissed him and brought another mason to do it in his place.

4. In the Cause of Brotherhood There Are No Titles

There are some souls who are similarly situated. When a work is entrusted to them by the Great Builder, they take it as a personal thing. They do as much of it as they think advisable according to their limited understanding or do not do it at all. In such a case the Great Builder without telling them anything about it, takes the work out of their hands and entrusts it to those who will dispatch it with the utmost rapidity. Personalities do not count in this Cause; work, enduring work, patient impersonal work is called for. There are no titles in this Movement. Let all the workers banish such dreams from their minds. In God's estimation the laborers are all equal. We are all His servants. 'Abdu'l-Bahá has taken the title of the "Servant of God' and the servant of humanity. Every sincere soul, according to his ability, must strive day and night to walk in this path. The divine path is the path of servitude, humility, evanescence—severance from aught else save God, and service.

5. 'Abdu'l-Bahá Inquires from the Persian Students about Their Teachers

At 8 o'clock 'Abdu'l-Bahá came and all the students were ready to receive him. He inquired about their health and if they were comfortable in their present quarters.

He asked them to tell him whether the teachers took pains to instruct the students, or if like some professors, they went through the lessons as machines without showing any feeling or interest in the progress of the pupils?

6. People Are Not Awake to the Danger of War

Holding in his hand several copies of his American addresses which had been published in the newspapers, he informed us that the people of Egypt were not interested in them and that any reference to them would bring only the answer, "very excellent," "very good." However, they were interested in the most unimportant news of the day. They are not thinking of those principles which will build up the future civilization of mankind; yet they acknowledge the fact that the world of humanity is in great danger and is going through a most crucial period. Although war may cease temporarily, yet there is an invisible war constantly carried on which is a tremendous economic loss. These unseen drains are breaking the financial backs of the nations. They do not know by what means or instruments the comity of nations, or the peace of the world can be achieved.

7. 'Abdu'l-Bahá Dictates Tablets for American Bahá'ís

Then he told me to have the letters ready, and in a few moments I was following him toward the garden. He was glad to be away from the people, and for three hours he dictated Tablets for the friends beyond the seas. Some of those who were honored with Tablets were the following: Miss Jean Masson, Mrs. Gertrude Diffet, the Editor of the "Master Mind" in Los Angeles, Mrs. Harriet Cline, Mrs. Mary C. Bell, Miss General Jack, Mrs. Thornberg Cropper, Mrs. Anna Killius, Mr. Horace Holley, Mrs. Fred Mortenson, Madame H. Maron, Mrs. Stansell, Miss Juliet Thompson, Consul-General

Topakeyan, Miss Edna MacKinny and Miss Maria Wilson.

Yesterday the Master's daughter left for Cairo with Bashír for a short stay. Today Shoghi Effendi joined his mother with Hájí Niyáz. In the afternoon four Bahá'ís arrived from Cairo.

8. Program for a National or Religious Feast

About 4 o'clock, 'Abdu'l-Bahá came again and gave us an interesting talk on how a religious, or national Fete should be celebrated.

The program for such fete days must be so prepared to yield a permanent result. As these are days of freedom from work, the leaders of the communities must discuss such problems as may be beneficial to the individuals and the outcome of which will be eternal. They must be occupied with prayers and thanksgiving and be grateful for the Favors and Bounties of God.

9. Driving around with 'Abdu'l-Bahá

Then he called me to follow him. Outside a carriage was waiting. He beckoned me to sit beside him and told Khusraw to sit next to the driver. We stopped at the Hotel Plaisance and took Mr. Atwood with us. The carriage drove for more than one hour on the shore of the Nile. We passed many large palm groves and the Arab hovels of Fellaheens. These Arabs live in real squalor. Pigs, hens, donkeys, goats sleep with them in the same mud rooms. Arriving at the Nozha, we drove through its shady avenues and our eyes were brightened by the wonderful flowers. The Master left the carriage and we passed into the place where the band was playing and where more than two hundred Englishmen were picnicking with their families. He walked through the Park and finally sat down on the side of a well. He was steeped in a world of thought. Then he went away from us and sat on the green grass. For nearly 15 minutes he remained there undisturbed. The sun was sinking behind the western sky when our carriage was driven homeward. The Master putting his arm around the shoulders of Mr. Atwood told him that he went driving today especially for him as he loved him very much. He was most pleased with him, because he had resigned his will to the Will of God.

Mr. Atwood thanked him for his kindness and said:

"Master, I think often of you and of your great work. I can never forget the time when you called at a mission school in Alexandria. The principal in greeting you, said: 'You are the father of the poor and I am their servant!' You answered: 'I am the servant of the poor, but you are their father!'"

RAMLEH, EGYPT, SEPTEMBER 6, 1913

1. The American Bahá'ís Must Make Great Efforts in Teaching the Cause of Peace.

When I stood in the Master's presence this morning, he asked me whether I had any news. Then in a talk he emphasized the fact that the American Bahá'ís must, with one accord, and one voice unite in raising the pillars of Universal Peace in their regions. God will reinforce them with the Powers of the Kingdom if they arise wholeheartedly in the service of this Cause. They have every means at their disposal, and no lack of extraordinary desire to do the will of God. By example and by deeds they have seen the workings of the Glorious Lord. Now that 'Abdu'l-Bahá is in the Orient, he loves to hear that the seeds of Truth which he has sown in the West are beginning to sprout, that the ideals of Peace which he has diffused are taking root in the hearts. They must gird up the loins of endeavor, enter the arena of activity and let the reports of their fresh triumphs gladden the heart of 'Abdu'l-Bahá.

2. Prof. Arminius Vambery's Letter to 'Abdu'l-Bahá

Before I left his presence, he handed me a letter written to him by Prof. Vambery of Budapest, who met him during his sojourn in that city. On his arrival in Port Said, 'Abdu'l-Bahá revealed for him a Tablet and sent him a Persian rug as a present. I will translate the letter as a matter of historical interest. The Professor's letter is in Persian:

> *I forward this humble petition to the sanctified and Holy Presence of 'Abdu'l-Bahá 'Abbás, who is famous throughout the world, the Center of Knowledge, and beloved by all mankind!*

O thou kind, noble friend, thou who art conferring guidance upon humanity—may my life be a ransom to thee!

The loving epistle which you have condescended to write to this servant and the rug which you have forwarded, came to hand safely. The meeting with your Excellency and being in your Presence, which is full of benediction, recurs to the memory of this servant and I am longing for the time when I shall meet you again. In reality, although I have traveled throughout many countries and cities of Islam, yet I have never met a lofty character and exalted personage to compare with your Excellency, and I bear witness that it is not possible to find one. On this account I am hoping that the Ideals and accomplishments of your Excellency may be crowned with success, and yield results under all circumstances; because, behind these Ideals and deeds, I easily observe the future welfare and prosperity of the world of humanity.

This servant, in order to gain firsthand information and experience, entered the ranks of various religions; that is, outwardly I became a Jew, a Christian, a Mohammedan and a Fire-worshiper. I discovered that the devotees of these different religions do nothing else but hate and anathematize each other; that all these religions have become the instruments of tyranny and oppression in the hands of rulers and governors, and that they are causes for the destruction of the world and of humanity. Considering these evil results, every person is forced by necessity to be enlisted on the side of your Excellency and embrace rejoicingly, the prospect of the Universal Religion which is being ushered in through your effort.

I have seen the father of your Excellency from afar and have realized the self-sacrifice and noble courage of His Son, and my admiration has been increasing. For the principles and aims of your Excellency, I express the utmost respect and devotion and if God, the most High, confers a long life upon me, I will be able to serve you under all conditions. I pray and supplicate for this from the depth of my heart.

(Signed) "Your servant, Vambery.

3. *The Persian Students meet Mrs. Getsinger*

In the reception room of the house of the Beloved the students met Mrs. Getsinger. She spoke to them most beautifully and they listened with rapt attention. None of them had yet seen or heard an American Bahá'í. She related for their benefit, the story of the Beloved's lecture in Columbia University of New York, and in Stanford University of California and when she told about Mortenson, and of how he traveled from Minneapolis to Green Acre under the trains, and of how he was received first by Mr. and Mrs. Ed. Kinney and later by 'Abdu'l-Bahá, all eyes were dim with tears. Then she spoke about spiritual knowledge, prayer, and the conformity of science and faith, and at the end chanted a prayer by Bahá'u'lláh.

4. *'Abdu'l-Bahá Speaks on the Power of Unity*

Then 'Abdu'l-Bahá came in and said that God had brought us together in Ramleh. No other power could ever have accomplished this. We were meeting with the utmost joy and fragrance. Spiritual attraction had united us. The Divine outpourings and the Bestowals of the Blessed Perfection had called us to this heavenly banquet. Just as in this material world we were brought together at this meeting, similarly may we associate with one another in the kingdom of Abhá.

In the afternoon the Beloved dictated several important Tablets, and later entertained the French Consul of Haifa who had come to meet him.

Many hours today were spent in writing and in listening to the delightful stories related by Mírzá Jalál Síná.

RAMLEH, EGYPT, SEPTEMBER 7, 1913

1. *The Story of the Mythical Republic and of a Curious Way of Electing a President*

Let me relate to you the story of a poor man and how he became the Ruler of one of the ancient Republics. Back of it you will detect the spiritual history of God and His relation with mankind.

Years and years ago the inhabitants of the country of . . . who enjoyed a sort of Republic, had a most curious way of electing their President. The people gathered once a year in the largest public square of the capital. Then they would bring out the golden cage of the bird, Humá, and place it at the head of the procession of dignitaries, amidst universal rejoicing, while the music of the national band played. After many ceremonies, and the delivery of eloquent addresses, they would open the gate of the cage and release the bird Humá before the eyes of all the citizens. The bird, gaining its freedom, would rise higher and higher toward the blue ether, and then descend on the head of an individual in the crowd, whom the people would hail as the next Ruler.

It was on such an important election day that a stranger entered the city. He observed decorations of flags and bunting, and the streets filled with seething humanity. Every avenue, like a tributary to the sea, emptied its rushing people into the great public square. All the seats, tier upon tier, were filled. After much pushing and pulling, the stranger found his way to the square, where a wonderful spectacle met his view. He was thunderstruck at the lavish splendor of this sight. While he was looking at it, he felt some one tapping on his shoulder. He was hot and pressed on all sides. "What do you want, man? Do you not see that I am nearly dying of suffocation?" "Wilt thou make me thy aide-de-camp if thou art elected President of the Republic?" "Pooh! Art thou gone insane, man? I have just entered this city and know not a single soul. I would like to know who would elect an absolute stranger to the highest position in the Republic?" "I think thou dost not know the laws of this country, neither is there any time for their explanation. Just give me thy word now." "All right," the stranger laughed aloud. "If I ever become the President of the Republic, thou wilt be my aide-de-camp."

Hardly was this promise given, when he felt the sudden weight of something upon his head. Then he heard the deafening hurrah of the great multitude which filled the air and which rocked the very foundations of the buildings. The bird Humí had sat upon his head, and he was already, by the sovereign will of the people, the President. The notification committee, followed by the most prominent citizens, informed him of his election, and with much solemnity conducted him to the capital. For one week there were great festivities in the capital. Fireworks and illuminations, athletic games and banquets, brilliant processions, and public receptions, attracted the attention of all the classes of citizens. The inaugural ball, which brought to a close these successive festivities, eclipsed all other events in points of brilliancy.

To the delight and satisfaction of Congress and the Cabinet members, the new President showed extraordinary knowledge on all public questions, and an intuitional grasp of necessary reforms. These reforms had been needed for a long time, but the nation had not been fortunate enough to have a man at the helm of the government who could make them possible for practical legislature.

Soon after his inauguration, the president received a letter from an unknown man, reminding him of his promise. He sent for him immediately and found in him the requirements of an aide-de-camp. In the course of mutual association, they became great friends and one day, the aide-de-camp said to the President in an off-hand manner: "do you know what is going to happen to you after the expiration of your Presidential term?" "No, I have never thought about it." "Well, I will tell you, because you have been very kind to me. When your term expires, the citizens will come to the Palace, drive you out of your executive office, ask you to put on your old clothes, take you through the streets, make you ride backward on a donkey, and at the head of a sneering, ridiculing mob, parade you through the avenues and bazaars. In this ignominious manner the procession will leave the city. They will proceed for several miles until they reach a broad river on the other side of which is an island. Then they will place you in a boat, and a boatman will row you to the other side. There he will leave you and return. As the island is surrounded by the water, there can be no communication with the outside world."

The President was quite disturbed by this account. "Why did you not tell me of this before?" "Firstly, I did not know you; secondly, this knowledge could not prevent Humí from alighting on your head; thirdly, even should you have known this, the people would not have accepted your refusal." "But, have I not given them a wise and efficient administration, and on that ground, am I not entitled to a second election?" "You must realize that the people are not electing you. It depends upon the caprice of a bird, and I am sure, that even if they let you stay in the public square on the election day, you would not have the remotest chance of being re-elected. On the other hand, no power on earth, except the will of the whole people of this Republic, can amend this provision of the constitution. It is simply impossible." "Then what must I do? Will you give me your advice?" "Well, you can do one thing. As long as you live in this Palace, you have a perfect right to expend your salary on any undertaking you deem most necessary and urgent. You are able to select a number of architects, masons, engineers and laborers, send them to the island, and give them the commission of building a commodious house, in which you may live during the remaining years of your life. I have been aide-de-camp to many former Presidents, and in every instance I have urged them to do this, but they were so occupied with the gratification of their own desires, that they did not heed my advice, and the time slipped by. Suddenly they saw that the year had expired, and they found themselves in manifest loss."

This President, however, was of a different disposition, and from that day on, he devoted his leisure hours to the construction of a house on the Island. When the term of his service expired, he went through all the strange rites prescribed by the law with a cool head, a confident heart, and a serene mind, because he knew that on the other side, everything was prepared to receive him....

After a few days on the Island, he started to explore it, and here and there came across a number of emaciated and starved looking men who were clothed in tattered garments. He asked them, "Who are you?" They answered: "We are the former Presidents of the Republic of X. We were not as wise and as far-seeing as you have proven to be. While we filled our Presidential Offices, we thought only of our own importance, and pursued the pleasures and vanities of life, instead of thinking of enduring and eternal principles. We never troubled our minds about our future; neither did we heed the admonitions of our friend. Thus this present misery is the result of our own past heedlessness."

2. 'Abdu'l-Bahá Spends a Busy Day

This morning the students were summoned into the presence of 'Abdu'l-Bahá, and he gave them a stirring talk on the union of the East and the West, and of how the Cause of Harmony was set aglow and the hearts of mankind and how its flame is getting stronger and stronger every day.

RAMLEH, EGYPT, SEPTEMBER 8, 1913

1. The Arab Bahá'ís Give a Feast to the Persian Students

Five of the young Arabian Bahá'ís acted as hosts to the students, and the friends. The feast was given in the garden of Nozha. The tablecloth was spread under the shade of the trees and forty of us sat around it. The dinner was delicious, and our Arabian friends dispensed true old-fashioned Oriental hospitality. During the day, Tablets were chanted, songs were sung, short speeches delivered and the spirit of Bahá'í friendship deeply felt. Although there existed no outward relation between the Arab and the Persian Bahá'ís, yet they conversed together with great sympathy as though they belonged to the same family. After dinner we were divided into small groups and walked through the Park. On our return, we found the Samovar boiling and tea prepared.

2. How an Arab Became a Bahá'í

One of the hosts told us how he was first attracted to the Cause: "Two years ago, a similar picnic was held here on this very spot by the Bahá'ís. I passed by, and looking at them, saw a divine happiness upon their faces. I became curious, and began to ask questions. Soon I obtained the privilege of entering the kingdom of Bahá'u'lláh. Now, all of these men who are passing by, looking at us with wondering eyes, who knows but there may be some who will become Bahá'ís, two years from now?"

3. Importance of Agriculture

When we returned home we found 'Abdu'l-Bahá dictating Tablets in the garden. Mírzá Munír was the secretary. Several new men were permitted to go into his presence. Later he sent for the students, because they had not seen him in the morning. He spoke with them on the subject of agriculture and the present need for it in Persia. He asked them whether such a course was given in the Beirut College. He laid great stress upon the study of scientific agriculture and encouraged them to become the teachers of this science and the spreaders of its principles. He concluded, saying that he expected the appearance of great things from them.

4. A Prayer for the Illumination of Mankind

One of the prayers chanted by the students today in the Nozha garden is the following:

He is El Abhá!

> O Thou pure God! Make thou this gathering the candle of the world and suffer this assembly to become a rose garden and a verdant meadow. Let its meeting become a delectable paradise and its horizon the dawning-place of the lights of the Merciful. Perfume Thou the nostrils of the dwellers of the Mount of the Friend with its Fragrance and rejoice the hearts of the pilgrims of the Holy city of the Desired One with its amber-scented breeze. Protect Thou these souls under the shadow of an asylum of Protection in the fortress of Thy Majesty, the One, the Most High! Shower upon us the Confirmations of Thy Abhá Horizon and bestow upon us the Graces of Thy Supreme Concourse. Although we are birds without feathers and wings, yet have we built our nests and homes in the gardens of Thy Cause. We have taken refuge at the Threshold of Thy Oneness, and we are begging of Thee Confirmation, help and aid. When we look upon ourselves, we are smaller than the atoms; when we behold the sea of Thy Generosity and Liberality, we see the atoms as brilliant suns, nay rather, more brilliant!

> O Thou Kind King! Cover the sins of these weak ones with the hem of the garment of Thy Mercy. Change the indifference of these heedless ones into the essence of fidelity, wisdom and understanding! Grant the souls a loftier effort and cast another tumult in the heads; so that they may sing the melody of the Supreme Realm, seek after the Everlasting Glory, long for the delicacies of the New World, soar toward the highest horizon, enter into the congregation of the Almighty and become the recipients of the Bestowals of the Kingdom of Abhá! Thus the dark world will become luminous, the satanic field will be transformed into the Court of the Merciful, this mound of earth will become the celestial heaven, and this terrestrial globe the Eternal Rose-garden. Verily Thou art the Powerful, the Mighty, the Hearer and the Seer.
>
> 'Abdu'l-Bahá 'Abbás.

5. The Object of the Coming of Bahá'u'lláh

'Abdu'l-Bahá writes in a Tablet:

> O ye real friends! And ye who are drawn to the Beauty of God! This is the time of attraction and acclamation, and the period of rejoicing and merrymaking. This is the morn of Glad-tidings! Is it not suffused with splendors? The Candle of the world is bestowing light upon all the assemblages. Is it not luminous? The Manifest Orb is rising from the dawning-place of the Most High! Is it not Glorious? The Blessed Perfection and the Most Great Name—may my life be a ransom to His believers—arose in the city of self-sacrifice like unto the banner of Guidance. While he was under the chain, He was a helper to every oppressed! From the Manifest horizon, He shone forth glorified by trials! In the midst of the world, He withstood the attacks of infinite persecutions; so that these withered ones might become enkindled, and these extinguished souls might be set aglow with the Fire of the Love of God. May we close our eyes to both worlds, and be ignited and burn with the Fire of Longing! Now, O ye spiritual friends! Is it just that we sit silent, become speechless, sorrowful and pessimistic! No by

God! This is not the attribute of fairness and gratitude, but the essence of unfairness and negligence.

RAMLEH, EGYPT, SEPTEMBER 9, 1913

1. A Bird's Eye View of the General Conditions of the World

Would you like to hear the translation of a Tablet which was read this morning? It contains a wonderful spirit and a most significant exposition of the general conditions of the world at this time.

He is God!

O Thou who art holding fast to the Pure Hem; thou who art the twig of the Blessed Tree!

Look thou with deep insight at the world and the inhabitants thereof! It is an immense theater upon the stage of which most spectacular plays are being enacted.

Here, thou wilt see upon its plains the victorious and vanquished legions of profit and loss and there, thou wilt observe the waves of the sea of folly, rising and falling with great impetuosity. Cries are heard on every side, and the agonies of revolution, revolt and unrest reach to the ears of every progressive man.

There is a tremendous clash and strife between capital and labor and the war between the aristocratic and the democratic adherents is carried on with relentless sword, javelin, bow and arrow. The phalanxes of the grand Army are drawn in battle array, each squadron taking its position. The world-raging armaments and the heavy artillery are prepared in every part of the field. The dazzling splendor of the swords of enmity blind the eyes from the most remote distance; the lightning effect of breastplates, the brilliancy of the lances and the sparkle of the bucklers of hatred brighten the gloomy night and bewilder our eyes.

In short, the weapons for strife, battle, and war are being prepared with the utmost celebration.

Thou wilt observe that from every house, the strains and notes of music are raised, the confusing melodies of harp, lyre, cymbal and flute are heard, and the mad revelers dance while in a state of inebriation with the wines of these vanishing pleasures and joys.

Here, thou wilt see wanton and soiled decorations, and there, flimsy shows of a gilded class of creatures. Here, embellishment and luxury are made possible through illicit wealth, and there are displayed the ravishingly beautiful appearances of this mortal and ephemeral existence. From one part of the world sighs of anguish, lamentations of poverty and agonies of misery are raised, and from another voices, acclamations and Jeremiahs calling for succor have reached the gates of heaven! Here, one sees the tears of the hopeless and listens to the appeals of the oppressed; there, the trembling murmurs of the helpless and the harrowing wails of the shipwrecked in the sea of perfection. The heat of the conflagration of separation spreads on all sides: the flame of the fire of longing is raging with great intensity, and the tongue of an avalanche of calamities leaps forth. Here, one observes the absolutism and oppression of kings, and the utter thoughtlessness of the Cabinet ministers, and there, one sees conflicts and wars on the battlefields of thoughts and ideals by ambitious generals, statesmen and administrators of the nations and countries. They consult together, they scheme, they plot, they exchange their views, they organize fallacious enterprises, they float superfluous companies, they circulate false notes, they destroy and they lay the foundation of their political careers.

In short, when thou considerest the reality, the outcome, and the fruit of all these theatrical performances, thou wilt see with thy real eyes, that they are the results of an illusory mirage and their sweetness is as bitter poison. A few days shall roll on their axis, and all these conditions will become non-existent, evanescent and completely forgotten. But when thou shuttest thine eyes to this dark world, looking upward and heavenward, thou wilt behold light upon light, eternity onward to eternity, and from everlasting to everlasting. Then thou wilt see the realities of Mysteries. . . . Therefore, happy is the pure spirit who does not attach himself to the changing conditions of this transitory world; and who clings rather to the Purity, Nobility and Grandeur of the Never-ending world.

Upon thee be Baha!

(Signed) 'Abdu'l-Bahá 'Abbás.

2. The Spread of the Bahá'í Cause in Germany Makes 'Abdu'l-Bahá Happy

This morning I had the great pleasure of finding myself in the Presence of 'Abdu'l-Bahá. A cablegram from Marseilles announced the departure of Mrs. Fraser and her approaching arrival in Port Said. 'Abdu'l-Bahá sent a telegram to Ahmad Yazdí to receive and direct her to Ramleh. Another telegram from America inquired about his health. Letters from Boston and Washington, as well as from Germany contributed to his happiness. The Bahá'í Cause in Germany is making splendid headway, and believers, enthused by the presence and example of the Master, have arisen to spread the Movement with a determination and strength never equaled before. As he walked back and forth, while I was reading the letter from Germany, he smiled and was much elated, saying: You see, you see! He wished the believers to spread the Cause of Bahá'u'lláh. If they do this, divine Confirmations shall encircle them from all directions.

The Cause, he said, has thrown a universal reverberation through the pillars of the earth, and the divine Power of Bahá'u'lláh shall encircle the globe. Rest thou assured of this.

3. Photographs Received from America and Germany Distributed Among the Persian Bahá'ís

This week I received five packages of photographs of 'Abdu'l-Bahá from Mr. and Mrs. Killius of Spokane, Wash., which were to be divided between Mírzá Mahmúd and myself. After making the division in equal parts I have distributed a number of them among the students and pilgrims. They are all made very happy by these presents. I also received some photographs from Consul Schwartz of Stuttgart which are already given away to many believers. In this way, the Western friends can impart the greatest joy to the hearts of their Eastern brothers.

[Editor: The entries go from No. 3 to No. 5; No. 4 is missing.]

5. *The Silence of 'Abdu'l-Bahá Is Eloquent*

In the evening the Master came in while the students were sitting on the veranda. As he entered they all arose. Before sitting he told us that this was a good gathering, a luminous gathering. He sat for ten minutes, but he did not speak one word. Silence, calm and eloquent, pervaded the whole atmosphere, and when he left we were quite as contented and happy as if he had given us an address.

RAMLEH, EGYPT, SEPTEMBER 10, 1913

1. *Good News Received from America and Europe*

I received a number of letters from the United States. Chicago, Spokane, New York, San Francisco and Washington were represented. I am sure that all the good news will make the heart of 'Abdu'l-Bahá very happy. I had also letters from Budapest and Stuttgart, London and Paris. In London the believers are already laying plans for the promotion of the Cause during the winter. The American friends, I have no doubt, will likewise carry away the wreath of triumph, and shall guide many souls into the green valley of Divine Faith.

2. *A Few Arabian Proverbs*

Here I would like to quote a few proverbs which the Arabs use in their conversation. The Arabs are generally very lively and dramatic. Their talk is enriched with numberless epigrams and is endowed with a wonderful power of expression and poetic fancy. They are simple, yet winsome, graceful and most chivalrous.

"Make neither your friendship a pretence, nor your hatred a menace."

"Don't ask a man about his origin; you can read it in his face."

"Patriotism is from faith."

"The boy is his mother's double."

"Avarice destroys what the avaricious gather."

"A ruler without justice is no better than a river without water."

"A man is often an enemy of things concerning which he is ill-informed."

"There is no honor like the possession of a good character."

"Disdain not a kind action, be it but to give water to one who is not thirsty."

"Knowledge without practice is like a bow without a string."

"No pious act is more beloved by God than the telling of the truth."

"Without Hope, no mother would nurse her child, nor would any peasant plant his land."

"The young who revere the aged will receive reverence themselves when they are old."

"The next best thing to belief in God, is sympathy with people."

"A true believer is not content while his neighbor is hungry."

"There are men who are keys to the good, and locks to the evil."

"Avoid vain hopes—contentment is prosperity."

"Wisdom lifts a slave unto the dignity of princes."

"Hearts, like bodies, become tired and should have recreation."

"A wise enemy is less harmful than a foolish friend."

"Man is not to be valued by the robes he wears, but by the character he shows."

"If you censure your friends for every fault they commit, there will come a time when you will have no friend to censure."

The beautiful spirit of the hospitality of the Arabs is often illustrated by the apt inscription of welcome engraved above the gates of their homes; for example:

"Welcome to him of whose approach I am all unworthy."

"Welcome to the voice announcing joy after lonely melancholy."

"Good tidings thine; off with the robes of sadness; for know, thou art accepted, and I myself will take upon me whatsoever grieves thee."

3. A Prayer by 'Abdu'l-Bahá for Detachment

I will here translate a prayer from the pen of the Master.

He is El Abhá!

O Thou kind, Incomparable God!

>Familiarize these hearts with Thy Mysteries and detach them from friends and strangers. Suffer them to drink from the cup of the Wine of the Morn of Eternity and intoxicate them with the Goblet of Everlasting Felicity. These servants long and yearn for Thee and these lovers are enamored and attached to Thee. They are dwellers in Thy Mount and attracted with the Beauty of Thy Face. They are the gazelles of Thy flock wandering in the wilderness of separation and scattered in the valley of regret. Send Thou to them the Messenger of Providence and cause to descend upon them the angel of guidance: so that the fragrance may waft from Thine Abode to their nostrils and effulgence from Thy Face may illumine the hearts of these servants; the impenetrable darkness be changed into light and the thorny place transformed into a rose-garden. Verily Thou art the Powerful, the Seeing and the Hearing.

In the evening Mírzá Abú'l-Fadl came and all the students gathered around him and he spoke to them about the early events of the Cause.

RAMLEH, EGYPT, SEPTEMBER 11, 1913

1. How the Persian Students Lived Together

Tomorrow our band of earnest students will depart, and everything will again be quiet for a few days before the second party arrives. The past days my room was a busy center; here a number of them were speaking, there some were writing letters. From morning till late in the evening they were constantly coming and going. Many of them were anxious to possess the Master's talks in America which I gave to them and of which in turn they made copies forwarding them to their homes. They were not only polite and courteous toward us, but also toward each other. They exercised the utmost kindness and consideration and did not lack the sense of true friendship and fellow-feeling. Like members of one family they inspired confidence and emulation. They were full of hope and each a true optimist. I can hardly remember a more united, a more congenial or a more devoted band of young men. Each one has set in his heart the accomplishment of a certain object and is intent on carrying it out. The photographs of the Master sent by Mrs. A. B. Killius of Spokane arrived in due time, and many of them were made happy by receiving this gift. In every one of his speeches, the Master has expressed to them his satisfaction and pleasure, because they are studying with zeal and their lives have been pure and uncontaminated. They are wonderful examples of the spirit of modern Persia.

Today 'Abdu'l-Bahá came to see them both in the morning and evening and each time he delivered a very eloquent and effective address, which I will share with you soon.

2. An Important Tablet Revealed by 'Abdu'l-Bahá for China

I will now give the translation of a very significant Tablet revealed for a learned gentleman in China. It may be taken safely that this is the first important Tablet which has been sent to the Chinese Republic. I would like to see it translated into the Japanese language and also into Chinese. Once translated into these two languages it will be well if it were printed in a small pamphlet with a short historical sketch of the Bahá'í Cause and distributed.

He is God!
O thou wooer of truth who art athirst for reality!
Your letter was received. Its contents were evidence to the

fact that from the horizon of consciousness the refulgent light has become manifest. It is hoped that after the appearance of the dawn, the brilliant sun may rise so gloriously as to cast its splendors upon all regions.

It is a fact well-known to your honor that the world of existence is in need of an educator and instructor. The educators are of two kinds. The educators of the world of nature, and the educators of the world of reality. If you leave the earth in its natural condition, it will become a jungle and a thorny place; but once it is entrusted to the hands of a skilled and kind gardener, the jungle will be changed into an orchard, and the thorny patch transformed into a rose-garden. Consequently, it has become evident that the world of nature is in need of training. Moreover, reflect carefully, for should humankind be deprived of the graces of culture and instruction, it would become a poisonous body; because the savage tribes have not acquired any of the separative distinctions which differentiate man from beast. For example: what is the difference between the African and the American black man? The former has not yet adorned himself with the ideals of culture while the latter has become intelligent, sagacious and civilized. During my journey throughout America, at the time when I was in Washington and elsewhere, I delivered detailed addresses in the universities, churches, conventions and meetings of the blacks, and found their audiences composed of most intelligent persons who could grasp the subjects under discussion as well as any other audiences of civilized and intelligent Westerners.

Thus a great chasm exists between these two communities; one in the lowest depth of ignorance; another rising toward the pinnacle of civilization and freedom. Then it is plain that education is the distinguishing mark. Undoubtedly, culture or instruction is the cause of the glory of the one, while the lack of education is the means of the degradation of the other.

Hence it is proven that education is the concomitant necessity of the world of modern civilization.

Furthermore: Civilization is of two kinds. The civilization

of the world of nature and the Civilization of the world of reality which belongs to the realm of morality. As long as the influence of these two types of civilization does not appear fully in the body politic, complete success and prosperity will not be obtained. Consider that the tent of material civilization is pitched in the European world; yet notwithstanding this how dark it is! The thoughts of all men converge upon the law of the 'Survival of the fittest' and the ideals of all the inhabitants revolve around the doctrine of the 'Struggle for existence.' The extravagant expenditures on armaments are daily increasing at a terrible rate, and the staggering expenses of the financial budget to support the preparations of the military storehouses, have brought the nations to the brink of bankruptcy. Civilized mankind is in a state of civil insurrection and under a too heavy burden; they are struggling, with wonder and astonishment, to free themselves. All this is because the civilization of morality, spirituality and attraction with the Fragrances of God is entirely lost sight of.

In short: Just as the Instructor and the Teacher are necessary in the material world; so in the Ideal realm, i.e. the Kingdom of spirit and consciousness, ethics and morality, infinite virtues and the perfections of humankind and salvation in both worlds there must needs be an Educator and Teacher. The founders of natural civilization are the philosophers of the earth, and the Teachers of the Ideal civilization are the Holy Divine Manifestations. Therefore if the human world is deprived of the training of the natural and ideal teacher, unquestionable it will fall headlong into the lowest stratum of the animal kingdom. Natural civilization is like unto a glass; divine civilization is like unto the light. Material civilization is similar to the body, Divine Civilization is the spirit. The lamp is in need of the light and the body is only quickened through the spirit. Read the work of Galen, the famous Greek Philosopher, which he has written on the progress of the civilization of the world of humanity. He says: 'Religious beliefs are the greatest means of impelling upward the world of civilization and humanity. As an example to this: We observe that a number of people contemporaneous with us are known as Christians. Inasmuch as they are firmly rooted and well-established in their beliefs, the common people of this sect are as true philosophers, are adorned with such ethics and manners that the greatest philosophers attain to them only after many years of study, troubles, hardships and discipline. The simple folk of this community are characterized with the infinite virtues and excellences of the world of humanity.' Hence it is established that mankind is in need of an Ideal, Universal Instructor, in order to unify under the shade of one Word the various nationalities, causing antagonistic communities to drink from one fountain; changing enmity and hatred into amity and love, and transforming strife and war into peace and salvation. In this manner His Holiness Mohammad—upon him be peace and greeting—conciliated the various contending warlike, barbaric tribes and nomads of Arabia, and ushered them into the shade of the Tent of agreement, upraised a lofty banner in the world of physical and spiritual sciences, and caused them to attain to the highest station of Everlasting Glory. Likewise, His Holiness Christ—upon Him be peace—gathered around one spring of Unity, the inimical, the quarrelsome and the warring nations of Greeks, Romans, Syrians, Chaldeans, Assyrians and Egyptians who exercised toward each other the utmost rancor and contempt. He established amongst them the ideal band of communications.

The above instances irrevocably demonstrate that the world of humanity is in need of Universal Teachers and Instructors, and that these are the holy, divine Manifestations. If certain souls pretend to be of the elect and in no need of education, it is similar to a pretension put forth by private soldiers that they are skilled and efficient, and do not require the instruction of the general. It is evident that such statements are baseless. All the individuals of the army, whether privates or officers, are in need of the supervision of the commander-in-chief, who is the general instructor.

This is enough and sufficient for those who have hearing ears and to this God bears testimony!

(Signed) 'Abdu'l-Bahá 'Abbás.

RAMLEH, EGYPT, SEPTEMBER 12, 1913

1. Departure of the Persian Students

Separation from the friends of God is a difficult thing. Although by this time we are more or less used to it, having already traveled so much, seen so many countries and associated with so many Bahá'ís, still we feel keenly when we meet and grow to love a number of the Bahá'ís, then suddenly they depart and in all probability, never will we meet again. However, in this separation, there is one consolation and that is: these friends go out into the world after attaining to the meeting of the Beloved, to teach the Cause of human brotherhood and to equip themselves to become more useful instruments. Thus in a spiritual sense there is no separation between those Bahá'ís who are truly devoted to the Cause of God and are striving in the path of Reality. Consequently, from an external standpoint, we were all sad, when we saw the body of students leave the house for the station. The Master received them in the afternoon and delivered to them his last word of advice and exhortation.

2. Russian Count Meets 'Abdu'l-Bahá and Talks on the Two Aspects of Reincarnation

The Master had sent for me to go to the hotel and translate. A prominent Russian Count who understands English and French was calling on him. In a moment I was there, and soon 'Abdu'l-Bahá plunged into a deep and most interesting discussion about the two aspects of reincarnation, the particular and universal, the return of generic and specific ideas, and a presentation of the logical proofs concerning the existence of a Divine, Supreme Power, animating and energizing all creation. The Count seemed greatly interested, and was going to ask more questions, when the Secretary of the brother of the Khedive was announced. Thus he

3. Strive That Love May Increase Day by Day

Strive ye as much as ye can, so that love and amity may increase day by day amongst the believers of God; all of you can help each other and be ever ready to sacrifice your lives for one another. This is the quality of the people of Bahá.

4. Tablet of 'Abdu'l-Bahá to the Author of Modern Social Religion

The following is a Tablet to Mr. Horace Holley, the author of the Bahá'í work called, *Modern Social Religion*:

> He is God!
>
> O thou son of the Kingdom!
>
> A copy of the book written by thee and forwarded to this spot was received. The friends are engaged in reading it. They praise and commend your book most highly and appreciatively. God willing, it will be translated and I likewise will read it. Thank God that thou art confirmed and assisted; thy aim is to render service to the Kingdom of Abhá and thy object the promotion of the Teachings of Bahá'u'lláh. Although the glory and greatness of this service is not known at the present it will in future ages, assume most great importance and attract the attention of scholars. Therefore strive more and more as far as thou canst in this service, so that it may become the Cause of thy everlasting glory; in the Kingdom of Abhá thou mayest be enkindled like unto a candle and in the horizon of majesty thou mayst shine like unto a star. Upon thee be Bahá'u'lláh.
>
> (Signed) 'Abdu'l-Bahá 'Abbás.

5. Pure Intention Is the Magnet of Heavenly Assistance

In another Tablet he says to Mrs. Killius:

> O thou who art attracted by the Love of God! Thy letter was like a mirror in which were reflected the pictures of Divine Confirmations. Thou hast a heart which is turned toward the

Kingdom of Abhá, a spirit rejoiced by the Glad-tidings of God and eyes illumined by beholding the Lights of God. Your aim is to render service to the world of Reality. Pure intention is the magnet of heavenly assistance and the only means whereby to attract a great power.

To another person whose house had been burned down he reveals:

6. "Strive to Quicken Dead Souls"

If thy earthly house is destroyed, be thou not sad! May the Palace of the Kingdom be upbuilt! O thou bird of reality! If thy terrestrial nest is ruined, be thou not unhappy, a heavenly nest is destined for thee. His Holiness Christ, the Holy Manifestations and the apostles possessed no nest whatsoever in this mortal word, but in the Universe of God a glorious Palace awaits. It is hoped that through the Divine Bestowals, on a lofty station, in the Universe of God, a radiant palace may become prepared for thee. Consider that the palaces of former kings from the day of Adam to the present age are ravaged by the relentless hand of time, while the towering Palace of the believers of God are built throughout Eternity and are never subject to destruction. Reflect carefully and thou shalt observe that all the buildings are uptorn, but the foundation of the apostles of Christ is becoming firmer and loftier every day. It is my hope that thou shalt likewise lay the basis of such a lofty palace. The foundation of this Palace is the Call of the Kingdom of God; its galleries are the Teachings of Bahá'u'lláh; its decorations the virtues of the world of humanity and its radiant lamps the lights of the Divine Kingdom. Therefore strive as much as thou canst to quicken dead souls, to guide erring ones, to cause to drink those who are thirsty and to invite those who are hungry to sit around the heavenly Table and partake of the Divine Foot.

RAMLEH, EGYPT, SEPTEMBER 13, 1913

1. From Ramleh a Mysterious Power Is Silently Quickening the World

Ramleh is honored with the presence of 'Abdu'l-Bahá. From this quiet summer resort of Egypt the mysterious power of God is felt in the uttermost corners of the world. Men, women and children belonging to all nationalities and religions are turning their attention to this spot. Here lives and moves the God-man amongst the people, as lived and moved Jesus over 1900 years ago along the shore of Galilee. His munificence and generosity embrace the world of humanity. His love is all-inclusive and the fountain of his sympathy flows without any interruption. With their burdens, sorrows and sufferings, the children of men come to him. With willingness and pleasure he shoulders their burdens; he cheers the despondent heart; he inspires the downcast; he strengthens the weak; he helps the poor and sows the seeds of wisdom in the garden of their minds. With fortitude he stands before the world and proclaims the coming of the kingdom of God. Those who are endowed with divine perception can easily realize that the spirit of God is moving over the world, the doors of the kingdom are open, and the Graces and Bounties of the Lord of Hosts are manifest. Thus awakened they arise to glorify their Lord and to summon mankind to the Banquet of Eternal Life and Everlasting Felicity.

2. Story of the German Consul in Haifa and How He Became the Victim of Bravo

This morning 'Abdu'l-Bahá accompanied by Shoghi Effendi came to our house and sat for about half an hour. Throughout his talk he laughed, giving us much happiness. He told us the story of a German Consul in Haifa, illustrating how certain people come to a sad end because they enjoy and believe the flattery of sycophants.

In Haifa there was at one time a German Consul who became 'Abdu'l-Bahá's friend. He used to call on him often, and 'Abdu'l-Bahá returned his visits. At one time he disappeared for a whole month. Suddenly, one day he entered 'Abdu'l-Bahá's room. He had a stick in his hand and was lame. "Oh, sir, how is it that you have not inquired about my health during the past month?" "Why, friend, what has happened to thee?" "Yes," he pitifully answered, "I am the victim of 'Bravo.' Let me tell you how it happened. The German colony had prepared a ball, a ball, to which I was bidden. The governor, the judges and the officials of Haifa were likewise invited. When the dancing was over, they had a jumping contest. One by one they started to jump, but in a clumsy manner. I saw that none of them had learned the secret of jumping a long distance, but I had learned it in boyhood, going to gymnasium in Germany. When the last one failed to reach the mark, I volunteered as a candidate. All eyes were on me now.

My first attempt was so successful that it elicited the hearty 'Bravo' of the governor. In my heart I was pleased and thought I would try again, and go beyond the first limit. I went back and back, then jumped forward, and when I landed on the other side, a tumultuous applause was raised from the governor and the officials. 'Bravo, bravo,' rang in my ears. By this time, I was puffed up with pride and became blind to my own limitations. 'Now I will show them,' I said to myself, 'what real jumping is,' and with this determination I started the third time. I wanted to go further, much further than the first and second time, and so, when I came down upon the earth with a great crash, I felt a most excruciating pain in my right foot. My leg was broken. I became unconscious, and when I opened my eyes, I found myself in bed. For the last thirty days I have suffered much. Thus you see now, how I became the victim of the 'Bravos' of the governor." There are many people in this world who will go to the limit of doing anything, even in attacking the purity and the motives of their friends just to gain a temporary applause and Bravo without thinking of the ruinous effect of such a thing upon themselves in the future, and the loss of public confidence.

3. 'Abdu'l-Bahá Dictates Tablets for Russia

The Master had received many letters from the East and America. He wondered to which direction he should turn his attention.

Seeing a package of letters in my hand, he laughingly asked: Is this the work I had prepared for him? How many hours did I want? It seemed to him that there was no end to my requests.

In the afternoon he dictated Tablets in the Garden to Shoghi Effendi for a long list of believers in Baku, Russia. Tea was served while he revealed the heavenly words. He also entertained the Arabic professor of the American College in Beirut. He spoke with him about the unification of religions and the principles of the Bahá'í movement. The professor went away with a new light in his heart.

RAMLEH, EGYPT, SEPTEMBER 14, 1913

1. The law of Universal Love and the Bahá'ís

In the garden of the heart plant only the flowers of Love. The fragrance of the hyacinths of Love, the influence of the divine Love, the efficacy of the spiritual Love must constitute the foundation of the life of every Bahá'í. You shall know the tree by its fruit. You shall recognize a real soul by the quality of Love he manifests. With Love in our hearts we are enabled to benefit humanity. Love being the magnet, its possessor is enabled to attract the hearts to the Kingdom of Peace. True love never changes, and has no similitude or shadow of turning. Love is the basis of human sympathy, and sympathy prompts us to be kind and compassionate to all those who are in sad circumstances. With Love the enemy is changed into a friend, the cheerless is comforted, the weary traveler is lodged, the hungry fed, the naked clothed, the destitute made rich, the weak reinforced, the hopeless made hopeful, and the barren life made to blossom like unto a rose. Love is the great panacea for the healing of all social, political and economic evils. Love is the Holy Fire enkindled in the hearts by the hand of God. The only Love that is all-enduring is the Love of mankind. Let the power of this Love take possession of our beings. Let the sea of this Love flow toward the countries of our hearts. Let the rays of this Love illumine the dark recesses of our minds. Let the sun of this Love flood the regions of our souls. Those who have experienced this Love will never become despondent; with shining faces and smiling lips they shall march through the storm of difficulty, scale the impassable mountains of trials and reach the goal with added zeal, increased energy, supreme faith and unfaltering courage. This Love exalts one's Ideals, purifies one's motives and glorifies one's thought.

The Bahá'ís are the servants at the Court of this Love; they adore and pay tribute to this king. Love, only Love, makes them invulnerable. With this weapon they gain victories over the cities of the hearts. With this torch they dispel the gloom. With this medicine they heal the sick and with this water they allay the thirsty ones. Out of this book they have learned the Mysteries of God; from this spring they have quaffed the wine of Knowledge, toward this exalted height they are soaring, and in this illimitable ocean they are submerged. They are the followers of the Lord of Truth, whose words, actions and ideals are spelled in letters of Love—Love for the world of humanity. Their watchword is Love. Their calling is Love and their avocation is Love. They eat Love, they drink Love, and they are clothed in Love and have their existence through Love. They have known the source of Love, and Love has made them free. They love God and they love mankind. With this omnipotent power they have arisen to serve the world. In all their transactions and dealings Love is their Instructor. They love to live a life of simplicity, prayerfulness, helpfulness and service. For them there is no more sorrow or hate. Life is an Elysian garden of joy and happiness where men may live together lovingly. Love is peace, peace is contentment, contentment is light.

2. *Tablets for German Bahá'ís*

This morning I was called into the presence of 'Abdu'l-Bahá. He has taught us what Love is, and how we should gain more capacity to become the custodians of Love. He called Khusraw to bring him a small cup of coffee, and when it was served, with a twinkle in his eye, he said:

"Who says that Mírzá Ahmad does not drink a cup of coffee? Khusraw, bring him one!"

Then he dictated several wonderful Tablets for the German believers. He was especially pleased with the letter of Miss A.

Knoblock, and with her splendid work in several German cities. He ordered the translation of her letter to be sent to all parts of the Orient. He started to dictate a Tablet for her: "O thou herald of the Kingdom of Abhá". Then he turned to me saying:

"Truly she is a herald of the cause of God. She has won this title by her noble work in guiding the souls."

Then he continued. At this time Mírzá 'Alí-Akbar was announced and later on Hájí Niyáz.

RAMLEH, EGYPT, SEPTEMBER 15, 1913

1. A Busy Day for 'Abdu'l-Bahá

We did not see the Master today. In the morning he was busy reading his letters; in the afternoon he dictated Tablets for the believers of Persia; in the evening he gave an interview to two correspondents of Arabic Dailies in Cairo. We were standing near the door of the Victoria Hotel, expecting him to come out when the interview was ended. About 10:30 P.M. we saw him descending the stairs. He was feeling well, but a little tired.

2. The Story of the King and the Thorn-picker

If you would like to hear the story of the king and the thorn-picker as related to me by Mírzá Jalál Síná, I will be glad to share it with you:

Once upon a time the king of the country of the North went hunting. While he was chasing a deer, he forgot all about his retinue and royal tent, and charged his steed through glen and dale; the deer ever evading him by leading him on. Suddenly the king realized that he was far away from his servants, the midday sun poured its hot rays down upon his head. He looked around, and to his amazement found himself in a vast desert full of thorns and briars. Then in the far distance he spied, with his eyeglass, an old man gathering thorns. The old man startled, looked up. "Who art thou?" the king asked. "I am a thorn-picker and maintain my large family by selling thorns in the city." "How many times a week dost thou come here?" "Oh, I come every day. If I miss one day, my people will go hungry." "But surely thou art not equal to this hard work." "What else can I do?" "Come, my brother," the king said, as he extended his hand to him. "If thou dost listen to me and obey all my orders, I will make thee the richest man in the world. I will teach thee the secret of the Philosopher's Stone which transmutes the baser metals into gold." "Very well, I will follow and obey thee under all circumstances." "But thou must first realize that the road is full of temptations. Thou must look neither to thy right nor to thy left, listen to me and renouncing all things, ever follow me." "Yea, yea, I will do anything thou dost command me." "Very well, then, come; I am willing to give thee a trial." The thorn-picker, throwing away his stiletto with which he used to cut the thorns, started to follow the king.

For one hour they walked till they reached a desert which was shining under the rays of the sun. The old man asked the king: "Why is this soil so brilliant?" "The ground of this desert is of silver." "Oh, oh, can I not fill my pockets with it?" he asked, all excitement. "Did I not tell thee that thou wilt encounter temptations in the path?" The old man, being thus rebuked for his apparent forgetfulness, became silent and said nothing, but in his heart, he coveted such free, abundant wealth. In order to keep his mind away from his secret thoughts, the king tried to entertain him with varied conversation until they had passed by this plain and entered another which was of a dazzling yellow color. "What is this?" the thorn-picker asked, while blinking his eyes. "The soil of this plain is of gold." "Gold, gold, my goodness! There is so much gold scattered here, and I am so utterly, so miserably poor; and my family always half-starved." Half bent, inclined by an uncontrollable desire, he was going to grab a nugget, when the king took him by the hand: "Come, come, my brother, I shall make thee so rich that thou wilt not deign to look at a mountain of gold." "Well, I don't know how! Here I see so much gold, a pocketful of which will make me rich beyond my fondest dreams." "Don't listen to the suggestions of thy heart. This desert of gold is not to be compared to the treasures which lie before thee." "I will wait and see."

At last they crossed the desert, but the old man was moody, his eyes wandering to the right and to the left, looking at the immense amount of gold dust scattered over the plain. Finally they entered another desert. Here their eyes were almost blinded by the dazzling brilliancy everywhere. "What is this plain made of? Please tell me at once," the old man asked excitedly. "I have never seen anything like it in all my life." "Oh," the king answered calmly: "Nothing especially valuable. This is the diamond plain." "Diamond!" His eyes were ready to fall from their sockets. "I have heard that it is the most precious gem in the world. Surely you will permit me to fill at least one of my pockets with these precious stones. Just think how one of them will make me quite independent!" "No, brother, thou must not act like a child. On this pilgrimage thou canst not carry anything with thee. Like a bird thou must be free. Thou must not soil thy wings with water and clay, otherwise thou wilt not be able to soar and reach the height." With much persuasion, the old man was at last prevented from loading himself with diamonds, and by and by they were out of this plain too. Now it was nearly sunset, when lo, on the Western horizon they saw a wonderful body of water shimmering under the last rays of the sun. the king pointed it out to the old man with an exultant cry: "Look, dost thou see the ocean lying before us? This is the sea of the 'Philosopher's Stone', one drop of which will transmute all the baser metals into the purest gold." The old man was, however, extremely tired by this time, and as he was thinking in an absent-minded way how to answer the king, he saw another thorn-picker, who was a friend of his, appearing on the scene. "What does thou do here?" he asked. "Today," he said, "several members of our guild went on a strike, so a load of thorns is fetching a high price in the city. Come along with me. We two, all our lives, have been non-union members, and for the next two or three days, before the strike is settled, we can make a nice profit by supplying the citizens with the necessary fuel." The old thorn-picker got very much excited over this unexpected news, and forgetting the king, the ocean of the Philosopher's Stone and the inexhaustible fortune awaiting him, turned back. The king, pitying their ignorance, cried out after them, promising that he would make both rich beyond their dreams. The younger man hesitated for a moment, but the old man would not listen. "He has fooled me all day, and now he is going to make another fool out of you. Let us run quickly before he persuades us again to obey and follow him."

For two days they gathered several loads of thorns, hoping that they would sell them at their own price and become independent and rich. But when they entered the city, they learned to their utter dismay that the price was even lower than its current standard, because there was no strike at all amongst the thorn-pickers, and the information given to the younger man was based on hearsay. Then the old man remembered the king, the plains of silver, gold and diamonds, and the ocean of the philosopher's stone. Wildly he ran out of the city, searched and searched all the neighboring plains, but he could find no trace of the king. Everything had disappeared like magic. "Why did I listen to another man? Why did I not obey the king? Why did I deprive myself of such a heavenly treasury?" Thus he was rebuking himself as he continued his search, ever hoping to find the king.

RAMLEH, EGYPT, SEPTEMBER 16, 1913

1. Arrival of Pilgrims and Other Incidents

This morning I could see the Master only for a few minutes and presented to him a number of letters just translated. We did not see him any more before sunset. At that hour he passed by our home going to Mírzá Abú'l-Fadl's apartment, where the Arab believers gather weekly to hear him speak. A number of Persians were also there. He sent for Mírza Mahmúd and told him that there were some pilgrims who would arrive at 7:30 P.M. from Port Said, and that we should go to the station to welcome them. We walked to Sidi Jaber and when the train rolled into the station, we were glad to receive two young Persians, one from Russia, another from Beirut, and Mrs. Stannard from Haifa. She has spent a pleasant summer on Mount Carmel and is going to stay at Ramleh, as long as the Master continues to live here. We conducted her to the Victoria Hotel. Miss Hiscock also has left her Hotel and is now at this one. I hear that Mrs. Getsinger will go to 'Akká and Haifa to visit the holy Tombs of Bahá'u'lláh and the Bab before starting on her journey to India.

2. Translation of a Tablet, Giving the Keynote of the Bahá'í Movement

He is God!

O ye friends of 'Abdu'l-Bahá! In this Divine Dispensation and lordly Cycle the fundamental principle and the supreme object is the establishment of the oneness of the world of humanity; so that through this oneness and agreement all wars and contentions will be wiped away from amongst mankind and the Beloved of Union appear in the Assemblage of the world.

The promulgators of this Union must be the believers of God, so that through the merciful power they may dispel from the horizon of the world the darkness of strangeness and the Adored One of Unity may unveil her sweet and heart-captivating Countenance. If the least ill-feeling exists amongst the friends themselves, how, then, can this great matter be realized? Therefore, everyone of the believers must strive valiantly with heart and soul; so that not the smallest speck of dust may sit upon the mirror of fundamental Unity; Love should increase day unto day, and the qualities of good-fellowship, intimacy, friendship and mutual kindness be clothed with resplendent realities amongst the believers.

O God, O God, I lay my forehead and place my face upon the dust of humility and submission—looking up toward the kingdom of Mystery and beg of Thee with a contrite, supplicating, entreating, humble, submissive, broken and pain-encircled heart, from the Threshold of Thy Holiness—in the world of Lights—to render asunder the veils of Pluralities, and with manifest signs reveal the Beauty of Fundamental Unity in the hearts.

O Lord! Make Thy believers the waves of the sea of Thy

Oneness, the Breezes of the rose-garden of Thy singleness, the stars of the heaven of amity and good-fellowship and the pearls of the ocean of Love and Guidance, so that they may drink from one fountain, breathe in one air, be illumined by one light, turn entirely their faces toward the world of renunciation and the Center of inspiration.

Verily Thou art the Mighty, the Beloved, the Glorious and the Most High!

(Signed) 'Abdu'l-Bahá 'Abbás.

3. Give Hearing to the Deaf, Sight to the Blind and Speech to the Dumb

O thou sign of Guidance! Thank God that thou hast advanced from the region of darkness toward the center of Lights and after crossing the desert of mirage, hast reached the sweet, cool and salubrious springs. The rays of Guidance thou hast beheld in the horizon of Unity, and in the Valley of safety, thou didst hear the soul-refreshing Call of God from the Blessed Tree. The honey of the Love of God thou didst taste, and hast become intoxicated with the Wine of the Knowledge of God.

Now is the time when thou mayst become the associate of the known and unknown and at every moment raise the cry of Yá Bahá'u'l-Abhá. Unloose thy tongue in the Most Great Guidance; give hearing to the deaf, sight to the blind and speech to the dumb. Bestow exhilaration and rejoicing upon the lukewarm, and happiness and joy upon the despondent. Confer intelligence upon the heedless, awake the sleepy ones, cause to drink those who are thirsty, guide the erring ones, make confident those who are deprived, and reinforce the weak. Verily thy Lord will assist thee and help thee; will inspire thee with the breaths of the Holy Spirit and cause thee to utter His proofs and arguments with great penetration and conviction.

RAMLEH, EGYPT, SEPTEMBER 17, 1913

1. The Spiritual Palace of International Brotherhood Is Being Built by the Peacemakers

All the palaces that are built are subject to destruction, save only the Palace of Love which is protected. So far as Love is the Ruler of hearts, there is no difficulty, but when it is replaced by indifference and the fire is extinguished. In order to remove the possibility of estrangement, we must look to the higher principles of the spiritual life. For life indeed is sterile, unless it produces the fruits of love, a Love which breaks through all the walls of national and racial prejudices, and enters upon the plane of universal brotherhood. The spiritual Palace, the foundation of which is the Love of God is never laid waste.

The Palace of the Bahá'í Cause is firm; because its architect is Bahá'u'lláh, its builder is 'Abdu'l-Bahá, its masons are the companions of God, its laborers are the friends of God, its foundation the Word of God; its cement the Law of God, its water the blood of the martyrs, its materials and principles of absolute Reality, its rooms the religions of God, its light the sun of righteousness, its decorations the virtues of the world of humanity, its imperishable flowers the glorious attributes of Divinity and its dwellers the people of Truth.

Men and women from East and West, North and South are daily working on the construction of this Palace. With noble self-sacrifice, with unparalleled enthusiasm, with confident self-reliance, they are continually adding new partitions to this heavenly Palace. They do not rest for one moment. For them spiritual treasures are destined and inestimable bounties are provided. Are they not joint-partners in the building of the Palace of International Peace and arbitration, the edifice of the equality of human rights and the structure of the economic adjustment of all the inescapable problems of this modern era? We are assured by the Divine Architect that the volcanic events of the times and the corroding effect of the coming ages, shall not leave their impressions upon this spiritual Palace.

2. *"Christian Commonwealth" and Bahá'í Articles*

Today 'Abdu'l-Bahá had a slight fever; notwithstanding this he wrote many Tablets for the believers of 'Akká with his own hand.

He received the newly arrived believer, Mírzá Sayyid Husayn, a fine young man, a graduate from the college of Beirut, and the son of the sister of the Master. Of course, he lives in His house. The rest of the students are expected to arrive tomorrow. In the afternoon the Master passed by and went to the garden. He stayed there for more than an hour, telling several stories to Hájí Niyáz who was in his presence. On his return we caught just a glimpse of him.

The Christian Commonwealth is publishing weekly articles and these are regularly translated into Persian and circulated in the Orient for the benefit of our Eastern friends, especially the August number which contained an article on the Prison Experiences of 'Abdu'l-Bahá. The Master has often expressed the wish that the friends should serve the Cause by subscribing to this paper. The other day a Tablet was revealed for the editor which I transcribe here; so that it may encourage the Bahá'ís to increase their subscriptions. They can do so through Mr. Joseph H. Hannen; because he is its Bahá'í correspondent. One of the latest copies will contain the Master's article on Universal Peace.

3. Tablet to the Editor of the "Christian Commonwealth"

He is God!

O thou kind, beloved friend!

The copies of your peerless paper which are in reality the proofs of your high ideals, the exaltation of your aims and the principles of the prosperity of the world aims and the principles of the prosperity of the world paper of yours, which is like unto a clear, transparent of mirror of humanity were received. Truly I say, this unique mirror, reveals the images of Reality. It is the reflection of Truths which mirror forth through the pages of this paper. All the Bahá'ís are grateful and thankful to you on account of your praiseworthy intentions. The significance of these articles is not realized at the present time, but in the future they will gain such importance that every copy containing an article on the Cause of Bahá'u'lláh will be framed, preserved and hung in the most honored place, and their contents quoted by people of culture. Therefore, rest thou assured that thou art sowing pure seeds in pure ground. Ere long they will grow and develop and many harvests will be gathered.

Upon thee be greeting and praise,

(Signed) 'Abdu'l-Bahá 'Abbás.

4. The Sojourn in Ramleh Has Been Fruitful

So far as I can judge at the present, our stay in Ramleh is coming to a close, though the next place to be honored by the presence of the Beloved is not definitely known. I hear talk about his going to Haifa. However, he will be here at least one month more. Our summer was altogether very delightful. 'Abdu'l-Bahá was a source of great joy and strength to the hearts of many believers who made the pilgrimage from all corners of the Orient to see him and to receive his spiritual instructions.

RAMLEH, EGYPT, SEPTEMBER 18, 1913

1. 'Abdu'l-Bahá Writes to the Believers in Russia

This morning the Master dressed in his beautiful soft cream-colored robe, entered our house. Mírzá 'Alí-Akbar handed him a few letters from Russia. He read them without delay and asked Mírzá Munír to bring paper, ink and pen. He dictated answers to each, and through them you can see how he adapts himself to the individual needs and the spiritual capacity of every person, and out of his abundant treasury, showers upon them the wealth of the Kingdom of Abhá. Although these believers live in the remote Empires of Russia, Persia, Turkey, or Arabia, yet he knows them and they know him. How they hunger for and preserve every Tablet which he reveals for them!

2. In the Bahá'í Cause There Are No Salaried Teachers

One of the believers asked him what should he do, what course of action should he take up? The Master told him to go and teach the Cause, spread the coming of the Kingdom and herald the dawn of the Sun of Reality. To convey the message is a confirmed matter. Whosoever arises in this service will always be aided by the angels of the Supreme Concourse. It is true that the friends will do everything in their power to help a person who devotes all his time to the service of the Cause, but let there be no doubt on this subject, that in this movement there are no regular salaried teachers. A paid teacher will not be able to accomplish as much work as if he were independent. In this Cause 'Abdu'l-Bahá desires to have teachers who sacrifice all their belongings, possessions, hearts, lives and spirits in the work of God. This would be very effective. The Cause must be promulgated with devotion and personal sacrifice, and not through financial operations.

3. Wit Is the Salt of Conversation

Then he told us that, although he did not feel well, he had written many letters to the believers of 'Akká with his own hand, because they were old and tried friends.

He mentioned their names, one by one, a long list, I assure you. Speaking about the Tablet written to Abú'l-Qásim, the gardener, he said that Abú'l-Qásim had sent some pomegranates to him from the garden, so that he might write back that the skin of the pomegranates were as rosy and pink as the cheeks of Jamilih (the gardener's wife), but that the former is through the creation of God, while the latter through the power of devotion. He laughed a great deal, finally saying that it is necessary to joke now and then, for joking is the salt of conversation.

4. The Second Party of Bahá'í Students Arrive

About ten o'clock the second party of Bahá'í students arrived from Haifa. They are all fine fellows, full of the spirit of the Cause, and devoted to their studies. Their names are as follows: Habíbu'lláh Khudábaksh,[24] Badí' Bushruyih,[25] Mír[zá] Jalál, Mír[zá] Kamál, Abú'l-Hasan Khán, Ghulám-Husayn Khán, Hasan Khán,

---

24. Better known as Dr. Habíb Mu'ayyad, the author of renowned diary titled, *Eight Years near 'Abdu'l-Bahá*.
25. A year later, Mírzá Badí joined the Bahá'í community of the Holy Land where he lived for several decades. He is the author of comprehensive diary on 'Abdu'l-Bahá titled *Núzdah Sál Shádmání* [Nineteen Years of Bliss]

'Abdu'l-'Alí and Tarazu'lláh. The first two are very brilliant young men and owing to their superior wisdom and intelligence exercise a most salutary influence over the student body. They are, in a way, leaders without the name of leadership. Badí' Effendi is a versatile poet as is well Habíbu'lláh. The former sings beautifully, and on account of this advantage, both of them have taught all the students Bahá'í songs and poems. As soon as they entered the house, the atmosphere was changed, and we heard snatches of songs, now in solo and again in chorus. After a while the Master sent for them and they had a short interview with him. He fired their hearts with words of encouragement and hoped that they would combine together literary knowledge with practical science. From now on they will stand daily in the presence of the Master and listen to his advice.

5. Mrs. Fraser Arrives from America

In the afternoon 'Abdu'l-Bahá passed by, followed by Shoghi Effendi. He called for me and I walked behind him in the rose-garden. A telegram sent to Port Said from the Master to Ahmad Yazdí: "Send Mrs. Fraser to Ramleh," brought back the answer that she had left at one o'clock. He told me to go with Shoghi Effendi to the station and bring her home. We were expecting her for a few days. I was delighted to hear the news.

6. Mrs. Fraser is Welcomed at the Station by Shoghi Effendi

It was a hot day, but the rose-garden is always cool, the fresh breeze wafting. The master asked Shoghi Effendi to bring him a bottle of Evian water. Meanwhile an Arab, who is a laborer, came in and saluted him. The Arab told a long story, illustrating it with poems, about the source of the Nile, that it is in paradise and flows from under a throne—a pretty legend. Then a few men came in to see the Master. He spoke to them in detail on trustworthiness and told them three stories about his own life. For three hours we sat in his presence listening with attention to every word he said. When he left the rose-garden, Shoghi Effendi and I went to the Sidi Jaber station to welcome our dear sister, Mrs. Fraser. We greeted her on behalf of the Master. After ten minutes, she stood before him. She is going to live with the Holy Family, and I have no doubt that the Bahá'í world will receive a rich and valuable treasure when her Diary is given out.

RAMLEH, EGYPT, SEPTEMBER 19, 1913

1. The American Bahá'ís Will Be Going to India

With the early departure of Dr. and Mrs. Getsinger and Mrs. Fraser to India, we will have three active teachers in that great field. May they work together in unity and hoist the banner of the Cause in that vast region! Each one of these three Bahá'ís is gifted with a particular spiritual talent, and when they combine their forces, they will be able to render a most brilliant service to the Cause. To India, a region of sects and creeds, this truth goes as a balm of reconciliation, a remedy for religious differences and a cooling water of knowledge for those who are thirsty. Their work will carry them through many cities and the assistance of God will be with them. A cable was received from Dr. Getsinger saying that he would be here in three or four days.

2. The Importance of the Art of Translation

This morning 'Abdu'l-Bahá sent for the students. They were all filled with hope and longing. When they stood in his presence, he welcomed them, and tea was served. Having received the constitution of "a central London Bahá'í Committee" which is in the process of organization, he gave it to Badí' Effendi to translate, and then delivered a short talk on the art of translation, advising them to write at least one page every day, either from English into Persian, or from Persian into English, thus they might acquire efficiency in this line of work. He recommended for the future that when the means are provided, a committee of translators be organized from both nationalities, who would know the two languages well, in addition to Arabic. Then the Tablets would be properly translated. Again he spoke about Persia and the part which they play in her reconstruction.

3. The Past Glory of Persia and Her Future Opportunity

He said to the students that there was a time when Persia was like a fragrant Bouquet, perfuming all nostrils. She was the center of the glory and honor of the world of humanity. The inhabitants of Persia from a social, industrial, political and moral standpoint were superior to the rest of mankind. Now conditions are reversed and the same high standard is not kept waving aloft. Like a great giant, she is prostrated on the ground, groaning with a pitiful voice. If the Persians could clearly see the sad and gloomy state of their own country, they would weep bitter tears of remorse, but they are all self-occupied. It is a natural and divine law that when a nation or country sinks to the lowest degree of degradation, then God, in His Bounty, comes to help her, uplifting and raising her to the highest zenith of glory. As Persia has experienced these sad events, the Lord in His Mercy has willed that that country be illumined, so that her future condition may become even more glorious than her past, ad that she may advance greatly along the path of science, industry and art. Now God has purposed that they may become a means of this reformation, and strive day and night that Persia may be enlightened. They must equip themselves with practical education; so that Persia may be benefited through them. The Confirmations of Abhá will always be theirs. If a person studies all the sciences and arts, without receiving heavenly Confirmations, he will not be able to accomplish very much. Now he hopes that they will become the Cause of the moral and scientific advancement of all the Persians.

4. The Bahá'í Students Meet Mrs. Getsinger and Mrs. Fraser in the Home of 'Abdu'l-Bahá

Afterwards he sent for Hájí Niyáz, Mírzá 'Alí-Akbar, Mírzá Mahmúd and me. I was carrying a package of Tablets just translated, which I gave to him. He took it out of my hands and gave me a hard blow on my right cheek. "Bravo," he said. Then for a few minutes he spoke about the events of Persia, and the attitude of the governors toward the Cause, and the believers. A package of petitions had just been received. He opened it and read a few. They all contained good news about the progress of the Cause in

Persia. Then he went into his own room and sent Mrs. Getsinger and Mrs. Fraser to see us. When they entered the sight of them brought me the significance of the Bahá'í Cause. Here we were, four Persians and two American ladies meeting on the ground of perfect spiritual friendship! Who has brought to us this divine edifice in which we abide? Those who have lived in the West all their lives, are not quit able to realize this wonderful transformation; this alchemical change of hearts. When we left them, I was yet under the spell of the realization of it and was more than ever thankful to Bahá'u'lláh for thus uniting the hearts of the East and the West by breaking away the barriers of nationalities, and causing the appearance of the light of Reality.

5. Bahá'í Meeting for the Americans

In the afternoon the students were taken to the garden of Nozha by Mírzá 'Alí-Akbar and Hájí Niyáz, after which they attended a meeting in Khurásání's house, where Mrs. Fraser, Mrs. Stannard and Miss Hiscock were present. Mrs. Fraser had her first experience of a Persian-Arabic Bahá'í meeting, and for her honor the students sang Mrs. Waite's poem of Alláh'u'Abhá and other pieces. This gathering composed only of men, must have appeared very picturesque and strange to her. The Master attended the meeting for a few minutes. In the evening several people visited him, and he spoke with them on the theological questions of the East, and of their futility. While the students were in the Park, he passed and asked for Mírzá Munír.

6. 'Abdu'l-Bahá Amid a Profusion of Thousands of Roses

After a few minutes Mírzá Munír returned, saying that the Master wanted us to go to the rose-garden. Mírzá Jalál Síná, Mírzá Mahmúd and I joined him. 'Abdu'l-Bahá was sitting under the shade on a tree, while the breezes played about him. This is a rose-garden divided into two parts, the first section overlooking the other and joined together by steps. Daily twelve thousand roses, pink, white, red, yellow, are sent to Alexandria and Cairo florists. The fragrance of these roses is exhilarating. The gardener is a simple Arab and most devoted to the Master. He always jokes with him.

7. Description of the Garden of Bahá'u'lláh in Tehran

After speaking and reciting several stories of the life in 'Akká, 'Abdu'l-Bahá reverted to the rose-garden, expressing his love and admiration for roses. He said that outside of Tehran his family had a great park planted by the father of Bahá'u'lláh. This was a wonderful garden. It contained four gates, Eastern, Western, Northern and Southern. As you entered the Eastern gate, the Western gate was visible, and similarly from the Northern you could see the Southern gate. In the center of the garden, a throne was built, the four great avenues branching off toward the gates, so that you could see all four gates as you sat on that throne. On both sides of these avenues, poplar trees were planted to the number of ten thousand. These trees rose erect and majestic toward the sky. Under them thousands of rose bushes were growing, the fragrance of which filled the air. Often 'Abdu'l-Bahá used to sleep in this throne at night. The moon clear, full, silvery, shone upon him. The galaxy of stars shedding their rays, now faintly, and again with a lustrous twinkle over the calm and mystic scene of the garden. Long before sunrise he would open his eyes and look with wonder at this infinite universe of God. Then the nightingales would break into a glorious concert of divine music; the gentle murmur of the rills flowing on all sides reached the ears, and the zephyrs wafting through the leaves made soft music, the branches hand-clapping and applauding. In the early morning the Blessed Perfection would rise and prepare tea for the family, and while the sun was dawning from the eastern horizon, they would gather about him, drinking tea and enjoying the heavenly scene.

Then he started to walk through the rose-garden, now and then standing before a rose on a bush, contemplating its structure and petals.

8. A Single Rose in the Garden of Constantinople

Looking at a rose which was very like an American beauty,

he said that it was just about this season when he arrived in Constantinople. The garden of the house where he lived contained one bush, or a branch of which a single rose bloomed forth after sunset. The believers, never having seen roses at this season were overjoyed, and until late at night were gathered around it.

RAMLEH, EGYPT, SEPTEMBER 20, 1913

1. *Thoughts on the Mediterranean Shore*

It is ten o'clock P.M. I have just returned home, after lying quietly on the shore of the Mediterranean for more than an hour. While my body was stretched on the soft sand, my eyes gazing at the infinite orbs of light, my spirit was holding communion with the friends beyond the seas. The night was dark and still, and my ears enjoyed the music of the waves, murmuring along the shore. Here I am, I thought, and where will I be in the future? Did I ever dream last year that I would be returning to the East in the service of 'Abdu'l-Bahá? Truly, how our own plans seem futile when compared with the glorious plan mapped for us by the Designer of the Universe! How often in a foolish fit of pride we prefer our own pigmy scheme to that of the Almighty! The Cause is great and our destiny is very high! I praise God for thus taking me out of the noise and clamor of the West into the calm and beautiful serenity of the East! As Mírzá Abú'l-Fadl said the other day:

"You are now in the school. Daily you are learning your lessons, but the time may come when 'Abdu'l-Bahá will send you away into the world to carry out his will and to serve the cause of humanity."

2. *'Abdu'l-Bahá Talks to Mrs. Fraser and Mrs. Getsinger About Their Trip to India*

This morning after the students had visited the Master, we were sent for, and he dwelt on the same subject on which he had spoken with them. It was on the internal condition of the Cause in Tehran and the history of one of the believers. Then he told me that I might come at any time to see Mrs. Getsinger and Mrs.

Fraser to talk with them about the details of the plan of their voyage to India and prepare for them a list of addresses. For an hour in the afternoon we discussed their approaching visit. The former gave me a copy of her diary of yesterday, and I will quote here a part of it:

> Suddenly turning to me, 'Abdu'l-Bahá asked, 'Can you think of an excuse to secretly take me to India with you? What plans have you made for India?' 'I have no plans,' I answered, 'except to obey the will of 'Abdu'l-Bahá!' Then turning to both of us, he said: 'What will you do if they dispute these teachings?' Mrs. Getsinger answered, 'I shall turn to 'Abdu'l-Bahá and call upon him for spiritual confirmation. After repeating the Greatest Name, I shall open my mouth and say what is given me to say.' 'What will you do if they beat you?' 'What will you do if they put you in prison' 'I shall thank God that I have walked in His path, and have been permitted to share what 'Abdu'l-Bahá has suffered for years.'

'Abdu'l-Bahá was silent for a moment. Then he raised his voice, giving it a dramatic emphasis, 'And what will you do if they kill you?' 'I shall realize that the first favor that I ever asked of 'Abdu'l-Bahá had been granted. And the minute my soul is freed from my body, I will fly to God from whom I hope it will never be separated through all eternity.'

There was a silence. The master's eyes were closed. Then he told us: When one goes forth to teach, he should think of all these things. He must be prepared at all times, for whatever comes in the path of God. During the many years that he was in prison, each moment he lived under the sword. He felt that perhaps tomorrow, or tonight, or in an hour, or on the very hour, an order might come from the Sultan to kill all of them. He never went to bed a single night all that time, thinking to see the morrow!"

3. Mr. Hooper Harris and Harlan Ober's Trip to India

In this connection let me bring to your attention the good and excellent Bahá'í work done in India, by our two American brothers,

Mr. Hooper Harris of New York and Mr. Harlan Ober of Boston. Both these brothers scattered far and wide the seeds of the Baha'i Cause, and their memories are always kept fresh in the hearts of those who have seen or heard them. Their services will never be forgotten. Like true, staunch pioneers, they worked nobly and faithfully, and when they returned, they laid many laurels of victory at the feet of 'Abdu'l-Bahá. With the lamps of guidance in their hands, these other teachers will soon hasten toward India, and will summon all to the kingdom of Abhá, and impart the Glad-tidings of Peace and Brotherhood.

RAMLEH, EGYPT, SEPTEMBER 21, 1913

1. The Story of the King and His Search for the Fountain of Life

"Please tell me a story," I asked Sayad Jalál Síná as I saw down in the front of my writing table.

"Once upon a time," he started without hesitation, "a king of antiquity who had conquered many countries and had raised the Flag of his authority over many climes, became restless and discontented with his lot. On the occasion of a New Year's Day, when all the Cabinet Ministers, Dignitaries of the States, colonial Governors and officials of remote countries had gathered in the capital to pay homage and tribute to their emperor, and while he was sitting on his diamond-studded throne, with all these men standing before him, he raised his voice addressing the concourse of officials, clothed in their dazzling robes of ceremony:

"'My friends! From my earliest youth, I have obtained everything for which my heart has wished. I have had the good fortune of receiving wise instruction from excellent teachers and statesmen. Then having attained the age of maturity, I ascended the throne after the death of my father. I have ever striven to keep peace within the vast heterogeneous elements of my empire, and have extended the boundaries of my possessions beyond the seas. The mighty arms of my generals have carried the authority of my government, and the influence of my laws to the confines of the earth. Notwithstanding these things, I am not contented.

My heart longs for the attainment of an object which seems to my mortal eyes unattainable. I do not know what it is, but I feel that there is something for the possession of which I am ready to give up my whole empire. The idea has occurred to me that I may ask each of you to relate the story and the experiences of your lives, perchance through your narration I may be able to learn the secret of this longing which is knocking at the door of my heart.'

"For several minutes the great throng of people in the audience-chamber fell into a deep silence, so deep that if a pin had been dropped, one could have heard its fall. They looked furtively at each other, and each wondered in his heart, 'What is this Something for whose possession the king is willing to forfeit his whole Empire?' At last, the prime minister arose from his seat, and related a long story about his experiences. He sat down, and others followed in the order of succession. All the while the king shook his head, showing that the problem had not been solved. Finally an old man, who had been the wise mentor and guide of the king from his early childhood, rose from his seat and, with a penetrating and convincing voice, spoke as follows:

"'Sire! I know the object of your Majesty's search. You are longing for the water of Life, the fountain of which is situated in the Kingdom of Darkness. I have been there. I have seen it with my own eyes and have drunk of it deeply. Now having attained to Eternal Youth, I am bound for the Kingdom of Light.' 'Oh! Oh!' the king exclaimed, rising from his throne, and shaking off his lethargy, 'that is the thing that I have wished for all my life but I did not know what it was. From this very moment I will make preparations to start the search and will close my eyes to all rest and comfort till I have found it.' Then he ordered his generals to summon the army and issued an edict for the Imperial Guards to prepare to start on a long journey. After a week of feverish work, everything was ready, and the king appointed his successor.

"On the last day, the inhabitants of the capital arranged a mammoth open air reception, and when the king had delivered a farewell speech, amid flying colors, and to the singing of the national anthem, he started at the head of his great army for the Kingdom of Darkness. After many months of journey through desolate deserts and over impassable mountains, the exhausted army reached the desired destination. But the king, to his great disappointment, remembered that the old man had told him in a private meeting, that there were about 2000 fountains in the Kingdom of Darkness, and as regard to color, taste and property, they were exactly alike.

"Therefore it would be a matter of impossibility to distinguish one from the other. Thinking that all the hardships of this arduous journey would be crowned with no success, and filled with apprehension and terror at the gloomy darkness enveloping his innumerable legions, with no possibility of escape, he resigned himself to the hand of Fate, and began to think how he and his army could manage to extricate themselves from the impenetrable gloom. At this juncture, the same old man appeared on the scene, and the king's hope immediately revived. He confided to him his great perplexity at not being able to find the real Fountain of Life, inasmuch as there were so many of them.

"'This is very easy,' the wise one said. 'I have come here to relieve your mind from further anxiety on this point. Here is a dead fish. Take it along with you. When you reach a fountain, drop it in. If it is revived, you will know, without a doubt, that you have the Fountain of Life before your eyes.'

"The old man disappeared in the same mysterious way. The king thus heartened by the advice of his mentor, ordered his army to decamp and to continue the journey. After several days, they reached a large fountain, and as soon as the king dropped the dead fish into the water, it became a living, moving creature. He prostrated himself on the ground, and thanked God for thus guiding him at last to the Fountain of Life. And so he camped there for a few days, and drank deeply of the water, gaining new life, new hope and new courage.

"Realizing that he had attained to the supreme object of his existence, he decided to return. Just before their departure, a great, invisible voice filled the air. 'Whoso ever takes away the stones from the bottom of the Fountain of Life will regret it afterwards, and whosoever does not take the stones will also regret.' The people were puzzled, and did not know what to do. Should they take, or should they not take? Finally a number of them filled their pockets, under the pretext that even if they did not take any, they would regret, so that it was just as well to take them; others argued, why they should burden themselves with any of these stones, and then regret it afterwards. So it happened that half of the army possessed themselves of the stones, and the other half returned empty-handed. When they came out of the kingdom of Darkness, they observed to their great astonishment, that these stones were precious gems. Those who had taken them regretted that they had not taken more, and those who were empty-handed, regretted that they had not taken any. Thus both sides were afflicted with remorse and regret.

"Now, instead of giving the full significance of this story, I will give you the key. The king, every man: Old man, reason; Fountain of Life, religion; Fish, the heart; Invisible voice, Intuition; Stones, good deeds; Kingdom of Darkness, material world; Kingdom of light, spiritual world; Eternal youth, Everlasting life; Two thousand fountains, Creeds and sect."

2. The Simplicity of Life, and How the Arabs Live on the Desert

In the morning the Master came to our house and as a preliminary to his talk, spoke about the renewal of the rent, which, of course, meant a longer stay in Ramleh. Then as naturally he fell into a description of the complexity of the means of modern life.

How complex are the means of life in the present age, and how much more complex are we making them daily! The people's needs seem never to come to an end. The more they accumulate, the more they want. There is only one way of freedom, and that is by shutting one's eyes and heart to all these things that distract the mind. The Arab of the desert teaches us a great lesson in the simple life. Living as he does, in the vast Sahara, he lacks all means except a tent, a rug or mat, a caldron, a sword hanging to the inside pole of the tent, and a javelin tied to the outside pole.

This is all his furniture. Then if he is wealthy, he has a mare, or a horse, a few camels, and maybe, adjoining his tent, a palm grove. It never occurs to his mind, that there is anything else in this world. He is happy and he has no worry. His food consists of a bowl of milk and a few dates, and he may well wonder how the city man can digest all the different kinds of dishes with their flavors and spices. He enjoys perfect health. His thought is peaceful and serene, contrary to the city people, who are always haunted by the nightmare of making a bare livelihood.

3. 'Abdu'l-Bahá Talks with Mrs. Fraser

Afterwards I went to see the Master. He was surrounded by many people and was talking and writing at the same time. In the afternoon, I visited Mrs. Fraser and Mrs. Getsinger and for quite a while we talked together about their forthcoming trip to India. Both are full of enthusiasm and are looking forward with great pleasure to their approaching experiences. In the evening, the Master sent for me and in speaking with Mrs. Fraser, told her that he was very pleased with her, because as soon as she received his cablegram, although there were difficulties in the path, she pushed them aside and came. The Confirmations of the Kingdom of Abhá shall descend upon her. She was going to India in the service of the Kingdom of God and the Angels of the Supreme Concourse shall assist her. Let her rest assured. Because her heart is pure, she will attract to herself the heavenly Bestowals.

RAMLEH, EGYPT, SEPTEMBER 22, 1913

1. 'Abdu'l-Bahá's Spiritual Moods

Last night, when Mrs. Fraser left the room, 'Abdu'l-Bahá continued to walk. He was fatigued. He sat down and closed his eyes, saying how glad he would be when he leaves this world; this world of darkness and sorrow, pain and suffering. He sighed. It seemed to me that he was too exhausted to speak another word, and I was going to retire. Then somehow, Mrs. Haney's letter came to my mind, so I said:

"I had a letter from Mrs. Haney the other day, in which she expressed great joy at reading the story of the Self-sacrifice of Mullá Mihdí Kandí."[26]

Immediately he opened his eyes, and looked like a different person, as though supplied by a tremendous force from an invisible source. As soon as the name of this martyr was mentioned he was energized, got up from his seat, and began to speak with inspiration and eloquent fervor, throwing additional sidelights upon the life of that divine martyr, and then just as unconsciously, a clear stream of words flowed from his tongue in praise of Mary Magdalene, and of how she became the cause of the constancy and steadfastness of the disciples of Christ.

2. Dr. Getsinger's Arrival in Alexandria

This morning Shoghi Effendi entered my room with a wireless message, just arrived from Dr. Getsinger, advising us of his arrival Monday morning, and as this was Monday, the Master sent word for me to go to the wharf to welcome him. I was on my way without delay and had to wait until noon. The "Prince Heinrich" of the German Line appeared, and after a few minutes, I spied Dr. Getsinger on the deck. We had to wait two hours in the Custom House before we were freed, and then taking a carriage, and putting his trunks and valise in front, we drove to Ramleh.

At four o'clock the Master greeted him in his house, and about six we called on Mírzá Abú'l-Fadl. He was very glad to welcome Dr. Getsinger back to the Orient and inquired about many believers in Washington, Chicago and New York. Then a historical discussion about the Bible and the exact date in which Zoroaster lived waxed hot until the Master came in. We all sat on the balcony for a few moments, 'Abdu'l-Bahá joked with Dr. Getsinger, reminding him of the days when he was traveling with him in America.

He dictated a long Tablet to the believers of Mazandaran in the garden. Returning from his walk he came to our house and

---

26. An early Bábí who served bravely at the battle of Shaykh Tabarsi.

spoke with the students. Thus he attends to his flock with care and solicitude Dr. Getsinger is going to have a room in the New Victoria Hotel as the guest of the Master.

3. Tablet of 'Abdu'l-Bahá to the Bahá'ís in Leipzig, Germany

He is God!

O ye sons and daughters of the Kingdom!

The heavenly daughter, Miss Knoblock, has given the utmost praise about your Faith and Love; that Glory be to God, you heard the call of the Kingdom, that your spirits gained the capacity of flight, your hearts were illumined with the Light of Guidance, you drank the Elixir of Bestowal from the Cup of Divine Knowledge and became intoxicated with the Wine of the Kingdom. Thank God that He has chosen you from amongst all the people of the world and has granted you such an eminent Gift, so that each one may enter into the Kingdom of God, and like unto the stars may shine and gleam. This Bestowal of the Most Great Guidance is not so apparent now, but in future ages, it will illumine the East and the West.

Consider that during the days of His Holiness Christ—upon Him be Glory—no one gave any importance to the guidance of the Apostles. The populace pretended that a number of insignificant souls, who were catchers of fishes, had gathered around a poor man and were talking foolishly. They laughed even at the Blessed Personage of Christ and spat upon that radiant, luminous and wonderful Countenance. But reflect that afterward the guidance of those catchers of fish became famous throughout all regions, and up to this time mankind is glorifying and praising them.

Upon ye be Bahá'u'l-Abhá!

(Signed) 'Abdu'l-Bahá 'Abbás.

4. Another Tablet to a German Bahá'í Asking How to Teach

He is God!

O thou respected youth!

How many holy souls in past ages have longed most

intensely to hear the name of the Divine Kingdom and live during the day of the Promised One of all the nations of the world; but they passed away and left this world with utter regret, because they did not attain to their wish. In this radiant century God has so confirmed thee that thou mayst step into the Universe of Life, be trained in the Cradle of God's Protection and Preservation, suck the milk of tenderness from the breast of Providence and take a share and a portion from the Light of Guidance. Consider what a great Favor is this! What a wonderful Bounty! Therefore loosen thy tongue in the glorification of this most Great Bestowal and summon the people to the Kingdom of God, so that others may receive a goodly portion from this Holy Cause.

Upon thee be Bahá'u'l-Abhá.

(Signed) 'Abdu'l-Bahá 'Abbás.

RAMLEH, EGYPT, SEPTEMBER 23, 1913

1. Speeches to be delivered at Public Meetings

As now and then the question of public speaking in the Bahá'í meetings has more or less agitated the minds of the believers, I desire to quote herein an extract from a recent Tablet which will show clearly the attitude of 'Abdu'l-Bahá on this rather important matter:

> Rest ye assured that the Breaths of the Holy Spirit shall inspire you with the power of speech. Consequently, loosen your tongues and speak in every meeting with undaunted courage. First, before beginning, turn your face toward Bahá'u'lláh, beg for the Confirmation of the Holy Spirit, and then open your tongues and speak out whatever is dictated to your hearts. Speak with the utmost serenity, conviction and dignity. I hope that day by day the circle of your meetings may be enlarged and that the investigators of Reality may listen to the proofs and arguments. With heart and soul, I am with you in every meeting. Be ye confident.

2. History of the Life of Arminius Vambery

This morning, with Dr. Getsinger, I called on Mrs. Getsinger and Mrs. Fraser and had a long talk with both of them. Then Mrs. Stannard came and the conversation turned upon the death of Prof. Vambery in Budapest, and his most significant letter written to 'Abdu'l-Bahá just a few days before he died. This letter will be published in the Egyptian Gazette and copies of the same will be sent to the European Press. He was well-known all over Europe on account of his travels in the interior of Asia, and on account of his writings. Mrs. Stannard thinks that this letter is one of the most wonderful documents of the Cause on account of the importance of the man, for he wrote with thorough understanding, and sympathy. The European Press prints long articles about his adventures and early life, and singles him out as a unique man.

Arminius Vambery was born in Hungary in the Village of Duna-Szerdahely, in March 1832. His father was a Jew in humble circumstances. He was apprenticed at the age of twelve, to a dressmaker, but having acquired some book learning, he presently became tutor to a publican's son. After enduring much privation, he had mastered, by the time he was sixteen, several other languages besides Latin. Four years later, he went to Constantinople, where he was engaged as tutor by Husayn Deen Pasha. In 1853, he brought out a German-Turkish Dictionary. He had now lived so long in the East, that he could pass for an Osmanli, and in 1862 he started on his long and arduous journey to Central Asia. He disguised himself as a Dervish which disguise he assumed at Tehran because of a knowledge of Persian and Turkish and of a careful practice, not only of the customs of Orientals generally, but also of the ways of the Dervishes—the mendicant friars of Islam. He made his way to Khive, where he was granted two audiences by the Khan. The Amír of Bukhara heard suspicious stories of the traveler, but having seen that Rashid Effendi, as Vamberey called himself, was a good Muslim and all that he professed to be, dismissed him with handsome presents. On his return to Europe, Vambery paid a visit to England, where he met with a reception both from the geographers and the public. His first account of his "Travels and Adventures in Central Asia" was published in London in 1864 and had a large circulation. He wrote also a "History of Bukhara," based chiefly on the works of Persian and Arab historians.

In recognition of his linguistic attainments, Vambery was appointed Professor of Oriental Languages at Budapest. He frequently visited England, and seldom missed an opportunity to give his opinions in European periodicals on any new developments of Eastern and Middle Eastern politics.

During the visit of 'Abdu'l-Bahá to Budapest, Vamberey met him twice. His knowledge of Oriental languages, especially Persian, Arabic and Turkish, was amazing. He was a pleasant looking old man of rather short stature and wrinkled face. In the course of conversation with the Master, he said:

"For many years have I followed your teachings and ever longed to meet you. I admire more than anything else your supreme courage in that at this advanced age you have left everything and are traveling all over the west to spread your humane principles. You are doing a great work. It will be crowned with success, because your sincerity, unwavering faith and high ideals have stamped themselves upon the minds of the World's thinkers."

His last words as 'Abdu'l-Bahá bade him farewell in his long drawing-room and library, were these:

"I hope to hear from you. Please when you return to the East, send me the writings and Treatises of your Father and I will do everything to spread them in Europe. The more these principles are disseminated, the nearer will be the age of peace and brotherhood."

The story of how Vambery, physically afflicted, for he was lame, fought for existence against hunger, and persecution, and gradually mounted the ladder of fame, furnishes one of the most remarkable pages of the history of the Jewish race. At school Vambery once said:

"Hunger, mockery and insult—I experienced them all in turn; but the greatest misery was not capable of darkening the serene sky of youthful mirth for more than a few minutes, and even my healthy color returned after a short interval of bodily collapse."

He was well received at the English Court both in the reign of Queen Victoria and in that of King Edward. On the occasion of his seventieth birthday, in 1902, his Majesty conferred upon him the title of Commander of the Victorian Order. The present King of England, when the Prince of Wales, proved equally amiable when the distinguished Hungarian Professor stayed at Sandringham.[27]

One day, while the latter was occupied with his correspondence, he received a message from Queen Alexandra, inviting him to join her in the garden. Vamberey wished to wash his hands before going, but there was no one in sight. At length the Prince appeared and asked him what he wanted. Vamberey told him, and the Prince disappeared, returning in a few minutes with a large jug in his hand, which he placed, smiling, on the washstand. Thus was a poor Jewish beggar-student of former days, waited upon by a Royal Prince, whom, moreover, he had the temerity to name "The Royal Jug-bearer."

In the afternoon and evening many people of various nationalities called on 'Abdu'l-Bahá, and the demands of several "gentlemen beggars" were satisfied. When I was walking in the evening with two others, we passed by a house, the windows of which were open; we looked in and saw the Master sitting on the Divan talking with the Pasha.

"God has created us that we may love each other"—were the words that came to our ears as we passed by.

RAMLEH, EGYPT, SEPTEMBER 24, 1913

1. *A Persian Bahá'í Student Delivers a Lecture in English*

Since the arrival of the students from Haifa, table-talks have

---

27. Sandringham House is a country house in the parish of Sandringham, Norfolk, England. It is the private home of Elizabeth II, whose father, George VI, and grandfather, George V, both died there. The house stands in a 20,000-acre estate in the Norfolk Coast area of outstanding natural beauty.]

become the fashion. These talks are delivered in English. Now and then one hears a good speech, short and to the point. It seems to me very interesting how these young men are eager to learn everything from everywhere and thus increase their fund of information, so that in the future they may become able to teach the Cause with eloquent tongues and fluent speeches. Why then, do they practice in English rather than in Persian one might ask? This in itself, of course, is another sign commingling of interests and ideals. The one all-absorbing thought of these young men is to equip themselves with the mental instruments whereby they may go out to war against ignorance, selfishness and greed. I may therefore quote one or two short addresses given by these budding orators. The following is an example:

"Gentlemen! Bahá'í Brothers! About seven thousand years ago, according to the religious history, God the Maker of all things through His Mercy and Providence created the world and made man after his own image and likeness. Since that time up to the present day, His Manifestations have successively appeared upon the earth and thus the dark world has been quickened and vivified through the spiritual vibrations of their divine Teachings. By this education mankind has attained to a higher degree of knowledge. It has passed over the arc of ascent, until now it has obtained the capacity for the recognition of the Manifestation of God. When His Holiness Moses appeared, thousands believed in him, and having received and lived according to his divine teachings, became leaders of other nations. God showed them His Love and showered upon them His blessings like unto a torrent. He freed them from the tyrannical yoke of Pharaoh, brought them out of Egypt, and established them in the Promised Land. He sent down for them manna from heaven, He cleft asunder the sea and made a safe passage for them to pass through. He called them His children and they became worthy of every praise and embodied every virtue. Later, they forgot the heavenly laws, followed their own inclinations and worshiped idols instead of the Almighty Jehovah. As a result they stopped progressing. Their civilization waned and their moral virtues retrograded. For many ages they were scattered, humiliated and scorned. But now, praise be to God, they are stirred with a new life, resuscitated with a new spirit, and many of them are quickened by the call of the Kingdom. The Lord of Hosts hath come; the King of Kings hath appeared. The rays of the sun of His Mercy have enlightened them and the Breeze of His Benevolence has wafted over them. Thus are they endowed with a seeing eye, a hearing ear and an understanding heart.

"One of these blessed souls is a brilliant young man of 30 years of age. His face is shining, his speech is winsome, his heart is radiant with the light of the Love of God, and his countenance is as pure and bright as the brightest diamond. His dark, ample brow, his towering forehead, his slender nose, and his graceful manners denote a sensitive nature and a true Bahá'í. His attitude is well-disciplined, his character, and his nature amicable. His intentions are pure, his desires holy and his aims philanthropic and he thinks ever of the welfare of the world of humanity. My humble delineation of this gentleman seems quite superfluous when we remember the repeated praises and commendations of 'Abdu'l-Bahá in reference to him. His word is a divine testimony, a heavenly witness and a celestial blessing. The name of this young man is Dr. Habíbu'lláh Khudábaksh. He is sitting now at this table, and is one of the promising Bahá'ís of this century of light and knowledge. We heartily congratulate him and offer him our best wishes, hoping that he will be assisted by God to cure the ills of humanity, both physical and spiritual; bestow eternal life upon every dead one, and cause mankind to obtain immortality by leading it to the fountainhead of light and bounty."

2. 'Abdu'l-Bahá Wishes the Bahá'í Students to Take Post-graduate Courses

This morning the Master received the students. His talk to them was about his lecture in Leland Stanford University, praising meanwhile, the President, Dr. Jordan, and his labors, in the field of International Peace. He encouraged the students to take post-graduate courses in that University, because he had spoken about this matter with Dr. Jordan. Already many are considering going there, and they mean to write to the President to ask for particulars.

3. The Mission of the Bahá'í Cause Is Universal and Not Local

Yesterday the new Persian Consul General arrived from Constantinople and the Master sent all the students to welcome him at the steamer and today, with Mírzá 'Alí-Akbar, he went to Alexandria to pay him a visit, in the hotel where he is staying for a few days before his departure for Jadda. In the course of conversation 'Abdu'l-Bahá pointed out to the Consul General the impartial attitude of the Bahá'ís in recent developments in Persia and how they are the lovers of Peace and progress. The mission of the Bahá'í Cause is universal and not local; its principles are for all humanity; its objects are world-wide. The Bahá'ís are the army of spiritual and intellectual advancements. Then he spoke a few words about the promotion of the Cause in America and Europe. The Consul General became very attractedand made an engagement to come next day and call on the Master. On his way back in the street car, the Master showed love and kindness to a little child with his mother. The child was so attracted, that he came and sat next to him. 'Abdu'l-Bahá gave him a present and kissed him, and the mother thankfully and happily carried him away, reluctant.

RAMLEH, EGYPT, SEPTEMBER 25, 1913

1. An Analysis of the Letters of UNITY by a Persian Student

The other day I was speaking with one of the students as we were walking along a broad avenue. The subject was "Unity," a word much used in the Bahá'í Movement. "Unity," he said, "is the foundation of all successful undertakings. With unity of purpose, a harmonious action is produced. When various elements are brought together, and basic unity is established, an organism is the result. In the political world, Union is the watchword of all the statements and in the Bahá'í world it has a deep significance. The aim of this Cause is, as we all know, a confederation of the world's religious systems, a consolidation of the political interests of the nations, and a truly grand realization of the brotherhood of man. To my mind, every letter in the world 'Unity' stands for a great principle or quality. For example, 'U' stands for 'understanding,' we must at all times try to understand truth impartially and improve our minds; 'N' stands for 'nourishment'; once we have acquired understanding, we must 'nourish' it with wisdom and knowledge and cleanse it with the water of intelligence; 'I' stands for 'investment'; if we have capital we should 'invest' it, in order to increase it. The Bahá'ís must teach the Cause and spread the Glad-tidings of the kingdom of Abhá and awaken those who are asleep. 'T' is for 'thoughtfulness'; before teaching we must think, or in other words, before teaching others we must teach ourselves. 'Y' means 'yield' to the truth. If you investigate an object and realize that it is reality, yield to it. Don't shut your eyes to the truth, once you have seen the glory of its beauty. Let us cling to the truth, as a shipwrecked sailor clings to the cliff. In short, our aim is to 'understand' everything in a comprehensive manner, to 'nourish' our understanding with the truths from every clime, to 'invest' our acquired knowledge in the best possible channel pleasing to our Lord; practice 'thoughtfulness' under all circumstances and 'yield' to Reality no matter from what horizon it dawns—thus may we become the cause of UNITY in the world of humanity."

2. *Story of the Stork, Fish and Prawn*

At this juncture Mírzá 'Alí-Akbar joined us and asked what we were talking about. We told him.

"Let me tell you a story,' he said, "which illustrates this very point. Once upon a time there was a stork, a fish and a prawn. They became friends and planned to travel together. They said to each other that they would do everything in 'Unity'; but the stork wanted to start on the journey by way of the air, the fish through the watery paths of the river, and the prawn by the track of a pond. The three formed a board of consultation to see which mode was the best for traveling together. They had several sessions, lasting for hours, but they could not determine upon any plan, each one insisting that his opinion was correct, and not willing to yield to the other. Finally they saw a little baby carriage not far away and decided to use it as a common vehicle for traveling. They came and hitched themselves to the carriage, confident that their differences were now brought to an end; but, no sooner did they start than they began to assert their varied natures. The stork flew 'upward,' the fish went 'forward' and the prawn was pushing 'backward.'"

RAMLEH, EGYPT, SEPTEMBER 26, 1913

1. 'Ishqabad, Russia, an Important Center of the Bahá'í Movement

The city of 'Ishqabad is an important Bahá'í center wherein the first Mashriqu'l-Adhkar [Temple] is built. The Bahá'ís are free to teach and pursue their religious principles without any molestation on the part of the Russian authorities. In that city the Bahá'ís are quite numerous and are respected by all classes. During the last few days the Master has been entertaining a believer from that city by the name of Ahmad Áqá and now he is going away, his life perfumed with Fragrances of the Love of God. 'Abdu'l-Bahá has revealed three Tablets for the believers in that city. He came this morning and after reading them aloud, handed them to Ahmad Áqá to be taken to 'Ishqabad. Here are the translations of two of these Tablets:

2. Tablets to the Bahá'ís of 'Ishqabad

O ye believers in the heart and spirit of 'Abdu'l-Bahá!

It has been well-nigh three years since this Servant at the Threshold of Bahá has been a wanderer over mountain and desert and a traveler upon plain and sea. One morning I was in this province and one night I spent in another. As the express train speeded over vast stretches of land and traversed long distances, thus joining together the remotest parts, I became associated with and the confident participator of every meeting and sang the praises of the Lord in each assembly. Day and night I was teaching and explaining and in public gatherings and important Congresses I upraised my voice. I imparted the Gladtidings of the Sun of Reality and made an exposition of Divine proofs and Arguments. I laid the foundation of the Teachings of God and elucidated the truth of the Merciful Effulgence.

After enduring infinite hardships, traveling through, and visiting many countries, diffusing the Fragrances of God and promoting His lordly instructions, I returned to the East. But the difficulties of this long voyage were so numerous, that toward the end, my body was attacked by a severe illness and I was at the point of breaking down. This is the reason why correspondence has been suspended for such a long time.

Now, praise be to God, my constitution is, to a certain extent, reinforced and the illness removed, and therefore day and night I am engaged in answering letters. Not for a moment do I rest or seek comfort. Continually do I remember the friends and as far as possible, I am writing to them. Truly I say, Ishqabad is the city of Love. Each one of the friends of God is occupied with service and engaged in adoration. They are the friends and the companions of 'Abdu'l-Bahá.

As regards the members of school committees, in reality they are serving with heart and soul and perform their duties with rejoicing. They put forward extraordinary effort in organizing and systematizing the school and in the instruction of the pupils while all the other believers are assisting and cooperating with them. On this account, I am greatly pleased with the friends of that region. Day and night do I supplicate and ask heavenly assistance; so that that city may become the envy of all the cities of the world.

O God! O God! This is a city wherein the Fragrances of Thy Holiness are spread, the delightful odors of the garden of Thy Mercifulness are diffused and from which the voices of glorification and thanksgiving, praises and commendations to the Lord of the Kingdom, are raised. For he has revealed Himself on Mount Sinai with a light of radiant effulgence wherefrom the regions are illuminated. Glory be unto Him who hath caused the appearances of the Morn! Glory be unto Him who sendeth the winds! Glory be unto Him who resuscitates the spirits! Glory be unto Him who breathes into the bodies of the world the inspiration of Existence!

O Lord! Accept their supplication toward Thee, their trust in Thee and their invocation between Thy Hands! Verily Thou art the Merciful! Thou art the Great! And Thou art the Ancient Lord!

(Signed) 'Abdu'l-Bahá 'Abbás.

The next Tablet is the following:

He is God!

O ye blessed souls!

The beloved pilgrim like unto an overflowing cup has a heart full of your praises. Continually this Servant expects that all the believers unloose their tongues in the commendation of the friends; nay rather, they may adore each other and sacrifice their wealth, comfort, life and spirit for the sake of one another.

O ye friends! This Cycle is the Cycle of Bestowal and this period is the period of Mercy. All the seasons are the seasons of spring and all the periods are the periods of the Grace of the Almighty. The Breeze of Providence is wafting, the Fragrances of the rose-garden of the realities and significances are perfuming the nostrils and the melody of the Kingdom of Mercifulness has stirred into joy and happiness the heart and the soul! What a delightful age is this! What a heart-attracting century! But a thousand times alas! that the spiritually dead are not awakened by the blowing of the trumpet of Revelation, that the blind are deprived of the sight of the world-illuminating Orb while those afflicted with colds cannot inhale the odor of sanctity. Praise be to God that ye have opened your eyes, have won the ball from the arena of self-sacrifice, prostrated yourself before the Threshold of His Highness the Merciful, become the manifestations of the Favors of the Incomparable Beloved and at all times are advancing and progressing!

Upon ye be Bahá'u'l-Abhá!

(Signed) 'Abdu'l-Bahá 'Abbás.

This morning the Master passed by our house, went into the garden and dictated many Tablets for the Eastern and Western believers. About eleven o'clock he returned and stayed a few minutes. The students were speaking together in English when he suddenly entered and laughed heartily over their speaking in a foreign tongue. Then he went to the Mosque, followed by Mírzá 'Alí-Akbar. Again in the afternoon he was in the garden revealing Tablets. Toward five o'clock we went to the meeting. Dr. Getsinger talked about the Master's address in the Jewish Synagogue of Washington.

RAMLEH, EGYPT, SEPTEMBER 27, 1913

1. Tablet in the Handwriting of Bahá'u'lláh

Have you ever seen the original writings of Bahá'u'lláh? Tablets written with His own blessed Hand? I had the privilege of seeing such a Tablet today. Just think to hold and read with your own eyes a Tablet written by Bahá'u'lláh's own Hand! For many minutes I looked at the writing. The Tablet belongs to Hájí Niyáz. He went to Cairo yesterday morning and returned in the evening bringing it with him.

When years ago he was in the presence of Bahá'u'lláh, he requested Him to reveal for him something. The Blessed Perfection took pen and paper and wrote the following prayer.

2. Prayer for Spiritual Strength by Bahá'u'lláh

He is the Knowing, the Wise!

O God! O God! I beg of Thee by Thy Radiant, Collective Name, to change the humiliation of Thy Chosen ones into Thy Glory; their weakness into Thy Strength; their impotence into Thy Omnipotence; their poverty into Thy Wealth and their fear into Thy Assurance.

O Lord! Illumine their hearts by the Light of Thy Knowledge!

O Lord! Behold Thou these thirsty ones journeying toward the River of Thy Bestowal and the Ocean of Thy Generosity. Verily Thou art the Powerful, The Mighty, the Benevolent.

3. Someone Must Arise to Write the Life History of Bahá'u'lláh

What would one not give to receive such a prayer from the Hand of Bahá'u'lláh. Truly this was a great bestowal. These old men who have seen Bahá'u'lláh many times are to my eyes very wonderful. I always look upon them with a peculiar reverence and respect. If someone had the time just to write down their stories, they would make, I am sure, most interesting reading. One of the most dramatic events connected with this Movement is the ascension of Bahá'u'lláh. Hájí Niyáz was living in 'Akká that time and for six months after the ascension. He has witnessed everything and having once heard his story, I will some day reduce it to writing; I am now waiting to hear of it from other eye-witnesses, and once I have all my material together, I hope to write the story in a consecutive manner. Up to this time no adequate history of the life of Bahá'u'lláh has been compiled. All that we have are fragments, or a mere outline. How I long for a man endowed with spiritual insight, divine faith, historical imagination and intellectual perspicacity to arise, and with patience and perseverance, to travel through the East, collecting the proper material, and then writing a connected history of the life of Bahá'u'lláh! Such a man will confer an eternal benefit upon mankind. It is a hundred times easier to undertake a work like this at the present time, than in the coming ages! Not only are there many people living who have seen Bahá'u'lláh and whose stories must be preserved, but we have amongst us 'Abdu'l-Bahá, who has lived and traveled with his Father in all His sufferings and wanderings and exile and imprisonment.

4. Pilgrims Arrive from India, Persia and Russia

Yesterday and today many pilgrims have arrived; four men, two women and three children, all Zoroastrian Bahá'ís; from the Persian Gulf, a prominent ex-governor; from Russia, an ardent believer, and from Persia an enthusiastic youth. Those who desire to see a religious Congress must come and stay with 'Abdu'l-Bahá, and observe how these men and women of various types and faiths appear from all parts of the world to receive heavenly knowledge from his Bounteous Table, and to then return to their respective homes, inspired with the celestial Spirit. A number of us went last night to the station to welcome our Zoroastrian brothers and sisters. Their faces were aglow with the fire of the Love of God. They were great, big-hearted men, with that stamp of nobility and dignity in their faces that does not wear off. How glad were they when they heard that the American Bahá'ís would go to India to spread the Glorious Message

"We long to see them," they said in a chorus, "we are ready to receive them and to sacrifice our lives for them. How wonderful! How wonderful! That God has given us the mighty privilege of witnessing His miraculous works. Are thy not our real brothers and sisters? All the believers in India are expecting their arrival and will cooperate with them to the extent of their capacity to spread the message of light and truth."

5. 'Abdu'l-Bahá Urges the Students to Practice Public Speaking on All Subjects

In the morning, 'Abdu'l-Bahá spoke in detail with the students about public speaking, and emphasized the fact that they must practice at all times, for, as the future teachers of the Cause, it is essential to develop this God-given faculty. They must choose various topics, physical and spiritual, and then speak amongst themselves and thus employ their imaginations.

RAMLEH, EGYPT, SEPTEMBER 28, 1913

1. Farewell Words to the Students

The Master received the students this morning. They are going to leave tomorrow for Beirut to be there before the opening of the College on October 5th. He reminded them of the former Glory of Persia and of her present decadence, and encouraged them to continue with their studies so that the confirmations of God might ever be with them, and wished for them to be as radiant stars on the horizon of Bahá. Afterward the Zoroastrian believers were ushered into his presence. They were so happy and glad because they have reached the destination of their long journey.

2. I Desire That Thou Mayst be Filled with Bahá'u'lláh

In the course of his conversation with Mrs. Fraser, the Master told her that he desired that she might be filled with Bahá'u'lláh. She must concentrate all her ideas and thoughts around the promotion of the Word of God. Just as the cup is filled with wine, so her heart must be overflowing with the Love of the Blessed Perfection. Let her look at him. How from early morning till late in the evening he is engaged in the service of the Cause. He devotes all his time to Bahá'u'lláh. He will help her. Whenever he sends someone to serve the Cause, he prays in his behalf and God will assist him. Let her rest assured that He will be with her and she will be enabled to render great services. Let her heart be at ease and have no fear.

3. Mrs. Stannard an Earnest Bahá'í

In the afternoon the Master was again in the garden dictating Tablets to Mírzá Muním. Mrs. Stannard was also permitted to be present. The Master is turning his attention to the believers of the Orient, and the Secretaries are kept busy copying his innumerable Tablets. Now and then a number of Tablets are revealed for the West, but the East is getting the lion's share. Before sunset, as I was walking outside of the house, I saw the Master coming out of the rose-garden followed by a number of believers, Mrs. Stannard and a newspaper correspondent. With the latter, the Master walked away, and I joined Mrs. Stannard and walked toward the beach. For nearly an hour we sat on the sand, watching the sea, and speaking about the Cause, and its future progress. She is a wonderful Bahá'í and the Master always praises her sincerity, her broad vision and her unfailing energy in many directions.

This being the last night, the students and resident Bahá'ís had a farewell meeting, and addresses were delivered both in Persian and English. Each one was followed by a Bahá'í song. We were singing and talking until late in the evening.

RAMLEH, EGYPT, SEPTEMBER 29, 1913

1. The Persian Bahá'ís Are Anxious to Know All About the Western Bahá'ís

Our ten students, after hearing a few farewell words from 'Abdu'l-Bahá, departed for Syria, and two Kurdish theological students of the University of Al-Azhar who were visiting him returned to Cairo. Tomorrow our ex-governor from the Persian Gulf will depart for Tehran with another Bahá'í via Russia. It has been a source of great joy to come in contact with these men of various countries and climes, who bring to us the good news of the progress of the Cause. They are all eager to hear of the promotion of the Bahá'í Movement in America. What are the believers doing? Are they happy now that the Master has been in their midst? Are they carrying on the great work he has started? Are they teaching new souls? Are the Western people susceptible to spiritual emotions? Are the friends enkindled with the fire of the Love of God? Are they going to assist us in bringing about the Cause of Human brotherhood? Is the light of reality shining in their hearts? Do they really think and believe that we are their spiritual brothers and sisters? How we long to see them and sacrifice our lives for them! These are the questions they ask me one after another, so tender in their feelings, so true in the expression of their innermost thoughts, so beautiful in their attitude, so wonderful in their faith!

"Yes," one of them told me, "I have heard that the American Bahá'ís are spreading the Cause very strenuously, and every night, before going to bed I pray for them from the depth of my heart. I beg of God to reinforce them with the angels of the Kingdom and to surround them with universal Confirmations."

2. Mahmal or the Holy Carpet

Today the Mahmal or the Holy Carpet was taken from Alexandria to be carried to Mecca. It arrived from Cairo and was paraded through the streets in a long procession, before it reached the steamer. As the story of Mahmal and its significance in the

Muslim world is very important, I will later devote a few pages to its narration, so that our Western brothers and sisters may have a clear conception in regard to it.

3. 'Abdu'l-Bahá Speaks to the Bahá'í Students before Their Departure for College

In his farewell talk to the students this morning at his own house, the Master praised God that they had come. For many days they have been here and with perfect joy and fragrance they associated together. These days passed in complete happiness. It is his hope that through the favors of the Blessed Perfection, they may finish their studies in the college of Beirut. Let them rest assured that they are confirmed. Many people are like unto sheep without a shepherd. They have no protector and no defender. But the students are the sheep and the Blessed Perfection is their Shepherd. He is kind to His flock. The majority of men are in great loss, but theirs is the spiritual profit. There are many who are retrograding, but they are progressing. Many trees are withered, but they are the young plants of the orchard of Abhá and daily they are growing in freshness and delicacy. Others are like unto the fallen stars, but they are rising with great brilliancy from the horizon of Reality.

Then he spoke about the Mahmal, and told them to go and see it before they departed for Beirut. Their steamer sailed at 4 o'clock P.M.

4. Mírzá Jalál and Wife Arrive from London

The Master and his family were surprised and delighted to welcome, unexpectedly, Mírzá Jalál and his wife. I have just heard this news. Tomorrow I will see him, and no doubt he will tell us of his experiences after our departure from Paris. Sometime ago I had a letter from London telling me that they were visiting some believers there.

5. All the Pilgrims Gone and the House Seems Deserted

It is now late and I am writing these few words. I look all around the room and there is no trace of last night's party of students. I do not hear their songs. They are all gone. I may meet them again or I may not. Everything is in the hands of a higher Power. He brings us together and then separates us, but an indelible impression is left on the pages of memory which will last during a lifetime. After all, we are travelers in this world. We stay a few days in this Caravanserai, but the home of our spirits is the world of light.

RAMLEH, EGYPT, SEPTEMBER 30, 1913

1. The Procession of Mahmal in Alexandria

Yesterday the Beloved ordered a number of us to go to Alexandria and see the gorgeous procession, carrying the Mahmal to Mecca. When we arrived, the main avenues through which the Mahmal was going to pass were thronged with thousands of Arabs—men and women and children, dressed in all the picturesque colors of the East. Egyptian soldiers and mounted guards kept the crowd in order. Although we could rent chairs in the front row by paying the royal sum of "two cents and a half," we preferred to mix with the holiday makers.... We had to wait two hours in the sun before the head of the procession appeared. It is popularly believed that whosoever touches the Malmal, God's blessings will descend upon him and his family. For this reason, there is always the fear that the crowd, in a burst of religious zeal, will gather around the Mahmal and in the confusion, trample many people under their feet.

Therefore the Government had ordered several regiments of soldiers to stand along the sidewalks, their rifles pointed at the crowd, who, enthused at the sight of the Mahmal, were singing Pilgrims' songs. The other day I was reading a book on the customs and manners of modern Egyptians. In one chapter the author gives an interesting account of this historic event and here I will quote a few extracts bearing on the subject:

2. Mahmal a Great Annual Event

"One of the greatest events of the year in Egypt is the starting of the Holy Carpet for Mecca. As regularly as the month of fasting comes to a joyful end in the Bayram Feast, the populace begin to look forward to the festival of the Mahmal, as not only marking the time of the setting off of the pilgrims to the Holy City, but as an event of great moment to all men religiously inclined, especially to the poor who have few hopes of making the journey themselves...."

3. Qur'an Verses Woven in Mahmal

"It would be better to speak of the holy 'Curtains' of which there are eight used in the complete covering of the Ka'aba.... The curtains are black, and the art of making them consists of weaving the Qur'an texts into the material, also in black, with an effect like that of damask, the lettering, which is large, being in the decorative Arabic. The watered-silk effect of the lettering is most striking, and in certain lights, when the cover is hung upon the Ka'aba, it can be read at a considerable distance....

"It was extremely interesting to be able to see and handle the famous band which encircles the Ka'aba. This magnificent belt is about two and a half feet deep. The following from the Qur'an, called the throne verse is heavily embroidered on it in gold: 'God! There is no God but He; the Living, the Eternal; nor slumber seizeth Him nor sleep; His whatsoever is in the heavens, and whatsoever is upon the earth.... His Throne reacheth over the Heavens and the Earth, and the upholding of both burdeneth Him not and He is the High, the Great.'"

6. How Mahmal Was Originated

"The Mahmal dates from the 13th century, when the first Mahmal was made by order of the Queen Shajaratu'd-Durr, to serve for the pilgrimage which she intended to make. The Queen's name signifies 'a tree hung with jewels' and the Mahmal is sometimes called by this name. In the following year she sent the empty palanquin, as a symbol of Egypt, and in memory of her own pilgrimage, and from this the annual custom grew up, to be followed by other countries, who take the occasion, as Egypt does, to send with their Mahmal the national tribute of money and food to the Holy City. The Court historian told me that he thought that the custom of sending a state symbol was older than the Queen's Mahmal, a special Camel termed the Mahmal, being sent with presents to Holy Ka'aba in pre-Islamic days. The prophet himself sent such a Mahmal from Medina to Mecca with presents.

8. The Hardships of Bahá'u'lláh to Become the Cause of the Awakening of the People

For the last few days 'Abdu'l-Bahá often spoke about the Mahmal and how people forget the spirit and cling to the letter; that while the fountain of the salubrious water was flowing, they were running after brakish water. This morning when the Zoroastrian believers stood in his presence, he asked them, what did they see yesterday? And then gave a detailed talk on the Mahmal and its significance.

In the afternoon before sunset, he called at Mírzá Abú'l-Fadl, and a number of friends, both Arabs and Persians were present. He talked on the severe trials and vicissitudes of Bahá'u'lláh, when he was exiled from Tehran to Baghdad and the hardships the party accompanying Him, had to go through. He hoped the results of those hardships would be the illumination of the world of humanity and the emancipation of men from the defects of the animal nature.

RAMLEH, EGYPT, SEPTEMBER 31, 1913

1. What It Means to Be with 'Abdu'l-Bahá

To be with 'Abdu'l-Bahá, to taste the sweetness of his love, to drink the elixir of his affection, and to be intoxicated with the wine of his tenderness is to be immersed in an ocean of spiritual lights; for is he not the essence of sweetness, the rose-garden of love, the source of affection, and the dawning-place of truth?

From the unattainable altitude and the unsearchable height of the heart, hidden beyond the mountains of his spiritual world, flow rivers of divine grace, broad and noble. And with majestic beauty and mystic light—these rivers ran through the arid land of the souls of humanity, causing miraculous transformations. Where formerly were thorns and briers, now there are hyacinths and violets; where before were wild jungles, now there are cultivated orchards; where in times gone by there was sterility, now there is fertility.

Like unto the rain, the Words fall from the heaven of his mind, creating thousands of rills and streamlets, and these in turn converging toward one center and impelled by a common interest, make a mighty river, on the banks of which a heavenly civilization is developing. This celestial river flows through many deserts, always with the same effect of changing them into fragrant gardens, wherein the flowers of friendship and mutual helpfulness blossom, perfuming the nostrils of all those who are far and near.

These days in Ramleh and with 'Abdu'l-Bahá! Ah, me! How divinely spiritual! These are days touched with Promethean fire; days taken out of the calendar of heaven; days flooded with the rays of the Sun of Reality; days blessed by the tender and loving presence of our Beloved and made significant and ever memorable by the revelation of holy tablets for the friends of the East and the West!

Daily he breathes into the half conscious body of the world the Breath of the Holy Spirits: reinforcing the visitors with heavenly Confirmation, vivifying them with the principles of righteousness. He receives the devotees of all religions; shoulders the burdens of all his people and welcomes the adherents of every sect with a beatific smile. In his presence all are welcome. The sun of his Love pours upon all humanity, illumines the chambers of every heart and ennobles the ambition of every soul. He is not the respector of persons but the lover of quality. If a man is a beggar but has a pure heart, he loves him more than a king in royal robes, surrounded by courtiers.

2. The Students Consist of a Large Delegation

As there is quite a large delegation of students and as they are to be the honored guests of the Master, he decided to divide them into two parties. The first party have come and gone. They stayed about ten days, received the benedictions of the Beloved, listened to his daily words and illumined their eyes by beholding his countenance. Then with songs of praise on their lips and paeans of thanksgiving in their hearts, they left for Haifa that they might be ready to enter the College.

The second party has just arrived, and will no doubt stay as many days as the Master wishes them to be here. The boys are from 12 to 25 years old. They live together, and the bond of Bahá'í love and good fellowship is strong and unbreakable between them. Unquestionably, they will not only form an invulnerable force for liberalism in Persia, but they will become the invincible army of the kingdom of Abhá, and with the sword of love put to rout the forces of darkness and banish the ghosts of ignorance. They have consecrated their lives to the service of the Cause and once their zeal and enthusiasm shake hand with knowledge and experience, they will carry the flag of Yá Bahá'u'-Abhá to the furthermost corners of the earth. They have set their ambition very high and have made up their minds to attain to it. What would be the effect of the accumulated result of science and experience, if they were not devoted to the propagation of the Cause of Abhá, which is the Cause of universal Peace, international brotherhood, and spiritual civilization?

3. The Students Sing Mrs. Shahnaz Waite's Anthems

Every one of the students studies and speaks English; they sing Bahá'í songs and the anthems of Mrs. Waite, which are translated into Persian verses by two of the great Bahá'í poets resident in Tehran.[28] These anthems they sing with great feeling; and all over the East, the poems of our "American nightingale," as the believers affectionately call Mrs. Waite in their poetic language, are sung by young men and women. She is loved and honored, because she is the poetic voice of the far West, crying in the wilderness of cold skepticism and summoning the people to the banquet of Bahá'í Peace and Love. How happy she would be—how grateful she would become, how her eyes would be filled with tears of joy if she could listen for one moment to the melodious voices of these

---

28. A reference to two poet brothers, Nayyar and Síná.

Eastern brothers, singing her songs with true understanding and sympathy!

4. Happiness and Tranquility of Heart

In order to bring my remarks to an end, I will share with you, the outline of two talks of 'Abdu'l-Bahá given to these students.

On one occasion, he stated that they are welcome to Ramleh. Are they happy? If they are not happy, then, in this wide world, who could claim happiness? Happiness is the most natural possession and immanent attribute of every Bahá'í. Praise be to God that they are free from every tie, are engaged in the study of spiritual and physical sciences and are beneath the protection of Bahá'u'lláh. God is with them, for they are not holding any thought which leads to intemperance and temptation.

The heavy-burdened people are afflicted with a hundred thousand sorrows and griefs and are at all times influenced and made unhappy by the changing conditions of life. In this world the greatest gift of God is the tranquility of the heart, especially when such a heart becomes the abiding place of the Love of God. This is the highest attainment in the world of creation!

But if, on the other hand, a man has all the wealth, comfort and luxuries of life, and does not possess tranquility of heart, all these things will become conducive of anxiety and nervous breakdown. When the tree is firmly rooted in the earth, no matter how much the hurricane rages, the furious winds blow and the rushing rains fall, this will only add to the firmness and verdancy of the tree, and it will loom toward the heavens with greater confidence and assurance. But if its root is not firm, even though the sun pours down, the winds blow, the rains descend and the breezes waft, there will be no foliage, no branch, no blossom and no fruit.

Now praise be to God, that the hearts of the believers are tranquil and assured in the favors and bounties of the Blessed Perfection. What bestowal is greater than this? No matter what affliction may befall upon us, the heart is in the utmost tranquility, serene and full of rejoicing. We can withstand all kinds of afflictions and resist all manner of persecutions with imperturbable courage and faith. Those souls, who are under the shade of the Cause of God, if they are not shaken and agitated, will advance through the infinite degrees of perfection. There is a vast difference between the bird which is already imprisoned in the cage, and the bird which after being set at liberty is caught again in the net through its own negligence.

5. *Lasting Enjoyment Is for the Moral Man*

In speaking to the students on another occasion, he stated, that, when the heart is confident, man knows that all is well. At one time in 'Akká, thirteen Bahá'ís lived in one room, but they radiated peace, joy and love.

Praise be to God, that they have come to Ramleh and stayed with him for nine days. They associated with one another and became his intimates. Their presence gave him much happiness. Likewise, they have spent many memorable days on Mount Carmel and in the vicinity of the tombs of Bahá'u'lláh and the Blessed Báb. Now they are going to return, but let them rest assured that these experiences have been permeated with ideal results and the invisible Confirmation shall ever descend upon them.

It is his hope that they will study with persistence and perseverance. He is well satisfied with their conduct in the College of Beirut. Truly they have borne themselves with urbanity and dignity. May they ever become better, sweeter, more perfect and more accomplished! In this path lies life's enjoyment. The success and pleasure of this physical life lies in uprightness! What a difference exists between those souls who live in accord with the good-pleasure of the Lord and those who are guided by their own thoughts and self-interests! The former are always attracted always enkindled, always immersed in the sea of God's Favors, always thinking of the well-being of humanity, always joyful and humble!

When you reflect carefully, you will observe that real and lasting contentment is in the possession of the moral man. Some may imagine that because they frequent theaters, accumulate wealth, or attend balls, they are always enjoying life; whereas in reality, these things often scatter thoughts, confuse the minds and dissipate the faculties. The effect of these amusements is like the effect of the wine upon the body; it exhilarates at first, but its after effect leaves one weak and the mental faculties exhausted. But the man who is chaste and moral receives his strength from the hidden spring of the universe; he is stirred continually by the Divine Glad-tidings; he is spiritual and godlike.

Praise be to God that their life is directed by ethical laws and molded by moral principles. He hopes that day by day their dignity and composure may increase; that they may strive with greater exertion in their studies; that the spring of their beatitude and happiness may gush forth unfailingly. The assistance of Bahá'u'lláh is with them and they shall precede all other students in their works.

6. The Meaning of Faith

Faith does not mean acknowledgment and mere confession. Faith means that one's conduct and behavior, one's character and life be in accord with the divine teachings. This is the quintessence of Faith. The greatest bestowal of the world of existence is a tranquil heart, and it is impossible to obtain a tranquil heart save through the good-pleasure of the Lord; i.e.; man should so adorn the temple of his being with lofty attributes and philanthropic deeds as to be pleasing at the Threshold of the Almighty. There is no other path! Consider the condition of kings, ministers, captains of industry and the leaders of mankind! Looking at them from the superficial standpoint, you would think their hearts to be in the utmost composure, joy and peace; but if you reflect carefully, you will observe, that they live in great agitation, surrounded with haunting fears and griefs. They do not enjoy one moment of ease and rest!

7. The Basic Principle of the Good-Pleasure of God

The point is this: let all their thoughts, their ideals, and aims revolve day and night around one common object, and that is: to live in accord with the good-pleasure of the Lord. Then all the doors of felicity will be opened before their faces, they will be successful in all their undertakings and will become confirmed in all their accomplishments. The basic principle is the good-pleasure of God and the good-pleasure of God is obtained through the tranquility of the heart and the tranquility of the heart is obtained by living in accord with the divine teachings and exhortations.

When a person attains to this station, he is contented and peaceful. Then he will become prosperous in all affairs. This station is joy succeeded by joy, confidence after confidence and paradise after paradise. Thus we read in the blessed Qur'an: O thou assured soul! Turn to thy Lord, confident and well-satisfied. If thou dost associate with my true servants, it is as though thou hast entered paradise. Having attained to this exalted station, man lives in paradise, although walking upon the earth; he lives in paradise when he departs from this world; his heart is ever in paradise; his spirit is in paradise; and he is encircled by the joys of paradise!

8. The Successful Student

Consider the condition of a student who attends school for five years and applies himself to a life of study. If at the time of examination he is not successful, he will become extremely despondent. He is living in a hell of despondency. But if, on the other hand, he passes examination with success, he is honored and beloved on all sides; receives his degree with pride and achieves great distinction in the world of humanity. In other words, he is living in a Paradise of fulfillment.

The students must, therefore, strive so that they may become thoroughly grounded in science and arts. Let them ever be thoughtful, supplicating, and entreating before God. Then when they are attending their classes, heavenly confirmations will uninterruptedly descend upon them.

The foundation of life is morality. They must exert themselves to improve continually the moral side of their nature. If the morals of man are merciful, although he may not be a great scholar, yet will his character be loving; but if his morals are corrupt, even though he be a master of sciences, he will be a harmful agency in the body politic. Instead of becoming the cause of illumination of the world of humanity, he will become conducive to its darkness.

Instead of helping the Cause of general construction, he will materially further the ends of destruction. Instead of adding to his energy for the cause of progress, he will enlist himself on the side of the cause of decline. On the other hand, if his character is merciful and he is also well grounded in sciences and arts—then, he will be light upon light.

9. *Light and Knowledge*

Here the Beloved paused for a few moments, and then gave a wonderfully, illuminative interpretation of a verse in the Qur'an, which is known as the "verse of Light." In phrase after phrase, he elucidated the Qur'anic words in the most comprehensive manner under the significance of knowledge. He closed his remarks with the statement, that, it is evident that light is knowledge. If the light is shining in a black and sooty lamp, it will not shed any radiance; but if the light abides in a transparent glass, in other words, if knowledge abides in a clear heart, imbued with merciful morality, characterized with faith, assurance and holiness, enkindled with the fire of the love of God and attracted by the Fragrances of God, such a heart will become a center for the outpouring of divine Bestowals and this will be light upon light!

10. *Letter to the Students from the President of the College*

I may quote herein a letter written to the Persian students by President Howard S. Bliss of the Beirut College. The letter is written on Board S. S. Royal Mail Steamship Pannona and mailed from New York, dated April 14, 1913:

> To the Persian students:
> Dear friends:
>   Before landing in New York, which we hope to do tomorrow, I wish to send you a special word of greeting and thanks for your very kind letter of farewell. I appreciate your thoughtful kindness very deeply and it has been a great pleasure to re-read your letter. We had, a long but pleasant journey. We are now eager to see land and to receive word from loved ones in Syria. Of course this includes the College and all the students.

I hope that the Persian students will have a prosperous ending to their years and all may be planning to return. I hope also that you may have addition to your numbers and that the good record that you have had during the past may be continued. I always look forward to returning to the campus which we love so ardently. My love goes to each one of you.

Your president,

(Signed) Howard S. Bliss.

Thus the East and the West join hands of communication! And these students, because they are acquiring material and spiritual sciences will be the greatest links of unity between America and Persia.

May they succeed as they have already succeeded all their undertakings!

11. *The Bahá'í Cause as Interpreted by 'Abdu'l-Bahá*

The Bahá'í Cause as lived and interpreted by 'Abdu'l-Bahá is a clarion call for the unification of the people of the Orient and the Occident. It is a light to lead the storm-tossed travelers to the haven of peace and brotherhood. Millions of people all over the world are praying for the coming of the day when truth will reign, and the clouds of prejudices will be dispelled from men's consciousness.

We as the followers of 'Abdu'l-Bahá are able to inspire these men and women with words of encouragement and examples of unselfish service. Let us unfurl the flag of the religion of God and gather in its shade all those who desire to enlist their names in the invincible army of the kingdom of Abhá. Our supreme Commander is Bahá'u'lláh; our General is 'Abdu'l-Bahá; our rule is the Word of God; our guide is the power of the Holy Spirit; our aim is to establish upon the earth the dominion of heaven; our hope is to defeat the soldiers of ignorance and fanaticism; our resolution is to make this world the paradise of the Almighty and our purpose is to gain victory for the forces of Justice, Truth and Liberty.

We as Bahá'ís have no other ambition, no other desire and no other plan. Let us fill the hearts with gladness; illumine the souls with the light of the Sun of Reality; refresh the minds with the breezes of the garden of universal Ideals and sing the thrilling anthem of the Union of the inhabitants of the East and of the West, of the North and of the South!

Isabel Fraser's Glimpses of Life in Egypt in 1913

The following report by Isabel Fraser was written in February 26, 1914, and published in *Star of the West*, vol. 4, pp. 316-17:

When 'Abdu'l-Bahá settled at Ramleh, he desired to have his old friend, Mírzá Abú'l-Fadl, near him. To do so he rented the upper part of a two story house set in a garden of date palms. To have provided a more pretentious place would not have been at all in accordance with Mírzá Abú'l-Fadl's modest habits. Here he lived alone. At first, 'Abdu'l-Bahá secured a cook who was to act as personal caretaker, for Mírzá Abú'l-Fadl's health was failing and he needed such an attendant.

But sick or well, the old philosopher was a hermit. He loved his circle of friends, and he also loved his hours of solitude and contemplation. He was not used to having anybody constantly around administering to what he regarded as merely trivial needs; but he soon discovered a way to compromise with the unaccustomed situation. One day when 'Abdu'l-Bahá called, he found his venerable friend waiting upon the servant and treating him as though he were an honored guest. Seeing that this was only an added burden to Mírzá Abú'l-Fadl, he had the man dismissed.

Mírzá Abú'l-Fadl's quarters resembled an unkempt library. There were books on every capable shelf and table, and even the floor was littered with volumes and papers. His place was a rendezvous for the learned shaykhs and mullás of the ancient city of Alexandria; for he was looked upon as an authority on history, Persian literature, higher criticism, and comparative religions.

His favorite outing was a visit to the house of 'Abdu'l-Bahá's secretaries which was just around the corner, and which beside housing the secretaries, was used as a guesthouse for visiting pilgrims to 'Abdu'l-Bahá. Here he would sit on the spacious veranda; the news would go forth and soon a little group would be gathered about him. On Friday afternoons a body of young native students from Alexandria came to him for lessons in the Sacred Books of Bahá'u'lláh.

To the many who were accorded the rare privilege of meeting this man of letters, both during his stay in America and on their pilgrim ages to the East, I need not speak of his peculiar personal charm. With all his book learning he was not at all "bookish." Gifted with one of those rare minds that explore all the channels of life with equal grace and facility the same dignity and impressiveness with which he discussed a verse of the Koran with the learned shaykhs, he put into the meeting of some sojourning American; often finishing with a personal peasantry for he was a ready humorist and made his guests instantly at ease.

He had the placidness of a child and the air of one who was never in a hurry and had plenty of time to make radiantly happy the place where God had placed him.

That was his attitude toward the world; but in the presence of the Center of the Covenant, 'Abdu'l-Bahá, with head bowed and downcast eyes, he became the essence of humility.

Even his voice, in answer to 'Abdu'l-Bahá's questions, became so low and subdued. Never have I seen such a perfect and instantaneous agreement of mind and body to express humility. One day when I was at his house, there were about twenty shaykhs who had come over from Alexandria to visit him. One who seemed to be the leader was a very learned and gorgeously attired young shaykh, who said with some pride that he had been educated in the oldest university in the world. He was the editor of a magazine in Alexandria and had come to interview Mírzá Abú'l-Fadl, who for more than an hour had been listened to with absorbed attention. His talk was interspersed with an occasional jest and his sharp eye would glance from one face to another to see if his point was understood. One might imagine the learned devotees in the early Christian era listening like this to the eloquence of St. Paul.

Suddenly 'Abdu'l-Bahá appeared. Mírzá Abú'l-Fadl faced the door, the rest of us had our backs to it and did not see him; there was a moment of silence and Mírzá Abú'l-Fadl stood with his head bowed, his whole attitude changed. He immediately became the most humble and respectful of servitors. Then quickly arranging a chair for 'Abdu'l-Bahá, he told him a low voice, in answer to his questions, the subject under discussion. 'Abdu'l-Bahá continued the subject, which was on the independent search for reality, further emphasizing the great necessity of investigating truth with a mind unbiased by theology or the limitations of other minds.

At the house of Mírzá Abú'l-Fadl he was an almost daily visitor. Whenever inquiry was made for 'Abbás Effendi, as the natives all call 'Abdu'l-Bahá, the conjecture invariably was that he was probably to be found either at the house of Mírzá Abú'l-Fadl or in the rose garden, opposite, dictating Tablets.

'Abdu'l-Bahá's love for his old friend, who for years had suffered banishment imprisonment and persecution for his faith, was remarked by all. He said of him one day: "Such men as Mírzá Abú'l-Fadl already belong to the Divine Concourse. All his interests are centered on the spiritual horizon rather than on this transitory phantasmagoria. Abú'l-Fadl's efforts are turned toward the heavenly kingdom. He has no other thought. Such souls are aided by heavenly confirmations."

Printed in Great Britain
by Amazon